CULTURE
and the
EVOLUTIONARY
PROCESS

Robert Boyd & Peter J. Richerson

CULTURE
and the
EVOLUTIONARY
PROCESS

The
University of Chicago
Press

Chicago and London

Robert Boyd is assistant professor of anthropology at Emory University. **Peter J. Richerson** is professor in the Division of Environmental Studies at the University of California, Davis. Their work on this subject has been published in many journals, including the *Journal of Theoretical Biology*, the *Journal of Economic Behavior and Organization*, *Human Ecology*, and *BioScience*.

The University of Chicago Press, Chicago 60637
The University of Chicago Press, Ltd., London
© 1985 by The University of Chicago
All rights reserved. Published 1985
Printed in the United States of America

94 93 92 91 90 89 88 87 86 85 54321

Library of Congress Cataloging in Publication Data

Boyd, Robert.
    Culture and the evolutionary process.

    Bibliography: p. 301
    Includes indexes.
    1. Social evolution.   2. Human evolution.
I. Richerson, Peter J.   II. Title.
GN360.B68   1985   304.5   84-24125
ISBN 0-226-06931-1

Contents

Preface

In 1974 we were assigned to co-teach an introductory environmental studies course for nonmajors. The course was supposed to present both the natural and social scientists' points of view on environmental problems. Previous offerings had focused on applied questions, but we decided to analyze environmental problems with a set of simple principles based on the notion that humans adapt to environments as other organisms do. Although both of us were trained as natural scientists, we knew that social scientists had made extensive use of concepts from ecology, particularly the notion of adaptation. For our limited purpose, it looked easy and fun to do the same. A little knowledge is always dangerous! Although it was true that social scientists had used the concept of adaptation, frequently even invoked analogies from biology, we could find no systematic theoretical argument for cultural behavior that paralleled the Darwinian theory of biologists. Anthropologists sometimes noted general similarities between culture and genes, but they usually stressed the differences, and therefore the autonomy, of anthropological theory. Furthermore, even the rather limited uses of evolutionary theory made in the study of human behavior were often quite controversial. Relatively uncontroversial syntheses, such as Dobzhansky's *Mankind Evolving,* seemed quite incomplete and unsatisfactory, despite the vigor of their assertions. Only the chance discovery of a very nice paper by Don Campbell gave us any encouragement at all. In the end we became convinced that what we had discovered was more promising as a topic for research than as a principle for organizing a freshman class.

Being ecologists by training, we had more enthusiasm than expertise to bring to this project. Our only other natural qualification for the task was a dubious one: we lacked the preconceptions that would have resulted from a more appropriate background. We were more than usually dependent on the help of unselfish colleagues and patient students. But we ought to begin by thanking several individuals, without naming any names, who honestly and candidly advised us not to waste time on such a questionable enterprise. We appreciate having friends who give such counsel even when we do not take it.

Several people read and commented on the whole text, often on multiple drafts, including Eric Smith, who made especially extensive and useful comments, Michael Wade and Susan Paulsen, who both carefully read the mathematical sections and saved us from several errors, and B. J. Williams, Bob Brandon, Joan Silk, and Lois Richerson. Joan was also responsible for the research on the tattooing example in Chapter 8 and for a number of technical comments on other points. Others read and commented in detail on several chapters, including David Hull, Rick Michod,

Jim Peoples, Robert Seyfarth, John Staddon, John Terrell, and Bill Wimsatt. Jim Cheverud gave us comments on Chapter 4, Emmy Werner and Larry Harper on Chapter 3, Daniel Rancour-Laferriere on Chapter 8, and Alex Rosenberg on Chapter 2. Avi Pervelotsky read several sections of the text and helped us manage the bibliography. Gary Macey, Ara Hakopian, and Marie Follo helped with bibliographic chores and with the index.

A number of people read early drafts of the book or related papers, or attended seminars, and gave us useful advice, help on technical points, and moral support. First among these individuals was Don Campbell. His intellectual contribution to our work is only partially described by citations in the text, and for his personal interest and many courtesies on our behalf we are especially grateful. Bill Davis gave us a long-running personal seminar in anthropology and sociology that contributed more than any other single interchange to our knowledge of these two disciplines. Michael Wade acted as RB's host during an NSF postdoctoral year at the University of Chicago and gave us help with the manuscript. Gerald Edelman and the Neurosciences Institute were our hosts during the last stages of preparing the text. Ron Pulliam suggested the basic elements of Chapter 4 and gave us other help. John Gillespie helped with the analytical techniques used in Chapter 4. Marc Feldman and L. L. Cavalli-Sforza allowed us to attend their class on cultural evolution in 1978, and Michael Turelli his graduate class in population genetics in 1979. Francisco Ayala helped us find financial support for the project on a couple of crucial occasions and was a source of several courtesies and bits of advice. Others with whom we had useful interactions of one kind or another include Richard Alexander, Stevan Arnold, Nancy Berte, Laura Betzig, Peter Brown, Napoleon Chagnon, Anne Clark, Dick Day, Tom Dietz, Bill Durham, Gerry Edelman, Lief Finkel, Mark Flinn, Morris Freilich, Vic Goldberg, Marjorie Grene, Bill Hamilton, Jack Hirshleifer, Bill Irons, Russell Lande, Charles Lumsden, Robert Merphy, Richard Nelson, Robert Richards, Ledyard Stebbins, George Stocking, Paul Sabatier, Paul Turk, John Werren, John Wiley, George Williams, Dave Wilson, Sidney Winter, and E. O. Wilson. Students in several seminars and courses, and anonymous reviewers of our papers and this book, provided useful suggestions and criticism.

Dolores Dumont typed, edited, and produced all too many drafts and copies of drafts of the book. Her organizational skills often covered for our lack of them. Bob and Ann Schneider were gracious and thoughtful hosts during RB's many stays in Davis. PJR would like to thank the School of Forestry and Environmental Studies, Duke University, and the John Simon Guggenheim Memorial Foundation. He is also indebted to the University of California–Davis for granting him a sabbatical leave in which to complete the book.

1
Overview

To study Metaphysics, as they have always been studied appears to me to be like puzzling at astronomy without mechanics.
                                   Charles Darwin, N notebook, p. 5, 3 Oct. 1838

Origin of man now proved.—Metaphysics must flourish.—He who understand baboon would do more toward metaphysics than Locke.
                                   Charles Darwin, M notebook, p. 84, 16 Aug. 1838

The year 1838 was an intense period in the life of Charles Darwin. He was busy unpacking and cataloging specimens he had collected on the *Beagle* voyage; he was courting Emma Wedgwood, whom he would shortly marry; and he was earnestly and eagerly searching for an explanation of the origin of species. After several false starts, in late September Darwin read Malthus and for the first time grasped the idea of evolution by inherited variation and selective retention. In July of the same year, Darwin began a new series of notebooks, the M and N notebooks. These notebooks, only recently transcribed (Gruber with Barrett, 1974), reveal that even before he understood natural selection Darwin was convinced that an explanation of evolution would profoundly affect our understanding of human behavior.

Darwin's reasoning was simple and compelling. The behavioral adaptations that characterize the human species are the result of the same evolutionary process that shaped all other species. If we understand that process and the conditions under which the human species evolved, we will have the basis for a scientific understanding of human nature. Trying to comprehend human nature without an understanding of human evolution is "like puzzling at astronomy without mechanics."

Nonetheless, until very recently evolutionary biology has made relatively modest contributions to psychology, anthropology, or any of the other social sciences. The rejection of a central role for Darwinism by the mainstream of twentieth-century social science has been a historical process of some complexity. Certainly one important factor was that Darwin's ideas were ill appreciated until the mid-twentieth-century synthesis of Darwinism and population genetics. Another was that until recently biologists had failed to produce an adequate account of the evolution of social behavior and therefore had very little to say about humans that was of interest to social scientists. Most important, we believe, was the apparent importance of culture in shaping human behavior. Many scholars, from both the social and biological sciences, have argued that because humans acquire so much of their behavior culturally rather than genetically, the human evolutionary process

1

is fundamentally different from that of other animals. However, since the neo-Darwinian theory of evolution does not explicitly account for the cultural transmission of behavior from one generation to the next, there has been no way of knowing whether this argument is cogent.

This book outlines a Darwinian theory of the evolution of cultural organisms. By "culture" we mean the transmission from one generation to the next, via teaching and imitation, of knowledge, values, and other factors that influence behavior. Cultural transmission may have a variety of structures. By "structures" we mean the patterns of socialization by which a given trait or set of traits are transmitted in a given society. For example, parents may enculturate their offspring or peers may enculturate each other. A Darwinian theory ultimately should be capable of answering two closely related questions about the evolutionary properties of cultural transmission. First, the theory should predict the effect of different structures of cultural transmission on the evolutionary process. For example, do particular kinds of behaviors become common when individuals imitate their peers? Second, the theory should allow us to understand the conditions under which different structures of cultural transmission might evolve. For example, when should natural selection favor the mutual enculturation of individuals by their peers? Clearly, we must be able to answer the first kind of question before we can address the second.

To amend neo-Darwinian theory so that it addresses these questions we proceed in two steps. First, we construct simple mathematical models of cultural transmission in which the assumed structures of cultural transmission are based as much as possible on the results of empirical research done by psychologists and anthropologists. Thus we restrict attention to the structures of cultural transmission observed in the human species. These models demonstrate that the cultural inheritance of behavior creates the possibility of novel evolutionary forces. By "forces" we mean causes of cultural change, the analogs of natural selection, mutation, drift, and so forth in the genetic system of inheritance. These forces can lead to behavior that would not be predicted on the basis of conventional neo-Darwinian theory. Second, we link these models of cultural transmission to models of genetic evolution and attempt to determine the circumstances under which natural selection might favor the modes of cultural transmission observed among contemporary humans. These models show that the same modes of cultural transmission that lead to novel evolutionary results can arise via conventional neo-Darwinian processes.

We call the resulting collection of models the "dual inheritance theory" of the human evolutionary process to emphasize that the potentially novel effects of culture result from the fact that the determinants of behavior are assumed to be transmitted via two structurally different inheritance systems. Like most theory in population biology, dual inheritance models are extremely simplified. Experience with modeling complex economic and ecological systems suggests that attempts to build realistically complicated models lead to impossible data requirements and uninterpretable, unreliable results. Our goal is not to make quantitative predictions, or to "show" that one or another interpretation of human evolution is correct. Instead, we hope that dual inheritance models will clarify the logical relationships between cultural transmission and other Darwinian processes and stimulate social scientists to make the empirical observations that may eventually allow us to make reliable general statements about the evolution of human behavior.

An Informal Sketch of the Dual Inheritance Model

Since in the remaining chapters we will address specific problems at some length, it is important to have the basic outline of our approach in hand before proceeding. In the remainder of this chapter we will sketch our basic argument and then outline what we think are the implications of this work for the social sciences.

Structure of inheritance and evolutionary forces

The first step in the argument is to clearly distinguish three concepts—genes, culture, and environment. The relationship between the genetic system of inheritance and the environment is the least problematic of these distinctions. Our nonbiologist readers should not be misled into thinking that the neo-Darwinian synthesis is completely secure, for there are fundamental issues outstanding. We are not sure how genes are assembled to produce macroscopic traits (Lewontin, 1974), nor are we certain how the generation-by-generation processes of natural selection, drift, and so on produce the large-scale patterns of adaptation observed in the fossil record (Gould and Lewontin, 1979). Nevertheless, compared to the state of our understanding of culture, there is broad agreement on the mechanics of genetic inheritance and on how the forces of evolution—natural selection, recombination, mutation, and drift—produce changes in the frequency of genotypes and thus the evolution of phenotypes.

These evolutionary forces result from the interaction of the structural features of genetic inheritance with the environment. A typical evolutionary model includes structural elements such as a specific mating system, a pattern of linkage between loci, and rules for translating genotypes into phenotypes. It also includes environmental elements that determine which phenotypes reproduce, how population size is regulated, and so forth.

Different inheritance structures can lead to different evolutionary forces even when otherwise similar organisms are subjected to the same environment. For example, the evolution of organisms that reproduce sexually is subject to forces that do not affect the evolution of organisms that reproduce asexually. For an asexual species the major force is selection, which acts nearly unopposed to increase the frequency of the most fit genotype. In a sexual species the shuffling of genes during sexual reproduction introduces the new forces of segregation and recombination. These forces can lead to a different distribution of genotypes at equilibrium in sexual and asexual species. Much more subtle interactions between the structure of inheritance and the environment are possible, but the general principle remains the same: different patterns of inheritance entail differences in the way evolutionary processes operate.

The synthetic theory of evolution is justifiably regarded as the centerpiece of biology. If we understand the genetic structure of a species and the environments to which it has been exposed, the theory allows us, in principle at least, to explain why the species is the way it is and predict how it might change if its environment changes. Just what is meant by prediction "in principle" and why we must be satisfied with less than lawlike statements in evolutionary biology will be explored in the next chapter. The essential point is that the synthetic theory does permit a deep and useful understanding of why organisms work the way they do.

The analogy between genetic and cultural inheritance

The synthetic theory is used in two ways here. First, we assume that the genetic factors which influence human phenotypes are governed by the same forces that affect genetic change in other species. Second, we will use the synthetic theory as a source of analogies and formal mathematical machinery with which to build a theory of the evolution of culture. There are important differences between the genetic and cultural inheritance systems, and the theory will by no means neglect them. However, the parallels are profound enough that there is no need to invent a completely new conceptual and mathematical apparatus to deal with culture.

At the most general level the analogy is fruitful because we want the same kind of explanation for the culturally determined components of the human behavioral phenotype that we have for the genetically inherited adaptations of other organisms. That is, given a knowledge of the structure of enculturation and of the expression of socially acquired skills and ideas, and of past and present (or future) environments, we wish to explain (or predict) behavior. We want to understand how the structural features of human cultural transmission interact with environmental contingencies to create the forces of cultural evolution. Some cultural evolutionary forces, like natural selection, have essentially the same character in both the cultural and genetic systems, and the analogy between genetic and cultural evolution is fruitful. Others, like the force produced by the inheritance of acquired phenotypic adaptation, have no clear analogy in genetic evolution.

Environment, learning, and culture

All organisms appear to have mechanisms that allow them to vary their phenotypes adaptively in response to environmental contingencies (Bonner, 1980; Staddon, 1983). The most elementary examples are the inducible enzyme systems in microorganisms. Bacteria typically have a genome that codes for several enzymes to metabolize different organic materials, but particular enzymes are not synthesized unless the appropriate substrates are available in the environment. Higher plants are able to modify their phenotype to suit their local environment (Bradshaw, 1965). In animals individual learning is an important mechanism of phenotypic adaptation. Given a criterion of reinforcement, such as a sense of pain or a taste for rewards, even random errors in behavior can be conditioned into elaborately organized adaptive behaviors. Of course, many environmental contingencies may not elicit adaptive phenotypic responses at all, or they may cause maladaptive responses because the determinants of learning are inappropriate.

Why not simply treat culture as a special case of phenotypic response to environmental variation in which the "environment" is the behavior of conspecifics? The reason is that cultural influences on behavior are transmitted from individual to individual. Variants acquired by individual learning and other common forms of phenotypic flexibility are lost with the death of the individual, and only the genes that underlie the capacity to learn are evolving properties of the population. In contrast, culturally acquired variations are transmitted from generation to generation and, like genes, they are also evolving properties of the population. Because of this we will say that culture has "population-level consequences." The concept of the population-level consequences of culture is crucial to understanding virtually every part of this book, so we will devote quite a bit of space to it here.

"Environment" should be restricted to those processes in the physical and biological realm that affect the population of interest but that are somehow external to the population itself. For example, the local climate, the kinds of food items available, and local predators are all part of the population's environment. The social behavior of individuals in a population is not part of the environment, even though behavior may affect individual fitness, because it is internal to the evolving population.

Most evolutionary models further assume that environmental conditions are not strongly affected by evolutionary changes in the population; in other words, environmental factors are exogenous to the evolving population. For example, the amount of rainfall in a particular location will affect virtually every aspect of the life history of a population of plants living there, but the amount of rainfall will itself be largely independent of the phenotypes or genotypes of that plant population. Clearly, this assumption will not always be satisfied. For example, host and parasite populations will usually affect each other at the phenotypic and genotypic levels. In order to make the distinction between culture and environment as stark as possible we also initially assume that the environment is exogenous. In Chapter 3 we will see how culture can be distinguished from environmental factors that are endogenous to the evolving system.

To see why culture should be distinguished from environment, let us diagram in the simplest possible form the evolutionary process in a noncultural organism (modified from Lewontin, 1974). We start with a population of zygotes just after fertilization. The distribution of genotypes in this population of zygotes will be denoted G_t. (There could be, for example, 1 percent genotype 1, 4.3 percent genotype 2, 63 percent genotype 3, and so on, until the frequencies sum to 100 percent.) Individuals in the population then develop mature phenotypes via various processes, including ordinary learning. If individuals with the same genotype are exposed to different environments, they may develop different phenotypes. That is, through the processes of ontogeny, including ordinary learning, a given distribution of genotypes interacts with the environment to produce a distribution of phenotypes labeled F_t. Then we could summarize the first step in the life cycle as follows:

$$G_t \xrightarrow{\text{Ontogeny}} F_t$$

Since we have restricted the term "environment" to mean processes independent of G_t and F_t, it can be conceptually included in the processes of ontogeny. Next, as adults interact with their environments to gather resources for reproduction, selection acts on the population to reduce the frequency of some phenotypes and increase the frequency of others. (We label the resulting distribution of reproductively active adult phenotypes F_t'.) Selection is followed by mating, segregation, and recombination, which result in a new population of zygotes with a distribution of genotypes G_{t+1}. (The subscript $t+1$ indicates the next generation after the focal generation, t.) The whole life cycle can be diagrammed as follows:

$$G_t \xrightarrow{\text{Ontogeny}} F_t \xrightarrow{\text{Selection}} F_t' \xrightarrow{\text{Mating}} G_{t+1}$$

For us the important fact about this diagram is that it can be conceptually simplified as follows:

$$G_t \xrightarrow{\text{Evolutionary Forces}} G_{t+1}$$

That is, we can understand the evolution of noncultural organisms as a process that transforms the distribution of genotypes from one generation to the next, because in a noncultural species each individual's phenotype depends only on its genotype and the environment in which it matures. Since the environment is independent of G_t, each genotype is associated with a fixed distribution of phenotypes. Subsequent processes such as selection affect the population in ways that depend on the phenotype alone. Thus as long as there is a statistically fixed association of genotypes and phenotypes, evolution can be understood in terms of genotypic change alone.

Culture has population-level properties

Unlike other modes of adaptive phenotypic flexibility, social learning causes the communication of phenotypic traits directly from individual to individual. This property of social learning is important because it ensures that culture is a population-level phenomenon. The following diagram of the evolutionary process of a cultural species shows why (F_t, F_t', and G_t have the same meaning as before, and the subscript $t - 1$ indicates the generation before the focal generation, t):

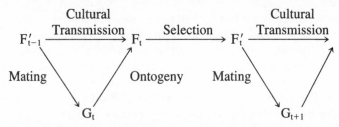

To predict the distribution of postontogeny phenotypes, F_t, during generation t we must know what genes individuals will draw from their gene pool and how these genes will interact with environmental contingencies, but we must also know what cultural traits were transmitted to the new generation. Obviously, the behaviors of two individuals with identical genotypes living in the same environment may differ strikingly if they are brought up in different cultures. Or, in terms of the diagrams, to predict F_t one must know G_t, the state of the environment, and the distribution of phenotypes in the previous generations, F_{t-1}'. Unlike the environment, however, the distribution of phenotypes is not exogenous to the ongoing evolution of the population. Therefore, any model of the evolutionary process of a cultural organism must keep track of the evolution of the distribution of phenotypes as well as the distribution of genotypes:

$$\begin{pmatrix} F_t \\ G_t \end{pmatrix} \xrightarrow{\text{Evolutionary Forces}} \begin{pmatrix} F_{t+1} \\ G_{t+1} \end{pmatrix}$$

That is, the evolution of a cultural organism is a process that transforms the joint distribution of genotypes and phenotypes. Put another way, phenotypic characters acquired via social learning can be thought of as a pool of cultural traits that coevolves with the gene pool in a way that characters acquired through ordinary learning without culture do not. Social learning causes the acquisition of phenotypes to be a population-level phenomenon.

This does not mean that cultures have mysterious lives of their own that cause them to evolve independently of the individuals of which they are composed. As in the case of genetic evolution, individuals are the primary locus of the evolutionary forces that cause cultural evolution, and in modeling cultural evolution we will focus on observable events in the lives of individuals. To understand the evolution of a cultural organism like *Homo sapiens,* we must understand the forces that affect the frequencies of different culturally transmitted phenotypes as well as the forces that affect the frequencies of different genotypes.

The structural properties of human cultural inheritance

Given a cultural system of inheritance based on social learning, the key problem is to understand its population-level consequences. Different structures of cultural inheritance will lead to different forces in cultural evolution, just as different structures of the genetic system lead to different forces in genetic evolution. For example, culture conceivably could have a pattern of transmission that makes it nearly an exact analog of genes insofar as evolutionary processes are concerned. Suppose that young individuals acquire certain behaviors from their parents, with each parent having the same expected effect on a given offspring's behavior. Further, suppose that the phenotypic copying is nearly error-free and that individuals retain traits acquired during childhood for life. Although the biochemical basis of such a system would be utterly different from that of genes, this difference would not have a dramatic effect on the evolutionary dynamics of the trait. The cultural system would behave like an extra genetic locus for all but the most technical considerations. The cultural evolution of humans is problematic precisely because the structure of cultural inheritance is often quite different from that of genetic inheritance.

What, then, are the structural differences between genetic and cultural inheritance?

1. The cultural "mating system" is different from its genetic analog. Every human society allocates roles in the enculturation process to individuals other than the two genetic parents. Members of an extended family frequently are very important, status as a teacher or priest may confer a formal role in socialization, prestigious individuals may be important, and so forth. Nor are the contributions of the biological father and mother to enculturation always so nearly equivalent as they are in genetic transmission. Either mothers or fathers may play a disproportionately important role in transmitting some cultural traits. We shall give the term "cultural parents" or "models" to the set of individuals who enculturate a given person. (We will use the terms "cultural offspring" or "naive individuals" for those who acquire traits by cultural transmission.) The possibility of having more and different people act as cultural parents than is the case in genetic transmission can lead to evolutionary effects that are strikingly different from those expected with purely genetic inheritance.

2. The cultural "generation length" is variable. The time scale of cultural evolution may be either shorter or longer than a biological generation. Individuals do not necessarily acquire all cultural characters from their parents or from members of the parental generation and do not in turn pass on cultural items only to children. Rather, the behavior of any individual can be copied—adults may copy adults and children may imitate other children. Sometimes older individuals may even imitate younger ones. Following Cavalli-Sforza and Feldman (1981) we will call such transmission within generations "horizontal." Horizontal transmission is analogous in some ways to the transmission of a pathogen, and Cavalli-Sforza and Feldman have used epidemiological models as a starting point for their development of theory. The item of culture being spread horizontally acts like a microbe that reproduces and spreads rapidly because it is "infective" and has a short generation length compared to the biological generation length of the "host." Fads and fashions and technical innovations are familiar examples.

3. Individuals are at least partly developed when they are enculturated. Cultural transmission occurs after birth, and even infants are mentally active, sentient individuals. Further, culture is acquired sequentially over time, rather than all at once at a single moment in the life cycle. These two structural differences cause the transmission of culture to be quite unlike that of genes. First, the existence of an active individual at the time of cultural transmission means that (1) genetic mechanisms can affect the probability of acquiring different cultural variants and (2) cultural traits acquired at one age can affect the cultural acquisition of traits at a later age. The only analog of these phenomena in genetic transmission is a process that geneticists call "meiotic drive," which apparently has not been an important force in genetic evolution. Second, both the set of cultural parents involved in transmission and the cultural generation time of cultural traits acquired at different ages can differ substantially. For example, during early childhood most traits in most cultures will be acquired from biological parents or other close relatives, while at later ages many traits may be acquired from peers via horizontal transmission.

4. Culture is acquired by directly copying the phenotype. The cultural information acquired by an individual may be affected by the events of his or her life, and, if so, the changes will be transmitted to an individual's cultural offspring. This property of cultural transmission makes for a kind of "Lamarckian" evolution, in the sense that acquired variation is inherited. In contrast, the genetic information transmitted by an individual is unaffected by the events of its life, and adaptive genetic evolution can only occur by the differential survival or reproduction of variant individuals in the population.

The forces of cultural evolution

The next question is, What evolutionary forces can be generated by the interaction between the cultural system of inheritance and the environment? This is not the point at which to judge which forces are more important or exactly how one force is linked to another. These are the questions that will occupy us for most of the book. At this stage, we simply want to enumerate all of the conceivable processes that can change culture through time.

1. Random variation. We all have had the experience of misremembering even important items of information. The neurological machinery of the mind must certainly cause errors at some rate. We can be confident that the cultural analog of mutation exists. A measurement of the error rate conceivably could be devised. For example, such a measure could be based on the rate at which an oral tradition corrupts the facts of a historical event known and datable from an independent source. Our intuition is that the rate of cultural mutation is much higher than the rate of genetic mutation. If this is so, accidental variation may play a somewhat different role in cultural evolution than it does in genetic evolution.

2. An analog of genetic drift. If the population of models active in cultural transmission is small, chance variations in which cultural variants are observed and remembered may cause substantial changes in frequency from time to time. Rare or rarely performed variants may be lost entirely. Diamond (1978) reviews evidence that the isolated Tasmanians lost many traits brought with them from Australia by this mechanism. Cavalli-Sforza and Feldman (1981) incorporate drift effects into several of their mathematical models.

3. The force of guided variation. Like many other organisms, humans adjust their phenotypes in response to their environments through learning and rational calculation. Unlike most other organisms, humans can culturally transmit the phenotypes so acquired to the next generation. Thus ordinary learning in combination with cultural transmission acts to create a kind of "Lamarckian" effect that increases the frequency of traits that are generated by the learning process. Both trial-and-error learning and more elaborate methods of adaptive modification of behavior based on rational calculation are almost certainly very important forces in human cultural evolution, and we will devote Chapter 4 to trying to understand how they might work.

The effect of the guided variation force on evolution depends on the existence of some adaptive standard such as taste or a sensation of pleasure or pain. For example, adaptation through rational calculation proceeds by the collection of information about the environment, the estimation of the results of various alternative patterns of behavior, and the evaluation of the desirability of the alternative outcomes according to some criteria. It is these guiding criteria that translate variation in the environment into a directional, often adaptive, change in phenotype, which then is culturally transmitted to subsequent generations. The source of these criteria clearly must ultimately be external to the guided variation process itself. In the final analysis, we will be driven to explain the guiding criteria as the product of some other process. This peculiar property of guided variation will become particularly important when we examine the application of sociobiological theory to human behavior in the context of dual inheritance theory.

4. Biased transmission. This force arises because the process of cultural transmission itself can favor some cultural variants over others. Biased transmission is closely akin to guided variation because both forces arise from the same capacities for learning and calculation. However, the forces arising from biased transmission are more complex than guided variation. We can conceive of three different kinds of biased transmission, each with different effects on cultural evolution.

In the simplest case, people may adopt some cultural variants rather than others based on their judgments about the properties of the variants themselves. We call this "direct bias." The enculturation of dietary preferences is a useful example. Parents know that it is easier to teach small children to eat some kinds of foods than others. Ice cream and candy are easy; spicy foods are hard. It seems likely that these childhood preferences have a genetic basis (Lumsden and Wilson, 1981: 38–43). By the time we are adults we have culturally acquired many preferences for food, including preferences that violate our genetically acquired tastes (peppery foods that cause painful sensations) and a host of seemingly arbitrary culture-specific preferences that determine dietary change in later life. Anglo-Americans prefer beef and pork and abhor dog, horsemeat, and fermented fish. Other cultures reverse these preferences. At all ages the decision to include novel food items in the diet will be influenced by some kind of preference. This directly biased transmission will then serve to increase the frequency of the preferred variants. We will devote Chapter 5 to trying to understand the effects of directly biased transmission in more detail.

More subtle kinds of biases are also possible. The tendency of an individual to acquire a particular cultural variant may be influenced by the commonness or rarity of the trait among that individual's cultural parents. We call this "frequency dependent bias." For example, a body of literature in social psychology (e.g. Keisler and Keisler, 1970) suggests that people are prone to adopt the opinions of the majority, even when such opinions are contradicted by their own experience. This tendency leads to an increase in the frequency of the most common cultural variant in a population. We will see in Chapter 7 that this phenomenon has interesting ramifications.

It is also conceivable that the possession of certain traits may cause an individual to be an attractive model for a wide variety of otherwise unrelated traits. For example, prestigious, powerful, or wealthy individuals are often attractive models, and we imitate their style of dress, their pattern of speech, and a variety of other traits that at first glance do not appear to be related to their attainment of prestige, power, or wealth. Thus, people may tend to acquire some cultural variants because they are associated with attractive variants of entirely different cultural traits. We will refer to this as "indirect bias." Among other things, indirectly biased transmission can cause an unstable "runaway" process analogous to the genetical process that is thought to account for maladaptively exaggerated male characters (e.g. peacocks' tails) in polygynous species. We will investigate the effects of this kind of indirect bias in Chapter 8.

It has been argued that directly biased transmission is the dominant force governing human evolution. Eugene Ruyle (1973), for example, has argued that human evolution is governed by the search for satisfaction. As with guided variation, however, the problem with this kind of explanation is the source of the criteria of satisfaction, and once again one will be driven to explain the guiding criteria as the product of some other force or forces.

5. *Natural selection can operate on culture.* Donald Campbell (1965, 1975) has argued that natural selection is a very general mechanism, one likely to operate on any system of inheritance. Darwin's original reasoning was that if inherited variation exists, and if this inherited information is an important determinant of the ability of organisms to survive and reproduce in a given environment, then variants that enhance survival and reproduction relative to other variants will increase in the population in question. Since cultural variants are inherited and many, if not all, culturally acquired behaviors have an effect on human survival and reproduction (both genetic and cultural), some cultural variants will increase relative to others.

Like Campbell, we believe that the empirically known properties of culture virtually guarantee that cultural variation is subject to natural selection. We will elaborate on this reasoning and review some of the relevant empirical data in Chapters 5 and 6.

Natural selection occupies an important place in our analysis because it can cause the results of cultural evolution to diverge systematically from the predictions of ordinary Darwinian theory. We have already seen how guided variation and biased transmission are dependent on some external process for their criteria of differential retention or transmission. Natural selection acting on genetic variation is an obvious candidate for this process.

Natural selection acting on cultural variation can cause the evolution of different behaviors from those one would expect as a result of selection acting on genetic variation when the pattern of cultural transmission is different from the structure of genetic transmission. If such structural differences exist, the behavior that enables an individual to maximize his chance to enculturate cultural offspring may not be the behavior that will maximize the transmission of genes to the next generation. For example, natural selection acting on culturally transmitted variation can conceivably favor behaviors through which an individual mobilizes the resources available to him to achieve a social role like "teacher" or "influential citizen." Such a role may confer prestige and a high probability of being imitated by "cultural offspring," at some cost in number of biological offspring.

We will say that two different inheritance systems are "symmetric" in structure if they have similar life cycles. For example, equal cultural transmission by both genetic parents to young children is symmetric to autosomal genetic transmission. Horizontal cultural transmission during adulthood is "asymmetric" with respect to both genetic transmission and cultural transmission from parents to children at an early age. If two inheritance systems are symmetric then it is likely that natural selection will favor the same phenotypic variants, regardless of how they are inherited. In contrast, when two inheritance systems are asymmetric, natural selection may favor one variant if the trait is transmitted by one system of inheritance and a different variant if the trait is transmitted by the other. For example, the traits favored in an adolescent prestige system with horizontal transmission may be quite different from those favored in the vertical transmission system from parents.

The Relationship between Genetic and Cultural Evolution

The theoretical approach described so far is useful because it provides a systematic framework for addressing a wide variety of questions about human behavior. Our goal is to account for all the processes by which the distribution of beliefs, attitudes, and values in a population are transmitted and modified. Understanding how these processes give rise to forces of cultural change allows us to link social, ecological, and psychological processes which act on individuals to large-scale and long-term patterns of behavior. Given detailed assumptions about the structure of cultural transmission and the nature of the social and natural environment, the theory allows predictions about the kinds of culturally transmitted behaviors that should characterize a particular population.

To understand the evolution of human behavior, however, it is not sufficient to know how the existing structures of human cultural transmission give rise to cultural change; we must also understand *why* human cultural transmission has these structures. To see why, suppose that guided variation, individual learning plus the imitation of learned behavior, is the only force affecting a particular culturally transmitted trait. The nature of the cultural variants favored by guided variation depends on the psychological criteria that determine how culturally acquired behavior is modified by learning. Given adequate empirical knowledge of the psychology of learning, we could predict which cultural variants would be common in any particular environment. This sort of understanding may be useful in many contexts. However, we would not yet understand why some variants and not others are favored by learning and therefore by guided variation. To understand the evolution of human behavior, we must understand how the structure of cultural transmission that is characteristic of humans might have evolved.

Most theorists in the social sciences do not feel any need to understand how the structures and processes that they posit might have evolved. We believe that this is a serious error. Ultimately, the human sciences must be unified with the physical and biological ones. The psychological factors which affect contemporary human behavior are products of organic evolution. Any theory of human behavior must be consistent with what we know about evolution in general and the evolution of behavior in particular.

The human sociobiologist's view of culture

The adherents of one school of thought, which we will call "human sociobiology," have tried to develop a theory of cultural evolution which is derived from the Darwinian theory of organic evolution. During the last two decades, evolutionary biologists have developed a subtle and, at least according to its practitioners, successful theory for explaining the evolution of animal social behavior, commonly referred to as sociobiological theory. A variety of biologists and social scientists have attempted to use sociobiological theory to understand human behavior (e.g. Wilson, 1978; Alexander, 1979a; Chagnon and Irons, 1979; Symons, 1979; Van den Berghe, 1979). Because human sociobiology represents the only really serious attempt to date to develop a logically complete theory of human behavior that is consistent with what we know about organic evolution, we frequently will compare its results with our own.

The most basic tenet of sociobiological theory is that we can usually predict the kinds of behavior observed in a particular ecological and social setting by determining the behavior that maximizes individual inclusive fitness in that setting, or at least in some relevant setting in the past. Individual inclusive fitness is a measure of an individual's reproductive success that includes the effect of an individual's behavior on its genetic relatives. For synthetic reviews of this theory and the supporting empirical evidence, see Wilson (1975) or Krebs and Davies (1981).

Human sociobiologists make predictions about patterns of human behavior by assuming that human behavior tends to maximize inclusive fitness. For example, several authors have asked why some societies are characterized by matrilineal social organization. Using sociobiological theory, they hypothesize that subsistence technologies or residence patterns that cause males to be uncertain about the paternity of any particular child should lead to matrilineal social organization (Greene, 1978; Alexander, 1979a: 159–176; Kurland, 1979).

Many social scientists have argued that sociobiological theory is not applicable to human behavior because human behavior is culturally acquired and therefore is somehow decoupled from genetic evolution. To answer these critics, human sociobiologists use a version of the deductive argument that we attributed to Darwin at the beginning of this chapter (e.g. Alexander, 1979a; Irons, 1979a): social learning is another form of phenotypic plasticity, just like individual learning in noncultural animals. The primate lineage that led to humans was almost certainly at some point acultural; as the capacities to acquire and transmit culture evolved in the lineage, natural selection must have acted on them to tend to maximize inclusive fitness.

Human sociobiologists differ over exactly how culture is kept on the fitness-maximizing "straight and narrow." Some, like Alexander (1979a) or Irons (1979a), deny that culture as we have defined it is important; human behavior can be understood in terms of learning and rational calculation based on genetically inherited preferences. Others, like Durham (1978), believe that culture is important in determining human behavior but that over the long run the forces of guided variation, biased transmission, and natural selection act to make genetically adaptive cultural variants more common than other cultural variants. Many others simply ignore the fact that behavior is culturally transmitted in the human species.

In essence, human sociobiologists believe that it is not necessary to take the details of cultural transmission into account when predicting human behavior. The organic origin of the human capacity for culture under the influence of natural selection acting on genes guarantees that, however it may work in detail, culture will usually enhance genetic fitness. This argument, which we will refer to as "the argument from natural origins," is common in evolutionary biology. If we want to predict the foraging patterns of a bird species in a particular habitat, we try to determine which strategy maximizes fitness in a given ecological setting. Usually, the evolutionary ecologist argues, it is not necessary to understand the neurophysiology or the learning mechanisms that characterize the species in detail to make useful predictions about its foraging behavior.

The argument from natural origins is a potent defense of human sociobiology. As critics within biology have pointed out, there are a number of reasons that the behavior (or any other phenotypic trait) of any particular species, including humans, may diverge from predictions based on what is adaptive (see Gould and Lewontin, 1979). Evolutionary accidents may occur, changes in one character may affect other characters, and populations may not have reached an evolutionary equilibrium. But most critics of the "adaptationist program" would admit that behavior generally tends to be adaptive. Unless the existence of cultural transmission makes human evolution fundamentally different from the evolution of other animals, sociobiological theory is likely to provide a useful source of hypotheses about human behavior. To deny the relevance of sociobiological theory to human behavior, one must either attack neo-Darwinian theory as a whole (not a promising enterprise) or be prepared to show how models that take culture into account actually generate more satisfactory hypotheses about human behavior without violating the assumption of natural origins. That the latter can be done is an argument we will defend repeatedly.

Inheritance as a shortcut to individual learning

Unlike human sociobiologists, we believe that the details of cultural transmission are likely to be essential to an understanding of the evolution of human behavior. The fact that culture is an inheritance system means that a variety of evolutionary forces affect behavior. Some of these forces can increase the frequency of behaviors that are genetically maladaptive. The capacity for cultural transmission can nonetheless persist because its, probably considerable, adaptive advantages also result from the fact that culture is an inheritance system, and therefore a cultural population can respond to weak evolutionary forces that act over many generations. If this view is correct, it means that understanding human evolution properly proceeds in two steps: First we determine how the costs and benefits of cultural transmission, averaged over many traits, have shaped its structure in humans, and then, taking this structure as given, we investigate how the forces of cultural evolution influence particular behavioral traits in different social and ecological settings.

In a variable environment, it is clearly useful to be able to develop the locally adaptive phenotype. But how does the organism determine what that phenotype might be? There are many ways, but in most species these processes share the same general features. The organism inherits criteria that determine what feels good and what feels bad; feelings of security and satiation are good, and feelings of fear and hunger are bad. It also inherits generalized behavior patterns and modes of learning; quail associate gastric distress with foods that are visually novel, while rats associate the same symptoms with foods that taste novel. The organism tries a variety of behaviors and retains those which are associated with rewarding sensations. In this way, complex patterns of behavior appropriate to local conditions can be generated.

Individual learning of this kind can be costly and error prone. Learning trials occupy time and energy that could be allocated to other components of fitness, and may entail a considerable risk to the individual as well. Because of these costs, the investment of individuals in determining the locally favored behavior must be limited, and individual learning can lead to errors. Individuals may fail to discover an adaptive behavior, or a maladaptive one may be retained because it was reinforced by chance. When these costs are important, selection ought to favor shortcuts to learning—ways that an organism can achieve phenotypic flexibility without paying the full cost of learning.

Cultural inheritance is adaptive because it is such a shortcut. If the locally adaptive behavior is more common than other behaviors, imitation provides an inexpensive way to acquire it. If the environment is not too variable, modest amounts of individual learning combined with cultural transmission lead to forces of guided variation and bias that are strong enough to cause available models generally to have adaptive skills. In this way, a cultural population can adapt to local conditions with a much smaller investment in learning than an acultural population.

To make this argument more concrete, consider the evolution of cultural transmission in a hypothetical population of acultural organisms in a temporally varying environment. In each generation, individuals modify their behavior through individual learning; on average, individuals develop behavior that is adaptive in the current environment, but because some individuals make errors, there is individual variation. Now, consider the evolution of a hypothetical mutant "imitator" gene that causes its bearers to eschew individual learning and copy the behavior of individuals from the previous generation. As long as the environment does not change too much between generations, the average behavior of these models will be close to the currently adaptive behavior. By copying behavior of individuals from the previous generation, imitators avoid costly learning trials, and, if they average over a number of models, have a better chance of acquiring the currently adaptive behavior than non-imitators. Thus, the imitator gene seems likely to spread when it is rare. As the imitator gene increases in frequency, however, more individuals will acquire their behavior by imitation. This will cause the population to track the changing environment less effectively and thus reduce the advantage of the imitator genotype. Eventually an equilibrium will be reached in which both imitators and non-imitators are present. If individual learning is sufficiently costly, and the environment not too variable, it seems plausible that imitators might predominate at equilibrium. Such a population would be adapted to the current environment even though only a small fraction engaged in individual learning.

This model is clearly artificial. A more realistic model would allow genetic modifiers to control the relative importance of individual and social learning in determining the behavior of each individual. In Chapter 4 we will show that such a model leads to qualitative conclusions like those of the simple model described here: selection favors increasing the importance of social learning in determining individual behavior relative to that of individual learning because social learning is a less costly way of acquiring the locally adaptive phenotype. As individual learning becomes less important, the population tracks the environment less effectively. Social learning can continue to be effective because a cultural population can respond to relatively weak forces that act over many generations.

There may also be circumstances that make it more profitable for an individual to imitate nonparental individuals than to imitate his or her genetic parents. For example, offspring frequently must emigrate. Individuals native to the new habitat are likely to be much better models than the immigrant's biological parents. Let us suppose that the structure of cultural transmission is affected by genetically transmitted traits. Then we might expect selection to favor an asymmetric system of cultural inheritance, again in order to reduce the costs of individual learning. Selection acting on such an asymmetric system can favor genetically disadvantageous behaviors, but as long as the effect of nonparental transmission, averaged over all the behaviors transmitted, is favorable, asymmetric transmission can evolve.

Selection could lead to cultural transmission that is biased in such a way that the forces due to transmission bias would counteract those due to selection acting on the asymmetric system of cultural transmission. Why doesn't it? An anthropomorphic answer to this question is that genes have to "know" what phenotype is favored by selection in any particular environment in order to bias cultural transmission in that phenotype's favor. However, genes have no way of "knowing" the relative fitness of different phenotypes in a local habitat without acquiring information through some process like trial-and-error learning. But we have supposed that cultural transmission is favored precisely because it allows individuals to avoid at least some of the costs of learning and calculating for themselves.

The same general argument applies to all the structural differences between genetic and cultural inheritance. A particular form of social learning may allow an individual to avoid the costs associated with independently evaluating the adaptiveness of alternative behaviors. Structural features such as an asymmetric life cycle, frequency dependent bias, and indirect bias may make it more likely that the offspring acquires an adaptive phenotype, but they also introduce novel evolutionary forces that make it impossible to understand behavior directly from the postulate of inclusive fitness maximization. So long as the net effect of social learning is positive, it can be favored by selection. At the same time, the resulting processes can cause particular behaviors or even whole suites of behaviors to diverge radically from the predictions of sociobiological theory.

This claim is stronger than the statement that different behaviors interact to affect fitness. Consider the following analogy. Biologists trying to understand the evolution of social behavior commonly take the nature of the genetic system as given, even though it can have crucial effects on the kind of social behavior a species has evolved. For example, some arthropods are "haplodiploid," meaning that females have two sets of chromosomes and males only one. Sociobiological theory suggests that haplodiploidy makes it more likely that altruistic cooperation will evolve between sisters (see Hamilton, 1972). Biologists trying to understand why haplodiploidy evolved from ordinary diploid ancestors should account for its "deleterious" effect on the cooperative behavior of sisters, along with all of its other effects. On the other hand, biologists trying to understand the evolution of social behavior in a particular species of wasp can take the genetic system as given because the time scale of evolution of the genetic system is much longer than the time scale of evolution of ordinary phenotypic characters like social behavior.

The evolution of the structure of cultural transmission in humans is analogous to the evolution of the genetic system. Changes in the structure of cultural transmission simultaneously affect all the characters that are culturally transmitted. If we want to understand the evolution of the structure of cultural inheritance itself, we have to average over all these effects. On the other hand, if we want to understand the evolution of social behavior in humans, we take the structure of the cultural inheritance system as fixed.

The General Utility of Dual Inheritance Theory

From the perspective of an evolutionary biologist, the relationship between genes and culture appears to be the most interesting scientific problem presented by human evolution, and this explains our preoccupation with the question. From the perspective of most social scientists, the relationship between genes and culture is of secondary interest. We believe that dual inheritance theory can be fruitfully applied to many other problems in the social sciences. To illustrate its utility, we use the models to address three other basic questions:

1. What is the relationship between ecological and evolutionary processes? Social scientists sometimes view synchronic and diachronic explanations as competing. More commonly, they are held to be complementary, but the mechanisms linking contemporary and historical causes are left quite vague. Dual inheritance theory accounts for historical effects through the cultural transmission process and for ecological ones through the forces that act on culture within one generation. Thus synchronic and diachronic explanations are aspects of the same causal processes in this system.

2. What is the relationship between individuals and society? This problem has generated a series of longstanding controversies. Methodological individualists (e.g. most economists), conflict theorists (e.g. Marxists, who emphasize the role of social classes), and macrofunctionalists (e.g. the followers of Durkheim in sociology and anthropology) identify different fundamental units of analysis and reach very different conclusions on this question. In our theory, the individual is linked to larger units by cultural transmission and its population-level properties. What this linkage implies for what behavior we can expect (e.g. should the function of behavior be interpreted at the individual or group level) turns out to depend on the details of evolutionary processes.

3. What is the role of symbols in human evolution? Much of human behavior consists of the use and production of symbols—language, art, religious ritual, and the like. No agreement has been reached whether or not such behavior can be explained in terms of functional theories. We can address this problem with models of the indirect bias force. Its runaway process can cause functional traits to become symbols.

In each case, dual inheritance theory clarifies these questions by formulating them in terms of explicit evolutionary models. Even though the models are far from complete solutions, they improve understanding of the logic of the problems and suggest what kinds of observations and measurements, and additional theory, are required for more definitive answers. We believe that many other problems of interest to students of human behavior can be similarly clarified by the construction of appropriate models of cultural evolution.

Conclusion

Throughout this book, we are concerned with two related theoretical questions: First, how do the structural features of cultural inheritance observed in contemporary humans produce observed patterns of human behavior? Second, are these structural features conceivably genetically adaptive? Our answers to these questions make it more difficult to apply the sociobiologists' argument from natural origins: If acquiring information by individual effort is costly compared to acquisition by social learning, an explicit theory of the mechanisms of cultural evolution may be necessary. At the same time, however, our results may provide novel explanations for otherwise puzzling patterns of human behavior. It has not been possible to solve the more interesting empirical questions definitively: Is an explicit theory of the mechanisms of cultural evolution necessary? And, if so, what exactly should it be like? However, a deductive theory which clearly sets out the logical relationships between genetic and cultural evolution does advance our understanding of such problems by more clearly showing what is at issue in controversies, such as those between human sociobiologists and their critics, which otherwise appear to be the result of irreconcilable "philosophical" differences. Our objective is to construct as wide a variety of simple hypotheses as seem logically sound and consistent with the available imperfect evidence. Present theory and data demand a considerable agnosticism about the various conventional explanations for human behavior and evolution, but dual inheritance models do suggest a compelling program for theoretical and empirical investigations that can eventually provide satisfactory explanations.

2
Some Methodological Preliminaries

I am a firm believer that without speculation there is no good and original observation.

Charles Darwin in a letter to A. R. Wallace, 1857
(Brent, 1981: 409)

False facts are highly injurious to the progress of science, for they often endure long; but false views, if supported by some evidence, do little harm as every one takes a salutary pleasure in proving their falseness; and when this is done, one path toward error is closed and the road to truth is often at the same time opened.

Charles Darwin, *The Descent of Man* (1871: II-385)

Charles Darwin was less than completely candid about the relationship between his theories and the many experiments and observations he used to support them. Sometimes he seems to have endorsed the inductive philosophy of science that was conventional in his day: first observe, then extract theories from the observations. For example, in *The Expression of Emotions in Man and Animals* (1872) he claims, "I arrived at these three Principles only at the close of my observations." As Howard Gruber (1974) has noted, however, all three principles are present in Darwin's M and N notebooks, which date from 1838. On other occasions, Darwin defended the more modern view that, without theory, fruitful observation is unlikely, that we must hypothesize in order to observe. Whatever his published views, Darwin's notebooks leave little doubt that as a working scientist he was an avid theorizer who more than once first developed a theory and then searched for evidence to support it.

This book is primarily about theory. It is based on the assumption that culture can be profitably viewed as a system of inheritance. Then we try to imagine how the observable events in the lives of individuals lead to the increase of some culturally transmitted variants and the decrease of others. To help answer these questions we have borrowed a style of mathematical theorizing, and many specific models, from contemporary evolutionary biology. Experience has taught us that many social scientists will find various aspects of this kind of theorizing confusing and objectionable. To some it seems too reductionistic, to others too simplified, and to still others reminiscent of either Social Darwinism or genetic determinism. In this chapter we briefly digress to defend our approach against these objections.

Darwinian Approach

We seek to develop models of cultural evolution which can link two kinds of observable phenomena, the macroscopic patterns of behavior that characterize societies and cultures and the microscopic details of the lives of individuals. Our goal is to understand how the day-to-day and generation-to-generation repetition of processes we can observe on the small scale can cause large-scale and long-run patterns of behavior within and between societies. Key among the assumptions in these models is that the transmission of culture in humans constitutes a system of inheritance. We introduced this idea in Chapter 1 and will defend it at length in Chapter 3. Here we will say only that humans acquire attitudes, beliefs, and other kinds of information from others by social learning and that these items of cultural information affect individual behavior. To understand the macroscopic patterns of social behavior, the theory must explain how the events in the lives of individuals change the frequency of different culturally transmitted beliefs and attitudes.

This approach to understanding the evolution of cultural organisms is analogous to the approach that Darwin first used to account for organic evolution. The basic element of Darwin's approach was the assumption that organisms inherit information that, in combination with the local environment, determines their phenotype. To understand why a population was characterized by some phenotypes and not others, he asked what processes in the lives of individuals increased the frequency of some variants relative to others. Ultimately, he came to believe that natural selection and the inheritance of acquired variation were the most important. Contemporary biologists reject the inheritance of acquired variation as an important factor in evolutionary change, and, based on a knowledge of genetics, they have added other forces such as segregation and recombination. Nonetheless, they have retained Darwin's basic approach to understanding the evolution of noncultural organisms.

Assuming that culture is a system of inheritance, it seems likely that Darwin's approach will be useful for understanding cultural change for the same reason that it provided the key to understanding organic evolution: it directs our attention to accounting for all the important processes that affect that variation carried through time by a succession of individuals. Today's cultural traditions are the result of cumulative changes made by past and present bearers of them. To understand why cultural traditions have the form that they do, we need to account for the processes that increase the frequency of some cultural variants and reduce that of others. Why do some individuals change traditions? Or invent new behaviors? Why are some variants transmitted, while others are not? Why do many variants remain rare or never occur at all? Answering such questions is the objective of our theory.

Recursion models

Like many of the models in evolutionary biology, all of the mathematical models presented in this book will be what are called "recursion equations." The form of these models provides an especially clear illustration of how we will connect assumptions about the nature of enculturation and life history of individuals with the larger-scale phenomena of cultural evolution.

The first step in building a recursion model of evolution is to specify a life cycle for the organism under consideration. For some trait we might wish to study, the following simplified life cycle of a cultural organism might suffice.

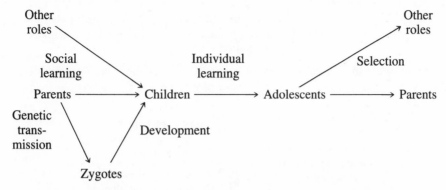

During the course of a single generation, various events occur in the lives of individuals in the population. Genetic transmission creates zygotes that develop into children who are enculturated by a set of individuals who typically occupy certain social roles. For example, for many cultural traits the biological parents typically play the most important roles in enculturation. In other cases, individuals occupying social roles such as grandmother, teacher, or priest may be important in enculturation. Children acquire some behaviors and modify others as they mature into adolescents. The result is a population of adolescents and young adults who interact with the physical and social environment. Some of these young adults acquire the resources necessary for cultural and/or genetic transmission.

The next step is to describe what happens to individuals in a population during each step of the life cycle. Some individuals will carry one genetic or cultural variant, some another, and often variants will differ in what happens to them at different stages of the life cycle. Consider two cultural variants, one placing a high value on domesticity, the other a low value—homebodies and hellraisers, respectively. We can begin constructing the model by starting anywhere in the life cycle, say with the events of social learning. How do children acquire a disposition to be homebodies or hellraisers? One of the simplest ways would be just to imitate one genetic parent or the other at random. If so,

$$
\begin{pmatrix}
\text{Number of homebodies} \\
\text{among children in} \\
\text{generation t}
\end{pmatrix}
$$

$$
= (1/2)
\begin{pmatrix}
\text{Number of homebodies} \\
\text{among parents of} \\
\text{generation t} - 1
\end{pmatrix}
\times
\begin{pmatrix}
\text{Average number of} \\
\text{children per homebody} \\
\text{parent}
\end{pmatrix}
$$

The equation is multiplied by one-half because each child has two parents and so each parent will, given our assumed rule of transmission, on average transmit the trait to half of them. The equation describing the socialization process for hellraisers is very similar:

$$\begin{pmatrix} \text{Number of hellraisers} \\ \text{among children in} \\ \text{generation t} \end{pmatrix}$$

$$= (1/2)\begin{pmatrix} \text{Number of hellraisers} \\ \text{among parents of} \\ \text{generation t} - 1 \end{pmatrix} \times \begin{pmatrix} \text{Average number of} \\ \text{children per hellraiser} \\ \text{parent} \end{pmatrix}$$

We can simplify the model considerably, without sacrificing anything for most purposes, by keeping track of frequencies or proportions of the variants instead of the numbers:

$$\begin{pmatrix} \text{Proportion of homebodies} \\ \text{among children in} \\ \text{generation t} \end{pmatrix} = \frac{\begin{pmatrix} \text{Number of homebodies} \\ \text{among children} \\ \text{in generation t} \end{pmatrix}}{\begin{pmatrix} \text{Total number of homebody} \\ \text{and hellraiser children in} \\ \text{generation t} \end{pmatrix}}$$

Since the proportion of hellraisers is just (1 − the proportion of homebodies) at this or any other stage of the life cycle, we only need an equation for one of the two types to specify the model completely.

Next, children mature to become adolescents. During this period many things happen, the most important of which might be that adolescents sample the pleasures of life; some children who began adolescence with a cultural disposition to become homebodies discover that hellraising is fun and switch, and vice versa. Keeping explicit track only of the proportion of homebodies now,

$$\begin{pmatrix} \text{Proportion of} \\ \text{homebodies} \\ \text{among adole-} \\ \text{scents in} \\ \text{generation t} \end{pmatrix} = \begin{pmatrix} \text{Proportion of} \\ \text{homebodies} \\ \text{among children} \\ \text{in generation t} \end{pmatrix} \times \begin{pmatrix} \text{Probability that} \\ \text{homebodies} \\ \text{stay} \\ \text{homebodies} \end{pmatrix}$$

$$+ \begin{pmatrix} \text{Proportion of} \\ \text{hellraisers} \\ \text{among children} \\ \text{in generation t} \end{pmatrix} \times \begin{pmatrix} \text{Probability that} \\ \text{hellraisers} \\ \text{become} \\ \text{homebodies} \end{pmatrix}$$

Next, adolescents mature into adults who will be the parents of the next, t + 1, generation. Perhaps homebodies and hellraisers have different probabilities of becoming parents:

$$\begin{pmatrix} \text{Proportion of home-} \\ \text{bodies among parents} \\ \text{in generation t} \end{pmatrix} = \frac{\begin{pmatrix} \text{Proportion of} \\ \text{homebodies among} \\ \text{adolescents in} \\ \text{generation t} \end{pmatrix}\begin{pmatrix} \text{Probability that} \\ \text{a homebody} \\ \text{becomes} \\ \text{a parent} \end{pmatrix}}{\begin{pmatrix} \text{Average probability that a member} \\ \text{of generation t becomes a parent} \end{pmatrix}}$$

Finally, by combining all of these steps, we obtain a model of events during one generation that influence the first stage of the next. This complete equation describing the events during one complete generation is called a recursion.

Recursions capture the nature of the evolutionary process on a microscopic time scale. The objective, however, is to predict the longer-run course of evolution. To accomplish this the equation is iterated recursively, stepped forward from generation to generation to determine how the frequency of different variants changes through time, and perhaps reaches some equilibrium, a value at which the frequency of the two variants becomes constant. Thus we can ask: Will the frequency of homebodies increase from the level maintained by chance development to almost 100 percent? Or will the frequency of homebodies stabilize at some intermediate value, say, one-half?

We say that distinct processes which cause the frequency of different cultural variants to change are *forces*. In this illustrative model, three forces are in operation, one resulting from life-style choice during adolescence, one from the different tendency of the variants to become parents, and one from the difference in the expected number of children raised by each variant. Some of the forces may increase the frequency of homebodies (homebodies may be more likely to become parents and have more children), and others may decrease it (more homebodies may learn to be hellraisers than vice versa).

Levels of explanation

The adherents of some schools of thought in the social sciences hold that to understand societies we must begin by understanding individual psychology and its effect on behavior. Large-scale social patterns are seen as the aggregate result of individual behavior. The otherwise diverse theories of Anglo-American economists, behavioral psychologists, and exchange theorists in both sociology and anthropology all share this general "reductionistic" approach. The members of other schools of thought hold that "the determining cause of a social fact should be sought among the social facts preceding it and not among the states of individual consciousness" (Durkheim, 1938 [1895]: 110). By this they mean that we should seek explanations for large-scale patterns in terms of causal processes acting on the scale of whole societies. These scholars argue that societies shape individual behavior rather than the reverse. Various kinds of functionalists in sociology and anthropology, symbolic anthropologists, and to some extent Marxists adhere to this "holistic" paradigm.

To some readers, it may seem that we must side with the reductionists because we attempt to discover the causes of the large-scale and long-term patterns of society in terms of events in the lives of individuals. This is a misperception. In our models the two levels are reciprocally linked; large-scale processes affect small-scale phenomena, and vice versa. We take the group (or population) of individuals as our fundamental unit. A group can be characterized by the number of individuals who exhibit each different cultural variant. We refer to this as the "distribution of cultural variants" (or phenotypes) within the group. To understand why a group is characterized by a particular distribution of cultural variants, we must understand the forces of cultural evolution that act on members of the group. Some of these forces have their origin in the psychology of individuals. Learning and rational calculation can affect the frequency of phenotypes through the force of guided variation, and various genetically or culturally acquired psychological predispositions may lead to biased cultural transmission. Other forces are the result of larger-scale social processes. Cultural transmission creates heritable variation in behavior between individuals and groups of individuals. Social processes which increase the frequencies of some kinds of individuals or groups lead to the force of natural selection. To predict the equilibrium distribution of cultural variants in a particular population we need to deduce the net effects of the various forces.

The way that dual inheritance models are used to link processes at different levels is illustrated by the simple example of a recursion model that was just outlined. Because there are only two variants, the distribution of cultural variants can be specified by the frequency of one of the variants, say homebodies. Some of the forces affecting the frequency of homebodies seem most plausibly the result of psychological factors. For example, life-style choice during adolescence might be determined mainly by the attractiveness of fast living. Other of the forces are more plausibly the effect of social factors. The number of children that a couple can have might depend on their income. In a peaceful agrarian society homebodies might have higher incomes, while in a society that relied on warfare and conquest, hellraisers might do better. In this way the nature of the social structure can affect which cultural traditions predominate.

Modeling Complex Phenomena

Human evolution is both extremely complex and extremely diverse. It is complex because to understand it we must understand the details of how individuals acquire and modify attitudes and beliefs, how different attitudes and beliefs interact with genes and environment to produce behavior, and how behavior and environment interact to produce consequences for individual lives, in addition to the complexities of organic evolution. It is diverse because we expect human populations to be quite different from one another. Each exemplar of the human evolutionary process not only is exposed to a different environment but also may have a unique cultural inheritance system.

The problem of how to construct useful theories of complex social and biological processes such as human evolution has preoccupied ecologists, economists, sociologists, and psychologists for several decades. The answer may seem obvious: to be useful, models must be realistic; they should incorporate all of the factors that scientists studying the phenomena know to be important. Models built following this reasoning will usually be quite complicated. This view is certainly plausible, and many scientists, particularly in economics (e.g. Hudson and Jorgenson, 1974) and ecology (e.g. Watt, 1964), have constructed such models.

We believe that building such detailed models is the wrong approach if one's goal is to arrive at a general understanding of a diverse class of evolutionary processes. We have adopted another modeling strategy that is also widely used in evolutionary biology and economics. We try to build a variety of simple models which can be completely understood but which still capture the generic properties of the processes of interest. Following Liebenstein (1976: Chap. 2) we will call the simple models "sample theories." Useful sample theories result from attempts to satisfy two competing desiderata: They should be simple enough to be clearly and completely grasped and at the same time approximate how the world actually does work. Within these constraints sample theories may be more or less specific. All of the sample theories we will present are designed to capture the qualitative properties of the whole class of processes which they are used to represent. The whole collection of sample theories and combinations of them creates a general theory of how the whole complex of processes work.

The population genetical theory of evolution provides a good example of such a general theory. Each of the basic processes (e.g. selection, mutation, drift) is represented by a large variety of simple models, some specific to a particular population, others quite general. These models are combined in different ways to represent interesting phenomena (e.g. sexual selection, speciation). This whole family of models, together with a knowledge of which models are appropriate for what kinds of situations, constitutes the theory.

In defense of simple models

All of the models presented in this book will be quite simple compared to the phenomena they are intended to represent. To keep the models simple we must deliberately omit many details that specialists in the relevant disciplines believe are important. We eschew more detailed models because (1) they are not useful for representing generic processes, (2) they are hard to understand, (3) they are difficult to analyze, and (4) they are often no more useful for prediction than simple models. Let us now consider each of these points in turn.

1. We do not seem to be able to construct models of social and biological phenomena that are general, realistic, and precisely predictive (Levins, 1966, 1968). That is, evolutionary biologists and social scientists have not been able to satisfy the epistemological norm derived from the physical sciences which holds that theory be in the form of universal laws that can be tested by the detailed predictions they make about the phenomena considered by the law. This failure is probably a consequence of the complexity and diversity of living things. Basic theoretical constructs like natural selection are not universal laws like gravitation; rather they are taxonomic entities, general classes of similar processes which nonetheless have a good deal of diversity within the class. A theoretical construct designed to represent the general properties of the class of processes labeled "natural selection" must sacrifice many of the details of particular examples of selection. On the other hand, a model tailored to the details of a particular case is unlikely to have much relevance beyond that case. Further, the most precise predictions may be obtained by statistical models which sacrifice realism and hence are useless as explanatory devices.

2. Complex, detailed models are usually extremely difficult to understand. As more realism is added, the myriad interactions within the model become almost as opaque as the real world we wish to understand. When a set of not-so-complex parts is linked together to form an interacting complex, it is often impossible to understand why the results behave as they do. To substitute an ill-understood model of the world for the ill-understood world is not progress. In the end, the only way to understand how such a model works is to abstract pieces from it or study simplified cases where its behavior is more transparent. Even when complex models are useful, they are so because we understand how they work in terms of simple models abstracted from them.

3. The analysis of complex models is also expensive and time consuming. The complexity of a recursion model is roughly measured by the number of independent variables that must be kept track of from generation to generation. It usually is not possible to analyze nonlinear recursions involving more than a handful of variables without resorting to numerical techniques. Until the advent of digital computers, obtaining numerical solutions was impractical. Since then, however, there have been many attempts made to simulate realistic computer models of complex social and biological processes. These projects have generally been quite costly. As the number of variables in a model increases, the number of interactions between variables increases even faster. This means that, even with the fastest computers, it is not practical to explore the sensitivity of a model to changes in assumptions about very many of its constituent interactions.

4. Detailed models of complex social or biological systems often are not much more useful for prediction than are simple models. Detailed models usually require very large amounts of data to determine the various parameter values in the model. Such data are rarely available. Moreover, small inaccuracies or errors in the formulation of the model can produce quite erroneous predictions. The temptation is to "tune" the model, making small changes, perhaps well within the error of available data, so that the model produces reasonable answers. When this is done, any predictive power that the model might have is due more to statistical fitting than to the fact that it accurately represents actual causal processes. It is easy to make large sacrifices of understanding (realism and generality) for small gains in predictive power.

That the general theory applied to the problems of biological and cultural evolution is built up of the analysis of simple sample theories does not mean that the general theory itself is simple. The objective is not to produce one universal theoretical model with one sample theory chosen for each component, although such a model may have great heuristic utility as a kind of elementary textbook reference point. Rather, general theory, as it matures, becomes a large family of sample theories and analyses of combinations of them. If the lessons of population biology are correct, this enterprise sometimes does lead to robust results, conclusions that are approximately correct for a wide variety of possible sample models. For kinds of phenomena that are truly diverse, the result is a classification of cases into types where different sample models must be used. For example, some organisms are haploid, some diploid and some are sexual, some asexual. Some evolutionary phenomena are rather robust with regard to such things, and a theorist might appropriately choose the simplest model. It may even be appropriate to use, say, a haploid sample model to analyze some theoretical questions where one knows the organisms of interest are diploid and that this assumption will lead to unrealism and modest predictive power. Such choices are often made because other parts of the model are complex and some particular patently unrealistic assumption seems unlikely to lead to qualitative changes in the results. However, if the behavior of diploid organisms is known to be quite different from haploid ones for the phenomenon under consideration, the assumption of haploidy may be not a convenient or desirable simplification but a serious error.

The utility of general theory

Does general theory based on a collection of simple sample models have any serious scientific purpose? Some might argue that their qualitative kind of understanding is, at best, useful for giving nonspecialists a simplified overview of complicated topics and that real scientific progress still occurs entirely in the construction of theories that actually predict. A sterner critic might characterize the attempt to assemble simple models into a general theory as loose speculation that actually inhibits the real work of discovering precisely predictable relationships. These kinds of objections implicitly assume that it is possible to do science without any kind of general model. All scientists have mental models of the world. The part of the model that deals with their disciplinary specialty is more detailed than the parts that represent related areas of science. Many aspects of a scientist's mental model are likely to be vague and never expressed. The real choice is between an intuitive, perhaps covert, general theory and an explicit, often mathematical one.

The most important function of general theory is to link the many disciplines contributing to the understanding of a complex problem like the evolution of human behavior. The general theory suggests what properties of sample theories are essential in order to make the theory complete. It makes it possible to deduce the consequences of alternative sample theories in one discipline for the phenomena studied by another. For example, in the next chapter we will be concerned with the details of how cultural transmission occurs, a subject studied by psychologists. Social learning theorists have made many, but not all, of the kinds of measurements that are necessary for specifying good sample theories of cultural transmission. Some of the crucial unknowns include the mechanisms by which variation and covariation are maintained in cultural traits. These properties have important implications for the process of cultural evolution because forces of the bias and natural selection depend on the maintenance of variation to be effective. The relative strength of the various evolutionary forces acting on culture in turn determines rates of evolution and the kinds of traits we expect to be common at equilibrium. These deficiencies of social learning theory are not at all apparent in the absence of a general theory linking the psychology of enculturation with the macroscopic phenomena of social institutions and long-run outcomes. When we force ourselves to construct models that make these links, even if they are simple caricatures, we often discover that processes with small, relatively hard-to-measure effects can produce major results. The frequency dependent bias force we will examine in Chapter 7 could have a large effect on the distribution of variation in populations, even if it is so small as to be difficult to measure in the psychological laboratory. Sensible social learning theorists would not undertake such arduous and costly experiments unless a general theoretical argument gave them reasonable confidence that the results would bear on an important problem.

By treating specific models as sample theories, a general theory may also help us decide when it may be worthwhile to sacrifice generality for prediction. At least in a mature general theory, a good many sample models will have been formulated and their behavior explored. The theory will contain information about which kinds of sample theories have proven to be useful approximations under various conditions. Robust results will be known. In other words, the general theory is a population of sample theories about which we know something. Given a particular situation where accurate prediction is desired, a general theory provides a compendium of potential sample theories that might be applied, together with some guidance for what kinds of models can be constructed and what sort of prediction can or cannot be sought.

As a matter of practical scientific strategy in biology and the social sciences, the use of general theory built up from simple models is not a substitute for a more sophisticated method, but the most sophisticated possible given the complexity and diversity inherent in the subject matter. Human behavior is certainly the product of the interaction of genes, culture, and environment expressed in phenomena as diverse as individual behavior and the social and political organizations of "world systems." No one discipline addresses more than a small fraction of this totality. Because we cannot build predictive general theories in the style of physics, the efforts of these disciplines must either be guided by simplified general theories or be left to drift in isolation. Under the latter condition, advancing understanding is extremely difficult. Long-run improvements in the ability of science to predict are dependent on a general theoretical understanding. Human behavior may be so complex that no single set of manageable sample theories will give even qualitatively correct predictions for all traits in all societies, but an adequate general theory might allow us to understand how to construct appropriately predictive sample theories under various conditions.

Testing the theory

Because simplified sample theories omit many important details, they usually only result in a qualitative understanding of the phenomena of interest. They cannot give us detailed, quantitative predictions about the outcome of any particular experiment. For example, neo-Darwinian theory is an elegant scientific account of why most plants and animals are closely adapted to the environments they live in, and microeconomic theory is a similarly elegant account of the role of price in equilibrating supply and demand. Neither is useful by itself for making precise quantitative predictions about the dynamics of particular populations or particular markets. Indeed, if we pressed them into service as predictive instruments, we would be pleasantly surprised if they worked at all.

It is difficult to subject a general theory assembled out of simple models to a direct empirical test because the failure to predict the outcome of a particular experiment or observation cannot falsify the theory. Sample theories usually omit many important processes from consideration. The theory may be correct and still fail in many particular instances as a result of the action of unincluded processes. No one would be surprised if any simple model of interspecies competition failed to predict the history of interaction in a particular community because such models typically neglect such factors as genetic variation within populations and environmental heterogeneity which could have important effects on population dynamics.

The relationship between a general theory of complex systems and empirical test or prediction is a subtle one. To insist upon empirical science in the style of physics is to insist upon the impossible. However, to give up on empirical tests and prediction would be to abandon science and retreat to speculative philosophy. A mature general theory like population genetics tells us which sample theories are likely to be relevant to any particular phenomenon or observation. These sample theories in turn make qualitative predictions, or perhaps even quantitative predictions in some special cases. If some sample theory is consistently at variance with the data then it must be modified. The accumulation of these kinds of modifications can eventually alter general theory, either by compelling the abandonment of some sample models or by systematizing knowledge about the variation of processes. In extreme cases, major discoveries in some of the components of a general theory can compel the reorganization of the entire edifice, as exemplified by the impact of Mendelian genetics on Darwinian theory in biology.

In the meantime, general theory is useful so long as its predictions are qualitatively correct, roughly conforming to the majority of cases. Nor is it necessarily an embarrassment if more than one alternative formulation of a general theory, built from different sample models, is more or less equally correct. In this case, the comparison of theories that are empirically equivalent makes clearer what is at stake in scientific controversies and may suggest empirical and theoretical steps toward a resolution.

Use of Data

Throughout this book we will use data from the social sciences and human biology to motivate the models of particular processes, and then to illustrate possible instances of the hypotheses that result. The social sciences and human biology constitute a huge body of knowledge. We do not claim to have thoroughly surveyed each of the many relevant fields, and we make no claim to have constructed a completely satisfactory general theory even in the limited sense suggested above. These are long-term tasks, and much of the work involved demands highly specialized knowledge. Psychologists will have to play a major role in the formulation and testing of theories of cultural transmission, and only anthropologists and sociologists have the kind of expertise necessary to judge which among several alternative formulations of a general theory gives the best overall qualitative fit to the macroscopic evidence.

Our more modest objectives are:

1. To be sure that the simple models we chose to represent particular processes are reasonable. Thus we have tried to motivate each model with data from the relevant areas in the social sciences or human biology. Even if our review is not entirely competent and our choices of sample models less than the best possible, we hope to have given our readers a clear point of argument if they disagree.

2. To represent the most controversial or least known part of a process with a variable term in the models. In this way, different readings of ambiguous data can be evaluated in a common theoretical framework by examining the quantitative properties of the model. For example, the models of learning and cultural transmission in Chapter 4 allow a given trait to be determined by any mixture of nonsocial learning and cultural transmission in order to represent the controversy over the degree to which humans behave as rational actors.

3. To show how the general theory can be used to gain a qualitative understanding of some of the observed macroscopic features of human behavior. For example, the scale of social organization is larger and the degree of cooperation among members of a given society is greater in humans than in other primates. In Chapter 7 we show how an empirically plausible form of biased cultural transmission can result in patterns of cooperation that seem to conform to those anthropologists and sociologists observe.

In short, our use of empirical information in theory construction is mainly illustrative. We have tried to use enough data in model construction and provide enough "tests" of models to show how our theory works and to demonstrate its power and utility. In so doing, we hope to have constructed a general theory sufficiently realistic to clarify the basic issues surrounding processes by which the interactions of genes and culture produce human behavior. We even entertain hopes that some of our specific hypotheses will turn out to be approximately correct. We beg our readers' indulgence of this last pretension and ask that it not be allowed to obscure the more fundamental arguments.

In Defense of Mathematical Models

Mathematical models are arduous to construct, analyze, and read, even for the well trained. They appear to contradict our argument for the virtues of simplicity, and, carelessly used, they can be quite misleading. However, mathematical analysis can also be extremely useful. By using this approach we can usually manage the logic involved in a model that is a bit more complex and realistic than would otherwise be possible. The human mind has very limited powers of deduction, especially when several processes interact in a quantitative or probabilistic fashion (see Chap. 5, pp. 168–170). Mathematical models often demand considerable simplification and abstraction to satisfy the constraints of analytical tractability, and for this reason they often seem objectionably artificial. However, attempting to deduce the answer to a complex problem by direct inspection and unaided intuition requires even simpler models and entails great risk of erroneous reasoning. In our own case at least, the formal exercise of reducing intuitive notions to mathematical propositions and deriving results has often led to unexpected conclusions.

However, mathematical analysis by itself is not sufficient; the well-known contemporary aphorism "garbage in, garbage out" applies to any logical analysis, not just computer calculations. Our nonmathematical readers, who may have to take the formal analysis pretty much on faith, should not despair. We have tried to explain in words as clearly as possible what assumptions are built into the models, what the results mean, and what their main limitations are. Quite aside from any desire to make the book accessible to such readers, our experience is that an inability to produce a sensible prose explanation of how a model works often indicates there is something wrong with the model.

In Defense of Analogies

The basic point of departure for the dual inheritance model is the analogy between genes and culture. Analogies between the behavior of humans and that of other animals have often been judged objectionable. Such analogies have often been misused, and much of their bad reputation is deserved. On the other hand, Masters (1973) argues that analogies between human and animal behavior are both inescapable and, when properly constructed, useful. Clarifying how we will use analogical reasoning may answer some potential objections that derive from experience with inappropriate analogies.

The main reason we are interested in using the inheritance system analogy is practical. To the extent that the transmission of culture and the transmission of genes are similar processes, we can borrow the well-developed conceptual categories and formal machinery of Darwinian biology to analyze problems. The work of Cavalli-Sforza and Feldman (e.g. 1981) has been particularly thorough in exploiting this use of the analogy.

However, we are as interested in the disanalogies between the cultural and genetic inheritance as in their similarities. If cultural inheritance were exactly analogous to genes, its existence would not present any interesting problems. We might wonder briefly why a system which duplicated the structure and function of DNA ever arose in the first place and go on to treat humans as if they had extra chromosomes of a rather odd kind. Human evolution is interesting, and difficult to understand, because there are important disanalogies between genes and culture. In fact, we will argue that the structural differences between the two systems may well have arisen because the two systems are functionally analogous, that is, both systems serve to enhance ordinary Darwinian fitness. For example, in Chapter 4 we show how the disanalogous inheritance of acquired variation can increase genetic fitness in some kinds of environments. On the other hand, the natural selection on cultural variation is closely analogous to natural selection on genes, but we will argue that it can lead to the evolution of behaviors that are not functionally close analogs of ordinary adaptations.

Conclusion

Constructing a satisfying explanatory theory of human behavior is clearly an ambitious undertaking. The topic is complex, and our empirical knowledge is woefully incomplete. However, we are convinced that the Darwinian approach we have sketched in this chapter is a sound one because it can clarify the logical relationships between evolution and human behavior and between various levels of explanation in the social sciences. However crude the initial attempts to construct theory and use it turn out to be, we are convinced that they will serve as a firm foundation for progressive improvement.

3

The Cultural Inheritance System

> Mohammedans are Mohammedans because they are born and reared among
> that sect, not because they have thought it out and can furnish sound reasons
> for being Mohammedans; we know why Catholics are Catholics; why Presby-
> terians are Presbyterians; why Baptists are Baptists; why Mormons are Mor-
> mons; why thieves are thieves; why monarchists are monarchists; why Repub-
> licans are Republicans and Democrats, Democrats. We know that it is a matter
> of association and sympathy, not reasoning and examination; that hardly a man
> in the world has an opinion on morals, politics, or religion that he got otherwise
> than through his associations and sympathies.
>
> Mark Twain, "Cornpone Opinions," in *Mark Twain on*
> *the Damned Human Race* (1923 [1962]: 24)

The essay "Cornpone Opinions" was found among Mark Twain's papers after his
death. In it, Twain tells how as a boy of fifteen he used to listen enraptured to the
sermons of an "impudent and satirical and delightful young blackman" named Jerry
who preached sermons from the top of his master's woodpile. One of his texts was:
"You tell me whar a man gits his corn pone, en I'll tell you what his 'pinions is."
Twain remembers Jerry and his sermons fondly, but he devotes the essay to
disputing Jerry's thesis. Instead of adopting cornpone opinions, Twain argues,
people adopt the opinions of those around them without giving much thought to
what those opinions might be. In our terminology, people inherit rather than choose
their views on religion, politics, and morals. To explain why thieves are thieves or
Republicans, Republicans, we must understand how and from whom they culturally inherited their beliefs.

As usual, Mark Twain is somewhat exaggerated in his opinions. People do not
believe what they believe solely because they inherit the beliefs of others. Some of
the evolutionary forces that affect the frequency of various beliefs in the population
result from "cornpone" effects such as rational choice. However, if Twain was even
partly correct that people inherit their beliefs and values, the population-level
properties of culture will be important.

In this chapter we explore the notion that cultural transmission in humans has the
properties of a system of inheritance. We begin by elaborating the definition of
cultural inheritance given in Chapter 1. Then we will review empirical evidence
from the social sciences that suggests that the cultural continuity of groups is due
to inheritance of beliefs and values, and is not merely a result of the effects of
individual learning and correlated environments. Finally, we will try to show in a
simple way how these structural features can be translated into mathematical
models that describe the changes in the frequencies of different behaviors from one
generation to the next. We hope to explicate the basic logic of the dual inheritance

approach, convince the reader that it is a reasonable depiction of social learning in humans, and at the same time introduce several kinds of mathematical machinery that are used throughout the rest of the book.

Defining Cultural Inheritance

What is culture? In anthropology, the term "culture" is used in many different and only partially overlapping senses. In 1952 Kroeber and Kluckhohn identified 164 definitions of culture proposed by historians and social scientists, and that number has undoubtedly grown. Their taxonomy of definitions required six major categories and ten subcategories, which gives some idea of the complexity of the culture concept. Social scientists seem to agree that culture is a socially transmitted heritage peculiar to a particular human society, but beyond this there is little consensus. In a recent review, Keesing (1974) argues that contemporary conceptions of culture fall into four distinct categories which differ in several fundamental ways. Consider just one dimension of the debate, the extent to which culture is seen as concrete behavior and artifact as opposed to a purely ideational concept. Members of one group, whom Keesing labels "cultural adaptationists," define culture in terms of observable, socially transmitted patterns of behavior. For example, Marvin Harris (1971: 136) offers,

> Cultures are patterns of behavior, thought and feeling that are acquired or influenced through learning and that are characteristic of groups of people rather than of individuals.

The other three categories of theories define culture exclusively in terms of ideas. For example, Ward Goodenough (1957: 167) suggests the following definition:

> [A] society's culture consists of whatever it is one has to know or believe in order to operate in a manner acceptable to its members. . . . We should note that culture is not a material phenomenon; it does not consist of things, people, behavior, or emotions. . . . It is the forms of things that people have in their mind, their models for perceiving, relating and otherwise interpreting them.

Other differences that Keesing reviews seem to be of nearly equal importance.

Like virtually all of the definitions of culture used in the social sciences, our definition emphasizes the notion that culture is a socially transmitted heritage:

> *Culture is information capable of affecting individuals' phenotypes which they acquire from other conspecifics by teaching or imitation.*

The information that a particular individual inherits culturally will be referred to as that individual's *cultural repertoire;* specific elements of the cultural repertoire are called his or her *cultural variant.* We will sometimes use the word *culture* by itself in two other ways: (1) to describe the information acquired by all the individuals in a particular group or society at a particular time, as for example, "Yanomamo culture," and (2) in a loose way to refer to the entire system of cultural inheritance, as for example, "genes vs. culture."

Our definition reflects several important conceptual distinctions that require elaboration. It is within the range of variation encompassed by other definitions in the social sciences, and, like them, it includes some distinctions but not others. It focuses on the process of cultural inheritance (or transmission) because that is the foundation of our analytical work and because we believe that it is the nature of cultural transmission that makes the evolutionary process of humans (and perhaps other cultural organisms) distinctive. Kroeber and Kluckhohn would have classified ours as a psychological definition with emphasis on learning. In contrast to other definitions they analyzed, it stresses the individual rather than society, the process of social learning rather than historical tradition, and it does not mention the functional properties of culture. As the analysis proceeds, we will find that these properties are implications of the process-based definition.

Why cultural inheritance is restricted to social learning

In the nature-nurture controversy, the concepts of culture, learning, and environment are usually regarded as nearly synonymous. We believe that each of these ideas plays a different role in explaining human behavior. The essential feature of culture is social learning, the nongenetic transfer of patterns of skill, thought, and feeling from individual to individual in a population or society. The social aspect of social learning can create novel evolutionary processes in cultural organisms through the existence of socially transmitted traditions that are not directly attributable to genetic factors and immediate environmental contingencies. To understand the evolutionary process of an organism with cultural transmission one must understand the forces that affect the frequency of different culturally transmitted variants in a population.

Social learning is only one of several nongenetic mechanisms by which individuals in a population can acquire a given pattern of behavior. Any mode of phenotypic flexibility will cause genetically similar individuals to resemble one another in similar environments. For example, a given European population's complexion will tend toward a given color. If a subset of the population moves to a sunnier climate, the typical color will become darker. In the human species both trial-and-error learning and rational calculation are potent mechanisms for producing similar patterns of behavior in similar environments because each individual independently tends to adopt the behaviors appropriate to that environment. Learning and other modes of phenotypic flexibility do have features in common with culture (Alexander, 1979a: 76–77), but it is the social transmission of culture that gives it an evolutionary dynamic different from ordinary learning and its analogs.

Not all social learning is cultural transmission

We have included the word "information" in our definition of cultural transmission to exclude certain simple modes of social influence on behavior, which cannot respond to evolutionary forces like natural selection in the same way as information does that is culturally transmitted. To see why this is true, consider the kinds of social learning that have been observed in animals other than man.

Bennet Galef (1976) provides an excellent review of the social transmission of acquired behavior in which he defines social learning as any "long-term homogeneity of behavior resulting from the transmission of patterns of behavior from individual to individual within a population as a consequence of social interaction."

Such transmission forms a graded series:

1. Traits for which the presence of a conspecific, usually the parents, is necessary for normal development, but variant behaviors are not transmitted. For example, young female rhesus macaques need social companions in order to develop normal maternal behavior later in life (e.g. Harlow and Harlow, 1969).

2. The acquisition of behaviors specific to particular localities through habitat imprinting. Many animals have home ranges that remain relatively fixed for many generations because the young form an attachment to the area in which they are born. The homing behavior of Pacific salmon and many migratory birds are well-known examples. In more complex cases, modification of the habitat constrains the behavior of new generations. For example, prairie dog territorial organization remains stable for many generations because of the effects of the complex burrow system (King, 1951, 1959).

3. Guided learning. Juvenile animals commonly follow adults. Similarly, dominant individuals tend to influence group movements. Both of these kinds of behavior will cause naive and subordinate individuals to be exposed to the same stimuli and reinforcements experienced by older or more dominant individuals. Guiding or following plus trial-and-error learning will result in the behavior of naive individuals resembling that of older or dominant individuals.

4. Social learning in the narrow sense. Animals may acquire behavior directly from conspecifics by imitating their behavior or because conspecifics (often parents) teach naive offspring by reinforcing appropriate behavior. Food preferences are one of the commonest traits nonhuman species acquire in this way. The spread of rather complex food handling traditions in Japanese macaques is a good example (Kawai, 1965). The observers introduced novel food items (sweet potatoes and wheat) which individual monkeys learned to process and eat. The learned techniques spread gradually throughout the troop, mostly from mothers to their offspring but also from juvenile to juvenile.

The incorporation of "imitation" and "teaching" with information in our definition of cultural inheritance is meant to restrict our definition of culture to social learning in the fourth, narrow sense. It is our intuition that only this kind of social learning is likely to have dynamic properties analogous to genetic inheritance. We use the term "information" to mean something which has the property that energetically minor causes have energetically major effects (Engelberg and Boyarsky, 1979). Because of this, information is cheap to store and replicate once acquired, and is easily transmitted to new individuals. For example, DNA, which represents a small fraction of the biomass of an organism, controls the energetically major features of metabolism and phenotype. Similarly, culture is cheaply acquired information, encoded in memory, that is capable of producing major phenotypic effects. Guided learning is not cultural transmission because the naive individual must acquire its own information by a process of reinforcement that is almost as costly as ordinary individual learning. It is the transmitted-information character of genes and the products of social learning that give organic and cultural evolution features not shared by cosmological or geological evolution, where information is not involved, or by the processes of individual learning, where the acquired information is costly and not transmitted.

To illustrate the importance of this distinction consider the question, Are prairie dog burrows culture? The inheritance of an artifact, the burrow, will certainly affect the behavior of a young prairie dog. Genetically identical prairie dogs which inherit burrows of different quality or in different locations may act very differently. However, burrows are a form of culture by our definition only if the shape and dimensions of a burrow are learned by prairie dogs who live there, are encoded in the memories of its prairie dog residents, and tend to be replicated by individuals who emigrate to new locations. Only then can burrows with advantageous geometry increase in frequency by natural selection (or some similar force). If, on the other hand, the form of the burrow is not so encoded, it will not have the potential to increase in frequency. Thus it cannot have evolutionary properties similar to genetically transmitted characters.

The cultural repertoire is analogous to genotype

"Information" was also included in our definition of cultural transmission because it is important to distinguish behavior and the products of behavior from patterns of thought and feeling. Harris, like many anthropologists, lumps behavior together with thought and feeling in his definition of culture. Many other definitions even include artifacts—tools, structures, and artwork—in the culture concept. We agree with Clifford Geertz (1973: 44, 143–146) that it is important to exclude behavior and the products of behavior from the definition of culture because behavior is contingent upon both patterns of thought and feeling and environmental circumstances. Two individuals with identical sets of culturally acquired dispositions may behave quite differently in different environments. Thus by our definition, the relationship between culture and behavior is similar to the relationship between genotype and phenotype in noncultural organisms.

Defining culture in terms of people's mental states (the "emic" concept of anthropology or the "cognitive" of social psychology) does not imply that culture is completely unobservable or that culture and behavior are not linked. As we shall see, the evidence from social learning theory (e.g. Rosenthal and Zimmerman, 1978) indicates that it is possible to observe the process of social learning and to obtain experimental evidence about the covert cognitive processes that govern its acquisition, storage, and influence on behavior. Only by distinguishing culture from behavior can we see clearly how social learning interacts with environmental contingencies to produce behavior.

Symbols

We will not make the common anthropological distinction that restricts culture to behaviors encoded by a system of shared symbolic constructs such as language, myth, or ritual (e.g. Schneider, 1976). The codification of culture in public symbol systems may have interesting effects on the human evolutionary process (see Chap. 8), but to our minds these effects are less fundamental than the effect of social learning per se. It is possible that language and other symbolic capacities were late developments in human evolution (Lieberman, 1975; Isaac, 1976; Marshack, 1976) and that the apparently effective food-foraging way of life that characterized hominids until the late Pleistocene was transmitted by direct phenotypic copying unmediated by arbitrarily meaningful codes. It is even plausible that much of human behavior is still so acquired (e.g. Rosenthal and Zimmerman, 1978).

Social norms

Goodenough's definition implies that culture is only that part of an individual's repertoire of socially learned traits that is acceptable to other members of the society. Freilich's (1980) suggestion that culture is "proper" behavior more explicitly calls attention to this dimension of variation in the cultural repertoire. Once again, our definition is more general. All variants acquired by social learning, including perhaps antisocial behavior, will be subject to evolutionary processes.

Culture as a property of individuals

Most anthropologists probably think of culture as a property of human groups, not of individuals, and for some the very essence of the culture concept is that groups of humans share a common set of culturally transmitted "meanings" (e.g. Schneider, 1968; Geertz, 1972). Many of the definitions reviewed by Kroeber and Kluckhohn stress the social unit. It may seem to our anthropological readers that by defining cultural transmission in terms of social learning by individuals we have improperly reduced a group phenomenon to an individual one. Such is not the case. As Ward Goodenough (1981: 54) has noted,

> People learn as individuals. Therefore, if culture is learned, its ultimate locus must be in individuals rather than in groups. . . . If we accept this, then cultural theory must explain in what sense we can speak of culture as being shared or as the property of groups . . . and what the processes are by which such sharing arises.

One of our goals is to understand how the psychological processes that underlie both ordinary and social learning interact with other social processes to produce the observed distributions of cultural variants in groups. It should be kept in mind, however, that the theory presented in this book takes the cultural population (i.e. the group or society) as its fundamental unit. To understand the dynamics of the cultural evolution we must understand how interacting individuals affect the distribution of culturally transmitted variants in the population.

The units of cultural inheritance

Our definition of culture is not at all specific about the nature of the information that affects phenotypes. In particular, we do not assume that culture is encoded as discrete "particles." In other recent work the existence of such particles is assumed, for example, Dawkins's (1976) "meme" and Lumsden and Wilson's (1981) "culturgen." (Lumsden and Wilson, 1981: 7, give a brief review of similar terms.) Relatively little can be said on this topic since our knowledge of the neurophysiology of social learning is primitive compared to our knowledge of the molecular biology of the gene. Moreover, as we will argue later in this chapter, it is possible to construct a cogent, plausible theory of cultural evolution without assuming particulate inheritance.

We have avoided a holistic element in our definition for similar reasons, although Tylor's (1871) classical definition and many others descended from it include such (Kroeber and Kluckhohn, 1952: 43–46). The degree to which cultural repertoires are integrated, and the mechanisms by which such integration is accomplished, are poorly understood and controversial empirical problems. They cannot be settled by definitional fiat. For example, Bandura and Walters (1963) argue from the evidence of social learning experiments that human behavior is very weakly integrated. We will analyze some elementary models of the linkage between elements of cultural repertoires in subsequent chapters.

Beliefs, values, and desires

We have also deliberately avoided the usual identification of culture with people's felt values, desires, and beliefs. Social scientists generally, and many cultural anthropologists in particular (e.g. Sahlins, 1976a), have freely treated the operational units of culture as the shared meanings available by introspection in one's own culture or by ethnographic study of others' felt meanings via empathetic observations and the reports of informants. The problem is that there is no guarantee that the actual culturally inherited determinants of behavior bear any close resemblance to our intuitive notions of what causes our own or others' behavior. Rosenberg (1980a) presents a very cogent series of deductive arguments on the difficulty of using the beliefs and desires of conventional experience as the basis for theory in the social sciences. These arguments are strengthened by a variety of empirical studies which suggest that self-reports and empathetic assessments of the determinants of behavior are not trustworthy (e.g. Milgram, 1965; Nuttin, 1975; Nisbett and Wilson, 1977; Nisbett and Ross, 1980).

In order to avoid awkward neologisms, we will continue to use words like "beliefs" and "values" to refer to the culturally transmitted behavioral dispositions, keeping in mind that the units of cultural inheritance must be discovered, or at least verified, by experiment, not introspection. Furthermore, we will use the ample data social scientists have collected about opinions, beliefs, and values to motivate and test the models on the assumption that they may bear a reasonable resemblance to actual dispositions. This assumption may very well have to be modified in the face of better information about the actual nature of cultural determinants of behavior.

Review of Data from the Social Sciences
How much culture is there?

The conceptual difficulties of distinguishing the effects of genetic, cultural, and environmental variation on human behavior pale beside the operational problems of actually measuring them. With rare exceptions, neither genetic variation, nor cultural variation, nor the complex processes by which developing phenotypes respond to different environments can be directly observed. The genetic system is reasonably well understood; the DNA code can be read and some simple cases of the interaction between genes and environment can be understood in their entirety.

Nonetheless, biologists are far from being able to give a complete account of how the genes interact with each other and with the environment to produce phenotypes. We are only beginning to understand the mental processes underlying the storage and expression of culture (Wickelgren, 1981). In practice scientists are reduced to inferring the effects of unobservable causal variables—genes, cultures, and environmental interactions—by studying their effects on phenotypes. This is not an insuperable task, witness the progress in genetics before Watson and Crick, but it adds difficulties.

The essential empirical problem is that genetic transmission, cultural transmission, and correlated environments all have similar effects on phenotypes. For example, suppose we were to measure the similarity between the economic behavior of fathers and sons. Further suppose that the data include both cases in which sons inherit ownership of a business from their fathers and cases in which they do not. It is likely that the data would show that the economic behavior of fathers and sons is similar, and that the extent of the similarity depends on whether ownership is transmitted. (See Glass and Hall, 1954, and Blau, 1965, on the statistical tendency for sons to remain in the same economic class as their fathers.) However, these facts alone would not help us distinguish the relative roles of genetic inheritance, cultural inheritance, and correlated environments in causing the similarities. The sons of businessmen might resemble their fathers because they inherited genes for business acumen, because they learned business practices from their fathers, or because the simple fact of inheriting the physical plant of the business constrained their choices.

In the analogous example of the inheritance of prairie dogs' burrows, an experimental solution to this dilemma suggests itself immediately. Sibling pups of known genetic relationship could be allocated at random among foster parents, and the parents randomly allocated to burrows. So long as gene-culture-environment interactions are not too complex, such an experiment might reveal the contribution of each cause to burrow-making behavior; some of the variation in the pups' behavior could be ascribed to common genotypes (observed similarity between genetic siblings), some to common cultural inheritance (observed similarity between foster siblings), and some to common environment (observed similarity between genetically and culturally unrelated individuals in similar burrows). Eventually, the effects of genes, cultural traits, and learning in determining burrow form might be dissected in the same detail as the factors affecting bristle number in *Drosophila*. Obviously such an experiment is impractical in the case of humans. Moreover, even the experimental determination of the importance of culture in other animals has proven to be quite difficult. We are aware of no experiments of this type in any species, and many apparent cases of nonhuman protoculture are suspect for this reason (Galef, 1980).

In the human case, the nature-nurture debate persists because of our inability to make precise measurements of the the influence of culture, genes, and learning in correlated environments. In the best-studied case, the causes of variation in scores on IQ tests, the contributions of culture, genes, and correlated environment have been extremely difficult to disentangle (for a recent review, see Henderson, 1982). Nevertheless, we feel that a great deal of the observed behavioral variation in humans can be attributed to cultural inheritance. The theoretical exercises in this book do not require the absence of genetic variation for behavior, or that de novo learning and individual strategizing are without effect. However, the models are most interesting if we can assume that some important fraction of behavioral variants are acquired culturally.

We will briefly review four different lines of evidence that we believe combine to make a strong, although certainly imperfect, case for the importance of stable, slowly evolving cultural variation in explaining human behavior:

1. Laboratory experiments show that humans learn from others with great facility. Social learning theorists have shown in some detail how an individual can acquire a very large cultural repertoire.

2. Studies of socialization in more naturalistic settings have shown that child-rearing patterns are correlated with behavioral variations in children.

3. A large body of psychometric and sociometric studies measuring correlations among offspring, genetic parents, and various classes of potential cultural parents provides ample evidence of cultural transmission despite an inevitable tendency for the effects of genetic, cultural, and environmental variation to be confounded.

4. Historians, sociologists, and anthropologists have found a number of striking examples of cultural inertia, situations in which cultural ancestry is important in changed situations or where traditional cultural differences persist in similar environments.

Neither a committed genetic determinist nor a devotee of the rational actor model of human behavior will necessarily be convinced by this evidence that cultural transmission has played an important role in human evolution. The evidence does not completely exclude the possibility that either genetic variation or individual rational calculation plays so large a role as to make cultural traditions relatively unimportant. On the other hand, the available data are certainly sufficient to make plausible the hypothesis that cultural variation is important. The models of this and subsequent chapters will at the very least serve to help deduce the consequences of this hypothesis so that it can be tested against other kinds of data.

Social learning

Following Galef, we have defined social learning as the transmission of stable behavioral dispositions by teaching or imitation. By stable dispositions, we mean ones that are substantially divorced from environmental contingencies. In other words, as environmental circumstances change, an individual's disposition (though not necessarily his or her behavior) must tend to remain the same for a significant period of time. What can psychologists tell us about how such dispositions are acquired? There are several competing accounts of social learning in contemporary psychology (Rosenthal and Zimmerman, 1978; Yando, Seitz, and Zigler, 1978). Of these the simplest, and perhaps most fully elaborated, is the social learning theory of Albert Bandura and his followers. We will begin by reviewing Bandura's theory of social learning and then indicate how the theories associated with other schools differ from Bandura's.

Bandura's social learning theory

In behaviorist learning theory, new behavior is acquired by conditioning. In classical conditioning, a reward or punishment schedule modifies the expression of an existing behavior (or "reflex"), and in operant conditioning a new behavior is developed by a system of reinforcement. Experienced enculturating individuals, or "cultural parents," commonly condition the behavior of children in order to develop responses that the parents consider appropriate (Williams, 1972). Children seldom escape being rewarded and punished by adults, although the extent and deliberateness of the conditioning regime varies greatly within and between societies (LeVine, 1973). Similarly, other people in positions of authority (policemen, teachers, priests, headmen, and so forth) reward and punish the behavior of people of all ages.

It is difficult to believe, however, that a large, sophisticated cultural repertoire can be acquired by socially controlled conditioning alone. The transmission of culture by socially controlled conditioning is not an economical process. It requires that the cultural information be inculcated in offspring fairly gradually by the repeated application of the reinforcement schedule. Children make errors which must be extinguished by the careful attention of parents. Even quite severe punishments may not result in the desired behavior unless their design and administration are quite sophisticated (Bandura and Walters, 1963).

Thus, the discovery by psychologists that direct imitation of modeled behavior, or "observational learning," is a highly effective means of communicating culture is a crucial advance. In the early 1960s (e.g. Bandura and Walters, 1963), Albert Bandura and his followers began to develop experimental methods for investigating the properties of observational learning. They have been able to use the observational learning paradigm and their experimental protocols to begin to demonstrate how the huge mass of cultural information is actually transmitted.

The observational learning paradigm

The typical observational learning experiment begins by exposing naive individuals to a model who exhibits a particular behavior or series of behaviors. Then the naive individuals are tested to see if they can replicate the behavior of the model. A classic experiment (Bandura and Walters, 1963) on the modeling of aggressive behavior will serve as an example of the technique and prototypical results. Grade-school children viewed films of an adult model exhibiting several stereotypic aggressive behaviors toward an inflated doll. There were three test conditions; in each condition children were presented with a slightly different version of the film. In one condition the model was punished, in a second rewarded, and in a third neither rewarded nor punished. First, the children were tested for acquisition of aggression toward the doll by being placed in a room with the doll and observed for imitative responses. In this case, the vicarious reinforcement effect was strong; observers of the rewarded model exhibited the most, and observers of the punished model the least, aggression. In a second test the children from all three treatments were offered rewards for imitating the aggressive behavior. The performance differentials then disappeared. Members of all experimental groups replicated the behavior with high frequency.

Observational learning theorists draw several conclusions from experiments like this one. The most important conclusion is that covert cognitive operations are central to the great bulk of social learning. This conclusion directly contradicts orthodox behaviorism, which holds that observational learning occurs by direct reinforcement of behaviors that resemble those of a model. In the traditional theory, the modeled behavior was categorized as a discrimination stimulus and social learning was said to occur when subjects were reinforced for match-to-sample behavior. Thus, social learning was characterized as a subclass of operant conditioning (Miller and Dollard, 1941; Gewirtz and Stingle, 1968).

Social learning experiments like the one outlined above show that people learn by observation in situations where they cannot perform the behavior. A whole pattern of aggressive behavior was acquired by observing the model in the film, despite the fact that some groups of children saw the model punished and none of the children had an opportunity to practice the behavior immediately. The children encoded both the behavior and the reward or punishment received by the model. When appropriate rewards were offered, the stored information could be retrieved and used, even by children who experienced the vicarious punishment of the model. Thus, the process of observational learning is partly decoupled from reinforcement.

In contrast to the operant conditioning model (stimulus→response→ reinforcement) of social learning, these experiments demonstrate that the following, more complex model applies:

Modeled Events→Attention Processes→Retention Processes→
             (depend on stimuli   (cognitive organ-
               and observer)   ization, covert
                                        rehearsal)
    Motor Reproduction→Motivation Processes→Matching
     (physical capabil-   (external, vicarious, Performance
     ities and skills)   and self-reinforcing)

Observational learning depends on a variety of factors characteristic of the model, the observer, and the environment. The key feature of the system is the observer's ability to collect and organize the information about behavior in the absence of immediate reinforcement. The fact that observational learning does *not* require such reinforcement enhances the resemblance between cultural and genetic transmission. As Bandura (1977: 37–38) summarizes the body of social learning experiments,

> In social learning theory, reinforcement is considered a facilitative rather than a necessary condition because factors other than response consequences can influence what people attend to. . . . When attention is drawn to modeled activities by the events themselves, the addition of positive incentives does not increase observational learning. Observers display the same amount of observational learning regardless of whether they are informed in advance that correct imitations will be rewarded or are given no prior incentives to learn the modeled performances. *After the capacity for observational learning has fully*

developed, one cannot keep people from learning what they have seen. [Our emphasis.]

In other words, people involuntarily "inherit" the cultural variants modeled for them in a way that is analogous to genetic inheritance.

It is plausible that these attributes of observational learning are adaptive. If it is an advantage to have a large cultural repertoire, traits must be rapidly acquired, efficiently stored, and largely free from immediate environmental control. In Bandura's (1977: 12) words,

> The more costly and hazardous the possible mistakes, the heavier is the reliance on observational learning from competent examples. Apart from the question of survival, it is difficult to imagine a social transmission process in which language, lifestyles, and institutional practices of a culture are taught to each new member by selective reinforcement of fortuitous behaviors, without benefit of models who exemplify the cultural patterns.

Another important feature of observational learning in humans is the ability to abstract rules from a series of modeled behaviors. In contrast to the behavioral model of imitation in which exact reproduction of specific behavior patterns was stressed, social learning experiments show that people are capable of acquiring general rules by observational learning. The relevant experiments involve language acquisition, moral concepts, and problem-solving techniques. The typical experimental paradigm is to expose children to a novel behavior, such as a complex, nonstandard grammatical form, and evaluate their ability to discover the grammatical rule used to generate the stimulus sentences. Such experiments demonstrate that children are able to abstract the rule from modeled sentences and use the rule to generate novel sentences (Rosenthal and Zimmerman, 1978: Chap. 2). Often, in an extension of the previous principle, direct reinforcement of learning is unimportant or even counterproductive.

The fact that social learning experiments indicate that humans acquire rules of behavior supports our intuition that the essence of culture is encoded information rather than the behaviors that result from this information. As we argued above, a given cultural rule may lead to different behavior in different environments, much as a given gene's effect on phenotype is dependent on environmental contingencies. This means that culturally acquired information is at least partially protected from the direct effects of environmental contingencies in a way that is somewhat analogous to genotype. The converse may also be true; a naive individual may be able to induce the rule that generates a model's behavior even though the model's behavior is changing in response to environmental contingencies. For example, although the details of political and social behavior organized around ethnic identity appear to be quite labile, the behavioral disposition toward in-group cooperation and out-group hostility could at the same time be very stable.

The implications of the social learning school for the understanding of culture have been forcefully summarized by Rosenthal and Zimmerman (1978: 79):

> Because of the emphasis on social observation and feedback as the primary means by which individuals learn and alter behavior, the continuity of cultural groups can be easily explained. Tradition and knowledge can be transmitted to

the youth who observes the rituals as well as the less formal behavioral practices of adults. From these modeling sequences, concepts or rules can be abstracted and refined by social consequences; these cognitions in turn guide the observer when he reaches adulthood. Witnessed by the next generation, his actions aid in perpetuating this socially mediated cycle for passing on important information.

Shortcomings of the social learning data

While the data from social learning experiments provide invaluable information about the mechanisms of cultural transmission, they suffer from two important drawbacks. First, the time scale of the typical observational learning experiment is very short, and the importance of the modeled information to the life chances of the offspring is usually small. The naive child is exposed to a particular modeling event, for instance a novel grammatical rule, and then shortly thereafter is tested to see if the rule was acquired. In some experiments the child is tested some time later to see if the behavior has been retained, but it is not clear whether the same mechanisms are at work over the longer time scale of the human life cycle. It is also unclear whether children acquire fundamental beliefs about the social and natural world at an early age in the same way that they learn novel grammatical forms and so forth in the laboratory. Clearly, experiments to answer such questions face severe ethical and practical difficulties, and without the answers we must make the reasonable inference that the results of the social learning experiments apply over longer time spans and for more important traits.

Second, social learning experiments have not yet been used to study some of the details of cultural inheritance that our models suggest may be very important. From our point of view, the most seriously neglected issue is how a cultural rule that a given individual acquires is affected by exposure to several modeling episodes involving different cultural parents. Although such problems are on the agenda of social learning researchers (Rosenthal and Zimmerman, 1978: 267–268), typical social learning experiments involve only one model for a brief period of time. The exceptions to this generalization involve models with different characteristics (e.g. male or female, nurturant or nonnurturant) in order to measure the effect of these characteristics on the imitation of other traits such as aggression (e.g. Bandura et al., 1963). As far as we are aware, the rule modeled and the modeling situation have not been varied in a way that addresses the following kinds of questions:

1. What happens when a naive person is exposed to two otherwise similar models with different rules for behaving in the same environmental circumstance? Is one model copied and the other ignored? Are the variant rules synthesized in some way, for example, by averaging? If the naive individual acquires both rules, what governs which rule is subsequently used?

2. What is the smallest unit of a complex rule that can be independently acquired? Does a complex rule that can be subdivided into smaller parts tend to be inherited intact from a given model, or are the smallest units freely mixed from various models?

The answers to these questions could turn out to be crucial to understanding the dynamics of cultural inheritance. The analogous questions for the genetic system were answered with the discovery of Mendel's laws. The genetic system is particulate, and the laws of independent assortment (modified by linkage) describe the way genes from two parents are recombined in sexual reproduction. Some claim that geneticists' main contribution to Darwinian theory was the discovery of these properties because, unlike blending inheritance, they act to conserve variation. Since evolution by the forces of biased transmission and natural selection depends on the preservation of variation and the size of the units that are transmitted independently, our ignorance of these structural attributes of cultural inheritance is a serious gap. We think that the experimental techniques of social learning research could be profitably applied to these problems.

Other views of social learning

A variety of other theories of social learning have also been advanced. In general, each of these theories paints a more complicated picture of social learning than does Bandura's theory.

1. Some structuralists such as Laughlin and D'Aquili (1974) or Chomsky (1976) argue for a much larger role for innate structures than do social learning theorists. In particular, they believe that there are genetically transmitted predispositions to acquire some traits rather than others. For example, they hold that humans are innately predisposed in favor of certain grammatical rules. In contrast, social learning theorists believe that the organic capacity to acquire culture is very general. Grammatical rules are held to be acquired through social learning.

2. Some scholars such as Piaget (1962), Kohlberg (1964), and Yando, Seitz, and Zigler (1978) place more importance on changes in cognitive abilities with age, as for example in Piaget's famous developmental stages. While social learning theorists acknowledge the importance of development, they suggest that Piagetian developmental stages may result from the fact that social learning at one age may often depend on what is acquired via social learning at earlier ages, rather than from organic development.

3. Some theories place a greater emphasis on affective ties with role models (e.g. Mowrer, 1960; Aronfreed, 1969). Although social learning theory incorporates attentional phenomena, it gives them less weight than do psychoanalytic theories that emphasize the role of identification with parents or other individuals in social learning.

4. Psychological theories which stress basic personality traits as explanatory variables assume a more complex integration of the cultural repertoire than do social learning theories. Social learning theorists hypothesize that the skills and dispositions acquired become more complex and differentiated as the repertoire grows, but they view an individual as possessing many separate, modular sets of cultural attributes. Thus Bandura's prescription for treatment of psychological disorders is to modify specific incompletely learned or deviant rules, rather than to search for deeply imbedded, general personality defects that would influence a large fraction of a deviant's behavior.

5. Social learning theorists assume a smaller role for reinforcement than behaviorists (e.g. Skinner, 1953; Gewirtz, 1971).

The controversies surrounding social learning theory are directly relevant to the current enterprise because each of the positions implies a different view of cultural transmission, and therefore of the evolutionary forces that might affect cultural variation. For example, the cultural evolution hypotheses of many human sociobiologists stress the forces of guided variation and direct bias, and the role of genetically transmitted traits in shaping the direction of these forces (e.g. Alexander, 1971, 1979a, b; Lumsden and Wilson, 1981). These views require that innate biases influence which cultural dispositions are acquired. Thus the usual sociobiological hypothesis is more consistent with a structuralist view of social learning than with Bandura's. In subsequent chapters we will analyze models which draw out the evolutionary implications that are inherent in these controversies.

Evidence from studies of socialization

Many studies of child development have focused on how child-rearing practices give rise to various behavioral variations in children through a mixture of modeling and reinforcement. Since quite basic traits (aggressiveness, helping behavior, school performance) are related to rearing practices, it appears plausible that cultural transmission is quite important in shaping behavior. Table 3.1 lists a sample of the studies in this research tradition and a brief account of their results. Child development textbooks (e.g. Mussen, Conger, and Kagan, 1979) can be consulted for a much more extensive review than we can give here. Werner (1979) reviews the cross-cultural evidence on the effects of child rearing.

Baumrind's (1967) study of the effect of parental practices on children's behavior is a good example of the child development approach. She first categorized 110 nursery school children with respect to five behavioral dimensions: self-control, approach tendencies (curiosity), subjective mood (happiness), self-reliance, and peer affiliation (friendliness). Three small subgroups of children were selected for further study. Group 1 included 13 children who scored high in each of the five dimensions and were judged to be the most mature, competent, and independent. Group 2 included 11 children who were moderately self-reliant and self-controlled but scored low on approach tendencies, subjective mood, and peer affiliation. Group 3 consisted of 8 children who scored low on self-reliance, self-control, and approach tendencies and who were judged the most immature of the original group. The child-rearing behavior of the parents of each group was assessed by naturalistic observations in the home, structured tests, and interviews of parents. Four dimensions of child-rearing style were evaluated: (1) control (efforts to influence children's behavior), (2) maturity demands (parental pressure on children to perform near the limits of their abilities, but also expectations of independence), (3) communication (reasoning with children to obtain compliance and obtaining information about the child's desires), and (4) nurturance (expressions of warmth and encouragement). The parents of mature children (Group 1) scored high on all four dimensions. The parents of the children in Group 2 scored high on the control dimension but low on the nurturance dimension. Parents of the

Table 3.1 Studies showing effects on children's behavior of parental rearing practices

Ahlstrom & Havighurst (1971)	Compared to controls, boys with persistent delinquency and failure to respond to work-study opportunities lacked competent male role models and lacked family support for scholastic activity.
Bacon et al. (1963)	Socialization practices in 48 mostly preliterate societies confirm patterns of association between child-rearing practices and frequency of theft and personal crime. Lack of a male role model for young children and excessively authoritarian child-rearing practices lead to more criminal behavior.
Hetherington (1972) Hoffman (1971)	Father absence has a subtle effect on the socialization of females, and a more substantial one on males. Daughters lack skills in interactions with males, whereas sons tend to suffer a wider range of deficits when a male role model is absent.
Lesser and Kendel (1969)	Danish and Americans show different frequencies of child-rearing patterns resulting in different patterns of adolescent independence. However, the same patterns of child rearing within each country have the same results.
Hoffman and Saltzstein (1967)	Parental child-rearing styles or techniques explain much of the variation in children's moral development.
Lynn (1974 and 1979)	Reviews of the role of father's child-rearing practices on children of both sexes, and a similar review of both parents' effects on daughters. Antecendents of sex role typing, achievement motivation, vocational choice, delinquency, personality, and other traits.
Maccoby (1980)	Sex identity can be assigned by parents (review of several studies) at least in cases where physiological sex is ambiguous, without apparent problems. This despite the apparent role of biases in the formation of sex identity. Other evidence indicates a substantial role for parents, particularly fathers, in teaching sex-typed behavior to normal children.
Maccoby and Jacklin (1974)	Children learn sex-appropriate behavior in part via parental socialization.
Simpson (1962)	Parental influence on career aspirations and prospective upward mobility are strong.

immature children (Group 3) scored quite low on the control, maturity demands, and communication dimensions but relatively high on nurturance. Baumrind (1967) termed the "competent" Group 1 parents *authoritative,* the high control Group 2 parents *authoritarian,* and the lax but nurturant parents of Group 3 *permissive.* Subsequent work by Baumrind and others has supported these and similar categorizations (Mussen, Conger, and Kagan, 1979: 445–447).

Werner's (1979) cross-cultural review of child-rearing attitudes reports a number of relationships like those uncovered by Baumrind and other investigators in Western countries. Differences between societies in presumably long-standing, traditional child-rearing practices have substantial effects on the cognitive capabilities and social behavior of children and adults. Werner presents considerable evidence that suggests that many societies have patterns reminiscent of Baumrind's rearing styles. In many societies mothers play a dominant role in child rearing and obedience to strict rules is stressed. In other societies fathers play a greater role in child rearing and there is a more nurturant family setting. Werner argues that each of these patterns produce adults who are well adapted to the contrasting ecological situations in which they live. Traditional or semitraditional stratified agricultural societies are disproportionately characterized by authoritarian child-rearing patterns. Such practices tend to produce children who are cooperative but not independent or self-assertive, which may be adaptive in societies which are authoritarian and emphasize cooperation in subsistence activities.

In contrast, less authoritarian parents are characteristic of unstratified agricultural societies, hunters and gatherers, and the middle class of Western industrial societies. The independent, competitive, but in some respects less socially skilled individuals produced by such practices appear better adapted to individual enterprise required by the economic and political organization that characterizes such societies.

The fact that parental child-rearing styles affect children's behavior is not convincing evidence of cultural transmission. Genetic determinants of warmth or authoritarianism might exist, or economic conditions might result in certain parental styles regardless of cultural transmission. Further, most studies of this type focus on behavior at quite different points in the life cycle. It is not entirely clear whether children's responses to different parental techniques are the result of modeling adult behaviors, or whether children will tend to imitate their parents' child-rearing traits when they become adults. A good deal of the evidence suggests that both inferences are correct, however. For example, the behavior of Baumrind's Group 1 children seems to be a nursery school age approximation of their parents' behavior toward them, a finding that is consistent with the picture of social learning drawn from laboratory studies. Other studies suggest that parental rearing behavior is indeed transmitted from parents to offspring. For example, parents who abuse children very frequently grew up in households where physical violence was used to enforce discipline (Spinetta and Rigler, 1972; Smith, 1975). Werner (1979: 300–303) reviews several studies suggesting that child-rearing patterns persist in the face of considerable social change. More narrowly, even if studies of parental style are insufficient to rule out genetic or correlated environmental explanations of parent-offspring similarities, they do show the pattern that would be predicted based on a social learning–cultural transmission hypothesis.

An overview of evidence from psychometric and sociological studies

The phenotypes of genetic relatives are usually positively correlated. For example, siblings, even siblings raised apart, are generally more similar in height than two individuals randomly chosen from the population. This fact has proven to be extremely useful for obtaining empirical information about the genetic basis of various characters, particularly in the practical world of plant and animal breeding. The experiments and observations of psychologists interested in social learning and child development reviewed above suggest that social learning in the human species is much like an inheritance system. If this view is correct, we should be able to observe statistical similarities in the behavior of "cultural relatives," that is, individuals who share some cultural models.

Psychologists and sociologists have extensively studied the behavioral similarity between various classes of individuals in human populations. Three general kinds of traits have been studied within this tradition: (1) psychological traits such as measures of cognitive ability, measures of personality and temperament, and tendency toward psychopathology, (2) sociological traits including criminal behavior and attitudes toward religious and political issues, and (3) interests, especially occupational choice. The bulk of these studies have been undertaken without any explicit model of cultural inheritance in mind. Most investigators have lumped the effects of cultural transmission with the effects of correlated environments.

There are several difficulties involved in using such data to estimate the importance of cultural transmission. Many of these data deal with the similarity between biological relatives, presumably because these data are the easiest to collect. Although the measured familial correlations are often quite high, their significance is ambiguous because the effects of genetic and cultural transmission and common family environment tend to be confounded. The data from unrelated individuals are much less complete and generally less quantitative, and the effects of correlated environments can rarely be excluded.

Nonetheless, we think the data are useful taken as a whole. The familial data can be used to estimate the importance of vertical cultural transmission for two reasons: first, in the most recent studies, sophisticated quantitative methods have been used to disentangle the effects of genes, culture, and environment. Though far from conclusive, these studies suggest that cultural transmission is important for at least some of the traits studied. Second, many studies show very high familial correlations for characters like religious preference that are unlikely to be genetic. In the case of nonfamilial effects, while none of the studies of nonfamilial effects unambiguously indicates horizontal or oblique cultural transmission, taken together they suggest, to us at least, that these modes of transmission are important.

Evidence from familial correlations

The results of a variety of studies of the similarity of biological relatives, mostly between parents and offspring, for various traits are given in Table 3.2. These data show that the correlations between parents and offspring for behavioral traits are often quite high. If the effects of genetic transmission or common, nontransmissible family environments could be excluded, these data would provide strong evidence that cultural inheritance exists. While this is not possible, several lines of evidence do indicate that, for some traits at least, there is an important cultural component.

The results of traditional psychometric studies of psychological traits such as IQ indicated that genetic variation was quite important compared to cultural or environmental variation. These studies generally relied on data comparing identical twins with other siblings, particularly dizygotic twins. If twins are raised together and can be assumed to have a common environment, then the genetic contribution to a trait can be estimated by comparing the correlation between identical twins with that between dizygotic twins. If the twins are reared separately, the data can also be used to estimate the effect of different family environments. Some of this latter kind of variation could be interpreted as being due to vertical transmission. In practice, twin studies suffer from a number of potential defects, and the traditional

Table 3.2 Studies showing evidence of vertical transmission

Bachman (1970) Bachman et al. (1978)	Longitudinal study of males from high school to young adulthood. Most of the personality variables, attitudes, and attainments studied were related to family background. Stability from high school age to young adulthood of most variables considerable.
Blau (1965) Duncan (1965) Lipset and Bendix (1964)	Sons tend to have the same occupational status as their fathers in industrial countries. Net upward mobility is substantial, but both upwardly and downwardly mobile sons tend to rise or fall to a status close to their fathers'.
Block (1973)	Variations in sex role conceptions within and between societies appear to reflect patterns of socialization that replicate parents' role conceptions.
Cavalli-Sforza and Feldman (1981) Cavalli-Sforza et al. (1982) Chen et al. (1982)	Surveys of college students and their parents used to obtain data on parent-offspring resemblances for a number of traits. Transmission matrices displayed and analyzed.
Coopersmith (1967)	Children with high self-esteem have parents with high self-esteem. Parents whose self-esteem is high also tend to be models of effective techniques to deal with everyday problems.
Glass and Hall (1954)	Mobility between occupational roles in Britain, as later found in the U.S., is far less than a perfect mobility model predicts. Sons are typically of the same or similar status as their fathers.
Flacks (1967)	Politically active students of the 1960s tended strongly to have liberal to radical parents, compared to nonactive students.
Hagman (1932)	Children's fears of dogs, insects, storms, and so forth are significantly related to mothers' fears. The number of mothers' and children's fears were correlated at the 0.67 level, and mothers and children showed a significant tendency to have the same fears.
Jessor and Jessor (1977)	Maternal ideology had a reasonable correlation with frequency of problem behavior in high school students. The children of traditional, religious, and tolerant mothers were less prone to marijuana use, alcohol abuse, sexual activity, and activism than children of other types of mothers.
Kirkpatrick (1936)	Modest correlations between mothers' and children's attitudes toward feminism ($r = 0.38$–0.34); insignificant relationships between fathers' and children's scores. Sharply higher values reported for parent-offspring correlations for religious attitudes.
McCall (1977)	Offspring attained adult education and occupational status correlated with parent's education and occupational status ($r \approx 0.6$). No independent effect of IQ.
Newcomb and Svehla (1937)	Parents' and children's attitudes toward church, war, and communism are correlated, ($r = 0.4$–0.7).
Rice et al. (1980)	Estimates of heritability of IQ from family resemblance data indicate that approximately 30 percent of the variance in IQ is due to cultural inheritance.

Table 3.2 continued

Roff (1950)	Review of a number of early statistical studies of parent-offspring and other intrafamily correlations for behavioral traits. Virtually all measures show at least some parent-offspring correlation.
Scarr and Weinberg (1976)	Transracial adoptions of black children into privileged white families result in black children's having IQs above white norms. Apparently the racial differences in IQ in the U.S. are due to cultural transmission or correlated environments.
Schiff et al. (1978)	Evidence from early adoption study shows that rates of school failure and of low IQ among adoptees compared with siblings raised by biological parents are entirely attributable to the socialization, not the biological parents.
Smith (1975)	A significant association exists between the tendency to abuse one's own children and having been subjected to severe physical punishment by one's parents; apparently such parents lack effective models of child-rearing behavior.
Vogel et al. (1970)	Sex role perceptions of college students affected by mother's employment status. Students whose mothers were employed view appropriate sex roles as less different.
Werts (1968)	College freshmen's indication of their occupational choice showed significant pattern of sons choosing the same or similar occupations as their fathers.
Weltman and Remmers (1946)	Attitude survey administered to high school students and their parents. Items tested included educational, political, and social items. Very high parent-offspring correlations found, with some decline between grades 9 and 11–12.
Whiting and Whiting (1975)	Cross-cultural study of socialization practices and children's behavior. Children's behavior reflects the need to acquire skills that will be useful in adult roles; socialization is training for adult roles. Some indirect indication that vertical transmission is important relative to other models.

studies have been sharply criticized (e.g. Layzer, 1974; Feldman and Lewontin, 1975).

However, more recent studies of psychological traits (Henderson, 1982) indicate a much smaller role for genetic effects. In these studies, more kinds of relatives have been considered and more care has been taken to measure such complicating factors as nonrandom mating, selective placement of adoptees, and cultural and environmental effects. New models have also been formulated that incorporate specific propositions about the effects of environmental and heritable cultural effects (Cavalli-Sforza and Feldman, 1973b, 1981: Chap. 5; Eaves et al., 1978; Rice et al., 1978; Cloninger et al., 1979a, 1979b; Karlin, 1980). In the much-analyzed case of IQ, the traditional models yielded estimates of genetic heritability in the neighborhood of 0.8. The availability of new and better data has reduced these estimates to roughly 0.5 (Henderson, 1982). When models with more complete specification of cultural transmission are used, typical results are that genetic variation, cultural variation, and nontransmissible environmental variation each explain about a third of the total variation in IQ (Rice et al., 1980; see also

Cavalli-Sforza and Feldman, 1978). For another character, Young et al. (1980) concluded that familial correlations on the "lie" scale of the Eysenck Personality Questionnaire were almost entirely due to cultural effects. (The lie scale may actually measure conformance to convention or degree of self-insight rather than propensity to dissemble.) It is equally true, however, that the best evidence still suggests that genetic variation plays a major role in explaining the variation in other personality traits (Scarr, 1981; Henderson, 1982).

As has long been recognized (Cattell, 1960), very extensive data are necessary to evaluate complicated models of human development realistically. The new models highlight this problem, and the older tendency to consider a reasonable fit to a purely genetic model as evidence of genetic transmission has given way to more cautious interpretations based on the realization that equally plausible cultural models may explain the same data. Often all that may be safely said is that there is a strong familial effect composed of an unknown mixture of genetic and cultural transmission and common family environment (Rice et al., 1980; Henderson, 1982). Improved data coupled with sophisticated models promise to continue to increase the accuracy with which the genetic, cultural, and environmental components of familial correlations can be distinguished. In the meantime, we take some comfort from the fact that cultural variation must now be invoked to explain variation that was once attributed to genes.

Sociological traits like skills, norms, and political and religious attitudes seem to us much less likely to be genetically acquired than basic psychological characteristics. Assuming that the reader agrees with this assessment, the observed parent-offspring correlations provide evidence of vertical cultural transmission. Unfortunately, recent psychometric studies have largely ignored these kinds of characters. However, the early literature in this area showed quite high parent-offspring and sibling correlations for this latter class of traits (see Fuller and Thompson, 1960, for a review). For example, Newcombe and Svehla (1937) measured first-degree family correlations from 0.57 to 0.76 for attitudes toward religion. This correlation is so high that the somewhat lower parent-offspring correlations indicate other transmission or decision effects. The highest measures of parent-offspring correlation for traits of this type are for political party affiliation, 0.80 to 0.94 (Weltmann and Remmers, 1946). Occupational interests show similar, although generally lower, parent-offspring correlations (Werts, 1968). Besides a general occupation and class effect, Werts's data also show a specific relationship between upward and downward occupational mobility and parental attitudes within classes. High-achieving children from lower-class families have parents who actively encourage and support their children's achievements, low-achieving children from middle-class families did not encourage their children, and so forth.

The unequal importance of mothers and fathers also gives evidence of cultural transmission. In many of the studies cited above, mother-offspring correlations are slightly higher than father-offspring correlations, an expected pattern in cultural transmission given the greater involvement of women in child rearing. The extensive studies of personality and mental and moral defects (Fuller and Thompson, 1978, give a long review) also often show that mothers and offspring have higher correlations for personality traits than do fathers and offspring, a finding that is consistent with cultural models but not with genetic ones.

Evidence for horizontal and oblique transmission

The hypothesis that a substantial proportion of behavioral variation in humans is culturally transmitted is supported by the evidence that a significant fraction of an individual's cultural repertoire is acquired by horizontal (from peers) and oblique (from nonparental adults) transmission. As the psychometric studies show, it is difficult to disentangle vertical cultural transmission from genetic transmission. Biological parents are usually extremely salient models for cultural transmission, especially to younger children. Nevertheless, social learning from friends, teachers, various nonparental relatives and admired public figures is expected to occur, especially as children grow up. Some data do support the intuitive impression that biological parents gradually become less important through adolescence and as children move from their natal household. Table 3.3 reproduces data (Bell, 1969) from a longitudinal study of adolescents' and young adults' self reports of the perceived influence of various categories of people.

Unfortunately, the effects of models outside the household are more diffuse and more difficult to measure than familial influences. Subjects selected for study can usually provide the experimenter with access to parents and siblings, whereas other potential models are harder to identify and contact. The result of this methodological difficulty is that the amount of horizontal and oblique transmission is probably underestimated by the available data. Also, a fair fraction of horizontal and oblique effects are likely to contribute to the measured parent-offspring correlation because of assortative "mating." Even a teenager's peers are likely to be drawn from the same social class, neighborhood, religious group, and so forth as his biological parents.

Table 3.4 summarizes the results of a sample of the studies measuring horizontal and oblique effects. Comparing Table 3.4 with Table 3.2 shows that some traits

Table 3.3 The relative importance of horizontal and oblique transmission at different ages

Social Role	Grade 9	Grade 19
Father	98	74
Mother	79	26
Parent Substitute	7	10
Sibling	42	24
Peer	8	54
Teacher	5	25
Adult Relative	25	68
Other Adult	9	36
Employer	0	21

Note: These data from Bell (1969) suggest that horizontal and oblique transmission increase in importance as children grow older. A group of boys were interviewed when they were freshmen in high school (grade 9) and then interviewed again when they had been out of high school for seven years. The table gives the total number of times individuals in different social roles were mentioned as role models.

Table 3.4 Studies showing evidence of horizontal or oblique cultural transmission

Bell (1963)	Peers of high school age students have some independent effects on social mobility aspirations.
Bell (1969)	Importance of various role models for males in grade 9 and age 25 evaluated from subjects' self reports. Parents and siblings and other relatives were overwhelmingly important in grade 9. By age 25 peers, teachers, employers, and "other adults" were proportionately much more important.
Boyle (1966)	A review of four independent studies found that part of the variation in high school students' aspirations could be attributed to the quality of the school program and to peer effects.
Brim (1958)	Sex role behavior partly learned from siblings, particularly role-specific behavior transmitted from older to younger siblings.
Brittain (1963)	At least in terms of hypothetical choices, adolescents conform to peer opinion regarding rapidly changing behavior or behavior with short-term consequences. The opposite classes of behavior showed conformity to parental norms.
Bronfenbrenner (1970)	The values of Soviet society effectively spread by the school system, even including children teaching those values to parents (contrasted with the U.S.).
Chaffee (1972)	Considerable statistical evidence that TV violence induces some aggressive behavior in adolescents.
Hartup and Coates (1967)	Peer imitation of altruistic behavior demonstrated in nursery school children in a social learning study.
Hartup (1970)	Review of peer socialization effects on a number of traits, including effects of younger child, older children, and siblings. Concord and discord with parental characteristics contrasted.
Inkeles and Smith (1974)	Education, work in factories and similar institutions, and mass media exposure result in a modern attitude set. Post adolescence exposure to modernizing influences strong.
Klaus and Gray (1968)	Intensive intervention by middle-class experimenters increases deprived children's performance in school and on school work-related tests. Also some evidence for horizontal effects among the children.
Kobasigawa (1968)	In a social learning study of young children, peers served as effective models for sex-appropriate and sex-inappropriate behavior.
Labov (1972)	Dialect variation spreads within speech communities by various forms of horizontal and oblique transmission in response to social variables. Rapid spread occurs especially because children acquire much dialect variation from peers.
Larson (1974)	Influence of parents and peers on adolescents studied by means of a survey instrument. Age, sex, and quality of relationship with parents affected the apparent salience of parents and peers.
Opie and Opie (1959, 1969, 1976)	Children's games and rituals are transmitted from older to younger children, not from adults to children. Some traditional games transmitted in this fashion appear to have recognizable roots millennia old.

Table 3.4 continued

Portuges and Feshbach (1972)	Children acquire incidental behaviors from a model mimicking a teacher; sex and social class of the child caused variation in the effect.
Rosenhan et al. (1968)	Children tend to adhere to a strict moral norm only when adult model both preaches and practices the norm. (Social learning study. For a review of the many experiments with adult models and child, see Rosenthal and Zimmerman, 1978.)
Simpson (1962)	Although parental influences on career aspirations and prospective upward mobility are strong, an independent effect of friends detected.
Yando and Kagan (1968)	Experienced, reflective teachers caused a decline in children's impulsiveness after several months in the teachers' classroom.
Yankelovich (1974)	Trends in survey data suggest that changing moral norms and social values originated among college youth and spread to noncollege youth with a time lag of 4-5 years.
Yarrow et al. (1973)	Generalized altruistic behavior was stably (6 months test delay) transmitted to children by models who both communicated altruistic rules and actually behaved altruistically to the children and others.
Young et al. (1980)	Psychometric analysis of lie scale data collected on twins and their parents shows a stronger effect of social interactions among twins than between twins and parents.
Zajonc and Markus (1975)	The decline in IQ with birth order is fit by a model in which siblings influence each other's intellectual development.

acquired by horizontal and oblique transmission are qualitatively different from those acquired vertically. For example, Opie and Opie (1959, 1969, 1976) document a childhood complex of sayings, rituals, and games that are transmitted among peers and remain remarkably stable for many years. Many other traits that are almost certainly strongly influenced by vertical transmission also show detectable horizontal and oblique effects, including language, educational and career objectives, IQ, and sex-role behavior. While these data do not constitute a rigorous test of the cultural transmission hypothesis, they are more consistent with it than with a large role for genetic transmission of a great range of important behavioral traits.

Though the psychometric and sociological evidence is unsatisfactory in many ways, it clearly supports the hypothesis that cultural transmission acts like an inheritance system. The calculated heritabilities for human behavioral traits are as high as or higher than measurements for behavioral and other phenotypic characters in natural populations of noncultural organisms (e.g. Arnold, 1981; Cheverud, 1982). Thus, it may be that cultural transmission is as accurate and stable a mechanism of inheritance as genes. Since social learning experiments and child development studies support the same conclusion, we feel that the "inheritance system" conception of culture is adequate.

Accounting for the variation between groups

So far we have been concerned with how the psychometric and sociological data can be used to partition behavioral variation observed within groups into genetic, cultural, and environmental components. The same kind of data have been used to evaluate the importance of genetic, cultural, and environmental variation in explaining the variation between groups. While only a handful of traits have been well studied, the conclusion of this work so far is that genetic variation underlies virtually none of the behavioral variation between groups. In the next section we will cite sociological and anthropological evidence which suggests that environmental variation is inadequate to explain all differences between human groups. In combination, this evidence indicates an important role for culture in determining between-group variation.

Once again the best data come from IQ studies. There is considerable evidence that little or none of the variation in IQ between racial groups can be attributed to genetic variation. Scarr and her colleagues (Scarr and Weinberg, 1976; Scarr et al., 1977; Scarr and Barker, 1981) have studied the variation in IQ between blacks and whites in the United States using three different sets of data: interracial adoptions, measurements of intellectual skills among individuals classified as black but with varying amounts of European ancestry, and a comparison of cultural and genetic effects on IQ in black and white twins. All three studies indicate that there is no genetic component to interracial variation in IQ. Black children adopted by advantaged white families have IQs above the mean for whites, the proportion of European ancestry is not correlated with measures of intellectual performance, and more of the variation in the IQ of blacks can be explained by cultural and environmental factors than can the variation in the IQ of whites. These facts are consistent with the hypothesis that the differences between the mean IQ of blacks and whites result from cultural and environmental differences between the two groups. This can be true even if variation within each group has a substantial genetic component.

The cultural analog of phylogenetic inertia

If culture acts like an inheritance system, there should be the analog of phylogenetic inertia for culturally acquired traits. That is, cultural traditions should not change instantly in response to changing environmental conditions. Rather, history should explain a significant fraction of present behavior and a common past should cause significant similarities between societies. We shall refer to this as "cultural inertia." Alexander (1979a: 76) has argued that, "Unlike a gene, a cultural trait can be suddenly abolished, and just as suddenly reinstated, across the whole population. At least in theory this can be done." Fads and fashions in Western societies almost fit this characterization. However, there is overwhelming evidence from many branches of the social sciences that most cultural traits persist for much longer than a human generation (Shils, 1981). Even the rapid spread of technological innovations in recent times via horizontal transmission is characterized by a definite pattern of historical change, albeit on a shorter time scale. Let us now consider some examples of the kind of data that can be used to estimate the strength of cultural inertia.

The ethnographic attitude toward rates of cultural change is expressed in the artifice of the "ethnographic present." Classical ethnography gives a present tense description of a society's culture that purports to represent a stable, traditional way of life. This conceit is based on the assumption that, in the absence of contact with a drastically different dominant society, cultures change very slowly. Since ethnographers rarely can observe rates of change under precontact conditions, the assumption is usually unverified.

Nonetheless, ethnographic accounts sometimes offer significant circumstantial evidence of the stability of cultural inheritance. A classical example is the contrast between the Melanesian and Polynesian occupants of the islands of the Western Pacific (Sahlins, 1963; Orlove, 1980). These two only distantly related groups have inhabited the volcanic and coral atoll islands of this region for many generations. Within the two groups, the size, isolation, and other ecological conditions of the islands occupied are fairly variable, but both groups occupy a similar range of islands. If cultural attributes were modified rapidly in response to environmental conditions, one would expect that most cultural variation would be present within the two groups, and the historical differences between the two should explain very little. The evidence indicates, however, that substantial differences have persisted between Polynesians and Melanesians. For example, Polynesian political organization is based on a system of ranked lineages, while Melanesians are characterized by a big-man system with free competition for political roles. As a consequence, Polynesians developed elaborate states on larger islands, headed by a hereditary king and governed with the aid of a series of specialists—soldiers and priests. In contrast, even on very large islands Melanesian political organization tends to remain small scale and societies unstratified.

Even when strong ecological pressure and the opportunity for diffusion of traits from one society to another combine to cause rapid cultural evolution, the effects of cultural inertia are detectable. Oliver (1962) discusses the case of the Plains Indians. After acquiring horses and guns, a number of previously horticultural and food-foraging peoples rapidly developed the familiar complex of traits surrounding nomadic horse hunting. A large number of specific traits entered into this adaptive complex over a span of perhaps 200 years, including patterns of social organization that were substantially different from the preexisting ones. Different parts of the complex were developed by different tribes and acquired by others by diffusion. Some groups, like the Apache, who acquired some parts of the complex (the Apache acquired the use of horses) but not others (the Apache did not abandon horticulture to become fully nomadic), were driven from the Plains by nomads whose way of life gave them superior military capabilities. By the early nineteenth century, the Plains were dominated by a group of tribes with a common basic pattern of adaptation. Nevertheless, important differences due to cultural tradition persisted. For example, tribes derived from horticultural ancestors had significantly more elaborate political traditions than those derived from food-foraging backgrounds.

Edgerton's (with Goldschmidt, 1971) study of four East African peoples quantified the relative importance of cultural background and ecological circumstances on a variety of psychological variables. Each of the four tribes included subgroups with widely differing mixes of cattle raising and farming in their subsistence economy. Two settlements in each of the four tribal areas were selected for study; in one farming was strongly emphasized, in the other pastoralism was emphasized. The environments of the four farming sites were quite similar; they were moist, cool, high elevation areas. Likewise, the areas in which pastoralism predominated were hot, semiarid lowlands. In terms of subsistence technology and ecological circumstances these two types of sites were near the extremes experienced by traditional African societies. All of the groups studied apparently moved to their present location from areas where a more evenly mixed farming-herding life was possible a few generations in the past, although precise historical control was not possible. Some contact with the larger tribal culture was maintained in each case. All four groups had minimal exposure to European acculturation.

In each of the four locations, Edgerton administered an extensive interview battery to a sample composed of about 60 married adults, half men and half women. The interview battery consisted of a series of projective psychological tests designed to tap values, attitudes, and feelings. For example, in his picture test, Edgerton presented a series of drawings that represented possible situations in which a subject might find himself or herself. Subjects were then asked to describe what was happening in the picture, and what ought to be happening. Pictures included situations such as a father confronting a misbehaving son, cattle damaging a farmer's maize, and a man either watching or interceding in a fight between two men. The results of the interviews were reduced to quantitative data by coding interview responses into nominal categories, for example, the number of times that respect for authority was mentioned in response to a question. In all, 116 primary response items, plus an additional 31 content analysis categories that included casual responses as well as direct responses to questions, were available for each subject. A variety of multivariate statistical techniques were applied to the data in order to estimate the effects of tribal group, ecological circumstances, European acculturation, age, and sex on the patterns of responses.

Edgerton's data permit a reasonably critical assessment of hypotheses regarding stability of cultural transmission as an inheritance system. If cultural transmission is less important than learning and rational calculation, we would expect that differences in responses should be explained largely in terms of ecological circumstance and subsistence technology; the pastoralists of all four tribes should resemble one another more than they resemble their co-tribesmen. If culture forms a stable system of inheritance subject to generally weak evolutionary forces, we should observe a substantial resemblance within tribes regardless of subsistence technology and ecological circumstance, but also some weak convergence of the attitudes, values, and feelings of farmers, and of pastoralists, regardless of tribe.

Edgerton's data strongly support the latter expectation. As Edgerton (with Goldschmidt, 1971: 273) summarizes,

> While it is true . . . that the variance in most of the variables is better accounted for by tribe than by economic mode, it is nevertheless also true that for almost all of these variables we would err in rejecting the null hypothesis that farmers and pastoralists do *not* differ only 5 times or fewer times in 10,000.

Many of the analyses of variance of the content analysis data also show marked interaction effects between economic mode and tribal affiliation, as if preexisting cultural traits had a substantial effect on the manner in which different tribes responded to the two economic circumstances. Nor should it be thought that the psychological traits distinguishing the four tribal groups were trivial or adaptively unimportant. They include such basic behavioral dispositions as attitudes toward sex, kinsmen, aggression, cattle, land, family size, and authority.

Edgerton also analyzed similarities and differences for a superordinate classification of the tribes into Bantu and Nilotic groups. Two of the tribes studied were Bantu and two were Kalenjin, a Nilotic subgroup. Even within these very broad cultural/ethnic classifications, 12 responses showed statistically significant Bantu/Kalenjin differences. These included such potentially important traits as expectations about military prowess, preferences for sex of children, attitudes toward in-group authority, attitudes toward land, and valuation of work.

Quantitative sociological studies of the attitudes and behavior of members of different immigrant groups in the United States indicate that differences in some traits due to national origin persist for several generations. Like the disparate behaviors of Melanesians and Polynesians, and the behaviors of the various African groups, these data suggest that differences between groups are not solely environmental. Greeley and McCready (1975) used survey data to compare Anglo-Saxon, Irish, and Italian Americans for personality, political participation, attitudes on moral issues, respect for democracy, and attitudes toward family. They generated a series of hypotheses from sociological studies of areas in Ireland and Italy that contributed disproportionately to American immigration, under the assumption that the mother-country culture would make a detectable contribution to differences between immigrant ethnic groups even several generations after they arrived in the United States. Their data showed substantial differences among the three ethnic groups studied. Many, but by no means all, of these differences corresponded to the predictions based on the culture of origin. For example, Greeley and McCready predicted that the high level of political activity and sophistication of the Western Irish compared to the low level in southern Italy should have resulted in higher levels of political participation by Irish immigrants. Six of their nine specific hypotheses along these lines were confirmed. Also, for both Irish and Italian Americans there was a weak correlation of political activity with number of generations that a particular individual's family had been in the United States.

If cultural inertia causes a substantial lag in response to new environments, we expect to observe not only the persistence of old traits in new environments but also different responses on the part of historically different groups to new circumstances. When such groups are confronted with novel environmental circumstances, we might expect some to manifest the phenomenon of "preadaptation"; groups which by the chance of history have one set of cultural variants may be more successful than others with different variants. A natural experiment to test for the existence of this effect has unfortunately been repeated many times in the past few centuries as European colonialization and trading activities suddenly brought non-Western peoples into contact with an entirely different political and economic system. Responses to this change have varied widely from group to group, and cultural preadaptation is one of the hypotheses offered to explain these differences.

LeVine (1966) considered how the precontact status and mobility system provides the basis for preadaptation to the entrepreneurial and commercial opportunities created by contact with the West. In his important comparative work in Nigeria, LeVine measured "need for achievement," a psychological trait hypothesized to be important in roles in a modernizing economy. He found that members of the Ibo tribe in Nigeria, whose precontact social structures emphasized achieved status, were also characterized by high individual achievement needs. People from these groups were disproportionately successful in the modernizing sectors of the Nigerian economy. By contrast, groups that had the most strongly ascribed hereditary statuses (Hausa) had lower measured needs for achievement and lower participation in the modernizing sectors. LeVine's hypothesis has been used to explain the remarkable speed with which some New Guinea peoples have entered the modern economy (Finney, 1972; also see Epstein, 1968; Pospisil, 1978).

Archaeological evidence also gives direct, if rather sketchy, evidence that culturally transmitted traits can persist for a long time. Archaeologists frequently use artifact traditions to reconstruct the spread of populations, and ethnographers and linguists use similarities between artifacts and language to estimate the historical relationship between contemporary societies. As with the analogous use of anatomical resemblances of contemporary animals and fossils to reconstruct phylogenetic and biogeographical history by biologists, the evidence is seldom perfect. However, in both cases it is sufficient to rule out frequent instantaneous creation and re-creation of cultural traits. To judge by the use of named cultural traditions, induced from durable artifacts, a typical item in an individual's cultural repertoire persists much longer than his own lifetime. Sometimes it seems plausible that such traditions have persisted even in the face of radically changing environments. Perhaps the most striking examples of this phenomenon are the Oldolwan and Acheulean tool traditions, which apparently lasted hundreds of thousands of years over wide geographic regions and persisted through the extreme climatic fluctuations of the early and mid Pleistocene (Isaac, 1976). The "life expectancy" of Pleistocene mammal species is only a factor of two or three longer than the duration of these tool traditions (Stanley, 1979; Schopf, 1982).

An enormous amount of circumstantial evidence suggests that culturally transmitted traits are stable over time and in the face of changing environments. As we develop the models of this book we will be able to say more specific, and interesting, things about this process.

Models of Cultural Transmission

In the remainder of this chapter we want to translate these findings from the social sciences into simple mathematical models of cultural transmission. In Chapter 1 we promised to make use of the analogy between genetic and cultural inheritance in building such models. Now we will digress for a moment to discuss the structure of genetic inheritance. The purpose of this digression is twofold. First, we hope to give our readers from the social sciences a feeling for the techniques that population geneticists use to analyze organic evolution. Second, we want to emphasize in the clearest way those features of genetic inheritance that make the analogy with culture plausible.

A simple model from population genetics

Let us consider the evolution at a single genetic locus of a haploid sexual organism. Such organisms actually exist (e.g. many fungi), but they are relatively rare compared to diploid organisms. We have chosen this kind of model for two reasons: (1) it is the simplest model with the qualitative features we want to illustrate, and (2) there are many circumstances in which the behavior of more complex genetical models can be approximated by a haploid sexual model. This approximation is the basis of the "modifier" or "evolutionarily stable strategy" approach that is widely used in evolutionary ecology (Maynard Smith, 1978; Slatkin, 1978). We will make frequent use of the modifier approach in subsequent chapters.

We will suppose that two genetic variants or "alleles," labeled a and b, are present in the population. Further suppose that at the time we census the population there are a number of individuals, N_a, in the population who are characterized by allele a and a number, N_b, who are characterized by allele b. We define the frequency of the allele a in the population, q, as follows:

$$q = \frac{N_a}{N_a + N_b} \tag{3.1}$$

The frequency of b is, of course, $1 - q$. In Chapter 1 we argued that in a non-cultural species evolution usually can be understood in terms of changes in the distribution of genotypes alone. In this simple model the distribution of genotypes can be specified by the frequency of either allele. (We have arbitrarily chosen a.) Thus to characterize the evolution of the population, a model must allow us to predict the frequency of a during future generations. To do this we must derive a rule that allows us to predict q in the next generation, given the value of q this generation. Such a rule is called a "recursion." As explained in Chapter 2, a recursion can, in principle at least, predict the frequency of the allele a during any future generation.

To derive the recursion, the life cycle of the organism is divided into a series of discrete stages; at each stage we keep track of the change in q. There are four genotypically distinct sets of parents. For example, one set of parents might consist of a female who carries the allele a and a male who carries b, in another set both parents carry the b allele, and so on. The "transmission rule" specifies the probability that a particular set of parents has an offspring characterized by genotype a. The transmission rule that is appropriate for a haploid sexual organism is given in Table 3.5.

Table 3.5 Transmission rule for haploid genetic transmission

Set of Models		Probability That the Naive Individual Is Genotype	
M	F	a	b
a	a	1	0
a	b	1/2	1/2
b	a	1/2	1/2
b	b	0	1

Let us denote the frequency of the allele a after transmission q'. If the population is very large then q' is equal to

$$q' = (1)\begin{pmatrix} \text{Probability} \\ \text{of an a} \times \text{a} \\ \text{mating} \end{pmatrix} + (1/2)\begin{pmatrix} \text{Probability} \\ \text{of an a} \times \text{b} \\ \text{mating} \end{pmatrix}$$
$$+ (1/2)\begin{pmatrix} \text{Probability} \\ \text{of a b} \times \text{a} \\ \text{mating} \end{pmatrix} \tag{3.2}$$

If the population is not large, then the value of q' is no longer certain; sampling error in the transmission of a from one generation to the next will cause q' to vary randomly. In this case the value of q' calculated using Equation 3.2 will be the expected, or average, frequency after transmission. In the simplest models it is assumed that mating occurs at random, that is, the frequency of a $\times$ a matings is equal to the product of the parental frequencies, q^2. This means that Equation 3.2 becomes

$$q' = (1)q^2 + (1/2)q(1 - q) + (1/2)(1 - q)q \tag{3.3}$$

which after a little algebra becomes

$$q' = q \tag{3.4}$$

Equation 3.4 says that when mating occurs at random in a large population, genetic transmission leaves the frequencies of different alleles unchanged. This remarkable fact is true in almost all genetic models, and it is responsible for many of the important properties of genetic evolution.

The forces of genetic evolution are the result of various events during the lives of organisms that differentially affect individuals with different genotypes, and thereby change the frequency of different alleles. There are many such forces, but in this simple example we consider only mutation. A variety of factors cause alleles to mutate occasionally. Suppose that the probability that an allele a mutates to allele b is μ_a and the probability that b mutates to a is μ_b. Denote the frequency of the allele a after mutation as q''. To calculate q'', subtract from q' the frequency of individuals who mutate from a to b and add the frequency of individuals who mutate from b to a as follows:

$$q'' = q' - q'\mu_a + (1 - q')\mu_b \tag{3.5}$$

Because it was assumed that mutation is the only force changing the frequency of genotypes, q'' is also the frequency of the genotype a among the parents of the next generation, q^*. Thus (recalling that $q = q'$), the recursion for the frequency of allele a is

$$q^* = q - q\mu_a + (1 - q)\mu_b \tag{3.6}$$

This recursion can be used to predict the frequency of a during any future time period. We are frequently interested in calculating the equilibrium frequency of different genotypes in the population. When a population is in equilibrium the gene frequencies do not change. This means that $q = q^*$. The equilibrium frequency of a, denoted $\hat{q}$, can be found by solving the simple equation

$$\hat{q} = \hat{q} - \hat{q}\mu_a + (1 - \hat{q})\mu_b \tag{3.7}$$

or

$$\hat{q} = \frac{\mu_b}{\mu_a + \mu_b} \tag{3.8}$$

The equilibrium frequency of the genotype a depends on the relative magnitudes of the two mutation rates. Notice that an equilibrium at $\hat{q} = 0$ or $\hat{q} = 1$ can occur only if one (or both) of the mutation rates is zero. Because of this, mutation is said to act to maintain the variability in the population.

A comparison of genetic and cultural transmission

The simple haploid model described above has several qualitative features in common with most models in population genetics. Cultural transmission in humans is characterized by some of the same features, and because of this the analogy between genetic and cultural evolution is a fruitful one. In what follows we highlight these structural features of genetic transmission and indicate the nature of their cultural analogs.

1. A stable structure is transmitted. The genotype of an individual is for the most part determined by what it has inherited from its parents. Mutation can act to change an individual's genotype spontaneously, but the rate of change is very slow. The evidence from social learning theory and from observed parent-offspring correlations suggests that some cultural traits are similarly transmissible and reasonably stable.

2. Parents are a small subset of the population. Each offspring derives its genotype by "sampling" two individuals from the population, its mother and father. Similarly, both the nature of human social learning and the statistical data from psychometric studies indicate that humans sample only a small number of individuals (although very often more than two) during the acquisition of any particular trait.

3. Different parents may have different roles in the transmission process. In the simple genetic model presented above, the mother and the father have the same probability of transmitting their genotype to an offspring. In other genetic models (e.g. sex-linked traits) the two sexes can have different probabilities. The number of different roles in cultural transmission can be substantially larger, with a variety of classes of individuals other than genetic parents influencing the acquisition of different traits.

4. The frequency of the a allele can be different in the two sexes. Again, in the simple genetic model the frequency of the genotype, a, was the same in both sexes. However, if the sexes occupy different ecological niches or if there is sexual selection, these frequencies can be different. This will affect the probability that different matings occur and, therefore, potentially lead to changes in the frequency of different genotypes. Similarly, we expect in some cases the frequency of different cultural variants among different kinds of cultural parents to be different.

The model of the cultural transmission of a dichotomous trait

With these analogies in mind, let us now build our first model of cultural transmission. Many cultural characters can reasonably be modeled as though there existed only a finite number of distinct variants. The simplest such characters would have only two alternative variants. This will be particularly true of "presence-absence" traits like smoker/nonsmoker or likes-cucumbers/dislikes-cucumbers. We will refer to such traits as "dichotomous cultural traits." Many traits may be better modeled as having several, or even a continuum of, variants. We will consider the latter case at the end of this chapter.

To model the transmission of a dichotomous cultural trait we begin by labeling the variants, say c and d. For example, c might represent the variant "likes-cucumbers" and d the variant "dislikes-cucumbers." The state of the population is determined by the distribution of different cultural variants. Since there are only two variants in this example, the state of the population can be specified by the frequency of individuals with the variant c, labeled p. In analogy with the genetic model sketched above, the task is to find a recursion that allows us to predict the frequency of p in the next generation given its frequency in the present generation. Again, let us break down the life cycle of an individual into discrete stages during which only one process changes the frequency of the two cultural variants.

At first, we restrict attention to vertical and oblique transmission, that is, transmission from members of one generation to naive members of the next generation. For the time being we suppose that each naive individual is enculturated by exactly three models, numbered 1,2,3, who occupy the same set of cultural roles. Later in this chapter we shall see that it is very easy to generalize this model to more than three models and to the case of horizontal transmission; in Chapter 5 we will show that it is easy to generalize to the case where the number of cultural parents and the nature of their social roles vary from one naive individual to another.

The cultural transmission rule gives the probability that a particular naive individual acquires the cultural variant c (or d) given that it is exposed to cultural parents with each different combination of cultural variants. There are a very large variety of conceivable cultural transmission rules. Here we consider a very simple "linear" transmission rule that is very similar to the haploid genetic model outlined above. Table 3.6 gives the transmission rule when there are three cultural models. The transmission process is characterized by the values of the parameters A_1, A_2, and A_3. These values must sum to one because the probability that a naive individ-

Table 3.6 A linear transmission rule for three parents

Cultural Variant Characterizing Model			Probability That Naive Individual Acquires Cultural Variant	
1	2	3	c	d
c	c	c	1	0
c	c	d	$A_1 + A_2$	A_3
c	d	c	$A_1 + A_3$	A_2
d	c	c	$A_2 + A_3$	A_1
d	d	c	A_3	$A_1 + A_2$
d	c	d	A_2	$A_1 + A_3$
c	d	d	A_1	$A_2 + A_3$
d	d	d	0	1

ual acquires some variant of the trait must be one. A large value of A_i means that the naive individual is disproportionately likely to acquire the cultural variant of the ith model. Thus these parameters can be interpreted as the importances or weights of models in different social roles in the transmission process. Notice that if all three models have the same cultural variant, the offspring acquires that variant with certainty. (For an extremely thorough analysis of a similar model for the case of two cultural parents, see Cavalli-Sforza and Feldman, 1981: Chap. 2.)

We want to use the cultural transmission rule to predict the frequency of c after transmission, p'. To do this we need to specify the probability that each distinct set of cultural parents is formed. Suppose that we label the probability of forming a set of models with ccd as Prob(ccd) and so on. Then, the rules of conditional probabilities result in the following expression for p':

$$p' = (1)\text{Prob(ccc)}$$
$$+ (A_1 + A_2)\text{Prob(ccd)} + (A_1 + A_3)\text{Prob(cdc)} + (A_2 + A_3)\text{Prob(dcc)}$$
$$+ (A_1)\text{Prob(cdd)} + (A_2)\text{Prob(dcd)} + (A_3)\text{Prob(ddc)} \tag{3.9}$$

Equation 3.9 says that the probability that a randomly chosen individual in the population of naive individuals is c is equal to the product of probability that a particular cultural "mating" results in c [e.g. A_1] and the probability that that mating occurs [e.g. Prob(cdd)], summed over all possible matings.

To evaluate Equation 3.9 we must specify the probability distribution of sets of models. First, let us assume that cultural parents are chosen randomly from the population before mating. This means that the probability of each set of cultural parents with I $(I = 0, . . ., 3)$ models with variant c and $3 - I$ models with variant d is $p^I(1 - p)^{3-I}$. Thus Equation 3.9 becomes

$$p' = p^3(1) + p^2(1 - p)[(A_1 + A_2) + (A_1 + A_3) + (A_2 + A_3)]$$
$$+ p(1 - p)^2(A_1 + A_2 + A_3) + (1 - p)^3(0) \tag{3.10}$$

Using the fact that $A_1 + A_2 + A_3 = 1$, we can simplify this expression to

$$p' = p^3 + 2p^2(1 - p) + p(1 - p)^2 \tag{3.11}$$

or

$$p' = p \tag{3.12}$$

In this simple three-model case with random formation of sets of models and a linear transmission rule, the cultural transmission rule causes no change in the frequency of cultural traits.

A more complex model

It turns out that this result is fairly general. To see this, let us consider the case of n models and nonrandom formation of sets of models. Because using a table to specify the transmission rule becomes inconvenient as the number of models increases, we often define transmission rules algebraically. To do this, we assign a numerical value to each cultural variant. In this case, assign the value 1 to the cultural variant c and the value 0 to the cultural variant d. Let X_i be the numerical value of the cultural variant of the ith model, in a particular set of cultural parents. Further, let A_i be the importance of the ith parent in transmission. Then in the case of n models the probability that a naive individual acquires the cultural variant c given that the n cultural parents have traits that take on the particular set of values $X_1, \ldots, X_n$ is

$$\text{Prob(offspring} = c|X_1, \ldots, X_n) = \sum_{i=1}^{n} A_i X_i \tag{3.13}$$

Once again the A_i must sum to one. Equation 3.13 illustrates the economy of expression that we can achieve using an algebraic representation of the transmission rule.

To predict the frequency of c after transmission, p', we weight the probability that the naive individual acquires variant c given that he or she is exposed to a given set of models $(X_1, \ldots, X_n)$ by the probability that that set of models is formed, $\text{Prob}(X_1, \ldots, X_n)$, and then sum over all sets of models. This leads to the following expression:

$$p' = \sum_{x_1=0}^{1} \cdots \sum_{x_n=0}^{1} \text{Prob}(c|x_1, \ldots, x_n) \, \text{Prob}(X_1 = x_1, \ldots, X_n = x_n) \tag{3.14}$$

To evaluate Equation 3.14 we must specify the probability distribution of sets of models. Define $M(X_1, \ldots, X_n)$ as the joint probability distribution of $X_1, \ldots, X_n$. Further, let $M_i(X_i)$ be the probability that the ith model has the cultural variant, X_i, averaged over all sets of cultural parents. $M_i(X_i)$ is said to be the marginal probability distribution of X_i. Suppose that the joint distribution of $(X_1, \ldots, X_n)$ is such that each of the marginal distributions has the following property:

$$\begin{aligned} M_i(1) &= p, \\ M_i(0) &= 1 - p \end{aligned} \tag{3.15}$$

This says that the frequency of c in each of the model roles is the same as the frequency of c in the population as a whole. The assumption that cultural parents are drawn at random from the population as a whole (a sort of cultural random mating) satisfies this condition, but so do a variety of other schemes, for example, ones in which models with similar behaviors are more likely to be found in the same set of cultural parents. When sets of cultural parents are formed in accordance with Equation 3.15, we shall say they are formed "nonselectively." It is shown in Box 3.1 that when the formation of sets of models is nonselective and the transmission rule is linear, transmission leaves the frequency of different cultural variants in the population unchanged.

This is an important result because it defines the conditions under which the transmission process itself does not result in evolutionary forces. We shall see that if the transmission rule is nonlinear or the formation of sets of cultural parents is selective, then cultural transmission does introduce evolutionary forces. We will defer analysis of these more interesting but more difficult cases until later chapters.

Random variation

Various events during the rest of the life history of an individual will lead to evolutionary forces that affect the distribution of cultural variants in the population. The simplest force is due to random variation, the cultural analog of mutation. By "random variation" we mean unpredictable changes in the cultural variant of an individual. There are three plausible sources of random variation: (1) the naive individual may erroneously perceive or erroneously cognize the behavior of an enculturating individual, (2) even if an individual accurately acquires a cultural

---

Box 3.1 The generalization of Equation 3.10 to the case of n cultural parents is

$$p' = \sum_{x_1=0}^{1} \cdots \sum_{x_n=0}^{1} \left(\sum_{i=0}^{n} A_i x_i \right) M(x_1, \ldots, x_n) \tag{1}$$

From the laws of conditional probability

$$M(x_1, \ldots, x_n) = M_i(x_i) \text{Prob}(x_1, \ldots, x_n \mid x_i) \tag{2}$$

where Prob $(x_1, \ldots, x_n \mid x_i)$ is the conditional probability of $(x_1, \ldots, x_{i-1}, x_{i+1}, \ldots, x_n)$ given x_i. Combining (1) and (2) and rearranging the order of summation results in

$$p' = \sum_{i=1}^{n} A_i \left\{ \left(\sum_{x_i=0}^{1} x_i M_i(x_i) \right) \left(\sum_{x_1=0}^{1} \cdots \sum_{x_n=0}^{1} \text{Prob}(x_1, \ldots, x_n \mid x_i) \right) \right\}$$

or

$$p' = \sum_{i=1}^{n} A_i ((1)p + (0)(1 - p))$$

$$p' = p$$

rule, it may be forgotten or misremembered at a later time, and (3) a correctly learned and remembered rule may be incompletely or erroneously performed in a given instance when it is being used as a model by another. Even though the proximate mechanisms of random cultural variation and genetic mutation are quite different, their properties are analogous.

We will model the effect of random variation exactly like mutation in the haploid genetic model. Suppose that the probability that an individual erroneously learns, misremembers, or transmits cultural variant c as d is μ_c and that the similar "error rate" for d to c is μ_d. Then the frequency of the cultural variant c after random cultural variation, p'', is

$$p'' = p' - p'\mu_c + (1 - p')\mu_d \qquad (3.16)$$

We assume that cultural transmission is linear and that the formation of cultural models is nonselective. These assumptions result in the following recursion for p:

$$p^* = p - p\mu_c + (1 - p)\mu_d \qquad (3.17)$$

We can calculate the equilibrium frequency of the cultural variant c, $\hat{p}$, exactly as we did in the haploid genetic case. This leads to the following expression for p:

$$\hat{p} = \frac{\mu_d}{\mu_d + \mu_c} \qquad (3.18)$$

This expression is completely analogous to the haploid genetic model described above. This results from the fact that the linear transmission rule has essentially the same properties as Mendelian genetic transmission. For another treatment of a closely related model, see Cavalli-Sforza and Feldman (1981: Chap. 2). As we proceed with our discussion, we will show step by step how various features that seem to characterize cultural transmission cause deviations from this linear model.

Horizontal transmission

It is very easy to modify the model of vertical and oblique transmission of a dichotomous character introduced in the last section to represent horizontal transmission. Consider a population of individuals of more or less comparable ages at a particular time, t. Suppose an interval of time Δt passes, and during this interval of time each individual encounters exactly $n - 1$ other individuals. We call these individuals "models" and label them 2,. . .,n, not necessarily in the order in which they were encountered. (We will show how this analysis can be generalized to allow individuals to encounter different numbers of models in Chap. 5.) Then at time $t + \Delta t$, each individual either retains his preexisting cultural variant with probability A_1 or adopts the cultural variant of the ith individual encountered with probability A_i. Then, the probability that an individual is characterized by variant c given that it had trait value X_1 at time t, and encountered individuals that had trait values $X_2,...,X_n$, is equal to

$$\text{Prob(Individual 1} = c \text{ at } t + \Delta t | X_1,...,X_n) = \sum_{i=1}^{n} A_i X_i \qquad (3.19)$$

Equation 3.19 has exactly the same form as Equation 3.10, which describes vertical and oblique transmission. The only difference is conceptual: to model horizontal transmission we allow an individual to be one of its own cultural parents, along with the $n - 1$ models. This allows us, for example, to model a situation in which individuals are unlikely to change their cultural variant by making an individual's own weight, A_1, approach one.

To compute the effect of horizontal transmission on the frequency of the variant c in the population, we need to specify the probability that individuals with variants are encountered. Let $M(X_1,...,X_n)$ be the probability that an individual with trait value X_1 encounters models with trait values $X_2,...,X_n$. Then as long as $M(X_1,...,X_n)$ represents nonselective formation of cultural parents as defined above, the episode of horizontal transmission leaves the frequency of the two variants in the population unchanged.

This is a very useful result, for it means that we can use the same mathematical machinery to model vertical, oblique, and horizontal cultural transmission. Results derived for one mode can be easily generalized to the others. We only need to keep in mind that the time scale has changed. In horizontal transmission the "generation time" is the length of time, Δt, in which individuals typically have some chance of changing their cultural variant.

Cultural drift

So far we have assumed that populations are very large. If populations are small, then sampling error will cause the frequency of the cultural variants to vary randomly. Consider a population of N individuals in which there are two cultural variants, c and d, with frequencies p and $1 - p$. When cultural transmission is linear, the individuals who make up the next generation can be thought of as a random sample of size N of the previous generation. Thus the frequency of c after transmission, p', is a random variable with mean p and variance $(1/N)p(1 - p)$. This means that if we started out with a large number of such populations, in some of them p' would be larger than p, and in others it would be smaller, but the average p' of all the populations would equal p. This process we will call "cultural drift" (because it is closely analogous to genetic drift).

In this book, we largely ignore the effects of cultural drift and concentrate instead on deterministic models. Deterministic models are easier both to analyze and to understand, particularly for the mathematically less sophisticated. It is our intuition that given the present state of development of the theory of cultural transmission, deterministic models return more insight per unit of effort invested in model building (or model reading) than do stochastic models. Both Cavalli-Sforza and Feldman (1973a, 1981) and Lumsden and Wilson (1981) provide extensive analyses of models of cultural transmission which include the effects of drift.

A model of the cultural transmission of a quantitative character

It is more natural to model many culturally transmitted characters as having a continuous range of values, instead of just two as we assumed above. For example, rather than characterizing an individual as either a Republican or a Democrat, we commonly place individuals on a political continuum running from right to left. It is probably even better to characterize an individual in terms of his or her position on a variety of different dimensions each of which represents his or her attitudes toward a particular issue. In this way it is possible to represent even quite complex sets of beliefs.

In modeling the cultural transmission of a quantitative character, we make the same general assumptions that we made in modeling the evolution of a dichotomous character, but add one major complication. In the case of quantitative characters we explicitly distinguish between the cultural variants, defined in terms of inherited information, and the directly observable behavioral differences that result from different cultural variants. This distinction is analogous to the distinction between genotype and phenotype in quantitative genetic models.

Imagine that the cultural variant individuals acquire through social learning can be characterized by a single number, X, which might, for example, denote their position on the left to right political spectrum. Further, suppose that an individual's behavior at any particular time can also be specified by a single number, Y, which might represent the individual's public statements on a particular issue.

We assume that different individuals with the same cultural variant (i.e. the same value of X) will in general be characterized by different behaviors (i.e. different values of Y). These differences could be the result of simple errors; for example, an individual may advocate a particular political position because he or she misunderstands the issues involved. Or the same cultural variant may result in different behaviors because it is expressed in a different environment. Two equally radical university professors may express different opinions on property taxes if one of them owns a house. We will also assume, however, that the individuals with different cultural variants will on average behave differently. The opinion of radical professors about property taxes will on average be different from that of conservative ones. These assumptions are shown graphically in Figure 3.1.

The population is characterized by the distribution of cultural variants. For a character which varies continuously, this distribution is a probability density func-

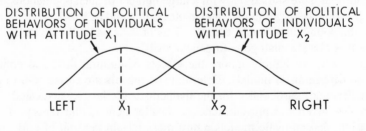

POLITICAL   ATTITUDE

Fig. 3.1 The horizontal axis gives a hypothetical cultural trait that affects political attitude measured on a left to right scale. The two curves plot the distribution of actual behaviors that might result from two particular cultural variants, X_1 and X_2.

tion which we will label P(X). This function has the following interpretation. Suppose that dX is a small increment in X. Then the probability that a randomly chosen member of the population has a cultural variant between X and X + dX is approximately P(X)dX. Suppose that we could measure the cultural variants of different individuals. Then we could get an approximation to the P(X) by measuring a large number of individuals and assigning them to classes of X as shown in Figure 3.2. The histogram that results is an approximation to P(X).

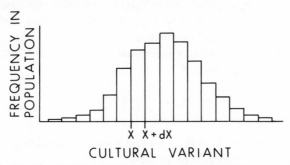

CULTURAL VARIANT

Fig. 3.2 The distribution of a hypothetical quantitative cultural trait in a population. The height of the histogram between X and X + dX is proportional to the fraction of the population with cultural variants that fall in that range.

Clearly the shape of P(X) will depend, in part, on the scale of measurement used. Experience from quantitative genetics and from psychometric studies suggests that it will often be possible to choose the scale of measurement so that P(X) can be approximated by a normal probability density. When this is true, it is possible to characterize the population by the mean value of X, $\overline{X}$, and the variance of X in the population, V. This greatly simplifies the task of modeling the evolution of the population because it means we only have to keep track of two numbers, $\overline{X}$ and V.

Blending inheritance

We will begin by describing a simple blending model of the cultural transmission of a quantitative character. As before, we suppose that each naive individual is enculturated by n models, numbered 1,. . .,n. Suppose that the cultural variant of the ith model is X_i. The offspring observes the behavior of each model, perhaps in a variety of environmental contexts, and then induces an estimate of the cultural rule that the model used to generate the observed behavior. We will label the naive individual's estimate of the ith model's cultural rule Z_i, which we will assume is given by

$$Z_i = X_i + e_i \qquad (3.20)$$

where the e_i are random variables with a multivariate normal distribution, $N(e_1,. . .,e_n)$, which represent the fact that a naive individual's estimate of the model's cultural rule may diverge from the inherited cultural rule of the model because of (1) environmental effects on the model's phenotype, (2) random variation of particular model performances, or (3) estimation errors by the naive individual. We assume that each e_i has a mean equal to zero and a variance equal to E_i. Because different cultural parents may model their behavior in a common environment, we also allow for the possibility that e_i and e_j may be correlated by assuming that the $Cov(e_i,e_j) = E_{ij}$.

One way to conceptualize cultural transmission is to imagine that the naive individuals are trying to estimate what behaviors have been favored by selection in previous generations using observations of a finite sample of the population, its models. Given this view, one plausible cultural transmission rule would be for naive individuals to adopt the average phenotype of its models. This leads to what has been called a "blending model" of inheritance (e.g. Fisher, 1958). Let X_0 be the cultural variant of a particular naive individual. Then a blending transmission rule is given by the following equation:

$$X_0 = \sum_{i=1}^{n} A_i Z_i \qquad (3.21)$$

where A_i is (in analogy with the dichotomous model) a constant giving the weight of the ith model in the transmission process.

As in the dichotomous case, we want to calculate the distribution of cultural variants in the population after cultural transmission, denoted $P'(X)$, given the distribution before transmission. Because we are assuming that $P(X)$ is normal, we need only to deduce the effect of transmission on the mean and the variance of $P(X)$. Let $M(X_1,. . .,X_n)$ be the probability that the set of cultural parents is characterized by the particular combination of cultural variants $(X_1,. . .X_n)$. Then the mean value of X in the population after transmission, $\overline{X'}$, is

$$\overline{X'} = \int\int M(X_1,. . .,X_n)N(e_1,. . .,e_n) \sum_{i=1}^{n} A_i(X_i + e_i) \, dX_1. . .dX_n de_1. . .de_n$$

$$(3.22)$$

This equation weights the average cultural variant that results from a given set of cultural parents, $\sum_{i=1}^{n} A_i X_i$, by the probability that such a set of parents is formed, $M(X_1,. . .,X_n)$, averaged over all possible sets of cultural parents. This equation is a modification of Equation 3.14 which allows for a continuum of cultural variants.

Once again we will assume that the formation of sets of models is nonselective. This means that the marginal distribution of cultural variants among models who occupy the ith social role, $M_i(X_i)$, is equal to $P(X_i)$. With this assumption it can be shown that (see Box 3.2)

$$\overline{X'} = \overline{X} \qquad (3.23)$$

The linear blending rule leaves the population mean of a quantitative cultural variant unchanged.

We can compute the variance after transmission, V', in a similar way. It can be shown (see Box 3.2) that this results in the following expression for the variance after cultural transmission:

$$V' = \sum_{i=1}^{n} A_i^2(V + E_i) + 2\sum_{i>j} A_i A_j(E_{ij} + V \, Corr(X_i,X_j)) \qquad (3.24)$$

Box 3.2 Equation 3.22 can be divided into a sum of two terms:

$$\overline{X}' = \int \ldots \int \sum_{i=1}^{n} M(X_1, \ldots, X_n)N(e_1, \ldots, e_n)A_iX_i \, dX_1 \ldots dX_n de_1 \ldots de_n$$

$$+ \sum_{i=1}^{n} M(X_1, \ldots, X_n)N(e_1, \ldots, e_n)A_ie_i \, dX_1 \ldots dX_n de_1 \ldots de_n$$

When we integrate over the estimation errors, e_i, the second term goes to zero and the first term no longer depends on e_i. Next, let Prob $(X_1, \ldots, X_n \mid X_i)$ be the conditional probability density of $(X_1, \ldots, X_{i-1}, X_{i+1}, \ldots, X_n)$ given X_i, and $M_i(X_i)$ be the marginal density of X_i. Then using the laws of conditional probability (see Box 3.1) this equation can be rewritten as

$$\overline{X}' = \int \cdots \int \sum_{i=1}^{n} \text{Prob}(X_1, \ldots, X_n \mid X_i)M_i(X_i)A_iX_i \, dX_1 \ldots dX_n$$

Next, we exchange the operations of summation and integration:

$$\overline{X}' = \sum_{i=1}^{n} \int \cdots \int \text{Prob}(X_1, \ldots, X_n \mid X_i) \, dX_1 \ldots dX_{i-1} \, dX_{i+1} \ldots$$
$$dX_n M_i(X_i)A_iX_i \, dX_i$$

The conditional probability density must integrate to one. Thus

$$\overline{X}' = \sum_{i=1}^{n} A_i \int M(X_i)X_i \, dX_i = \overline{X}$$

The variance of X in the population after transmission, V', is

$$V' = \int \cdots \int M(X_1, \ldots, X_n)N(e_1, \ldots, e_n)\left(\sum_{i=1}^{n} A_i(X_i + e_i)\right)^2 dX_1 \ldots$$
$$dX_n de_1 \ldots de_n - \overline{X}^2$$

After squaring the sum this becomes

$$V' = \int \cdots \int N(e_1, \ldots, e_n)M(X_1, \ldots, X_n)\left(\sum_{i=1}^{n} A_i^2(X_i^2 + 2X_ie_i + e_i^2)\right.$$
$$\left. + 2 \sum_{i>j} A_i A_j(X_iX_j + X_ie_j + X_je_i + e_ie_j)\right) dX_1 \ldots dX_n de_1 \ldots de_n - \overline{X}^2$$

Since the e_i and the X_j are assumed to be independent and the means of the e_i are zero, all terms linear in e_i are zero. The remaining expression can be simplified to 3.24 in the text using the rules of conditional probability as in the case of the mean.

The term $\text{Corr}(X_i, X_j)$ is the correlation of X_i and X_j. If sets of cultural models are formed at random, the $\text{Corr}(X_i, X_j) = 0$. The data from psychometric studies indicate, however, that sets of models assort in such a way that similar individuals are in the same sets of cultural models. If models i and j assort in this way, $\text{Corr}(X_i, X_j) > 0$.

The most important thing to notice about Equation 3.24 is that the variance after transmission does not necessarily equal the variance before transmission. Blending inheritance, even with a linear transmission rule, affects the distribution of cultural variants in the population. To get a better idea of how this happens, we will first econsider a very special case. Assume that mating occurs at random so that $Corr(X_i, X_j) = 0$ for each pair of models. Next suppose that $A_i = A_j = (1/n)$, so that all models have equal weight, and finally assume that $E_i = E_j = 0$, so that there is no error in the transmission process. In this case

$$V' = (1/n)V \tag{3.25}$$

This equation says that in this special case the transmission process decreases the variance of X in the population by a factor of $1/n$. This makes sense because the naive individual is averaging the phenotypes of a sample of n models, and experience with statistics tells us that increasing the sample size decreases the variance of the mean. Thus the simplest blending rule has the property that heritable variation rapidly disappears.

Now, suppose we return the complications one at a time to Equation 3.24. First, suppose that the parents have different weights in the transmission process. Then

$$V' = V\sum_{i=1}^{n} A_i^2 \tag{3.26}$$

Notice that Equation 3.26 is the same as Equation 3.25 except that $(1/n)$ is replaced by ΣA_i^2. When cultural parents have unequal weights in transmission this has the effect of reducing the "effective number" of cultural parents. (To see this, think about what should happen if $A_i = 0$ for a particular model.)

Next we suppose that the formation of sets of cultural parents is assortative, so that $Corr(X_i, X_j) = R$ (where R is a constant) for each pair of models. Then

$$V' = V[(1/n) + (1 - 1/n)R] \tag{3.27}$$

Thus, if similar individuals are more likely to be found together in a set of models than chance alone would dictate, the effect of blending inheritance on the variance is reduced. Again this is easy to understand in terms of the extreme case $R = 1$. This means that the cultural variants of different models are perfectly correlated and, therefore, there is in effect only one model. In this case it seems reasonable that there should be no blending effect.

Next, we allow errors by naive individuals in estimating the cultural rules of their parents. This means that $E_i > 0$, for $i = 1, \ldots, n$. We will continue to assume that $E_{ij} = 0$. In this case

$$V' = (1/n)V + \overline{E} \tag{3.28}$$

where $\overline{E} = (1/n)\Sigma E_i$ is the average value of E_i for the set of models. This equation says that the errors made in estimating the models' cultural variants increase the variance of the distribution of cultural variants each generation by an amount $\overline{E}$.

Blending inheritance and the conservation of variation

In each of the cases described in the previous section the blending transmission rule reduced the amount of variation in the population. The strength of this effect depends on the effective number of models, the extent to which the formation of sets of models is assortative, and the amount of new variation introduced each generation by errors. Despite these qualifications it seems hard to dispute that blending inheritance creates a powerful evolutionary force reducing the variance of quantitative characters.

Geneticists often claim that their main contribution to Darwinian theory was the discovery that genes are particulate units because, unlike blending inheritance, particulate inheritance conserves variation. During the nineteenth century most biologists thought that organic inheritance was also a blending process, and Darwin adopted this view in *The Origin of Species*. A Scottish engineer named Fleeming Jenkin (1864) pointed out the effect of blending inheritance on the variance, and argued that it would rapidly destroy the variation necessary for natural selection to work. Darwin's correspondence reveals that he thought that Jenkin's argument was a serious blow to his theory (Eiseley, 1958). It was not until R. A. Fisher (1918) showed how particulate inheritance could be reconciled with quantitative phenotypic variation that Darwin's ideas were completely immune to this argument.

Several people have raised a similar objection to us in the case of culture. The hypothesis that culture is subject to evolutionary forces, like natural selection or biased transmission, depends on the assumption that cultural transmission preserves variation. Therefore, they argue, cultural transmission must be particulate. We believe that this argument, as hoary as it is, is a non sequitur. It is certainly true that variation must be preserved for evolutionary mechanisms based on selection and biased transmission to work, and that particulate inheritance is one such mechanism that will serve that function. However, it does not follow that it is the only such mechanism or that particulate inheritance by itself guarantees the conservation of variation.

In the absence of selection and mutation, the particulate nature of genetic inheritance does ensure that the variance of a quantitative character in a population will achieve a stable positive equilibrium value (Fisher, 1958). In the absence of mutation, however, most forms of selection will rapidly deplete this variation. Only recently have attempts been made to show (Kimura, 1965; Lande, 1976) how particulate inheritance, in combination with measured mutation rates, can account for the observed variation in quantitative characters. These authors argue that the main effect of particulate inheritance is to allow very small mutation rates to maintain observed amounts of variation (see Turelli, 1984, for a contrasting view).

Are there any circumstances under which blending inheritance can maintain significant variation? To answer this question we calculate the equilibrium value of V assuming that transmission creates the only forces affecting the variance. The equilibrium value of the variance is found by setting V' equal to V in Equation 3.24 and solving for V. This results in the following expression for the equilibrium variance, $\hat{V}$:

$$\hat{V} = \frac{\sum_{i=1}^{n} A_i^2 E_i + 2 \sum_{i>j} A_i A_j E_{ij}}{1 - \sum_{i=1}^{n} A_i^2 - 2 \sum_{i>j} A_i A_j \operatorname{Corr}(X_j, X_i)} \tag{3.29}$$

As long as at least one of the E_i is greater than zero, the equilibrium value of V is greater than zero. This is not surprising since as long as new variation is introduced each generation $\hat{V}$ cannot become exactly zero. It would be more interesting to get some feeling for the magnitude of $\hat{V}$. To accomplish this we assume that for all i and j (1) $E_i = E$, (2) $E_{ij} = EC$, (3) $A_i = A_j = (1/n)$, and (4) $\text{Corr}(X_i, X_j) = R$. This means that R is the correlation between the cultural variants of the parents and C is the correlation between the estimation errors for each parent. With these simplifying assumptions the expression for the equilibrium variance becomes

$$\hat{V} = \frac{E(1 + (n - 1)C)}{(n - 1)(1 - R)} \tag{3.30}$$

This expression indicates that the equilibrium variance can be any value between zero and infinity depending on the relative values of the four parameters, E, R, C, and n. If $E(1 + (n - 1)C)$ is large compared to $n - 1$ and/or R is close to one, $\hat{V}$ will be large. Thus we can conclude that a substantial variance can be maintained with blending inheritance if enough new variation is introduced into the population each generation [i.e. $E(1 + (n - 1)C) > n$] or if the formation of sets of cultural parents is sufficiently assortative (i.e. R near 1).

Whether blending inheritance will maintain enough variation for selection and other evolutionary forces to work is an empirical question. If the rate of introduction of new variation is low (as it is in the genetic case), then the answer is probably no. If the cultural error rate is high, blending inheritance will present no difficulties. In the absence of empirical estimates of the cultural error rate we cannot exclude blending inheritance as a plausible model for the cultural inheritance of a quantitative character.

An alternative to the blending model

It is often assumed, incorrectly, that blending models and particulate models are the only possible alternatives. In fact, other models are conceivable. In this section we outline a model of the cultural transmission of a quantitative character that does not assume any kind of particles exist, but which nonetheless maintains variation in a way that is exactly analogous to genetic transmission. We refer to this model as the "multifactor model" for reasons that will become apparent as we go along. We begin again with the simplest (and least realistic) case and then add features that make the model more realistic.

We start with the same assumptions as in the blending case. Each offspring is enculturated by n parents who are characterized by the cultural variants $X_1, \ldots, X_n$. The offspring uses each model's actual behavior to estimate his or her cultural variant. These estimates are labeled $Z_1, \ldots, Z_n$. However, we now assume the following transmission rule, which is quite different from blending inheritance. We imagine that the naive individual chooses one of the cultural parents as a "role model" and adopts its estimate of that model's cultural rule as its own cultural variant. We can express this mathematically as follows:

$$\text{Prob}(X_0 = Z_i | Z_1, \ldots, Z_n) = A_i \tag{3.31}$$

where X_0 is the naive individual's cultural variant and A_i is the probability that the ith model is chosen as a role model. Thus the naive individual acquires cultural variant $X_0 = Z_i$ with probability A_i. The probability that the naive individual adopts any cultural variant other than $Z_1, . . ., Z_n$ is zero.

To compute the effect of this kind of cultural transmission on the mean of the population we proceed as before. Since on average the e_i are zero, the mean of the cultural variants that result from a set of models with the cultural variants $X_1, . . ., X_n$ is

$$E(X_0|X_1, . . ., X_n) = \sum_{i=1}^{n} A_i X_i \qquad (3.32)$$

where $E(X_0|X_1, . . ., X_n)$ is read "the expected value of X_0 given the values $X_1, . . ., X_n$." The mean value of X_0 in the population after transmission is

$$\overline{X}' = \int . . . \int E(X_0|X_1, . . ., X_n) M(X_1, . . ., X_n) \, dX_1 . . . dX_n \qquad (3.33)$$

where $M(X_1, . . ., X_n)$ is the probability density function governing the likelihood that various sets of cultural parents are formed. Combining Equation 3.32 and Equation 3.33 results in an expression for the mean that is identical to that of the blending case. (See Eq. 3.22.) Thus, this model of cultural transmission leaves the mean unchanged.

Next we compute the variance of X_0 after transmission, V'. The expected value of X_0^2 given a particular set of models with cultural variants $X_1, . . ., X_n$ is

$$E(X_0^2|X_1, . . ., X_n) = \int . . . \int N(e_1, . . ., e_n) \sum_{i=1}^{n} A_i(X_i + e_i)^2 \, de_1 . . . de_n \qquad (3.34)$$

The variance in the whole population after transmission is

$$V' = \int . . . \int E(X_0^2|X_1, . . ., X_n) M(X_1, . . ., X_n) \, dX_1 . . . dX_n - \overline{X}^2 \qquad (3.35)$$

If the formation of cultural parents is nonselective, then combining Equations 3.35 and 3.34 shows that

$$V' = V + \sum_{i=1}^{n} A_i E_i \qquad (3.36)$$

If there is no additional variation introduced by the estimation process (i.e. $E_i = 0$ for all i), the variance is unchanged. The presence of any estimation errors will cause the variance to increase, and if there are no other forces acting to oppose this process the variance will grow without bound. It turns out that this model of cultural transmission is formally identical to the one-locus haploid genetic model with an infinite number of alleles and shares the property of this and other genetic models that relatively low rates of introduction of new variation can maintain substantial variation.

The multifactor model does not assume that inheritance is in any way particulate. Just as in the blending model, each offspring makes an estimate of the cultural rule that each of its cultural parents is using to generate offspring behavior. This estimate is a continuously varying quantity. The only difference between this model and the blending model is that in the multifactorial model the offspring ultimately acquires the phenotype of only one of its cultural parents, although it "chooses" this role model from a larger set, and different parents may be chosen as role models for different traits. It is the quasi-uniparental aspect of the model that causes the variance to be conserved.

The simple version of the multifactorial model outlined above is not a plausible description of cultural transmission. To see why, consider several naive individuals who share the same set of two cultural models. The model outlined above predicts that the distribution of culturally acquired behavior among these "cultural sibs" should be bimodal; some of the imitators like one model and others like the other model. While this may be true for some characters, it seems more likely that in general the distribution of imitator phenotypes will be unimodal and that the mode will be intermediate between the parental types.

It is easy to modify the multifactorial model to meet this objection. To do this we imagine that the phenotypic character or behavior of interest is the cumulative result of a number of different components or factors. For example, consider the way bread is made. The outcome, measured in terms of taste, depends on a variety of factors, the kind of flour chosen, how much shortening and sweetener are added, how long the bread is kneaded, how hot the oven is, and so on. Each different combination of the factors will lead to a different kind of bread. Suppose that we could characterize each kind of bread by a single number, Y. Then if we are free to choose the measurement scales of each of the component factors that determine the kind of bread, we might represent the aggregate effect of these factors in terms of their sum. That is,

$$Y_i = \sum_{j=1}^{m} X_{ij} \qquad (3.37)$$

where X_{ij} is the value of the jth factor in the ith individual. So, for example, X_{i1} might represent the amount of sweetener and X_{i2} the amount of shortening that the ith individual thought should go into making bread.

Now, suppose we generalize the simple transmission scheme discussed above to multiple factors in the following way. Each naive individual is exposed to n cultural parents. The naive individual estimates the value of each of the factors in each of its model's cultural rules. Let Z_{ij} be the estimate of the jth factor for the ith model. We suppose that

$$Z_{ij} = X_{ij} + e_{ij} \qquad (3.38)$$

where e_{ij} are independent normal random variables with zero mean and variance E_{ij} that represent the effects of errors made in the estimation process.

Now suppose that the naive individual constructs its own cultural rule by "mixing and matching" from among the various factors of all its cultural parents.

For example, the individual adopts mother's ideas about sweeteners, cooking time, and temperature, grandmother's ideas about shortening, and a neighbor's ideas about flour. This idea can be formulated mathematically by assuming that the probability that the jth component of the imitator's cultural rule, X_{0j}, will be Z_{ij} with probability A_i.

With these assumptions, the effect of transmission on the mean and variance of each of the factors will be the same as in the simple one-factor model described immediately above. The mean value of each factor will be unaffected by transmission, and the variance will be increased by an amount that depends on the accuracy of the offspring's estimations. It is also possible that the values of the different factors may covary. However, as long as there are more than a few cultural parents and the covariances of the estimation errors are small, any initial covariance between the values of the factors will rapidly disappear. (We will return to the topic of covariances in Chap. 8.)

If the formation of sets of cultural parents is nonselective, a derivation closely analogous to the one given in Box 3.2 shows that $\overline{Y}' = \overline{Y}$ and that the variance of Y, U is equal to

$$U' = U + \sum_{i=1}^{n} \sum_{j=1}^{m} A_i E_{ij} \qquad (3.39)$$

Thus the effects of transmission on the variance are much the same as in the simpler case in which there was only one factor.

The difference between the two models is that in the multifactorial model the distribution of cultural offspring that result from a single set of cultural parents will usually be unimodal, and the mode will be located between the cultural variants of the two parents. This results from the fact that each element in the sum that makes up the cultural rule of a particular offspring is a random variable with several discrete outcomes, the estimates of factors in its parents. Sums of such random variables are multinomially distributed, which has the requisite properties.

In subsequent chapters we will be concerned mainly with how the means of the cultural variants in the population change in response to various forces of cultural evolution, and we will be much less concerned with the variance. In most cases the qualitative predictions of the theory do not depend on how the variance is maintained as long as it is maintained at a finite, stable level. In the absence of more detailed information about the cultural transmission of quantitative characters, we will simply assume that one of the mechanisms discussed above maintains a constant, finite variance and concentrate on the mean.

Conclusion

In this chapter we have tried to convince the reader of two different things. First, we argued that empirical work in the social sciences supports the notion that social learning in the human species has the properties of an inheritance system. Individuals observe the behavior of others, induce the cultural rules that generated the observed behavior, and then incorporate these rules into their own cultural repertoire. Second, we showed how this qualitative description of cultural transmission could be translated, albeit in a stylized way, into mathematical models. These models, at least in principle, allow us to deduce the long-run, population-level consequences of particular forms of cultural transmission.

One property of the simple models we have analyzed so far is that cultural transmission by itself does not cause any change in the frequency of the different behavioral variants. The models have that property because we assumed that naive individuals unselectively acquire the cultural rules that are modeled for them. Unselective copying must be represented with a linear model of transmission which always has the property that cultural transmission itself leads to no evolutionary forces.

It is interesting to consider this result in the context of the following commonly held view. Many authors, including us, have argued that cultural transmission is adaptive because it is an efficient shortcut to trial-and-error learning. By imitating the cultural rules of others, individuals can avoid the cost of learning. Rosenthal and Zimmerman (1978: 208) illustrate the argument with the following vivid metaphor:

> Imagine being suddenly abandoned on a mythical island. One finds oneself amid lurid vegetation, weird fauna, and surrounded by burbling streams and geysers of many colors. What can one do? The intrepid but unwary castaway might try direct experimentation to gain sustenance, hoping that experience will be a successful teacher . . . . But hasty trials with unknown contingencies also invite punishing, perhaps fatal effects of permanent time out. The more cautious adventurer could greatly improve prospects by observing the exotic animals . . . . If the area were populated, watching or asking the local inhabitants would be still more informative.

They conclude that "learning by observation minimizes the need for trial and error practice." This argument only makes sense if the individuals observed are behaving adaptively: that is, if adaptive cultural variants are in higher frequency than maladaptive variants. As we have seen, however, if everyone acquires their behavior unselectively, there will be no force that will act to increase the frequency of adaptive traits—cultural transmission is a useful shortcut to ordinary trial-and-error learning only if some force acts to increase the frequency of favorable cultural variants. In the next chapters we consider several such forces.

4

Guided Variation and the Evolution of Cultural Inheritance

Custom is the principal magistrate of man's life. [Its predominance] is every-
where visible. Men do just as they have done before; as if they were dead
images and engines moved only by the wheels of custom.

Francis Bacon

In 1573, at the age of twelve, Francis Bacon entered Cambridge University. A little
more than two years later he returned home disappointed and without his degree.
Bacon was little impressed with the scholasticism that dominated the university in
his day. He described his tutors as "Men of sharp wits, shut up in the cells of a few
authors, chiefly Aristotle, their Dictator" (quoted in Eiseley, 1973). Throughout the
rest of his scholarly life he was to stress the conflict he perceived between learning
and tradition. For Bacon, learning meant trial-and-error learning, gaining knowledge directly by observation or experiment. The alternative to learning was passive
acceptance of the cultural beliefs and traditions of the previous generation. For
Bacon, induction was important because it was an "engine" for overcoming the
stultifying effects of custom and tradition.

Bacon's view of the relationship between learning and social tradition seems to
differ sharply from that of many contemporary sociobiologists (e.g. Alexander,
1979a; Bonner, 1980) who see social learning and individual trial-and-error learning as fundamentally similar. These scholars believe that all kinds of learning cause
individuals to acquire adaptive behavior by interacting with their environment.
Social learning is notable only because the "environment" includes the social
environment as well as the physical and biotic environment. From this point of
view, learning and custom are not opposed; instead, evolution should have shaped
the processes of ordinary learning and social learning (these authors argue) so that
they usually act in concert to enhance individual fitness.

These conflicting perceptions of the interaction between ordinary learning and
social learning present the following intriguing puzzle: Can a system of social
learning which inhibits individuals from learning new adaptive behaviors for themselves be favored by natural selection? The data reviewed in the previous chapter
and common experience suggest that Bacon was correct; adherence to culturally
inherited beliefs often causes people to ignore the dictates of ordinary, individual
learning. Generally, we expect that individual capacities for learning (and other

81

kinds of phenotypic plasticity) will have been shaped by evolution so that they improve the fit of the organism to its environment. When culturally transmitted tradition conflicts with learning, it is reasonable to surmise that the tradition is maladaptive. It also seems likely, however, that the sociobiologists are correct in assuming that the capacity for the cultural transmission of beliefs is adaptive.

In this chapter we suggest a possible solution to this puzzle. We proceed in three steps. First, we briefly review the empirical evidence about the nature of individual learning. Trial-and-error learning is but one of many mechanisms by which organisms modify their phenotype in response to environmental contingencies. In the human case, at least, these mechanisms range in complexity from the simplest kinds of conditioning to the complex processes of rational choice. For simplicity, we refer to this whole range of processes as "individual learning." On the basis of our review, we propose a simple model of individual learning that captures the qualitative properties of the range of learning processes.

Next, we will combine our model of individual learning with the simple models of cultural transmission introduced in the previous chapter in an attempt to understand how learning interacts with cultural transmission to affect the dynamics of the distribution of phenotypes in a population. When individuals learn, phenotypic variation is not random. Instead, the frequency of certain (usually favorable) variants is increased. If such learned variants are culturally transmitted, the result is a force that increases the frequency from one generation to the next of the same variants whose frequency is increased within a generation by learning. We call this the force of "guided variation." Early evolutionary theory placed great weight on this force, often attributed somewhat erroneously to Lamarck. Darwin (e.g. 1874: 3) stressed its importance under the rubric of "the inherited effects of use and disuse." Although students of genetics have all but ruled out "Lamarckian" effects in that system of inheritance, it is likely that they are important in the case of culture.

With these results in hand, we then address the question, Are there any circumstances in which natural selection will cause cultural transmission to be more important than learning in determining individual phenotype? The answer to this question is particularly important for understanding the origins of cultural transmission. It seems likely that the capacity for culture evolved in a primate with extensive learning abilities and prolonged parental care but only a rudimentary ability for social learning. In such a species, the only forces increasing the frequency of favored variants would be natural selection and the force of guided variation. We will conclude that under some environmental conditions (but not others) cultural transmission can be favored.

These results are interesting in light of the curious fact that the cultural transmission of phenotype is apparently rare in nature, and where it does exist it is generally restricted to a narrow range of traits (for reviews, see Immelman, 1975; Galef, 1976; Bonner, 1980; Mainardi, 1980). Given the apparent benefits of cultural transmission in the human species, the rarity of culture seems paradoxical. Of course, there are always many possible reasons a trait has not evolved. Nonetheless, it will be interesting to consider this problem in the context of the results of this chapter.

Models of Learning

In their book *Programmed to Learn,* Ronald Pulliam and Christopher Dunford introduce a particularly apt metaphor to describe the relationship between genotype and phenotype. Genes, they say, are like investors who are setting up a blind trust. The investors can give their brokers a set of initial instructions, which cannot subsequently be changed or canceled. Some investors might wish to give their brokers detailed instructions about which stocks to buy and sell at each future time. In an unpredictable environment like the stock market, such an investment strategy is likely to be disastrous. Wiser investors would give their brokers a flexible set of instructions. For example, they might specify that a certain proportion of the trust be held in blue chip stocks, some in growth stocks, and so on, with the overall specification that the broker try to maximize revenue within these constraints. Similarly, in an uncertain world genes are more likely to be successful if phenotypes are free to adapt flexibly to the environment in which they find themselves.

It seems likely that virtually all organisms have mechanisms that allow learning and other forms of phenotypic plasticity, general genetic "instructions" that permit considerable flexibility in the way anatomy, physiology, and behavior are actually adapted to particular environments. Reviews of the kinds and extent of learning in nature can be found in Waddington (1957), Bradshaw (1965), Wilson (1975), Bonner (1980), and Staddon (1983). Humans modify their behavior in response to environmental changes through a variety of mechanisms. These mechanisms range from the simple conditioned responses that are studied by behavioral psychologists to the cognitively complex processes of rational choice studied by cognitive psychologists and economists.

To model the interaction of individual learning and cultural transmission we clearly require a model (or models) of learning. We would like this model to be as simple as possible and still capture the qualitative features of the full range of processes that fall within our definition of learning. Surprisingly, evolutionary theorists have largely ignored phenotypic adaptation and instead focused on the way that populations adapt genetically to heterogeneous environments. Because of this there are no standard models of learning within evolutionary biology. Therefore, in this section we will briefly review models of learning used in the social sciences. We will focus on two very different models, the linear learning model (Bush and Mosteller, 1955) used by behavioral psychologists to describe certain kinds of trial-and-error learning and the Bayesian model of rational choice used by economists, decision theorists, and cognitive psychologists (e.g. Hirshleifer and Riley, 1979). We shall see that these two models are qualitatively very similar, and because of this fact we can capture the important qualitative features of learning in a single, simple model.

Learning from the point of view of behavioral psychology

Behavioral psychologists have studied learning extensively in both animals and humans. The goal of this work has been to discover general laws that describe the process of learning in all species. To do this psychologists have examined how animals learn in extremely simplified controlled laboratory conditions. In most cases the animal is presented with a novel association between a "stimulus" (such as a light or a bell) and some form of reward (a food pellet) or punishment (an electric shock). The experimenter tries to find out how the animal learns to associate the stimulus with the reward or punishment. By carefully controlling the details of the setting in which the learning takes place, the experimenter hopes to discover the fundamental processes that underlie all learning.

The following experiment by Garcia and his co-workers (Garcia and Keolling, 1966) illustrates the approach. A naive rat is placed in a chamber with a water bottle which is rigged so that every time the rat's tongue touches the spout, lights flash and a raucous noise is made. In roughly every other trial the noise and lights are followed a few seconds later by an electric shock to the rat's feet. The rat is allowed to remain in the chamber for a fixed period of time. The same process is then repeated with each of several rats. After a relatively short time rats learn to avoid drinking "bright-noisy water." Usually, different rats learn at different rates. In the typical experiment a large population of rats shows the kind of results shown in Figure 4.1. The rate at which rats drink the "bright-noisy" water decreases according to a smooth, convex curve.

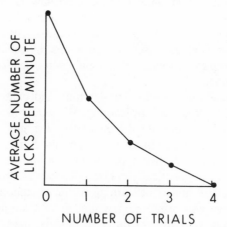

Fig. 4.1 Learning curve for rats being conditioned to avoid bright-noisy water. (Redrawn from Garcia and Keolling, 1966.)

The linear learning model. Behavioral psychologists have invented a variety of mathematical models that describe learning in a simple experimental setting like the one described above. Here we discuss one of the earliest of these models, the linear learning model of Bush and Mosteller (1955). Although there are a variety of competing models (reviewed in Atkinson, Bower, and Crothers, 1965), the linear model captures the general properties of learning and its simplicity allows us to add cultural effects easily.

The basic assumption of this model (and many others in this field) is that learning can be modeled as a change in the probability that the rat chooses to drink the bright-noisy water. For a particular rat, let P_i be the probability that the rat drinks the bright-noisy water during the ith trial. Then the probability that the rat drinks during the next $(i + 1)$ trial is assumed to be

$$P_{i+1} = a_iP_i + (1 - a_i)\Gamma_i \qquad (4.1)$$

The parameters a_i are called the learning parameters and may vary between zero and one, according to the outcome of the trial. The a_i give the importance of previous trials relative to the most recent one in determining behavior during the current trial. If the a_i are near one, a single trial has little effect on the rat's behavior; it learns slowly. If the a_i are near zero, the rat's behavior is almost completely determined by the most recent outcome. The Γ_i are parameters which also range between zero and one and give the reinforcement value of the outcome of the ith trial. A plausible set of values for the Γ_i might be

$$\Gamma_i = \begin{cases} 0 \text{ if the shock is administered} \\ 1 \text{ if the shock is not administered} \end{cases}$$

Every time the shock is administered after the rat drinks the bright-noisy water, the probability that the rat will drink on the next trial decreases an amount $(1 - a_i)P_i$, and every time the rat drinks without being shocked the probability that it will drink on the next trial is decreased an amount $(1 - a_i)(1 - P_i)$. (See Box 4.1.) It can be shown that this model, called the "two-operator linear model," results in a negatively sloped, convex learning curve like that shown in Figure 4.1. (See Atkinson et al. for solution techniques.)

This extremely simple model gives three important insights into the learning process. First, in order to learn the rat must be able to evaluate different outcomes that result from its behavior. In this case, it must "know" that shocks are to be avoided. Second, the rat cannot learn without making some assumptions about the nature of the environment. In this example it must "assume" that events that occur close together in time (i.e. the drinking of bright-noisy water and the subsequent shock) are likely to be causally associated. Third, the time path of the learning process depends on the initial predispositions of the rat. In this experiment rats initially had no aversion to bright-noisy water, and even after several trials some rats had not learned to use the light and noise as cues to avoid the shock. According to the linear learning model, if the rats had started with an aversion to bright-noisy water, they could have avoided many costly learning trials.

Box 4.1 Suppose that a rat drinks bright-noisy water on trial i and receives a shock. We want to calculate the decrease in the probability that the rat will drink on trial $i + 1$. From 4.1

$$P_{i+1} = a_i P_i + (1 - a_i)0$$

$$= a_i P_i$$

The decrease in the probability of drinking is

$$P_i - P_{i+1} = P_i - a_i P_i$$

$$= P_i(1 - a_i)$$

Learning as adaptation

These three properties of the learning rule make sense if we think of learning as a mechanism by which the rat acquires information about its environment and then uses that information to modify its phenotype adaptively. The ability to do this requires a priori "knowledge" about the nature of the environment. The rat must be able to "decide" what kinds of events can reduce its fitness. Painful events usually reduce fitness, although in this particular case the association may be coincidental rather than evolved. The rat must make assumptions about what events in the environment can be used as predictive cues to avoid the painful events. It is probably a good rule of thumb that disturbances such as sudden light and noise are frequently associated with contemporaneous events that the rat wants to avoid. As we shall see, however, this rule of thumb does not always work. Finally, the rat must begin with some initial "assumptions" about the environment. In this case water was assumed to be all right until proven otherwise.

Until the early 1970s most behavioral psychologists would have looked askance at this kind of adaptive interpretation of laboratory learning experiments (e.g. Skinner, 1966). However, the experiments of Garcia and others examining the acquisition of food preferences provide very strong evidence that animals have learning rules that make adaptive sense. (For reviews of this work, see Seligman and Hager, 1972, and Barker, Best, and Domjan, 1977.) The experiment described above was part of a larger experiment that was crucial in convincing psychologists of this fact. The larger experiment had four separate treatments. In addition to bright-noisy water, rats were also exposed to "tasty" water which had saccharin added to it. After drinking the tasty water, the rats were shocked in the same way as before; however, they were unable to learn to associate the taste cue with the subsequent shock. In another pair of treatments, sickness was induced in rats after they had drunk tasty water or bright-noisy water, either by exposing them to X-rays or by injecting them with a poison. The rats exposed to tasty water quickly developed an aversion to it, while those that became sick after drinking bright-noisy water did not develop any aversion.

The results of this experiment, summarized in Table 4.1, suggest that rats act as if they have a prior belief that there is a causal relationship between novel tastes and subsequent gastric distress but that there is no such prior association between taste and external events like an electric shock. Similarly, rats "expect" auditory and visual cues to be associated with external consequences like shocks but not with internal ones like gastric distress. These assumptions about nature seem very sensible given that rats are nocturnal, live in a wide variety of habitats, and are opportunistic foragers utilizing many different kinds of foods (Barnett, 1975). It

Table 4.1 The relationship between cue and reinforcement in the experiments of Garcia et al. (1966)

Cue	Reinforcer	
	Shock	Sickness
Taste	No response	Response
Lights/noise	Response	No response

seems likely that rats must frequently learn to avoid novel, toxic food substances whose main distinguishing feature is that they lead to gastric distress.

This adaptive interpretation of Garcia's results is strengthened by the fact that other experiments show that different patterns occur in other species. For example, Wilcoxon, Dragoin, and Kral (1971) gave rats and quail blue, salty water and then induced illness. When both species were subsequently offered blue water and salty water, the rats avoided the salty water while the quail avoided the blue water. This makes sense given that birds are diurnal foragers that use visual cues to avoid noxious food items like certain brightly colored caterpillars in contrast to nocturnal rats that must use taste cues.

There is evidence that this kind of simple food aversion learning does not involve any complicated cognitive abilities (Kalat and Rozin, 1972) but instead represents a kind of reflexive aversion. It seems likely that humans, rats, and many other animals do engage in much more complicated learning. In the next section we consider one model of complex learning, the Bayesian theory of rational choice.

The Bayesian model of rational choice

The Bayesian theory of rational choice was developed by mathematicians and economists as a normative theory of human decision making in the presence of uncertainty (see Savage, 1954). At the root of the theory are several axioms that the authors of the theory believed captured the meaning of rationality. For example, one of the axioms is that rational choice must be transitive. This means that if an individual prefers A to B and prefers B to C he must, if he is rational, prefer A to C. It turns out that it can be shown that these axioms of rational choice are satisfied only if people follow certain rules of behavior. These rules constitute the Bayesian theory of rational choice, sometimes called Bayesian decision theory. There are two key concepts in Bayesian decision theory. The first of these is the notion of "utility." If individuals are rational, it can be shown that they must be able to assign to each outcome of a particular decision (or, more generally, to each state of the world) a single number that represents the desirability, or utility, of the outcome. The second key concept of Bayesian decision theory is the notion of subjective probabilities. Again, it can be shown that rational individuals must be able to specify the probability of each of the outcomes of a particular decision. The rational decision is said to be the decision which yields the highest expected utility. If an individual fails at either of these tasks, then it is likely that his choices will violate one of the axioms of rational behavior.

The problem of the Bayesian horticulturalist.
To see how the Bayesian model works, consider the following simple example which has been adapted from Hadley (1967: 438). Suppose that a group of tropical horticulturalists has just moved into a new area. Each family clears a plot and plants its crops. The head of a particular family, a "Bayesian horticulturalist," can estimate the probability distribution of yields from his plot from his experience in other areas. His best guess is that the long-run average yield in this particular location will be M and the variance of the yield from year to year will be V. The Bayesian horticulturalist knows that there is some chance that his plot will not supply enough food for his family. According

to the customs of his group, he can hedge against this eventuality by helping in his neighbors' fields, which entitles him to a portion of their harvest if his own is insufficient. Each day of labor donated to his neighbors entitles him to h units of yield, but only if his family does not have enough; otherwise his neighbor keeps all the food from his own garden. If at the end of the season the amount of food the Bayesian horticulturalist has access to is still less than the amount his family needs, D, he must borrow food from the headman, who charges substantial interest rates. The Bayesian horticulturalist figures that, on average, the borrowed food costs him twice as much labor in the long run as working in his neighbors' fields. Being rational, the Bayesian horticulturalist seeks to feed his family with the least amount of extra work.

To solve this problem, the Bayesian horticulturalist starts by writing down the total amount of labor on his neighbor's field and for the headman, λ, as a function of (1) the eventual yield of his field, z, (2) the amount of time he decides to invest in helping his neighbors, h, and (3) his family's need, D:

$$\lambda = \begin{cases} h & \text{if } z + h \geqslant D \\ h + 2(D - z - h) & \text{if } z + h < D \end{cases} \tag{4.2}$$

The rational choice of the level of investment in helping his neighbors is the level that maximizes his expected utility, which we have assumed is the same as minimizing the expected amount of his labor, $E(\lambda)$. This is computed as follows:

$$E(\lambda) = \int_0^\infty h\, f(z)dz + 2\int_0^{D-h} (D - z - h)f(z)dz \tag{4.3}$$

where f(z) is the Bayesian horticulturalist's subjective probability distribution for the yield of his plot. It is shown in Box 4.2 that $E(\lambda)$ is minimized when the following rule is satisfied:

$$\text{Prob}(z + h < D) = 1/2 \tag{4.4}$$

The left-hand side of Equation 4.4 is the probability that his own harvest plus the share he can get of his neighbor's harvest is less than his family's needs. Equation 4.4 says that the Bayesian horticulturalist should invest in helping his neighbors up to the point at which this probability is equal to the ratio of the cost of investing in his neighbor's field to the cost of borrowing after the harvest. Since he believes that his yield, z, is distributed normally with mean M, the optimal value of h, h^*, is

$$h^* = \begin{cases} D - M & \text{if } D - M > 0 \\ 0 & \text{if } D - M < 0 \end{cases} \tag{4.5}$$

The rational decision is to invest just enough in helping his neighbor so that the average yield of his own garden plus what he can get from his neighbor is equal to his needs. Notice that this rule depends on the ratio of the cost of helping his

> **Box 4.2** Since $f(z)$ is a probability density, $\int f(z) = 1$. Using this fact, we can simplify Equation 4.3 as follows:
>
> $$E(\lambda) = h + 2(D - h) \int_0^{D-h} f(z)dz - \int_0^{D-h} zf(z)dz$$
>
> We want to find the value of h, labeled h*, that minimizes $E(\lambda)$. This will occur when
>
> $$\frac{d}{dh}E(\lambda) = 0 \quad \text{or} \quad \frac{d}{dh}E(\lambda) < 0 \text{ and } h^* = 0$$
>
> To calculate the derivative of $E(\lambda)$ we use the fundamental theorem of calculus which states:
>
> $$\frac{d}{dz} \int_0^{G(z)} F(z)dz = F(G(z))\frac{d}{dz}G(z)$$
>
> Thus
>
> $$\frac{d}{dh}E(\lambda) = 1 - 2 \int_0^{D-h} f(z)dz - 2(D - h)f(D - h) + 2(D - h)f(D - h)$$
>
> $$= 1 - 2 \int_0^{D-h} f(z)dz$$
>
> $$= 1 - 2 \text{ Prob}(z < D - h)$$
>
> Suppose that a particular value of h, h', satisfies this condition. Then, if h' > 0, h' = h*. Otherwise, h* = 0.

neighbor to the cost of borrowing after the harvest. If this ratio were different from one-half, then the optimal decision would depend on the variance of his yield as well as the mean.

A Bayesian view of learning. In the context of Bayesian decision theory, learning is thought of as using observations to modify one's prior probability distribution of the outcomes that result from different decisions. We will illustrate how this works in the context of the decision problem of the Bayesian horticulturalist. In particular, we will show how he could use his experience to revise his estimate of the average yield of his plot. The Bayesian horticulturalist knows that his estimate of the long-run average yield, M, may be in error; the actual long-run average yield may be another value. In fact (because he is a Bayesian) he can specify the density, $f(M_a)$, that specifies the probability that the actual long-run yield will take on a different value. As shown in Figure 4.2, we assume that $f(M_a)$ is initially normal with mean M and variance V_m. After his first year's harvest our horticulturalist measures the yield from his garden and the result is a yield of y. If he assumes that his actual long-run mean is M_a and his estimate of the year-to-year variance is correct, the density function specifying the probability that this yield takes different values is proportional to

$$f(y|M_a) \propto \exp[-(y - M_a)^2/2V] \tag{4.6}$$

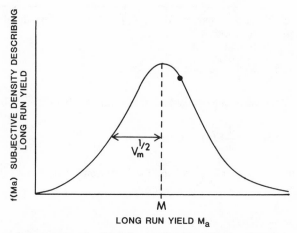

Fig. 4.2 Shape of the assumed subjective probability density function of the Bayesian horticulturalist that describes his beliefs about the long run yield of his plot, M_a. M is the mean and V_m the variance.

The Bayesian horticulturalist uses this information to revise his estimate of the probability distribution of M_a by calculating the conditional probability density of M_a given y using Bayes's theorem:

$$f(M_a|y) = \frac{f(y|M_a)\, f(M_a)}{\int f(y|M_a)\, f(M_a)\, dM_a} \tag{4.7}$$

The mean of $f(M_a|y)$, M', is his new estimate of the long-run mean. As is shown in Box 4.3, $f(M_a|y)$ is normal with the following mean and variance:

$$V_m' = a\, V_m,$$
$$M' = a\, M + (1 - a)\, y \tag{4.8}$$

where

$$a = \frac{V}{V + V_m}$$

These equations say that the year's experience has two effects on the Bayesian horticulturalist's estimate of the average yield. First, notice that the variable a is always between zero and one, and therefore the variance of his estimate is always decreased by a fraction a. Second, his estimate of the mean is moved toward y a fraction a of the distance between his initial estimate, M, and the measured yield, y. Notice that a will be near one if $V \gg V_m$. This means that if the annual variation is much larger than the variance of the Bayesian horticulturalist's estimate of the mean, a will be nearly one, and one year's experience will have little effect on the horticulturalist's beliefs. If, on the other hand, $V_m \gg V$, the yield from a single year

Box 4.3 First, note that Equation 4.7 can be rewritten as

$$f(M_a \mid y) = C \exp\{-(y - M_a)^2/2V\} \exp\{-(M_a - M)^2/2V_m\}$$

that is, as a constant, C, which is chosen so that the integral of $f(M_a \mid y)$ is one, multiplied by the product of two Gaussian functions of M_a. Expressions with the form of Equation 4.7 will occur repeatedly in this book. This expression can be rewritten as

$$f(M_a \mid y) = C \exp\{-(y - M_a)^2/2V - (M - M_a)^2/2V_m\}$$

The quadratic expression in the exponent of this expression can be rewritten as the sum of a perfect square in M_a and a term not involving M_a using the method of completing the square, i.e.,

$$(y - M_a)^2/2V + (M - M_a)^2/2V_m = (M_a - M')^2/2V' + (y - M)^2/2(V + V_m) \tag{1}$$

where

$$M' = \frac{yV_m + MV}{V + V_m} \quad \text{and} \quad V' = \frac{V_m V}{V_m + V}$$

The reader can verify that this identity is true by squaring out both sides and checking for equality. Because the second term on the right-hand side of (1) doesn't involve M_a it can be incorporated into the constant term. Thus

$$f(M_a \mid y) = C \exp\{-(M_a - M')^2/2V'\}.$$

We have specified that C should be chosen so that the integral of $f(M_a \mid y)$ is one. This means that it is a normal probability density with mean M' and variance V'.

will have a substantial effect on the horticulturalist's estimate of the long-run mean and will also sharply reduce the variance of that estimate.

During the next year the Bayesian horticulturalist will use his revised estimate of the long-run average yield of his plot to decide how much labor to invest in helping his neighbor. Because his estimate of the yield of his garden is different from his estimate the previous year, his behavior will also be different. The Bayesian horticulturalist can once again use the actual yield of his plot to update his estimate of the long-run average yield of his plot. Each year the Bayesian horticulturalist will improve his estimate of the yield of his plot, and so each year the change in his behavior will diminish. Thus, the average behavior of a number of Bayesian horticulturalists will show a learning curve like that pictured in Figure 4.3.

The problem of the Bayesian horticulturalist illustrates that behavior governed by rational choice has the same three essential features as the much simpler models of learning used by behavioral psychologists. First, the Bayesian model of rational choice requires that the actor be able to assign a utility value to different outcomes. The Bayesian horticulturalist ranked alternatives according to the amount of outside labor required. Similarly, rats ranked the absence of shock over being shocked. Second, the Bayesian model of learning requires that the actor make assumptions

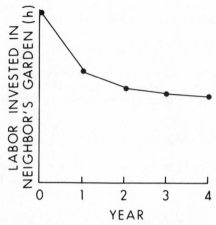

Fig. 4.3 The average learning curve for a population of Bayesian horticulturalists.

about the nature of the environment. To update his estimate of the average yield of his plot the Bayesian horticulturalist had to know the relationship between this year's yield and the long-run mean (i.e. he had to know the likelihood function). This is analogous to a rat's "assumption" that events close together in time are causally related. Finally, the Bayesian model of rational choice requires that the actor make an assumption about the initial state of the environment in the form of a prior probability distribution. Thus, the horticulturalist's initial guess about his yield is analogous to the rat's initial "assumption" that bright-noisy water was safe.

The problem of the Bayesian horticulturalist also illustrates a fourth general feature of learning: Individuals must infer the state of the environment from "noisy" observations, and because these observations are sometimes misleading, learning is subject to errors. Suppose, for example, that the Bayesian horticulturalist's initial beliefs about the yield of his garden are approximately correct, but that the first year is extremely dry, so that yields are extraordinarily low. Using Bayes's law will cause him to reduce his estimate of the most likely yield of his plot erroneously. The simple conditioned responses of rats can also lead to errors. Consider, for example, a rat who coincidentally becomes sick after eating a nutritious food item. Subsequently the rat will avoid foods that taste similar, even though they may be quite nutritious.

Rational choice, learning, and behavioral rules of thumb

The problem of the Bayesian horticulturalist also illustrates the fact that rational choice is both difficult and complex. To satisfy the canons of rationality, the Bayesian horticulturalist had to specify precisely an unrealistically large amount of information about the environment in the form of the prior probability distribution and the likelihood function and then perform computations that are too difficult for anyone but mathematicians. As posed, the problem of the Bayesian horticulturalist is an extremely simple problem—much, much simpler than any real decision facing a tropical horticulturalist. The difficulty and complexity of most real problems is so great as to preclude normatively rational choice. Even modern corporations that can afford to expend enormous resources in gathering and analyzing data are unable to conform to the canons of Bayesian rationality (Cyert and March, 1963).

Nonetheless, both humans and other animals seem to behave in an understandable, adaptive fashion. How do they achieve the semblance of rationality? It seems likely that the answer to this question is that both humans and other animals use simple "rules of thumb" to make decisions. It is plausible that simple rules of thumb may greatly reduce the cognitive complexity of decisions but still result in behavior that closely approximates normatively rational behavior in some restricted range of environments.

The best evidence for the existence of such rules of thumb in nonhuman animals comes from optimal foraging theory. Recently, several authors have used Bayesian decision theory to try to understand how animals learn to forage in unpredictable environments (Arnold, 1978; Krebs, 1978; McNamara and Houston, 1980; Pulliam and Dunford, 1980; Houston and McNamara, 1981). The work of Houston and McNamara is of particular interest because it suggests that two patterns of behavior very commonly observed in a variety of species by behavioral psychologists can be understood as resulting from simple rules of thumb. McNamara and Houston (1980) use Bayesian decision theory to analyze the problem of an animal foraging in a patchy environment. In particular they ask, How long should an individual forage unsuccessfully before it moves to another patch? They show that the answer to this question depends on the previous rate of success in the patch. If the previous rate of return was high, then even a short interval without success should provoke the animal to leave. If, on the other hand, the patch has been only intermittently rewarding, then the animal can forage unsuccessfully a long time before it is optimal to leave. McNamara and Houston argue that this result is consistent with the "partial reinforcement effect" that has been widely observed in behavioral psychology. Animals that are always rewarded for a particular response ("continuous reinforcement") stop responding quickly if reinforcement ceases. In contrast, animals that are rewarded only intermittently for giving the response ("partial reinforcement") persist for quite some time after reinforcement is terminated. Houston and McNamara (1981) also show that the "probability matching" behavior that has been observed by psychologists can be understood as a rule of thumb approximating the optimal behavior in a variety of choice experiments.

Considerable experimental evidence suggests that humans also rely on simple rules of thumb to guide their behavior. These rules of thumb, called "heuristics" by psychologists, often work well, but occasionally they lead to behavior that is irrational according to the canons of Bayesian rationality. People frequently must assess the likelihood that a particular event, A, will occur based on knowledge of the processes that cause the general class of events to which A belongs. Tversky and Kahneman (1974) argue that people use what they call the "representativeness heuristic" to answer this kind of question. Nisbett and Ross (1980) illustrate the representativeness heuristic with the following experiment. Undergraduates are asked, Which of the following three sequences of births of boys (B) and girls (G) is more likely to occur in the next six births in a particular hospital (a) BBBBBB, (b) GGGBBB, or (c) GBBGGB? Most people choose (c) because it is representative of the underlying random process, that is, most sequences of births will have G's and B's intermixed. The correct answer is that all three sequences have almost equal probability. The representative heuristic will frequently work quite well, but as in this case it will occasionally fail. We will return to this area in psychology in the next chapter.

There is also evidence from economics that humans make extensive use of suboptimal rules of thumb. Conventional neoclassical economic theory assumes the behavior of both individuals and firms is purely rational. However, economists within the subdiscipline of behavioral economics have argued that this ideal is unlikely to be realized because rational behavior is extremely costly. Detailed data on the behavior of firms (e.g. Cyert and March, 1963) suggest that firms do not optimize but rather use simple rules of thumb. Models of economic behavior that rely on suboptimal rules of thumb developed by Simon (1957), Day (1967), Day et al. (1974), and Winter (1966) share the qualitative features of the other models described in this section.

The Force of Guided Variation
A simple model of learning

Behavioral psychologists and decision theorists developed their models of learning in order to understand very different kinds of phenomena. Nonetheless, these models (as well as the models of Simon, Day, and Houston and McNamara, which are intermediate between these two extremes) share four features:

1. Individuals have objectives or guiding criteria that allow them to rank possible outcomes of their behavior.

2. Individuals make assumptions about the relationship between observed events in the environment and the outcome of future decisions.

3. Because the observed events are imperfect indicators of the outcomes in the local environment, learning leads to errors.

4. Individuals have an initial guess about what forms of behavior are best in the local environment.

We think that the following simple model of learning captures these four features of learning models. Suppose that each organism begins with an initial guess about the kinds of behaviors that constitute the optimal mature phenotype in its local environment. We will refer to this guess as the individual's "initial phenotype," recognizing that it may often be a covert cognitive structure. We will suppose that the initial phenotype can be quantified as a single number, X. In the case of the Bayesian horticulturalist, the value of X would represent the horticulturalist's initial guess about the right amount of labor to invest in his neighbor's garden, and in the case of the rat, X would represent the rat's initial rate of drinking bright-noisy water. Next, we will suppose that the mature phenotype of the individual can also be specified by a single number Y, which is measured on the same scale as X. For the Bayesian horticulturalist the value of Y would represent the amount of labor invested in the neighbor's field after a year's observation of his own yield, and for the rat Y would be the final rate of drinking bright-noisy water.

Organisms learn by experiencing their local environment and then modifying their phenotype according to some criteria. This means that knowledge of a particular individual's determinants of learning should allow us to predict the phenotype which that individual will develop in a given environment. We formalize this relationship between learning and the environment as follows:

$$Y = \frac{V_e X + L(\Gamma(H) + \epsilon)}{L + V_e} = aX + (1 - a)(\Gamma(H) + \epsilon) \qquad (4.9)$$

where L is a parameter which measures the propensity of an individual to rely on individual learning, $\Gamma(H)$ is the objective (or goal) of the learning rule in environment H (for habitat), and ϵ is a normally distributed random variable that represents the effect of errors made during the learning process. We assume that ϵ has a mean of zero and a variance V_e. In general, we expect learning to improve the fit of the mature phenotype to the environment. This means that the objective of the learning rule, $\Gamma(H)$, will usually be different in environments in which the optimal phenotype is different. Thus, Equation 4.9 says that learning causes the mature phenotype to lie a fraction $L/(L + V_e)$ of the distance between the individual's initial phenotype, X, and the objective of the learning rule in the local environment, $\Gamma(H)$. Thus, the parameter a, $= V_e/(V_e + L)$, gives the fractional importance of cultural transmission in determining mature phenotype. Notice that the relative importance of individual learning depends on both an individual's propensity to rely on individual learning (measured by L) and the accuracy of the learning process (measured by V_e). When $L \gg V_e$, individual behavior is mostly determined by individual learning; when $L \ll V_e$, learning will have little effect on the initial phenotype. It is worth noting that this model of learning is formally identical to the Bayesian model of learning outlined in the previous section.

In what follows we assume that $\Gamma(H) = H$. This assumption simply means that we are using the objective of the learning rule in a particular environment as a way of characterizing the environment. We have made this assumption because it simplifies the notation, and relaxing it does not cause any fundamental change in the following argument.

The force of guided variation

Consider a hypothetical population in which young individuals acquire their initial phenotypes by imitating the behavior of adults or, in other words, by some combination of vertical and oblique transmission. After cultural transmission, these individuals modify their initial phenotypes according to the learning rule just described. Because individual learning will usually cause mature phenotypes to be different from initial phenotypes, the distribution of mature phenotypes will, in general, be different from the distribution of initial phenotypes. Variants favored by learning will be more common, and those that are not favored will be less common. Finally, suppose that mature individuals then serve as models for young individuals in the next generation. This will cause the distribution of initial phenotypes in the next generation to be different from the distribution in this generation. Thus, cultural transmission of the initial phenotype and its subsequent modification by learning combine to produce a force increasing the frequency of the variants favored by learning, even in the absence of natural selection. This effect is the essence of guided variation.

To build a model of cultural evolution under the influence of the force of guided variation, we proceed in two steps. First we determine the effects of learning on the distribution of cultural variants within a single generation. Then we combine this model with the blending model of the cultural transmission of a quantitative character derived in Chapter 3. The result is a recursion that describes how guided variation changes the distribution of cultural variants from one generation to the next. This recursion can be iterated to determine the long-run effects of this force.

To derive an expression that describes how individual learning changes the distribution of initial phenotypes, we assume that the distribution of initial phenotypic values in a population before learning is P(X). Suppose this distribution has mean $\overline{X}$ and variance V. It is shown in Box 4.4 that the mean, $\overline{Y}$, and the variance, U, of the distribution of phenotypes after learning, F(Y), are given by

$$\overline{Y} = a\overline{X} + (1 - a)H$$

$$U = a^2V + (1 - a)^2V_e$$

(4.10)

where, as above, $a = V_e/(L + V_e)$. Equation 4.10 says that the mean of the distribution of phenotypes after learning lies a fraction a of the distance between $\overline{X}$, the mean before learning, and H, the objective of the learning rule. Learning has two opposing effects on the variance of X in the population. First, learning causes individuals to modify their phenotypes toward a common goal, H, and this tends to decrease the variance of X in the population. This effect is represented by the term a^2V. Second, however, errors made during learning increase the variance of

---

Box 4.4 From Equation 4.9 the mature phenotype, Y, of an individual with initial phenotypic value X in environment H is

$$Y = aX + (1 - a)(H + \epsilon)$$

where $a = L/(L + V_e)$ and ϵ is a normally distributed random variable with a mean of zero and variance V_e that represents the effects of learning errors. The mean value of Y in the population after learning, $\overline{Y}$ is

$$\overline{Y} = \iint P(X)N(\epsilon)\{aX + (1 - a)(H + \epsilon)\} \, dX \, d\epsilon$$

$$= a\overline{X} + (1 - a)H$$

The variance of Y in the population is given by

$$U = \iint P(X)N(\epsilon) \{aX + (1 - a)(H + \epsilon) - a\overline{X} - (1 - a)H\}^2 \, dX \, d\epsilon$$

$$= \iint P(X)N(\epsilon) \{a^2(X - \overline{X})^2 + (1 - a)^2\epsilon^2 - 2a(1 - a)\epsilon(X - \overline{X})\} \, dX \, d\epsilon$$

and since the mean value of ϵ is zero

$$= a^2 V + (1 - a)^2 V_e$$

X in the population. This effect is represented by the term $(1 - a)^2 V_e$. Thus, the net result of learning may be either to increase or to decrease the value of U relative to V.

Equation 4.10 formalizes the idea that social learning and individual learning are *alternative* ways of acquiring a particular behavioral variant; if an individual's mature phenotype is mostly determined by individual learning, then what he or she acquired from his or her parents is not too important. The parameter a gives the relative importance of cultural transmission in determining individual behavior expressed as a fraction. When a is close to one, individuals are little influenced by their own experience and instead simply imitate their parents. According to Equation 4.10, this causes the population mean to be mostly determined by the mean behavior in the previous generation; the current environment has little effect. When a is small, individual learning predominates. In this case the mean behavior of a population is mostly determined by environmental conditions; there is little cultural inertia. Finally, when a is around one-half, cultural transmission and individual learning have about equal effects.

If no other forces act to change the distribution of phenotypes, the distribution of mature phenotypes among the individuals who serve as models for the next generation is simply F(Y). If we further suppose that cultural transmission proceeds according to the n model blending rule described in Chapter 3, then the mean value of X in the next generation, $\overline{X}'$, is

$$\overline{X}' = a\overline{X} + (1 - a)\,H$$

$$V' = (1/n_e)(a^2 V + (1 - a)^2 V_e) + \overline{E} \tag{4.11}$$

where n_e is the effective number of models and $\overline{E}$ is the effective amount of random variation introduced during transmission. See Chapter 3, page 74, for an explanation of how these terms are calculated.

Equations 4.11 give the change in the distribution of cultural variation in a single generation resulting from the action of cultural transmission and individual learning. Equations 4.11 say that when the determinants of learning are transmitted culturally, learning itself causes the mean phenotypic value in the population to move a fraction of the way toward the objective of the learning rule. The combination of learning and cultural transmission creates a force, guided variation. If the objective of the learning rule is adaptive, this force improves the fit of the population to the local environment (i.e. it moves $\overline{X}$ toward H) even in the absence of natural selection. The strength of the force of guided variation depends only on the parameter a, $= V_e/(L + V_e)$, which represents the fractional importance of transmission. Unlike natural selection, the force of guided variation does not depend on the amount of variation present.

The effect of guided variation over many generations. By iterating Equations 4.11 we can determine the long-run effects of guided variation. We will begin by assuming that the environment is both constant and uniform. When this is true, the equilibrium values of the population mean, $\hat{X}$, and variance, $\hat{V}$, can be found by solving the equations

$$\hat{X} = a\hat{X}+(1 - a)\,H$$

$$\hat{V} = (1/n_e)(a^2\hat{V}+(1 - a)^2V_e) + \overline{E} \tag{4.12}$$

That is, equilibrium occurs when the forces due to transmission and learning exactly balance, leaving the distribution of cultural variants unchanged.

Solving Equations 4.12 yields the following expressions for the equilibrium mean and variance in the population:

$$\hat{X} = H \tag{4.13a}$$

$$\hat{V} = \frac{(1/n_e)(1 - a)^2V_e + \overline{E}}{(1 - (1/n_e)a^2)} \tag{4.13b}$$

Equation 4.13a says that if the environment does not change the population eventually will reach an equilibrium at which the mean value of X in the population is the value which is the goal of the learning process. This means that the most common individuals are ones with the optimum initial phenotype. This result holds as long as a is not exactly zero. Even if individual learning is weak, the population mean will eventually achieve the optimum value. Equation 4.13b says that many individuals in the population will be characterized by initial phenotypic values which are larger or smaller than that value. This variation is due to errors made during the learning process (measured by V_e) and random variation introduced during cultural transmission (measured by $\overline{E}$). The effects of changing a on the equilibrium variance will depend on the relative magnitudes of V_e and $\overline{E}$. If individual learning is much more error prone than social learning ($V_e \gg \overline{E}$), increasing the relative importance of cultural transmission decreases the equilibrium variance. If social learning is more error prone, then the reverse occurs.

The Evolution of Cultural Transmission

The models in this book assume that culture has the properties of an inheritance system. In the last section we saw that culture can have these properties only if individual learning is not too important in determining behavior. In Chapter 3 we reviewed several lines of empirical evidence which suggested that this assumption was justified. In this section we ask, What are the conditions, if any, under which a system of social learning with the properties of an inheritance system might have evolved?

We begin by making some assumptions about how individuals acquire the psychological predispositions that control the relative importance of learning and cultural transmission. If these predispositions are acquired genetically, then they can be understood in terms of the theory of genetic evolution. If they are acquired culturally, then the specific nature of the cultural forces that affect their acquisition will be important, and genetic theory will not be sufficient. We will begin by assuming that the traits that determine the relative importance of individual and social learning are themselves determined by genetically transmitted characters. We do this for two reasons: First, when the capacity for culture in the human species was first evolving, this probably was the case. A knowledge of how cultural transmission could have been genetically adaptive will help us understand the origin of cultural transmission. Second, this is the most extreme sociobiological assumption that one can make. If we start with this assumption but still show that cultural transmission leads to the evolution of genetically maladaptive traits, then we have the strongest indication that the forces of genetic and cultural evolution do not always coincide.

Even assuming that the determinants of learning are transmitted genetically, we will show that natural selection may act to reduce the importance of individual learning and increase that of cultural transmission. In such cases novel forces may affect the dynamics of cultural change. Many of these forces lead to outcomes that are at variance with the usual predictions of sociobiological theory. Thus, the existence of a plausible range of conditions in which it is adaptive for individual behavior to be largely determined by social learning supports the hypothesis that the existence of culture causes human evolution to be fundamentally different from that of noncultural organisms.

We analyze the evolution of cultural transmission in three steps.

1. We describe a simple model in which alleles at a genetic locus affect the relative importance of cultural transmission and individual learning, that is, the value of the parameter L.

2. We analyze the evolutionary properties of the model in a homogeneous environment. In this kind of environment individual learning will not be important in determining behavior at evolutionary equilibrium unless random variation is quite important.

3. We generalize the model to allow the environment to vary in space or time. It is very plausible that natural selection should favor individual learning in a variable environment since it causes individuals to develop the locally optimal variant in each of a variety of different habitats. Nevertheless, we also find that there are conditions under which selection favors weak learning.

A model of the genetic modification of the learning rule

To analyze the evolution of the relative importance of cultural transmission and individual learning, we employ the model of cultural transmission with guided variation just outlined. To allow the learning rule to evolve, we suppose that the importance of learning in determining an individual's mature phenotype is modified by a haploid genetic locus with two alleles, e and f. Individuals who carry the allele e have a learning rule characterized by the parameter $L = L_0$; individuals who carry the allele f have a learning rule characterized by the parameter $L = L_0 + \delta L$. We assume that δL is positive and small enough that terms of order δL^2 can be ignored when compared to terms of order δL. Let the frequency of allele f just after genetic transmission be q.

To simplify the analysis, we make the following special assumptions: (1) the cultural and genetic parents are drawn at random from the same pool of adults, and (2) the genetic parents are no more likely to transmit the cultural trait to their genetic offspring than any other individual in the population. The first assumption is crucial, and we consider the effects of relaxing it in detail in Chapter 6. The second assumption greatly simplifies the analysis because it means that each genotype experiences that same pool of cultural variants. If only genetic parents are important in cultural transmission, then guided variation (and other forces as well) may lead to a persistent nonrandom association between particular cultural variants and particular genotypes. (This is analogous to linkage disequilibrium in genetic evolution.) We have analyzed a model in which genetic parents participate in the socialization of their own children. This more elaborate model yields similar results as long as the magnitude of the force of guided variation is not too strong and individuals other than the genetic parents have some role in enculturation.

With these assumptions, the distribution of initial phenotypes among individuals of both genotypes, $P(\underline{X})$, is the same among individuals of both genotypes. This distribution has mean $\overline{X}$ and variance V. By setting $L = L_0$ in Equation 4.10 one can determine the distribution of mature phenotypes among individuals carrying the allele e, $F(Y)$. Similarly, by setting $L = L_0 + \delta L$ in Equation 4.10 one can determine the distribution of mature phenotypes among individuals with allele f, $F^*(Y)$. Because individuals with different genotypes are characterized by different learning rules, $F(Y)$ and $F^*(Y)$ will usually be different. The learning process does not affect the frequency of the two alleles, and thus the frequency of f after learning is also q.

The effect of natural selection

So far, we have assumed that the distribution of X does not change from the time at which learning takes place until mating, genetic, and cultural transmission occur. This assumption means that all mature phenotypes have the same probability of becoming both parents and models. It seems likely that in many cases individuals characterized by different phenotypes will have different probabilities of surviving and acquiring the necessary resources to become parents. When this is the case, natural selection will change the distribution of mature phenotypes. Because different genotypes will on average be associated with different mature phenotypes, natural selection will also change the frequency of the two alleles that affect the nature of individual learning.

Fitness functions. In order to model the effect of natural selection, we must specify the probability that individuals who are characterized by different mature phenotypes become parents. We assume that the probability that an individual with the mature phenotype Y becomes a parent in a particular environment, H, is given by the function $W(Y,H)$, which has the following Gaussian form:

$$W(Y,H) = \exp[-(Y - H)^2/2S] \tag{4.14}$$

As is shown in Figure 4.4, the optimum phenotypic value in environment H is the value H. This means that the objective of the learning rule is also the optimal phenotype in the local environment. This is a very important assumption because it means that the learning rule causes individuals to develop adaptive mature phenotypes. The farther away an individual's phenotype is from the optimum, the

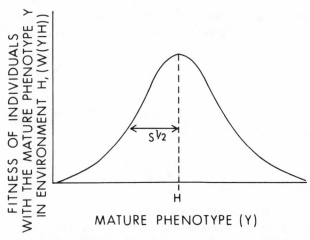

Fig. 4.4 A Gaussian fitness function. The ordinate measures the fitness of individuals as a function of their mature phenotype, measured by Y.

less likely it is that he or she will become a parent. The intensity of selection is measured by the parameter S. As S becomes larger, the difference between the fitness of the optimum mature phenotype and the fitness of any nonoptimum phenotype becomes smaller. This kind of natural selection, called "stabilizing selection," generally has the effect of moving the population to the optimum and then keeping it there. If the distribution Y is normal, the Gaussian form of W(Y,H) preserves the normality of the distribution of Y, which allows us to characterize this distribution by its mean and variance alone.

To deduce the effect of selection on the frequency of the two genotypes, we first calculate the average fitness of each genotype. The probability that an individual with genotype e becomes a parent, W_e, is

$$W_e = \int W(Y,H)\, F(Y)\, dY \qquad (4.15)$$

Equation 4.15 says that the average fitness of the e allele is computed by multiplying the probability that a particular mature phenotype survives by the probability that an individual carrying allele e acquires that phenotype and then integrating over all mature phenotypes. Similarly, the probability that an individual with genotype f becomes a parent is

$$W_f = \int W(Y,H)\, F^*(Y)\, dY \qquad (4.16)$$

The two alleles have different average fitness because they affect the probability that individuals carrying them will acquire any given mature phenotype. Also notice that because F(Y) and $F^*(Y)$ depend on P(X), the distribution of initial phenotypes in the population, the average fitness of the two genotypes will also depend on P(X).

A condition for culture to be favored. Suppose that initially there were N parents in the population. The number of individuals characterized by the gene e was

$(1 - q)N$ and the number characterized by f was qN. Assuming that N is large, the frequency of the allele f among parents after selection, q', is

$$q' = \frac{(qN)W_f}{(qN)W_f + [(1 - q)N]W_e} = \frac{qW_f}{qW_f + (1 - q)W_e} \qquad (4.17)$$

By subtracting q from both sides of Equation 4.17 we can compute $q' - q$, the change in the frequency of f caused by selection:

$$q' - q = \frac{q(1 - q)[W_f - W_e]}{qW_f + (1 - q)W_e} \qquad (4.18)$$

Equation 4.18 indicates that the allele f will increase if it has higher average fitness than the allele e. Put another way, f, the genotype that depends slightly more on learning, will increase in the population if a small increase in the propensity to rely on individual learning (i.e. a small increase in the value of L) increases the chance that individuals will acquire the optimal mature phenotype, H.

Assuming selection is weak, Box 4.5 shows that selection will favor larger

---

Box 4.5 Let $\tilde{W}(L|\overline{X},V)$ be defined as the expected fitness of an individual whose learning rule is characterized by the parameter L given that the distribution of cultural variants in the population, P(X), is normal with mean $\overline{X}$ and variance V. Thus

$$\tilde{W}(L|\overline{X},V) = \iint W(Y,H)\text{Prob}(Y|X,L)P(X) \, dXdY$$

with this definition $W_e = \tilde{W}(L_0|\overline{X},V)$ and $W_f = \tilde{W}(L_0 + \delta L|\overline{X},V)$. If δL is small enough, we can express W_f as follows:

$$W_f = W_e + \delta L \frac{d}{dL} \tilde{W}(L|\overline{X},V) \bigg|_{L=0}$$

where the derivative is evaluated at $L = L_0$. We have assumed that the incremental effect of the allele f, δL, is greater than zero, and thus $W_f > W_e$ implies that

$$\frac{d}{dL} \tilde{W}(L|\overline{X},V) \bigg|_{L=L_0} > 0$$

When selection is weak, W(Y,H) is approximately

$$W(Y,H) = 1 - (1/2S)(Y - H)^2$$

Then, by combining this expression with the definition of average fitness, one can show that

$$\tilde{W}(L|\overline{X},V) = 1 - (1/2S)\{a(L)^2[(\overline{X} - H)^2 + V] + [1 - a(L)]^2 V_e\}$$

where $a(L) = V_e/(V_e + L)$. Differentiating this expression yields Condition 4.19 in the text.

values of L (i.e. $W_f > W_e$) whenever

$$L < (H - \overline{X})^2 + V \qquad (4.19)$$

By weak selection we mean that the change in the distribution of phenotypes within any single generation is small. Since evolutionary change is usually slow, this assumption is probably nearly always satisfied. As is shown in Figure 4.5, weak selection requires that the width of the selection function be much greater than the variance in mature phenotype, or, more formally, $S \gg U$.

To intepret Equation 4.19, assume for a moment that $\overline{X}$ and V are held constant. Then if the initial value of L is less than $(H - \overline{X})^2 + V$, L will increase until $L = (H - \overline{X})^2 + V$. Similarly, if the initial value of L is greater than $(H - \overline{X})^2 + V$, L will decrease until 4.19 is an equality. We will say that $L = (H - \overline{X})^2 + V$ is the equilibrium value of L given that $\overline{X}$ and V are held constant. In general $\overline{X}$ and V will change as L changes, and we will take this fact into account in a moment.

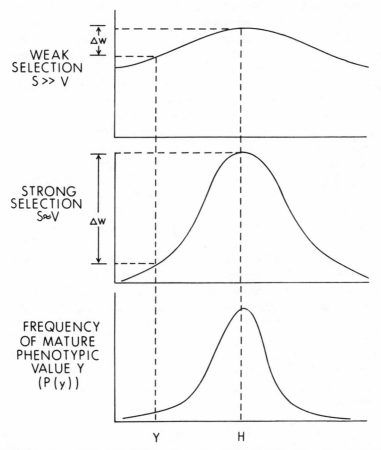

Fig. 4.5 Illustration of the assumption of weak selection. H is the optimal phenotypic value, and Y is a given nonoptimal value. As selection becomes stronger, the difference in the fitness of Y and H increases.

This result has a satisfying intuitive explanation. Inequality 4.19 says that the relative importance of a given mode of phenotypic acquisition should be inversely proportional to its error rate. To see this, recall from Equation 4.11 that $L/(L + V_e)$ and $V_e/(L + V_e)$ give the relative importance of individual learning and cultural transmission, respectively. The parameter V_e is a measure of the likelihood that individual learning will cause an individual to develop a maladaptive phenotype. Similarly, the right-hand side of 4.19, $(H - \overline{X})^2 + V$, is a measure of the likelihood that a maladaptive phenotype will be acquired by cultural transmission. Thus, if $L = (H - \overline{X})^2 + V$, the relative importance of individual learning will be proportional to the likelihood that cultural transmission will lead to a maladaptive phenotype, and the relative importance of cultural transmission will be proportional to the error rate of individual learning.

The equilibrium amount of cultural transmission in a constant environment

Equation 4.19 gives the equilibrium value of L, the propensity to rely on individual learning, given that the distribution of phenotypes is constant with mean $\overline{X}$ and variance V. However, the distribution of cultural variants is not constant; it is evolving, and the speed and direction of cultural change will depend on the learning rule that characterizes the population. Therefore, to complete the analysis of the evolution of individual learning and cultural transmission we must consider the coevolution of the genes that affect the relative amount of individual learning and distribution of cultural variants that determines the fitness of those genes.

To accomplish this task, we assume that guided variation acting on cultural variation is much stronger than the force of natural selection. This allows us to simplify the analysis in two important ways: First, natural selection will act to change the frequency of cultural variants in much the same way that it changes the frequency of alternative genetic variants. However, if the force of guided variation is much stronger than selection, we can ignore the effects of selection acting directly on cultural variation. This is a conservative assumption; including the effect of natural selection on cultural variation increases the equilibrium importance of cultural transmission (thus decreasing the equilibrium value of L). We return to the effect of selection of cultural variations briefly later in this chapter and in detail in Chapter 6. Second, the assumption that guided variation is stronger than selection means that the rate of cultural change is much more rapid than the rate of genetic change, which in turn means we can assume that the distribution of cultural variants is always in equilibrium when we consider the dynamics of gene frequencies.

The equilibrium mean value of X in the population is equal to H, the optimum phenotypic value. Thus, assuming that the distribution of cultural variants is in equilibrium, Equation 4.19 says that natural selection will cause the value of L to increase whenever

$$L < \hat{V} \tag{4.20}$$

We know from Equation 4.13, however, that $\hat{V}$ is a function of L. By substituting the value $\hat{V}$ given in Equation 4.13 into Condition 4.20, we can determine when the propensity to rely on individual learning (L) will increase, now allowing the distribution of cultural variants to coevolve as the genes determining the balance of individual and social learning change in frequency:

$$L < \frac{(1/n_e)L^2V_e + \overline{E}(L + V_e)^2}{(L + V_e)^2 - (1/n_e)V_e^2} \qquad (4.21)$$

The value of L that satisfies 4.21 (expressed as an equality) is the "evolutionary equilibrium" value, L^*. This value characterizes populations in which the distribution of cultural variants and the frequency of genes affecting learning are in equilibrium simultaneously.

To get an intuitive understanding of 4.21 it is useful to consider two special cases:

1. Most of the cultural variation is due to errors made during individual learning ($V_e/n_e \gg \overline{E}$). It is shown in Box 4.6 that in this case Condition 4.21 is not satisfied for any value of L. This means that the evolutionary equilibrium value of L is zero; at equilibrium individuals' phenotypes are completely determined by cultural transmission and learning has no effect. This makes sense given the assumptions of the model, since once the population reaches equilibrium the only effect of learning is to increase the variance of X. This result should not be interpreted literally; we do not expect that selection would really favor the complete absence of individual learning. Rather, when the main source of cultural variation is errors made during individual learning, selection will favor individuals who rely mostly on cultural transmission and not on individual learning.

2. Most of the cultural variation present is due to errors made during social learning ($V_e/n_e \ll \overline{E}$). This condition could arise in two ways. If $V_e \approx \overline{E}$ but n_e is large, then 4.21 says that L will increase whenever $L < \overline{E}$. When the number of cultural parents is large, the equilibrium amount of variation in the population is equal to the amount of new variation introduced each generation. Thus, the evolutionary equilibrium value of L is equal to $\overline{E}$. Notice that if n_e is large, it might

---

Box 4.6 If $V_e/n_e \gg \overline{E}$, then 4.21 becomes approximately

$$L < \frac{L^2 V_e}{n_e(L + V_e)^2 - V_e^2} \qquad (1)$$

The right-hand side of expression 1 decreases monotonically as the effective number of cultural parents is increased, and thus cannot be satisfied unless it is satisfied for the minimum value of n_e, $n_e = 1$. Making this substitution and simplifying yields the following condition, which must hold for L to increase:

$$1 < \frac{V_e}{L + 2V_e}$$

This condition can never be true and thus L cannot increase when $n_e = 1$. But since the right-hand side of Expression 1 is smaller for any larger values of n_e, Expression 1 can never be satisfied.

be that $V_e > \overline{E} \gg V_e/n_e$, and therefore that the importance of individual learning, $L/(L + V_e)$, could still be quite small. This condition could also arise if $\overline{E} \gg V_e$. In this case one can show that $L^* > \overline{E}$, and therefore that the amount of social learning at equilibrium is small.

The most significant conclusion so far is that natural selection acting on genes will favor weak individual learning (and therefore a system of social learning with the properties of an inheritance system) anytime that (1) the environment is constant and (2) the error rate of individual learning is substantially greater than that of social learning. If imitation is reasonably accurate, as it seems to be, for example, in the case of language, then we would expect that selection would favor strong learning only for those traits for which individuals can accurately determine the optimal behavior based on their own experience. This suggests that selection would favor the acquisition of many traits by cultural transmission rather than individual learning.

Guided variation in a heterogeneous environment

So far we have shown that for a population in evolutionary equilibrium in a constant, uniform environment, it is plausible that social learning will usually be more important than individual learning in determining individual behavior. Perhaps this result should not surprise us. It is usually thought that the primary function of individual learning is to enable organisms to respond to variable environments. Given that the population mean reaches an equilibrium at the optimum value, the main effect of learning is to introduce random variation. In a variable environment, the mean phenotypic value may be quite different from the optimum. Therefore, it seems plausible that in a variable environment the benefits of phenotypic flexibility might compensate for the errors introduced during the learning process.

To investigate this question, we must add environmental variability to the model of individual learning and cultural transmission. In this section, we will modify the model so that different members of the population experience different environments. In the next section, we will allow environment to fluctuate in time. We refer to the first kind of variable environment as heterogeneous and to the second kind as fluctuating. We will show that in both cases there are plausible conditions which favor cultural transmission and only weak individual learning.

A model of heterogeneous environments. There are two essential features of a heterogeneous environment: (1) different individuals in the population experience different environments and (2) there is some chance that naive individuals will experience a different environment than the environment experienced by their models. Environmental variation could occur for many reasons. For example, the environment might be spatially variable, with different individuals living in different habitats. Environmental heterogeneity could also arise from social causes: different individuals might have different professions or belong to different ethnic groups.

To formalize these ideas, we assume that individuals in the population learn and do or do not become parents in environments characterized by different values of

H. The probability density governing the likelihood that an individual experiences an environment characterized by the value H, f(H), is normal with mean 0 and variance V_H. We can set the mean to zero without loss of generality since it merely specifies the origin of the coordinate system in which environments are measured. The variance of f(H), V_H, is a measure of the amount of environmental hetero-geneity. If V_H is large compared to S (recall that $1/S$ is a measure of the strength of selection), we will say that there is substantial heterogeneity.

The mean and variance of the distribution of cultural variants will usually be different in habitats characterized by different values of H, since learning will tend to increase the frequency of the most adaptive variant. Let $\overline{X}(H)$ and V(H) be the mean and variance before learning among individuals who will experience environment H. From Equation 4.11, the mean and variance after learning are

$$\overline{Y}(H) = a\overline{X}(H) + (1 - a)H \qquad (4.22)$$

and

$$U(H) = a^2V(H) + (1 - a)^2V_e \qquad (4.23)$$

Once again we assume that any selection that occurs is weak when compared to any effect of the transmission of guided variation, and therefore we can ignore the effect of selection on the distribution of cultural variants.

To formalize the idea that individuals may experience different environments than did their models, consider an individual who will experience environment H. We suppose that there is a probability $(1 - m)$ that any of this individual's models also experienced environment H and a probability m that they were drawn randomly from the population as a whole. Thus m is a measure of the extent of cultural contact between individuals experiencing different environments. For example, m might be a migration rate; a fraction $(1 - m)$ of the individuals in a particular habitat remain in that habitat, while a fraction m emigrate and are replaced by individuals drawn randomly from other habitats.

Box 4.7 shows that with these assumptions the mean and variance of initial phenotypes in the next generation as a function of H are

$$\overline{X}'(H) = (1 - m)\overline{Y}(H) + m\tilde{Y} \qquad (4.24)$$

$$V'(H) = (1/n_e)\Big\{(1 - m)U(H) + m \int U(h) f(h)\,dh$$
$$+ m\int [\overline{Y}(h) - \tilde{Y}]^2 f(h)\,dh + m(1 - m)[\overline{Y}(H) - \tilde{Y}]^2\Big\} + \overline{E} \qquad (4.25)$$

where $\tilde{Y} = \int \overline{Y}(h) f(h)\,dh$, the average phenotype in all environments. Equation 4.24 says that mixing models from different environments moves the mean in a partic-ular environment a fraction m of the distance toward the mean initial phenotype in all habitats. According to 4.25, mixing has two effects on the variance: first it causes the variance in a particular environment to move toward the average vari-ance in the population (just as in the case of the mean), and second it increases the

---

Box 4.7 Let $F(Y|H)$ be the distribution of mature phenotypes in habitats character-ized by environment H. Consider a naive individual in a habitat characterized by the environment H. The probability that the naive individual draws a model from his or her own habitat is $(1 - m)$, and the probability that a model is drawn from some other habitat characterized by an environment between h and h + dh is mf(h)dh. Thus, the mean value of mature phenotypes among the models of individuals in environment H, $\overline{Y}'(H)$, is

$$\overline{Y}'(H) = (1 - m) \int YF(Y|H)dY + m \iint yF(y|h)f(h)dh \, dy$$

$$= (1 - m)\overline{Y}(H) + m \int \overline{Y}(h)f(h)dh$$

Similarly, the variance of mature phenotypes among models of the individuals in environment H, $U'(H)$, is

$$U'(H) = (1 - m) \int Y^2 F(Y|H) \, dY + m \iint y^2 F(y|h)f(h)dh \, dy - \overline{Y}'(H)^2$$

Integrating and then adding and subtracting $m \int \overline{Y}(h)^2 f(h)dh$ and $m\tilde{Y}^2$ to the right-hand side of this expression yields 4.25 in the text.

---

variance in environment H an amount proportional to the average of the squared difference between the mean in that environment and all other environments. Thus, mixing will generally act to increase the variance of the initial phenotypes, and this effect will be strongest in the most extreme environments.

Equilibrium in a heterogeneous environment. To compute the equilibrium im-portance of individual and social learning in a heterogeneous environment, we proceed as we did in the case of a uniform environment. First we determine the equilibrium distribution of cultural variants, holding the relative importance of individual and social learning constant (i.e. the value of L). Then, assuming that cultural evolution occurs much more quickly than genetic evolution, we determine the value of L that can resist invasion by modifying alleles assuming that the distribution of cultural variants is in equilibrium.

It follows from the symmetry of the model that at equilibrium the average of $\overline{X}$ over all environments must be zero. Using this fact and Equations 4.22 and 4.24, it can be shown that the equilibrium mean in environment H, $\hat{X}(H)$, is given by

$$\hat{X}(H) = \frac{(1 - m)(1 - a)H}{1 - (1 - m)a} \tag{4.26}$$

The mean behavior in any particular environment results from the balance of two forces. The force of guided variation acts to move the mean toward the local optimum (H); the influx of models from other environments moves the population toward the mean of the entire population (which at equilibrium must be zero). Equation 4.26 says that the point at which this balance occurs depends on the relative strength of these two processes, measured by $1 - a$ and $1 - m$, re-spectively.

The equilibrium variance in environment H, V(H), can be computed by combining Equations 4.23 and 4.25. This results in a complicated expression for $\hat{V}(H)$ which is proportional to H^2, which means that there is more variation among individuals living in extreme, uncommon environments than among those living in central, common environments. At equilibrium the average variance in all environments, $\tilde{V}$, is given by

$$\tilde{V} = \frac{(1 - a)^2 V_e + V_H(1 - (1 - m)^2)\left(\dfrac{1 - a}{1 - a(1 - m)}\right)^2 + n_e \bar{E}}{n_e - a^2} \tag{4.27}$$

According to Equation 4.27, the average variance in all environments depends on the amount of error introduced by individual learning (V_e), the error rate during cultural transmission ($\bar{E}$), and the amount of environmental variability confronting the population (V_H). Increasing any of these values increases the average value of the variance.

The equilibrium amount of cultural transmission. Determining the equilibrium amount of cultural transmission is complicated by the fact that different values of L will be favored in different environments. Recall that in deriving Relation 4.19, we made no assumptions about the environnent. This means that in any particular environment, alleles increasing L will be favored by selection whenever 4.19 is satisfied, that is,

$$L < (\hat{X}(H) - H)^2 + \hat{V}(H) \tag{4.28}$$

Since both $\hat{X}$ and $\hat{V}$ increase as H increases in absolute value, larger values of L, and therefore less cultural transmission, will be favored in more extreme environments. This makes sense because in extreme environments the distribution of cultural variants is not as closely adapted to local conditions as it is in more common environments.

Here we will assume that the genes that control the relative importance of individual learning and cultural transmission respond to the average conditions in all environments. This assumption will be reasonable if the amount of gene flow between habitats is large compared to the strength of selection on alleles affecting the value of L. Once again assume that there are two alleles, e and f; individuals carrying e have a learning rule characterized by the parameter L_0, and those carrying f have a rule characterized by $L_0 + \delta L$, where δL is a small positive number. It can be shown that the allele f, and therefore larger values of L, are favored whenever

$$L < V_H\left(\frac{m}{1 - (1 - m)a}\right)^2 + \tilde{V} \tag{4.29}$$

This condition is a straightforward generalization of 4.19 to the case of a heterogeneous environment. It says that the optimum value of L is equal to the average quality of information available from models and that individuals using the optimal rule will weight individual learning and cultural transmission according to their respective error rates.

The population will be in evolutionary equilibrium when the left-hand and right-hand sides of 4.29 are equal. While we have not been able to determine analytically the values of L that satisfy this condition, they are easy to determine numerically. Figure 4.6 plots the relative importance of cultural transmission in determining behavior, a(L), when L is at its evolutionary equilibrium value, L^*, as a function of the error rate during individual learning (V_e) for three levels of mixing (m).

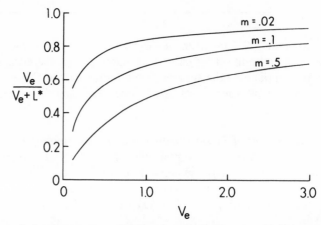

Fig. 4.6 The relative importance of cultural transmission, $a = V_e/(V_e + L^*)$, assuming that L is at its equilibrium value, L^*, in a heterogeneous environment as a function of the error rate during individual learning for three rates of mixing (m), assuming $\overline{E} = 0$ and $n_e = 1$.

These figures show that the evolutionary equilibrium amount of culture in a heterogeneous environment depends strongly on both the amount of error introduced by individual learning and the amount of mixing between environments. When it is difficult for individuals to determine accurately what behavior is best in their environment (i.e. V_e is large) and there is not too much mixing of models between environments (i.e. m is small), natural selection acting on genes can favor a system of social learning with the properties of an inheritance system. These results make sense. When V_e is large, individual learning is error prone and there-fore costly. When m is small, small amounts of learning generate a strong enough evolutionary force to keep the mean in each environment near the optimum. Thus, a population that relies mostly on cultural transmission can achieve the benefits of phenotypic flexibility and still avoid most of the costs of individual learning.

Guided variation in a temporally fluctuating environment

To model a fluctuating environment, we assume that the optimum phenotypic value, H_t, fluctuates from generation to generation. We assume that the error rate of individual learning (measured by V_e) is constant. This assumption greatly simplifies the analysis. Recall that the recursions for the variance of X in the population did not depend on the mean or the value of H. Thus, as long as V_e is constant, the variance of X in the population will approach its equilibrium value deterministically without regard to fluctuations in H. We simply assume that the variance at equilibrium is given by Equation 4.13.

The nature of the environmental fluctuations is determined by the sequence of values H_1, H_2, H_3,. . .,H_t. We assume that this sequence of numbers is an auto-correlated time series with the following moments:

$$\text{Mean}(H_t) = 0 \tag{4.30a}$$

$$\text{Var}(H_t) = V_H \tag{4.30b}$$

$$\text{Cov}(H_t, H_{t-j}) = V_H R^{|j|} \tag{4.30c}$$

Equation 4.30a says that the long-run mean of the values of H_t is zero. Once again this assumption really just specifies the origin on the line which we use to measure H_t. Equation 4.30b determines the amount of variability in the environment. If the variance in the values of the H_t, V_H, is much greater than the variability in fitness within a single generation (S), then we say that the environmental fluctuations are large. If, on the other hand, $V_H \ll S$, then the environmental fluctuations are small. Equation 4.30c specifies the extent to which the environments in consecutive generations are similar. If $R = 1$, the environments in consecutive generations are identical; if $R = 0$, the environment in one generation is completely uncorrelated with the environment in the next; finally, for intermediate values of R there is an intermediate similarity between environments in successive generations.

The stationary distribution of $\overline{X}_t$. When the environment fluctuates from generation to generation, it presents the evolving population with a "moving target." In each generation guided variation moves the mean value of X in the population toward the current optimum. Then the optimum shifts position, and the population moves toward the new value. The mean phenotype of the population never comes to equilibrium, but instead endlessly chases after the current optimum as it fluctuates randomly around the long-run optimum. The appropriate generalization of an equilibrium in a randomly fluctuating environment is the "stationary distribution." After an initial period in which the population is influenced by the initial conditions, it comes to a kind of probabilistic equilibrium, in which the probability that the mean takes on any particular value is a constant. The distribution of these long-run probabilities of $\overline{X}_t$ is called its stationary distribution.

To calculate the stationary distribution of $\overline{X}_t$, we begin by explicitly solving 4.11 to obtain $\overline{X}_t$ as a function of the initial value of the mean, $\overline{X}_0$, and t. As is shown in Box 4.8, this results in

$$\overline{X}_t = \overline{X}_0 a^t + (1 - a) \sum_{i=1}^{t-1} a^{t-i-1} H_t \tag{4.31}$$

If $0 < a < 1$, the first term in this equation becomes smaller as t becomes larger. This means that the population eventually "forgets" its initial position as it is jostled around in a random environment. Because of this effect, the stationary distribution can be calculated using only the second term in 4.31. As it turns out, we do not need to calculate the entire distribution; we only need to calculate the mean and variance. To see why, we must consider how to measure genetic fitness in a temporally varying environment.

Box 4.8 To see why Equation 4.31 is the solution of Equation 4.11, we begin at time $t = 1$. Then

$$\overline{X}_1 = a\overline{X}_0 + (1 - a)H_0$$

Next consider $t = 2$:

$$\overline{X}_2 = a\overline{X}_1 + (1 - a)H_1$$
$$= a(a\overline{X}_0 + (1 - a)H_0) + (1 - a)H_1$$
$$= a^2\overline{X}_0 + (1 - a)[aH_0 + H_1]$$

Next consider $t = 3$:

$$\overline{X}_3 = a\{a^2\overline{X}_0 + (1 - a)[aH_0 + H_1]\} + (1 - a)H_2$$
$$= a^3\overline{X}_0 + (1 - a)[a^2H_0 + aH_1 + H_2]$$

It should be clear that repeating this process i times will result in 4.31. The reader can also verify that 4.31 is the solution of 4.11 directly, by substituting 4.31 into 4.11.

The evolutionary equilibrium amount of cultural transmission in a fluctuating environment. We want to determine the value of L, the propensity to rely on individual learning, favored by natural selection acting on genes in a fluctuating environment. There are a variety of ways to approach this question (see Karlin and MacGregor, 1974; Slatkin, 1978; or Roughgarden, 1979, for reviews). We have chosen to simply find the value of L that maximizes geometric mean fitness. We are motivated by the fact that a variety of studies have shown that modifying alleles can invade a population in a temporally fluctuating environment only if they have a higher geometric mean fitness than the alleles already present in the population (Haldane and Jayakar, 1963; Gillespie, 1981a). (The reader should be warned however that Gillespie, 1981b, has demonstrated at least one case for which this condition does not hold.)

To model selection in a fluctuating environment, we assume the genetic fitness function given by Equation 4.14, except that now the fitness-maximizing phenotype, H_t, fluctuates from generation to generation. In particular, we assume that the width of the fitness function, S, is a constant. (This model of natural selection in a random environment is adapted from Slatkin and Lande, 1976.) The geometric mean fitness of a population is defined as e to the expected value of the logarithm of the average fitness, or

$$\text{Geom}(W_t) = \exp[E\{\ln(\overline{W}_t)\}] \tag{4.32}$$

where

$$\overline{W}_t = \int W(Y,H_t)\, F_t(Y)\, dY \tag{4.33}$$

The expectation, $E\{\cdot\}$, is calculated using the stationary density of $\overline{W}_t$. $\overline{W}_t$ is a function of L because L will affect the distribution of mature phenotypes, $F_t(Y)$.

> **Box 4.9** Using the definitions of W(Y, H) (Eq. 4.14) and F(Y) (Eq. 4.10), the average fitness, $\overline{W}_t$, can be written
>
> $$\overline{W}_t = \int (2\pi U_t)^{-1/2} \exp\{-(Y - \overline{X}_t)^2/2U_t - (Y - H_t)^2/2S\}dY$$
>
> Completing the square in the exponent as in Box 4.3 and integrating the resulting expression with respect to Y yields
>
> $$\overline{W}_t = \left(\frac{S}{S + U_t}\right)^{1/2} \exp\left\{\frac{-a^2(\overline{X}_t - H_t)^2}{2(U_t + S)}\right\}$$
>
> If selection is weak enough, terms of order $(U/S)^2$ can be ignored. Thus in $(\overline{W}_t)$ is approximately
>
> $$\ln(\overline{W}_t) \approx - (1/2S)\{U_t + a^2(\overline{X}_t - H_t)^2\}$$
>
> Substituting the expression for U_t given in Equation 4.10 and taking the expected value with respect to the stationary distribution of $\overline{X}_t$ yields
>
> $$E\{\ln(\overline{W}_t)\} \approx -(1/2S)(a^2[E\{(\overline{X}_t - H_t)^2\} + \hat{V}] + (1 - a)^2 V_e)$$
>
> Differentiating this expression with respect to L (recall that a is a function of L) yields 4.34 in the text.

(We actually find the value of the natural logarithm of the geometric mean fitness because this transformation simplifies the calculations and does not alter the result.)

It is shown in Box 4.9 that increasing L will increase geometric mean fitness whenever

$$L < E\{(\overline{X}_t - H_t)^2\} + \hat{V} \tag{4.34}$$

To evaluate the expectation in 4.34 we use the expression for $\overline{X}_t$ as a function of H_t, H_{t-1}, H_{t-2}, and so on, given in 4.31. This expression is substituted into 4.32, which results in an expression that only depends on the variances and covariances of the H_t. It can be shown (Boyd and Richerson, 1983) that this process results in the following expression for $E\{(\overline{X}_t - H_t)^2\}$:

$$E\{(\overline{X}_t - H_t)^2\} = \frac{2V_H(1 - R)}{(1 + a)(1 - aR)} \tag{4.35}$$

To find the evolutionary equilibrium value of L, L^*, we reexpress 4.34 as an equality and solve for L. Figure 4.7 plots the values of $V_e/(V_e + L^*)$, the relative importance of cultural transmission when $L = L^*$, for several values of R.

The results shown in these figures are strikingly similar to those obtained assuming a heterogeneous environment. They suggest that natural selection acting on genes will favor extensive amounts of cultural transmission whenever it is difficult for individuals to determine the optimal behavior (i.e. V_e is large) and the environment is sufficiently predictable (i.e. when R, our measure of generation-to-generation similarity in environments, is large). The fact that these two quite different models yield very similar results also suggests that these results are robust.

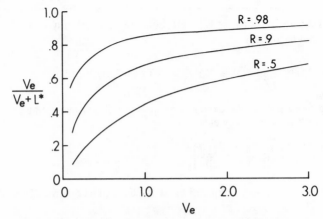

Fig. 4.7 The relative (fractional) importance of cultural transmission, $a = V_e/(V_e + L*)$, as a function of the variance of errors made during individual learning, V_e, for three values of the environmental autocorrelation, R, assuming that L is at its equilibrium value, $L*$, and that $\bar{E} = 0$ and $n_e = 1$.

Adding learning costs

So far we have assumed that the accuracy with which individuals can assess the local environment (measured by the parameter V_e) is fixed. It seems plausible that in many circumstances individuals may be able, at some cost, to improve the quality of the information upon which individual learning is based. This assumption is important because the accuracy of individual learning strongly influences the optimal balance between individual learning and cultural transmission in both heterogeneous and fluctuating environments. When individual learning is sufficiently inaccurate, natural selection acting on genes will favor the evolution of cultural transmission. It could be argued that natural selection would not favor such inaccurate individual learning, and thus if the accuracy of individual learning is allowed to evolve, cultural transmission will not be favored. In this section we modify our model so that the accuracy of individual learning can evolve. Based on the analysis of this model we will argue that culture still can be favored.

To model the evolution of individual learning, we must modify the fitness function so that increasing the accuracy of individual learning has costs. By this we mean that increasing the amount of resources allocated to increasing the accuracy of individual learning decreases the amount of resource devoted to some other aspect of the phenotype. This assumption makes sense if one thinks of learning as analogous to a sampling problem in statistics. For a given sample size, the variance of an estimator is fixed. To increase the accuracy of the estimate, one must decrease the variance of the estimator, which in turn means one must increase the sample size. But increasing the sample size increases the cost of the experiment. If this were not the case, selection would always favor perfectly accurate learning.

We formalize the costs of learning by modifying the fitness function as follows:

$$W(Y,V_e) = \exp\{-(Y - H)^2/2S\} - C(V_e) \qquad (4.36)$$

where $C(V_e)$ is a convex function with the form shown in Figure 4.8. This form of

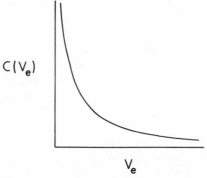

Fig. 4.8 The assumed form of $C(V_e)$ which gives the fitness cost of changing the accuracy of individual learning assuming all other aspects of phenotype are held constant.

$C(V_e)$ formalizes the assumption that an incremental decrease in V_e becomes more costly as V_e becomes smaller. This assumption is consistent with the sampling analogy outlined above.

We want to determine the value of V_e that maximizes fitness in a heterogeneous environment. We have analyzed an analogous model assuming a fluctuating environment, and the results are very similar. Assuming that L is at its equilibrium value, L^*, it can be shown that the following condition must be true for V_e to be an optimum:

$$-\frac{(L^*)^2}{S(L^* + V_e)^2} = \frac{d}{dV_e} C(V_e) \tag{4.37}$$

The left-hand side of Equation 4.37 represents the incremental decrease in fitness caused by a change in V_e due to more accurate learning, and the right-hand side represents the incremental decrease in fitness due to the costs of more accurate learning. In Figure 4.9, incremental cost and incremental benefit in terms of fitness

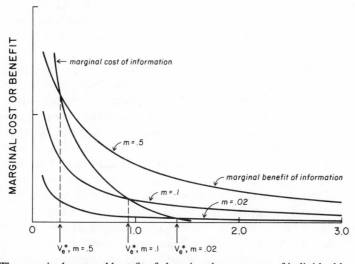

Fig. 4.9 The marginal cost and benefit of changing the error rate of individual learning (V_e) in a heterogeneous environment for three values of m. Optimal values of V_e occur at the intersections of the marginal cost and benefit curves.

are plotted as a function of V_e, for several values of m, the appropriate measure of environmental predictability. There are two qualitative results of interest: First, increasing the cost of information increases the optimal value of V_e. Thus, as individual learning becomes more costly, selection favors investing in less of it. From our previous results, we know that decreasing the quality of information increases the optimal amount of imitation. Thus making individual learning more costly will tend to favor more imitation. Second, increasing the predictability of the environment decreases the optimal amount of individual learning. This makes sense because as the environment becomes more predictable, the behavior of models is, on the average, closer to the optimal behavior, and thus a smaller investment in acquiring costly information by individual learning is justified.

Reprise: The evolution of cultural transmission

In the last several sections we have been building an argument that natural selection, acting on genes, can lead to the evolution of a system of cultural transmission with the properties of an inheritance system. The behavior of contemporary primates suggests that the human species evolved from a hominid with elaborate individual learning abilities but only a limited reliance on social learning. The models indicate that, under the appropriate conditions, natural selection could favor an increased reliance on social learning relative to individual learning in such an organism.

The key assumption in the argument is that individual learning is imperfect. Individuals observe their environment and, based on these observations, determine how to behave in the local environment. Because the information available to individuals is incomplete, and because individuals have limited cognitive abilities, individual learning leads to errors. The error rate of individual learning can be reduced, but because the time and energy devoted to acquiring better information cannot be allocated to other fitness-enhancing activities, such reductions are costly. Thus the quality of individual learning for any given trait should depend on the costs of learning. When it is easy to determine the locally best behavior, we expect learning to be quite accurate, but when it is difficult, individual learning should be inaccurate.

Given that learning is imperfect, the models analyzed in the last several sections indicate that natural selection will favor an increased reliance on culturally inherited beliefs whenever (1) the error rate of individual learning is substantially greater than that for social learning and (2) the environment is reasonably predictable. When behaviors modified by individual learning are subsequently transmitted to others, the force of guided variation affects both the mean and variance of behavior in the population. The strength of the force affecting the mean depends on the importance of cultural transmission relative to individual learning in determining individual behavior. If individual behavior is determined mostly by individual learning, then the force of guided variation is strong and the population mean moves rapidly to the value favored by learning. In the limit of no cultural transmission, this occurs in a single generation. If individual behavior is mostly determined by cultural transmission, then guided variation is weak, and the population will move more slowly toward the value favored by learning. The relative importance of individual learning and cultural transmission also affects the variance of the population. If individual learning dominates, then most of the errors made during individual learning are translated into behavior; if cultural transmission dominates, a smaller amount of error affects behavior. When the force of guided variation is strong, more variation is introduced into the population in each generation and the equilibrium variance is larger than when guided variation is weak. Thus the results of our models make sense: when individual learning is inaccurate, increasing the importance of cultural transmission reduces the variance in the population; when environments are predictable, a weak force is adequate to keep the mean of the population near the optimum.

It is our intuition that it is often difficult for individuals to determine the locally optimal behavior. Consider, for example, the problem of the Bayesian horticulturalist. The experience of any single year is affected by a large number of random factors, the weather, insects, the luck of his neighbors, the political fortunes of the big man, and so on. To get an adequate estimate of the best behavior might take a sample of many years, yet the horticulturalist must decide what to do the first year he farms. We believe that many human decisions have this character. Because they have many effects that are spread out over a long period of time, it is difficult for individuals to determine the best choice by trial and error; because the consequences of alternative choices depend on a complex, variable, hard-to-understand environment, it is difficult for individuals to deduce the optimal behavior. The result is that a reliance on individual learning will lead to frequent errors. If this intuition is correct, and if the social learning theorists (whose work we reviewed in Chap. 3) are also correct that information can be acquired easily and accurately by social learning, then the models analyzed here suggest that a strong dependence on cultural transmission usually provides a better way to acquire beliefs about the environment than a strong dependence on individual learning.

Comparing Genetic and Cultural Transmission

So far in this chapter we have shown that social learning is favored relative to individual learning when environments are predictable and it is difficult for individuals to determine the locally favored phenotype. It could be argued that these are exactly the conditions which would also favor the genetic transmission of behavior, since in predictable environments selection will increase the frequency of genes leading to the development of the locally favored phenotype. This intuition has some theoretical support. Cavalli-Sforza and Feldman (1983) have analyzed a model in which individuals acquire one of two phenotypic variants either culturally or genetically. Assuming a constant, uniform environment, they show that genetic transmission will replace cultural transmission as long as the error rate of cultural transmission is higher than that of genetic transmission. It is important to note that Cavalli-Sforza and Feldman's model does not include the effects of the transmission of guided variation.

To make the argument for the adaptiveness of cultural transmission persuasive, we must also demonstrate that there are conditions under which it is better to acquire one's initial behavioral predispositions by social learning than to inherit them genetically. Contrary to Cavalli-Sforza and Feldman, we think such conditions exist. To demonstrate this, we compare the geometric mean fitness of a "cultural" population with a "genetic" population in a fluctuating environment. In the cultural population, an individual's mature phenotype is transmitted to the next generation as in previous sections of this chapter. In the genetic population, it is the initial "phenotype" (or, more properly, the genes that determine it) that is transmitted. Both populations are assumed to have identical capacities for individual learning. The crucial difference between them is that the force of guided variation does not affect the evolution of the distribution of initial phenotypes in the genetic population. We shall see that this difference creates a plausible range of conditions under which the cultural population has a higher geometric mean fitness than the genetic population.

Genetic transmission of the learning rule

To derive a recursion for the distribution of values of the initial phenotype, X, under the assumption that X is genetically transmitted, we assume that the life cycle has three stages, genetic transmission, followed by learning, and finally selection. We begin the life cycle just after genetic transmission. At this stage we assume that the distribution of X in the population is normal with mean $\overline{X}$ and variance V.

Since Weismann (1893), one of the fundamental tenets of evolutionary theory has been that developmental events in an individual's life do not affect its germ cells and thus cannot affect the genetic material that the individual transmits to the next generation. This means that learning has no effect on the distribution of X. Hence, the mean and variance after learning are still $\overline{X}$ and V, respectively.

The effect of selection. To deduce the effect of selection on the distribution of initial phenotypes, we calculate the average fitness of an individual with the initial phenotype X. We denote the probability density that an individual develops the mature phenotype Y in environment H given that it has the initial phenotype X as Prob(Y|X,H). Then the probability that an individual with initial phenotype X survives to reproduce in environment H, $W_{av}(X,H)$, is

$$W_{av}(X,H) = \int W(Y,H) \, \text{Prob}(Y|X,H) \, dY \qquad (4.38)$$

Equation 4.38 says that the probability that an individual with initial phenotype X survives in environment H, W_{av} (the average fitness), is equal to the product of the fitness of an individual with mature phenotype Y in environment H and the probability that an individual with initial phenotype X develops a mature phenotype Y, integrated over all values of Y.

With the assumptions already made about the nature of learning (Eq. 4.9) and selection (Eq. 4.14), we can calculate the form of $W_{av}(X,H)$. It is shown in Box 4.10 that

$$W_{av}(X,H) \propto \exp[-(X - H)^2/2S_{av}] \qquad (4.39)$$

where

$$S_{av} = \frac{S + V_e(1 - a)^2}{a^2}$$

Box 4.10 From Equation 4.10 the probability that an individual with initial phenotype X develops mature phenotype Y is normally distributed with mean $aX + (1 - a)H$ and variance $(1 - a)^2 V_e$. Thus the integrand in Equation 4.38 is the product of two Gaussian functions of Y. Once again we can use Expression 1 from Box 4.3 to show that 4.38 has the form

$$W_{av}(X,H) = \int \left(\frac{1}{2\pi(1 - a)^2 V_e}\right)^{1/2} \exp\left\{\frac{-(Y - M_x)^2}{2V_x}\right\}$$
$$\exp\left\{\frac{-[H - (aX + (1 - a)H)]^2}{2((1 - a)^2 V_e + S)}\right\} dY$$

where M_x and V_x are parameters that could be computed by completing the square as in Box 4.3. Performing the integral with respect to Y yields the expression

$$W_{av}(X,H) = \left(\frac{S}{(1 - a)^2 V_e + S}\right)^{1/2} \exp\left\{\frac{-[H - (aX + (1 - a)H)]^2}{2((1 - a)^2 V_e + S)}\right\}$$

which is proportional to

$$W_{av}(X,H) \propto \exp\left\{\frac{-a^2(X - H)^2}{2((1 - a)^2 V_e + S)}\right\}$$

Figure 4.10 shows that $W_{av}(X,H)$ represents stabilizing selection on the initial phenotype, X. The optimal initial phenotype in a particular environment is H, the optimal mature phenotype. The width of W_{av}, given by S_{av}, is inversely proportional to the strength of selection on X. Notice that the strength of selection on the initial phenotype (measured by $1/S_{av}$) is always weaker than selection on the mature phenotype (measured by $1/S$). Two factors cause this result: errors made during learning and development weaken selection on X (i.e. $V_e > 0$), and learning itself weakens selection because it causes the mature phenotype of individuals to move closer to the optimum phenotype. To understand this effect, consider the case when $a = 0$. In this case all individuals develop the optimum phenotype independent of their initial phenotypes. As one would expect, as $a \to 0$, $S_{av} \to \infty$, which means that selection has no effect on X.

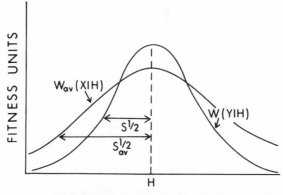

Fig. 4.10 The relationship between the expected fitness of genotypic value X, $W_{av}(X|H)$, and the fitness of mature phenotypic value Y, $W(Y|H)$.

We can now derive the effect of selection on the mean phenotype in the population. Once again, suppose that just after transmission the distribution of X in the population, $Q(X)$, is normal with mean value $\overline{X}$ and variance V. Then the distribution of X after selection, $Q'(X)$, is

$$Q'(X) = \frac{Q(X)\ W_{av}(X,H)}{\int Q(X)\ W_{av}(X,H)\ dX} \qquad (4.40)$$

That is, to calculate the frequency of a particular value of X after selection, one multiplies the frequency of those individuals before selection by the probability that they survive and then normalizes by the average probability of survival (or average fitness) so that the frequencies integrate to one. Given the distribution of X in the population after selection we can calculate its mean, $\overline{X}'$. It is shown in Box 4.11 that the mean value of X after selection is

$$\overline{X}' = \gamma\overline{X} + (1 - \gamma)H \qquad (4.41)$$

where

$$\gamma = \frac{S_{av}}{S_{av} + V}$$

Thus, selection moves the mean of the population a fraction γ of the distance between the mean before selection and the optimum in the environment. Notice that as S_{av} becomes large, γ approaches one, or in other words, as selection becomes weaker the population moves a smaller distance toward the optimum of X in a

---

Box 4.11 The numerator of the right-hand side of Equation 4.40 is proportional to

$$Q(X)W_{av}(X,H) \propto \exp\left\{\frac{-(X - \overline{X})^2}{2V} + \frac{-(X - H)^2}{2S_{av}}\right\}$$

From Result 1 in Box 4.3, we know that

$$Q(X)W_{av}(X,H) \propto \exp\left\{\frac{-(X - \overline{X}')^2}{2V}\right\}$$

where

$$\overline{X}' = \frac{S_{av}\overline{X} + VH}{S_{av} + V}$$

and

$$V' = \frac{S_{av}\,V}{S_{av} + V}$$

Since the denominator normalizes the ratio so that it integrates to one, $Q'(X)$ is a frequency distribution with mean $\overline{X}'$ and variance V'.

single generation. Recall that S_{av} becomes larger as learning becomes more important in determining the mature phenotype of the population (i.e. a $\rightarrow$ 1). Thus, efficient learning makes for weak selection on the determinants of learning.

Genetic transmission. In order to derive the effect of genetic transmission, we will assume that the value of X in any given individual is determined by alleles at a number of different genetic loci and that each of these alleles has only a small additive effect on the value of X. The genetical theory of the evolution of such polygenic, quantitative characters is discussed in Falconer (1960), Lande (1976, 1977, 1979, 1980), and Bulmer (1980). We further assume that mating takes place randomly with respect to the value of X. It is shown in all of these references that with these assumptions the mean value of X after transmission, $\overline{X}'$, is simply $\overline{X}$. An expression can also be derived for the effect of transmission and mutation on the variance of a character under polygenic control (Lande, 1976, 1977). These calculations are beyond the scope of this book; however, it turns out that under some circumstances the recursion for the variance does not depend on the mean of the population. This means that once the variance reaches an equilibrium it will remain constant, unaffected by any fluctuations in the mean. Generally, we will simply assume that the variance is at equilibrium at a value, V_g.

These results should not be surprising. In Chapter 3 we saw that genetic transmission by itself had no effect on the frequency of alleles at a single locus. When there are many loci, both the segregation of alleles at a single locus and the recombination of alleles at different loci cause a shuffling of the genome. This shuffling affects the variance of the character in the population in a fairly complex way. However, because the frequency of different alleles remains constant, and their effects are additive, the shuffling has no effect on the mean. While this result may seem obvious, as we have seen, it differs sharply from the case in which the initial phenotype is inherited culturally.

This simple model of the genetic transmission of one of the determinants of learning illustrates three points. First, learning by itself has no effect on the frequency of the determinants of learning in the population. Second, selection acts to shape the determinants of learning just as it would any other character. Third, as learning becomes more effective in causing the organism to develop an adaptive phenotype the effect of selection on the initial phenotype is weakened. That is, as the organism's skill at moving toward the optimum increases, selection for a good a priori guess about the environment decreases.

The interaction of guided variation and natural selection

Natural selection will affect the distribution of phenotypes within a generation in the cultural population in much the same way that it does in the genetic one. After individual learning, selection increases the frequency of some mature variants and decreases the frequency of others. In the first part of this chapter we assumed that selection was weak enough compared to guided variation so that its direct effect on the distribution of cultural variants could be ignored. To compare the effects of genetic and cultural transmission fairly, however, we need to investigate the interaction of the force of guided variation and natural selection. By analogy with

Equation 4.40, the distribution of mature phenotypes after selection, $F'(Y)$, is

$$F'(Y) = \frac{F(Y)\ W(Y)}{\int F(Y)\ W(Y)\ dY} \qquad (4.42)$$

In contrast to Equation 4.40, we weight the frequency of the mature phenotype after learning by the fitness of the mature phenotype. A derivation similar to that given in Box 4.11 shows that the mean value of Y after selection, $\overline{Y}'$, is

$$\overline{Y}' = c\overline{X} + (1 - c)H \qquad (4.43)$$

where

$$c = \frac{aS}{S + U_c}$$

Since it is the mature phenotype that is transmitted, the mean value of the initial phenotype in the next generation is also $\overline{Y}'$. We assume that the variance of initial phenotype is at equilibrium at V_c and the variance of mature phenotype is at equilibrium at U_c.

Equation 4.43 says that the combination of learning and selection moves that mean mature phenotype a fraction c of the way toward the optimum phenotype. The magnitude of c is determined by the product of two factors, a, which represents the force of guided variation alone, and $S/(S + U_c)$, which represents the effect of selection alone. Thus, increasing the strength of learning increases the rate at which the population approaches the optimum phenotype when the determinants of learning are culturally transmitted. This is in sharp contrast to the case of genetic transmission where learning slows the evolution of the initial value of the learning rule.

Comparing the change in the mean over one generation

We can now compare the adaptive consequences of cultural and genetic transmission. The recursions that were derived in the previous section show that the magnitude of the change in the mean and variance of the distribution of initial phenotypes in a population over one generation will depend strongly on whether the initial value of the learning rule is transmitted genetically or culturally. These differences will cause a cultural population to respond differently to a changing environment than a genetic population. This, in turn, will cause the genetic fitness of individuals with genetic transmission to differ from the genetic fitness of individuals with cultural transmission.

We begin by comparing the dynamic response of the mean of the population to selection under the two modes of inheritance. When the determinants of learning are genetically transmitted, increasing the effectiveness of learning (i.e. a→0) reduces the response of the population. In contrast, when the determinants of learning are culturally transmitted, we see the opposite result. This suggests that the force of guided variation will cause populations with cultural transmission of the determinants of phenotype to respond more rapidly to environmental change. We can use the results that we have already derived to show that this intuition is generally correct.

First, notice that Recursions 4.41 and 4.43 (which give the change in the mean over one generation for each mode of transmission) differ only in the definition of the constants γ and c. That is, they have the same linear form:

$$\overline{X}' = \mathcal{A}\overline{X} + (1 - \mathcal{A})H \tag{4.44}$$

where $\mathcal{A} = \gamma$ in the genetic case, and $\mathcal{A} = c$ in the cultural case. This tells us that the population with genetic transmission will respond more quickly to selection only if $c > \gamma$. The relative magnitude of c and γ depends on the strengths of selection and learning and the magnitudes of the variances, V_g, V_e, and V_c. We can determine the combinations of these parameters for which $c > \gamma$ if we make the assumption that selection is weak. It is shown in Box 4.12 that $c > \gamma$ when

$$V_g/S > (1 - a) + U_c/S \tag{4.45}$$

where U_c is the equilibrium variance of the mature phenotype under cultural transmission. This condition has a very simple interpretation. U_c/S and V_g/S are measures of the strength of selection on culturally and genetically transmitted variation. The parameter $(1 - a)$ is a measure of the effectiveness of learning, and therefore also a measure of the strength of the force of guided variation. Thus, Inequality 4.45 says that a genetic population responds more quickly than a cultural one whenever the effect of natural selection alone in the genetic population exceeds the effects of the force of guided variation plus that of natural selection in the cultural population.

The strengths of selection under the two modes of inheritance depend on the relative magnitudes of the variances V_g and U_c. It is important to keep in mind that U_c is the variance in mature phenotype in a cultural population while V_g is the variance in initial phenotype in a genetic one. Using Equation 4.10 we can write U_c in terms of the equilibrium variance in the initial phenotype in a cultural population, V_c:

$$U_c = a^2 V_c + V_e(1 - a)^2 \tag{4.46}$$

To interpret this relation, first assume that there is no learning (a = 1) and that equilibrium variances of the initial phenotype are the same ($V_g = V_c$). In this case the two populations respond to selection in exactly the same way because learning has no effect on the variance of the mature phenotype. Allowing learning to become important (so that $a < 1$) has two effects: Individual learning acts to decrease the amount of variance in mature phenotypes because individuals tend to acquire similar individual phenotypes by individual learning, but it also acts to increase the variance because more of the errors made during learning are transmitted. Finally, there is no reason to suppose that equilibrium variances should be equal. A variety of factors affect the relative magnitudes of these variances. It seems likely that new variation will be generated at a higher rate in the case of cultural transmission

Box 4.12 A genetic population responds more quickly to changes in the environment than a cultural population when $c > \gamma$. Here we want to find the combinations of values of a, S, U_c, V_e, and V_g that cause this inequality to be satisfied. Using the definitions of γ and c, the condition $c > \gamma$ becomes

$$\frac{a}{1 + U_c/S} > \frac{1 + (1 - a)^2 V_e/S}{1 + (1 - a)^2 V_e/S + a^2 V_g/S}$$

First, we expand both denominators using Taylor's series

$$a\left(1 - U_c/S + (U_c/S)^2 - \ldots\right) > (1 + (1 - a)^2 V_e/S)$$

$$\left(1 - ((1 - a)^2 V_e + a^2 V_g)/S + \{((1 - a)^2 V_e + a^2 V_g)/S\}^2 \ldots\right)$$

If selection is weak, $S \gg V_e, V_g, U_c$. This means we can ignore terms of order $(V_e/S)^2$, $(U_c/S)^2$, and $(V_g/S)^2$. Doing this yields the approximate expression

$$a(1 - U_c/S) > (1 - a^2 V_g/S) \tag{1}$$

Now consider the special case when $\gamma = c$. Then Expression 1 becomes the following equality:

$$-a^2 V_g/S - a(1 - U_c/S) + 1 = 0$$

We can use the quadratic formula to solve for a, which yields the following expression:

$$a = (1/2)\{(1 - U_c/S) \pm [(1 - U_c/S)^2 + 4V_g/S]^{1/2}\}$$

We expand the square root as a Taylor series and once again ignore the terms of order $(V/S)^2$ to obtain

$$a \approx (1/2)(1 - U_c/S \pm [1 - U_c/S + 2V_g/S])$$

Since the $-$ root is always negative, only the $+$ root is relevant. Thus

$$a \approx (1/2)(1 - U_c/S \pm [1 - U_c/S + 2V_g/S])$$

From this it is clear that $c > \gamma$ when

$$V_g/S > (1 - a) + U_c/S$$

because all the environmental and learning errors are inherited. However, for the same reason more of the variation is also subject to selection in each generation than in the genetic case. The amount of variation in the cultural population also depends on the model of inheritance chosen. The blending model will act to reduce the amount of variation in each generation while the multifactorial model will not. Finally, learning itself has the effect of reducing the variability in the cultural population. Thus, we cannot predict what the relative magnitudes of these variances (V_g and V_c) will be.

What is clear from 4.45, however, is that in a cultural species even very weak learning processes can have an important impact on the rate of change of the mean phenotype in a population. If selection is weak, we expect the ratios U_c/S and V_g/S to be relatively small, on the order of a few percent. This means that learning processes which move an individual's phenotype only a few percent of the way toward the optimum in a single generation can be as important as the effect of selection on the distribution of phenotypes in a population. Learning processes that on average have a stronger effect than this on the behavior of an organism will generally swamp the effects of selection.

Comparing the fitness of genetic and cultural transmission in a fluctuating environment

The cultural transmission of the mature phenotype has two main effects. First, transmission of phenotypes modified by learning creates a force that increases the frequency of favorable phenotypic variants. This means that a cultural population will respond more rapidly to a changing environment. Second, the nature of the inheritance system affects the amount of variation in the population. Differences in the variation of the mature phenotype affect the mean fitness of the population directly. Differences in the proportion of this variation that is transmitted also affect the strength of selection and thus the rate at which a population responds to changing conditions.

With the qualitative effects of cultural transmission in mind, let us now consider when cultural transmission might be favored by natural selection in a fluctuating environment. Assume that the environmental fluctuations are described by the model outlined earlier in this chapter. Once again we use geometric mean fitness as a measure of the relative advantage (or disadvantage) of cultural transmission over genetic transmission. It can be shown that the logarithm of geometric mean fitness of a cultural population less the logarithm of the geometric mean fitness of a genetic population, ρ, is given by

$$\rho = 0.5 \ln\left\{\frac{S + U_g}{S + U_c}\right\} - \frac{a^2 E\{(\overline{X}_{c,t} - H_t)^2\}}{2(S + U_c)} + \frac{a^2 E\{(\overline{X}_{g,t} - H_t)^2\}}{2(S + U_g)} \quad (4.47)$$

where U_g is the variance of mature phenotypes in the genetic population and $\overline{X}_{g,t}$ and $\overline{X}_{c,t}$ are the means in genetic and cultural population, respectively. If $\rho > 0$, then the geometric mean fitness of a cultural population is greater than that of a genetic population.

Initially we will assume that the equilibrium variances of initial phenotype under the two modes of inheritance (V_g and V_c) are equal. When $V_c = V_g$, it follows that the variances of mature phenotype are equal, that is, $U_g = U_c$. This means that ρ will be greater than zero whenever $E\{(\overline{X}_{g,t} - H_t)^2\} > E\{(\overline{X}_{c,t} - H_t)^2\}$. Or, to put it in words, if we constrain the variances to be equal, the ratio of the geometric mean fitnesses depends only on the expected squared difference of the mean initial phenotype and the optimum phenotype, which, in turn, depends on the rate at which the mean initial phenotype in the population responds to environmental fluctuations. Since the recursions for $\overline{X}_{g,t}$ and $\overline{X}_{c,t}$ have the same linear form given in Equation 4.44, we can use Equation 4.35 to obtain these expectations by making the substitution $\mathcal{A} = a$.

What is the optimal rate of response? When we first considered this problem we reasoned that the mode of inheritance that led to more rapid adaptation would always be favored. Our intuition was incorrect. By differentiating the expression for $E\{(\overline{X}_t - H_t)^2\}$ given in Equation 4.35 with respect to $\mathcal{A}$, it is easy to show that there is an optimal value of $\mathcal{A}$, $\mathcal{A}^*$, that minimizes $E\{(\overline{X}_t - H_t)^2\}$:

$$\mathcal{A}^* = \begin{cases} (1 - R)/2R & \text{for } R > 1/3 \\ 1 & \text{for } R < 1/3 \end{cases} \tag{4.48}$$

Equation 4.48 says that in weakly autocorrelated environments ($R < 1/3$) the slowest possible response is favored, $\mathcal{A} = 1$. For more highly correlated environments ($R > 1/3$) there is an optimal rate of response, $\mathcal{A}^*$, which is slower than the fastest possible response, $\mathcal{A} = 0$. Surprisingly, this result is independent of the magnitude of the environmental fluctuations, V_H. It is important to keep in mind that this result assumes that the variance is held constant.

We suggest the following heuristic explanation of this interesting result. In any generation, a population's response is always toward the optimum in that generation. In an uncorrelated environment in which there is no statistical similarity between the optimum phenotype in consecutive generations, a rapid response of the mean phenotype does not improve the fit of the organism to the environment. In fact, in an uncorrelated environment the motion of the mean phenotype is simply a random walk around the long-run optimum. Increasing the rate of response simply increases the variance of this process and therefore the value of $E\{(\overline{X}_t - H_t)^2\}$. If the optimum phenotypes in consecutive generations are correlated (so that $R > 0$), movement toward the previous generation's optimum will, on average, also be movement toward the present generation's optimum. This effect will tend to decrease $E\{(\overline{X}_t - H_t)^2\}$. Apparently these two effects balance at $R = 1/3$.

The rates of response of genetic and cultural populations depend on the values of γ and c, which in turn depend on the parameters a, V_c, V_g, and V_H. Figures 4.11a–c give the combinations of values of R and a for which the logarithm of geometric mean fitness of a genetic population exceeds that of a cultural population by a constant amount. In each figure the magnitude of the environmental fluctuations, V_H, is different, but the general pattern is very similar in each case. Genetic transmission is favored for low values of R, and cultural transmission is favored for higher values of R. The difference is most pronounced for moderately weak learning (i.e. $a = .7–.8$) and large values of V_H. This reflects the fact that increasing the strength of learning ($a \rightarrow 0$) or decreasing environmental fluctuations ($V_H \rightarrow 0$) increases the absolute magnitude of the geometric mean fitness of both modes of transmission.

Next, we allow the variances of the initial phenotype to differ. In this case all the terms in Equation 4.47 are important. The first term gives the direct effect of the variances on the relative fitness of the two modes. Notice that this term is positive whenever cultural transmission has a smaller variance than genetic trans-

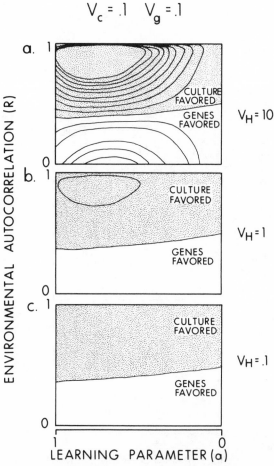

$$V_c = .1 \quad V_g = .1$$

Fig. 4.11 A contour plot of the logarithm of the difference of the geometric mean fitnesses of populations with cultural and genetic transmission as a function of environmental autocorrelation (R) and the relative importance of cultural transmission (a) for three amounts of environmental variability (measured by V_H). Unshaded areas represent parameter combinations for which genetic transmission is favored, and shaded areas indicate situations in which cultural transmission is favored. In this figure $V_c = V_g = 0.1, S = 1.0$, and $V_e = 0.1$. Note that at very high autocorrelations genes become favored again in all cases, though this effect shows up poorly in the figure.

mission and negative when the reverse is true. The second two terms give the effect of the response of the population discussed above. To deduce the relative importance of these effects, in Figures 4.12a–c we have plotted contours of constant ρ under the assumption that the variance in the cultural population is ten times that in the genetic population ($V_c = 10V_g$). In Figures 4.13a–c it is assumed that the variance in the genetic population is ten times larger than that in the cultural population. From these figures we conclude that the direct effect is important only when the amount of environmental variation is small.

$$V_c = .1 \quad V_g = .01$$

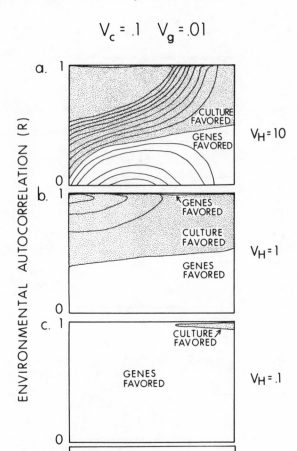

Fig. 4.12 The same as 4.11 except that $V_g = 0.01$. That is, it gives a contour plot of the logarithm of the difference of the geometric mean fitnesses of populations with cultural and genetic transmission as a function of environmental autocorrelation (R) and the relative importance of cultural transmission (a) for three amounts of environmental variability (measured by V_H). In this figure $V_c = 0.1$, $V_g = 0.01$, $S = 1.0$, and $V_e = 0.1$. Again, genetic transmission is favored, when R is near one.

Conclusion

At the beginning of this chapter we posed the following question: Can a system of social learning which requires individuals to ignore the dictates of individual learning be favored by natural selection? We began our investigation of this question by reviewing models of learning drawn from the social sciences. These models are all very similar—in each case learning is portrayed as a process that modifies some initial phenotype according to some guiding criteria. It is reasonable to expect that, on average, learning will usually increase an individual's adaptation to its environment, but for any particular individual, learning can lead to errors. Each newborn individual must inherit its initial phenotype, either genetically or culturally through the processes of social learning.

$$V_c = .01 \quad V_g = .1$$

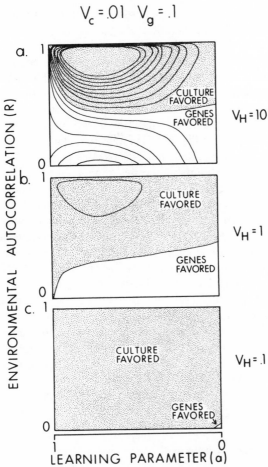

Fig. 4.13 The same as 4.11 except that $V_c = 0.01$. That is, it gives a contour plot of the logarithm of the difference of the geometric mean fitnesses of populations with cultural and genetic transmission as a function of environmental autocorrelation (R) and the relative importance of cultural transmission (a) for three amounts of environmental variability (measured by V_H). In this figure $V_c = 0.01$, $V_g = 0.1$, $S = 1.0$, and $V_e = 0.1$. Here cultural transmission is favored near $R = 1$ because the genetic variance, V_g, is assumed to be greater than the cultural variance, V_c.

We first considered the dynamics of a population in which phenotypes modified by learning were culturally transmitted. In such a population the interaction of cultural transmission and learning creates forces which affect both the mean and the variance of the initial phenotypes in the population. The cultural transmission of such guided variation creates a force which increases the frequency of variants which are favored by learning. If individual learning is important in determining mature phenotypes compared to cultural transmission, then the force affecting the mean is strong and the population mean moves to the phenotypic value favored by learning in a short time. When this is the case, however, most of the errors made during individual learning affect behavior, and therefore the variance in the population is substantial. When cultural transmission is more important in determining individual behavior, the mean approaches the optimum more slowly, but less error variation is introduced each generation.

We then supposed that the parameter L, which determined the relative importance of culture and individual learning in determining individual behavior, was under genetic control and asked what value of L is favored by natural selection. We showed that in both a heterogeneous and a fluctuating environment small values of L (meaning that culture is much more important than learning) were favored if (1) social learning is more accurate than individual learning, (2) individual learning is costly and therefore inaccurate, and (3) environmental variability is predictable. When these conditions hold, the model suggests that natural selection will lead to a system of social learning with the properties of an inheritance system, even though such a system causes individuals to ignore the dictates of individual learning.

Predictable environments and inaccurate learning would also seem to favor genetic transmission. To determine the circumstances under which cultural transmission is a superior mode of adaptation to genetic transmission, we considered the case in which the initial phenotype was genetically inherited. We then compared the dynamics of cultural and genetic populations in a fluctuating environment. Because the cultural population is affected by both the forces of selection and guided variation, it responds more rapidly to environmental fluctuations than does the genetic population. However, cultural transmission also affects the variance of the trait in a complicated way. Using these results we compared the geometric mean fitness of genetic and cultural populations in a temporally fluctuating environment. From this comparison we concluded that cultural transmission is most likely to be favored when (1) environmental fluctuations are large and at least moderately autocorrelated and (2) learning makes only modest improvements in the phenotype of any individual during any generation.

Why is culture so rare in animals?

The model described in this chapter predicts in a very general way the kinds of conditions that are likely to favor the origin of a system of cultural transmission. In evolutionary biology such predictions are typically evaluated using the method of comparative natural history. To apply this method to the question at hand we would collect as much evidence as possible about the ecology and behavior of a number of closely related species that varied in the extent to which phenotypic traits were culturally transmitted. If we found that cultural transmission was most common in species living in habitats that fit the predictions of the model, then we could reasonably infer that the model had some basis in reality.

The difficulty with this approach is that cultural transmission seems to be extremely rare in nature, and where it does exist it is apparently confined to a very narrow range of traits. The literature on cultural transmission in nonhuman animals has been reviewed extensively by Immelman (1975), Wilson (1975), Galef (1976), Bonner (1980), and Mainardi (1980). These authors report a large number of instances of very simple kinds of cultural transmission in nature. There are, for example, many examples of habitat imprinting and the inheritance of song dialects in birds. However, there are very few examples of species in which complex novel behavior patterns have been shown to be culturally transmitted.

There are at least two possible explanations for the limited occurrence of complex forms of cultural transmission among other animal species. The first is that complex cultural forms of transmission are actually more common than the limited number of published examples would lead us to believe. This may be due in part to the difficulty of distinguishing the cultural and genetic components of any behavioral trait. Moreover, since examples of complex cultural transmission are so rare, it is usually assumed that most behaviors are transmitted genetically or learned de novo. Hence, the burden of demonstrating cultural transmission falls on the investigator. Given these problems it is plausible that there are many more examples of cultural transmission than has been realized.

It is also possible, however, that complex forms of cultural transmission are genuinely rare in nature. If so, this is an interesting and curious occurrence. The results of our model suggest that cultural transmission should be favored over genetic transmission under a fairly wide range of circumstances. The fact that cultural transmission is not common suggests that some additional explanation is required. One possibility is that some rare preadaptation is necessary in order for culture to evolve (Lumsden and Wilson, 1981: 325–331). Given that rudimentary forms of culture are common, this does not seem likely. Another possibility is that there are other costs associated with cultural transmission that we have not taken into account so far. As we shall see in subsequent chapters, this explanation is very plausible.

5

Biased Transmission and the Sociobiology Debate

> The *universal* ideas do not exist everywhere in identical form, but they vary. . . . [T]hese variations are either external, that is founded on the environment . . . or internal, that is founded on psychological conditions.
>
> The effects of psychical factors are also being studied. . . . Inquiries into the mutual relations of tribes and peoples begin to show that certain cultural elements are easily assimilated while others are rejected.
>
> Franz Boas, *Race, Language and Culture* (1940: 271, 272)

Donald Campbell (1960) has suggested that all learning processes are analogous to the process of natural selection. Consider, for example, trial-and-error learning: individuals generate behavioral variants, try them out, and then select the best variants according to some standard of merit. Social learning can also be analogous to natural selection. The same sense of pleasure and pain that allows individuals to select among the variants that are generated as part of trial-and-error learning also allows selection among preexisting cultural variants. Similarly, the more elaborate cognitive processes whereby people plan and invent new behaviors can also act to discriminate among preexisting ones. If individuals are predisposed to adopt some variants, then these favored variants will increase in frequency. We term this process "biased transmission." A number of theorists have proposed that the evolutionary forces that result from biased transmission play a dominant role in cultural evolution (Ruyle, 1973; Durham, 1976; Boehm, 1978; Cavalli-Sforza and Feldman, 1981; Lumsden and Wilson, 1981). Cavalli-Sforza and Feldman and Lumsden and Wilson analyze evolutionary models of biased cultural transmission under the rubrics of "cultural selection" and "epigenetic rules," respectively.

We believe that the role of biased cultural transmission in human evolution is crucial in the human sociobiology debate. Many authors have argued that sociobiology fails as a theory of human behavior because it does not account for the fact that humans rationally choose their behavior. Even Marshall Sahlins (1976b) and Marvin Harris (1979), who concur on little else, agree that it is through the invention of cultural variants and the choice among existing ones that genetic imperatives are transcended. In our terminology, these authors are arguing that human behavior cannot be predicted by sociobiological theory because the forces of guided variation and biased transmission dominate cultural evolution.

Whether this view is correct depends on the origin and strength of the forces of guided variation and biased transmission. If panhuman, genetically transmitted rules allow humans to choose fitness-maximizing cultural variants in many habitats, as Alexander suggests (1979a: Chap. 2), or if epigenetic rules can respond to selection in particular local habitats, as Lumsden and Wilson argue, then bias and guided variation will create strong forces favoring the evolution of cultural variants which enhance reproductive success. If such genetically transmitted rules cannot readily evolve, then other forces may predominate in cultural evolution, forces which do not necessarily act to maximize genetic fitness.

In this chapter, we have two aims. First, we want to consider the evolutionary properties of biased cultural transmission. We begin by defining biased transmission in general and developing a taxonomy of different kinds of biased transmission. Then we develop models of the simplest type of biased transmission, direct bias. Finally, we consider models in which the strength and direction of direct bias are genetically controlled, and we attempt to use these models to understand how direct bias might evolve. From these models we conclude that genetically transmitted biases can evolve if (1) they are not too costly and (2) they increase the chances of acquiring locally favored cultural variants in a wide variety of habitats. However, the evolution of habitat-specific biases appears much less likely.

Our second aim is to reconsider the sociobiology controversy in the light of the concepts presented in this chapter and the preceding one. Our models suggest that two unresolved issues are at the crux of the controversy:

1. How much choosing do people actually do in the course of acquiring or transmitting their cultural repertoire? How strong are direct biases relative to other evolutionary forces acting on cultural variation?

2. Where do the rules that direct choice (including cognitive structures, senses of pleasure and pain, and objectives of rational calculation) come from and how do they work?

If biased transmission and guided variation are strong forces closely controlled by genes, then a sociobiological hypothesis seems plausible. If biased transmission and guided variation are typically weak, or if their direction is determined by other forces of cultural evolution, then other hypotheses are possible. We conclude our discussion with a review of some empirical evidence relevant to these questions. Our conclusion is that this evidence is consistent with the following interpretation: strong general biases that favor genetically advantageous cultural variants may govern the evolution of some traits, but for others biases seem to have only a weak influence. For this latter important class of traits, other forces need to be considered.

An Overview of Biased Transmission
An analogy with statistics

We saw in Chapter 3 that although linear cultural transmission may affect the amount of variation of a trait in a population, it produces no evolutionary forces affecting the mean of the trait. It is useful to consider linear cultural transmission as analogous to statistical estimation. Each naive individual is exposed to a sample of the cultural variants present in the population, those variants that characterize his set of cultural parents. If we assume that sets of cultural parents are formed at random, then each such set of cultural variants constitutes an unbiased sample of the population. (This is not an unduly restrictive assumption; it means that we are defining changes in the distribution of variants in the population due to selective formation of sets of cultural parents as a form of natural selection. Such changes are analyzed in the next chapter.) The cultural variant acquired by each naive individual can be thought of as an estimate of the average value of the cultural trait in the population based on the sample to which that individual was exposed. To make this analogy more concrete, consider the case of vertical and oblique transmission of a quantitative character via the blending rule. This transmission rule is analogous to a weighted average of the (unbiased) sample, and as such it is an unbiased estimator of the mean value of the character among the pool of parents.

Transmission, by itself, will lead to evolutionary forces only when an offspring is disproportionately likely to acquire some variants, that is, when the cultural transmission rule is analogous to a biased estimator. When this is the case, we say that the transmission rule is biased. In the next section we sketch a taxonomy of biased cultural transmission and consider why the various kinds of bias might make adaptive sense.

Three types of biased transmission

It is useful to think of biased transmission as arising from the attempts of offspring to evaluate the adaptiveness (that is, their effects on genetic fitness) of the different cultural variants to which they are exposed. This is not to say that all, or even most, biases are necessarily adaptive, especially in contemporary societies. However, thinking about biases in this way enables us to generate predictions concerning which kinds of biases might be widely observed, predictions which then can be tested empirically.

Suppose that individuals are exposed to several different variants of a particular trait. Further suppose that some evolutionary force, such as the force of guided variation, has acted to increase the frequency of adaptive variants and reduce the frequency of maladaptive ones. Given these assumptions, the locally adaptive variants will also be the most common variants, and, therefore, a naive individual who simply picks a model at random and adopts his or her cultural variant would have a probability equal to the frequency of the variant of behaving in the locally adaptive manner. As we saw in the last chapter, such unbiased cultural transmission can be genetically adaptive.

It seems plausible, however, that a naive individual might increase its chances of acquiring the most adaptive variant by using some procedure to evaluate the cultural variants to which he or she is exposed. There are undoubtedly many different ways that this might be done. However, we believe that the three general classes of mechanisms are likely to be important in human cultural transmission. Each results in a different kind of biased transmission which we label "direct bias," "indirect bias," and "frequency-dependent bias." The following simple example illustrates the differences among these three kinds of biased transmission.

Suppose that a child is learning to play ping-pong by observing the play of several adult models and that there are two different ways to grasp a ping-pong paddle—the "pencil grip" and the "racquet grip." Once a player has adopted one grip, it is unusual to switch. Suppose each of the grips is used by at least one of the models. How might the child choose which grip to adopt? One way would be to randomly (with respect to grip) choose one model as a "role model" and copy his or her grip. For example, the child might imitate a parent. This would lead to unbiased transmission. The other answers to this question correspond to the different classes of biased transmission.

Direct bias. One way would be to try both kinds of grip and see which one seemed to work best. This is an example of direct bias. In general, we will say that a cultural transmission rule is characterized by direct bias if one cultural variant is simply more attractive than others. The direction of the bias need not be the same for all individuals; individuals with large hands or access to expensive paddles might prefer one grip while individuals with small hands or cheap paddles prefer the other. The problem with this method of evaluating the different grips is that it might take a lot of practice with a grip to become proficient enough to evaluate it. A fair test of both grips might occupy time that could be better spent perfecting one grip, especially if one has to be a fairly expert player before accurate judgments are possible.

Indirect bias. A second method of evaluating the grips would be to choose the grip used by the model who is the most successful ping-pong player. This is an example of indirect bias. In general, indirect bias results if offspring use the value of a second character that characterizes a model (e.g. success at ping-pong) to determine the attractiveness of that individual as model for the primary character (e.g. mode of gripping the paddle). This method of evaluating which grip to use is likely to be much less costly than directly evaluating both grips. It may also be less reliable. The best ping-pong player among the set of cultural parents may use the inferior grip and excel anyway because of some other factor such as reflex speed or strategic ability. Or it might be that the best player's grip is best for him, but that it is not best for a given child because they differ in some way.

Frequency-dependent bias. Another method of choosing between the two grips would be to pick the one used by most of the models. This is an example of frequency-dependent bias. In general, frequency-dependent bias will occur if the probability that offspring acquires a variant depends nonlinearly on the frequency of the variant among the set of cultural parents. Once again this method of judging the merit of different grips is much less time consuming than evaluating them directly. However, it will be a good method only if some process, like guided variation, ensures that the best grip is the most common.

Each of these three kinds of biased transmission can be thought of as resulting from attempts by naive individuals to evaluate the cultural variants to which they are exposed in a setting in which information is incomplete or costly to acquire. In this chapter we focus on directly biased transmission. Most procedures for evaluating which behaviors are adaptive in a wide range of habitats are likely to entail some kind of experimentation. As long as this experimentation is not too expensive, it is plausible that directly biased transmission might evolve. As we shall see, there is abundant empirical evidence that direct bias exists. When it is difficult or costly to evaluate the consequences of the variants available in the population directly, then indirect or frequency-dependent bias may be more advantageous. We will see in Chapters 7 and 8 that these modes of evaluation can be effective without any direct evaluation of the adaptive merits of the different variants and that empirical evidence suggests they are significant factors in human cultural transmission.

Comparing directly biased transmission and guided variation

The forces of directly biased cultural transmission and guided variation are similar because they both depend on "guiding criteria" for their direction. Recall that the force of guided variation results from the cultural transmission of behavior as modified by learning, where learning is taken to include the whole range of processes from simple conditioning to cognitively complex rational calculation. We argued that all of these processes require a guiding criterion that specifies the merit of different alternatives. Directly biased transmission is similar, except that now individuals select from among the alternative cultural variants that have been modeled for them rather than choosing among self-generated alternatives. In both cases, the guiding criteria allow the individual to rank the various alternatives. As in the case of simple kinds of learning such as operant conditioning, this selection process can be unconscious. As with guided variation, the guiding criteria that shape the direction of the directly biased transmission could be inherited genetically or culturally or learned independently.

One might sensibly ask, Is directly biased transmission of any use to an individual if it is so similar to guided variation? One answer is that the two processes are not mutually exclusive. The same cognitive apparatus used for ordinary learning could be equally well applied to sorting among culturally presented alternatives. A second answer is that it may be easier to sort among existing alternatives than to invent new ones. It seems intuitive that in most situations the search for alternatives is more costly than the evaluation of behaviors that have already been discovered. In such situations directly biased transmission can be effective even when ordinary learning is too costly to be significant in the determination of behavior.

Despite their fundamental similarity, the transmission of guided variation and directly biased transmission have different population-level consequences. The force of directly biased transmission depends on the existence of variability in the population. Naive individuals choose only from among the variants to which they are exposed. If they are exposed to only one variant, directly biased transmission can have no effect. If there is little variability in a population, most sets of parents will contain only one variant and the force that results from direct bias will be weak. In contrast, guided variation involves selection among internally generated alternatives. This process does not depend on the cultural repertoire of other individuals in the population. Thus the magnitude of the force of guided variation is independent of the amount of cultural variability in the population (see Eq. 4.11).

Models of Direct Bias

In this section we describe two classes of models of cultural transmission with direct bias, one based on the transmission of a dichotomous character and the second on the transmission of a quantitative character. Both of these models show how directly biased cultural transmission can increase the frequency of the culturally transmitted variants that are favored by the bias. Like natural selection, the magnitude of the force caused by directly biased transmission depends on the amount of variability in the population. In the subsequent section we consider the adaptive consequences of directly biased transmission.

A model of directly biased transmission of a dichotomous character

In this section, we modify the linear transmission rule discussed in Chapter 3 so that it allows for the possibility of direct bias. We begin with the simplest possible version of the model. Suppose that (1) there are two cultural variants, c and d, (2) cultural transmission is vertical, (3) there are two parents, and (4) both parents have equal weight in the transmission process. With these assumptions the linear transmission rule takes the form shown in Table 5.1. In Table 5.2 the linear rule has been modified by introducing a new parameter, B, which represents the effect of directly biased transmission. Notice that if $B = 0$, this rule reduces to a linear rule. If $B > 0$, then offspring who are exposed to cultural parents with different cultural variants will be more likely to acquire variant c than variant d. When $B > 0$ we say

Table 5.1 Rule for linear transmission with two models of equal weight

Variant of Model 1	Variant of Model 2	Probability That Offspring Acquires Cultural Variant	
		c	d
c	c	1	0
c	d	1/2	1/2
d	c	1/2	1/2
d	d	0	1

Table 5.2 Rule for directly biased transmission with two models

Variant of Model 1	Variant of Model 2	Probability That Offspring Acquires Cultural Variant	
		c	d
c	c	1	0
c	d	$\frac{1}{2}(1+B)$	$\frac{1}{2}(1-B)$
d	c	$\frac{1}{2}(1+B)$	$\frac{1}{2}(1-B)$
d	d	0	1

that the transmission rule is biased in favor of variant c, and when $B < 0$ we say that transmission is biased in favor of d. Since the probabilities that an offspring acquires c and d must sum to one, it follows that $0 \leq B \leq 1$.

To deduce the effect of biased transmission on the frequency of the two variants in the population, we proceed exactly as we did in Chapter 3. Suppose that the frequency of variant c before transmission in a particular generation is p and that sets of cultural parents are formed at random. Then the frequency of p after transmission, p', is found by computing the frequency of each different set of cultural parents, multiplying this times the probability that a particular set of cultural parents results in an offspring with a particular cultural variant, and then summing over all possible sets of cultural parents. In the case of two parents,

$$p' = p^2(1) + p(1 - p)(1/2)(1 + B) + (1 - p)p(1/2)(1 + B) \quad (5.1)$$

which can be simplified to become

$$p' = p + Bp(1 - p) \quad (5.2)$$

Equation 5.2 says that if $B > 0$ transmission will increase the frequency of variant c. This means that directly biased transmission creates a force that increases the frequency of the culturally transmitted variant that is favored by the bias. The magnitude of this force depends on the variance of the character in the population, $p(1 - p)$, and on the strength of the bias measured by the parameter B. The magnitude of the variance is important because the strength of the force caused by directly biased transmission depends on the probability that sets of parents with different cultural variants are formed. If one variant is very common, then most sets of cultural parents are characterized by the same variant. These transmission events have no effect on the frequency of the different variants in the population because directly biased transmission can only be effective if the offspring is exposed to parents with different cultural variants. In Equation 5.2 this condition is represented by the fact that the quantity $p(1 - p)$ approaches zero as p approaches one or zero.

The model also suggests that directly biased transmission has the property that relatively weak biases can have important effects on the frequency of different cultural variants in a population. The parameter B measures the extent to which a particular transmission event is biased. Equation 5.2 shows that small values of B can lead to relatively rapid change in the frequency of cultural variants in a population. For example, suppose that $B = 0.1$. This means that in 20 offspring exposed to one model with variant c and another with variant d, we would expect 11 offspring with variant c and 9 with variant d. To detect biases of this magnitude reliably would require the observation of a fairly large number of transmission events. As is shown in Figure 5.1, however, a bias of 0.1 can cause a rare variant to increase to high frequency in a few tens of generations. This property of cultural transmission is very important in the context of both the nature-nurture question and the sociobiology controversy because it means that weak, hard to measure, genetically transmitted biases can have large effects.

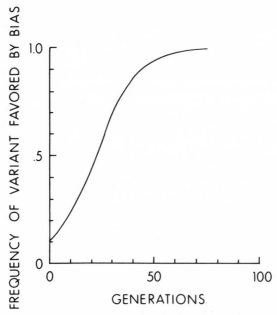

Fig. 5.1 The time path of the frequency of a cultural variant favored by directly biased transmission. The initial frequency of the favored variant is 0.1 and the bias parameter, B, is also 0.1.

A more complicated model

In many cases of interest, cultural traits are transmitted horizontally among peers. As we saw in Chapter 3, this requires a modification of the model to allow for the possibility that different cultural parents have different weights. In this section we will modify the model of directly biased transmission to allow for this possibility. We will see that there is an interesting interaction between unequal transmission by different parents and directly biased transmission.

In Chapter 3 we modeled horizontal transmission of a dichotomous trait as follows: Suppose that the frequency of trait c in the population is p. Then, each individual encounters $n - 1$ other potential models. The probability of encountering models characterized by a particular cultural variant will depend on the frequency of that variant in the population and perhaps on other factors as well. After encountering the $n - 1$ models, each individual then either retains his or her initial cultural variant or adopts the cultural variant of one of the models. Recall that in order to express the transmission rule algebraically we denoted the cultural variant of each model by a numerical value, X_i, where $X_i = 1$ if the ith model was characterized by the variant c and $X_i = 0$ if the ith model had the variant d. With these assumptions the probability that a particular individual is characterized by variant c after cultural transmission given that he was X_1 and was exposed to cultural parents with variants $X_2, \ldots, X_n$ is given by

$$\text{Prob}(c|X_1, \ldots, X_n) = \sum_{i=1}^{n} A_i X_i \qquad (5.3)$$

According to 5.3, each individual has a probability of A_1 of retaining its initial cultural variant and a probability of A_i of adopting that of the ith model. Such a rule causes no change in the distribution of cultural variants in a population (see the discussion in Chap. 3 on vertical transmission).

The essence of directly biased transmission is that the probability that a particular model is imitated should depend on whether the model is characterized by variant c or variant d. This means that the weight of the ith model should be a function of X_i. One simple way of doing this is as follows: let the function $\beta(X_i)$ be defined

$$\beta(X_i) = \begin{cases} B & \text{if } X_i = 1 \\ -B & \text{if } X_i = 0 \end{cases}$$

Then we can define the importance of the ith model, A_i, with X_i:

$$A_i = \frac{\alpha_i(1 + \beta(X_i))}{\sum_{j=1}^{n} \alpha_j(1 + \beta(X_j))} \tag{5.4}$$

Equation 5.4 says that the ith model has a "basic" weight, α_i. As argued in Chapter 3, these values may be different if some kinds of models are more salient than others. This basic weight is increased by a factor $1 + B$ if the ith model is characterized by variant c (assuming $B > 0$) and decreased by a factor $1 - B$ if the ith model is characterized by variant d. Finally, the weights are normalized by the denominator so that A_i gives the weight of the ith model relative to the other models encountered by the individual in question.

This model is not easy to solve for all values of B and n. In this section we consider the case in which individuals potentially change their cultural variant after each encounter with a potential model, which corresponds to $n = 2$. In the next section we will analyze a very similar model assuming a quantitative character for arbitrary n but small values of B. Suppose that the frequency of c before an episode of horizontal transmission is p. If we assume that each individual encounters a model with cultural variant c with probability equal to p, then the frequency of variant c after transmission, p', is given by

$$p' = p^2(1) + p(1 - p)\left(\frac{\alpha_1(1 + B)}{1 + B(\alpha_1 - \alpha_2)} + \frac{\alpha_2(1 + B)}{1 - B(\alpha_1 - \alpha_2)}\right) \tag{5.5}$$

where α_1 is the basic weight the individual places on his own previous cultural variant and α_2 is the weight of the model. Using the fact that $\alpha_1 + \alpha_2 = 1$, it can be shown that Equation 5.5 can be simplified to become

$$p' = p + p(1 - p)\left(\frac{4B\alpha_1\alpha_2}{1 - B^2(\alpha_1 - \alpha_2)^2}\right) \tag{5.6}$$

This result is qualitatively similar to Equation 5.2. As before, directly biased transmission creates a force that always increases the frequency of the variant that is favored by the bias. As in Equation 5.2, the magnitude of this force depends on the variance of c in the population and the magnitude of B. However, the relative importance of the model, α_2, and the ego, α_1, in horizontal transmission now affects the strength of the force of directly biased transmission. If the ego and the model are equally important (i.e. $\alpha_1 = \alpha_2 = \frac{1}{2}$), then Equation 5.6 reduces to Equation 5.2, as one would expect. However, if their weights are unequal, the magnitude of the force increasing the favored variant is always decreased. This effect is most important when B is small. This means that the force of direct bias is strongest when the variance *within* sets of parents is large.

Direct bias and quantitative characters

Chapter 3 includes discussions of two models of the cultural transmission of a quantitative character, a blending model and a multifactorial model. Both of these models have the property that cultural transmission by itself does not change the mean value of the character in the population. Transmission did affect the variance of the character in the population in both of the models, but in very different ways. In this section we modify the blending model so that it allows for the possibility of direct bias. We only analyze the effect of directly biased transmission on the mean. It can be shown that the effect of direct bias on the mean in the multifactorial model of quantitative inheritance is exactly the same as in the blending model.

Once again, suppose that cultural transmission is horizontal, and an individual (ego) who has the cultural variant X_1 encounters $n - 1$ other individuals (models) with variants X_i. Based on the observed behavior of the ith, Y_i, model, ego forms an estimate of his or her cultural variant, labeled Z_i. As in Chapter 3, we assume that

$$Z_i = X_i + e_i \tag{5.7}$$

where e_i is a normally distributed random variable with mean zero and variance E_i that represents the fact that a naive individual's estimate of the model's cultural rule may diverge from the inherited cultural rule of the model because of (1) environmental effects on the model's phenotype, (2) random variation of particular model performances, or (3) estimation errors by the naive individual. Here we consider only the special case in which the e_i are independent and have the same variance (i.e. $E_i = E_j = E$). According to the blending model, the ego's cultural rule after transmission will be

$$X_1' = \sum_{i=1}^{n} A_i Z_i \tag{5.8}$$

We introduce direct bias into this model in the same way as we did for the case of a dichotomous character. First we define a bias function $\beta(Z_i)$ that measures the extent to which different cultural variants are perceived as attractive. We then define the importance of the ith parent, A_i, exactly as in Equation 5.4, that is,

$$A_i = \frac{\alpha_i (1 + \beta(Z_i))}{\sum_{j=1}^{n} \alpha_j (1 + \beta(Z_j))} \tag{5.9}$$

In principle the distribution of cultural variants after transmission can then be calculated using Equation 3.22. However, in practice the fact that the right-hand side of 5.9 is a nonlinear function of Z_i makes this task difficult. To simplify the analysis we will assume that the biases are relatively weak. This means that the change in the distribution of cultural variants due to any single episode of cultural transmission is small. This assumption is represented mathematically by assuming that the bias function, $\beta(Z_i)$, is small compared to the value one for all possible values of Z_i.

With this assumption it can be shown that the mean value of X after the episode of cultural transmission, $\overline{X}'$, is given by

$$\overline{X}' = \overline{X} + [1 - 1/n_e]\text{Var}(Z) \, E\{\text{Reg}(Z,\beta(Z))\} \tag{5.10}$$

where

$$n_e = \sum_{i=1}^{n} \alpha_i^2$$

and $E\{\text{Reg}(Z,\beta(Z))\}$ is the regression of the bias function $\beta(Z)$ on Z averaged over all possible sets of models. This regression measures the extent to which a change in phenotypic value affects the probability of transmission. For example, if $E\{\text{Reg}(Z,\beta(Z))\}$ is positive, models with larger values of Z are on average more likely to be imitated. The greater the absolute value of $E\{\text{Reg}(Z,\beta(Z))\}$ the greater the effect. It is important to realize that both the sign and the magnitude of $E\{\text{Reg}(Z,\beta(Z))\}$ may depend on the distribution of Z. To see why this is so, consider Figure 5.2. In part a, the mean cultural variant in the population is smaller than Z^*, the value which maximizes $\beta(\cdot)$. In this case larger values of Z are favored by biased transmission and, therefore, $E\{\text{Reg}(Z,\beta(Z))\} > 0$. On the other hand, if the mean cultural variant in the population is larger than Z^*, $E\{\text{Reg}(Z,\beta(Z))\}$ is less than zero.

Equation 5.10 also shows that the change in the mean of a quantitative character due to the effect of directly biased transmission has the same qualitative properties as the model which assumed a dichotomous character. The magnitude of the force depends on the variance of the character in the population, Var(Z). All other things being equal, the larger the variance of the character the stronger the effect of directly biased transmission. The magnitude of the force also depends on the number of models (n) and the disparities in their weights. The term $(\sum_{i=1}^{n} \alpha_i^2)$ can be thought of as representing the "effective" number of cultural parents, n_e. If all parents have the same weighting, then $n_e = n$. If parents have unequal weightings, $n_e < n$.

This definition of the cultural transmission rule requires that $\beta(Z_i)$ be chosen so that $1 + \beta(Z_i)$ is greater than zero for all possible values of Z_i. One plausible form of $\beta(\cdot)$ that satisfies this condition is a Gaussian bias function

$$\beta(Z_i) = b \, \exp[-(Z_i - Z^*)^2/2J] \tag{5.11}$$

where $b \ll 1$. Equation 5.11 says that, given a choice between cultural parents with different variants, naive individuals will tend to imitate the cultural parent whose observed behavior is closest to the value Z^*. We will say that Z^* is the cultural variant favored by direct bias. The strength of this effect is measured by J. If J is

(a)

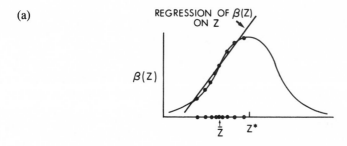

(b)

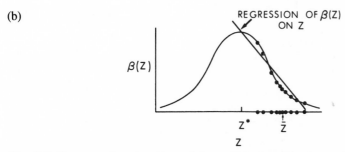

Fig. 5.2 Illustrates that the sign and the magnitude of the force of directly biased transmission acting on a quantitative character is proportional to the expected regression of the bias function on the character. In (a) the mean value of the character $\overline{Z}$ is less than the maximum of the bias function $\beta(Z)$, and therefore bias acts to increase the mean value of the character. In (b) the mean value of the character in the population is greater than the maximum of the bias function, and therefore bias acts to decrease the mean value of the character.

small, then small differences in the value of Z can have a large effect on the probability that a model is imitated. If J is large, then differences in observed behavior among models will have only a small effect on the probability that they are imitated.

With this assumption it is shown in Box 5.1 that the mean after biased transmission, $\overline{X}'$, is given by

$$\overline{X}' = \overline{X} + b(\overline{X}) \tag{5.12}$$

where

$$b(\overline{X}) = b(1 - 1/n_e)\left(\frac{(V + E)(Z^* - \overline{X})}{V + E + J}\right)\left(\frac{J}{V + E + J}\right)^{1/2} \exp\left(\frac{-(\overline{X} - Z^*)^2}{2(V + E + J)}\right)$$

The function $b(\cdot)$ gives the magnitude of the change in the mean cultural variant due to biased transmission and has the form shown in Figure 5.3. This figure indicates that if no other forces are operating on the population, the population will reach a stable equilibrium with a mean equal to Z^*, the cultural variant that is favored by biased transmission. Notice, however, that the magnitude of the force due to biased transmission first increases as the mean of the population is displaced from Z^* and then decreases. Thus, if a sudden environmental change caused the

---

Box 5.1 From Equation 5.10 we have

$$\overline{X}' = \overline{X} + [1 + 1/n_e][E\{\beta(Z)Z\} - E\{Z\}E\{\beta(Z)\}]$$

Using Equation 5.11 and result 1 from Box 4.3, we can calculate the two expected values

$$E\{\beta(Z)Z\} = \int (X + e)\beta(X + e)P(X)N(e)dX\ de$$

$$= b\left(\frac{J}{V + E + J}\right)^{1/2}\left(\frac{Z^*(V + E) + \overline{X}J}{V + E + J}\right)\exp\left(\frac{-(\overline{X} - Z^*)^2}{2(V + E + J)}\right)$$

$$\overline{X}E\{\beta(Z)\} = \overline{X}\int \beta(X + e)P(X)N(e)dX\ de$$

$$= b\overline{X}\left(\frac{J}{V + E + J}\right)^{1/2}\exp\left(\frac{-(\overline{X} - Z^*)^2}{2(V + E + J)}\right)$$

where $N(\cdot)$ is a normal density function with mean zero and variance E.

---

population to be very distant from the equilibrium, the force restoring the population to equilibrium would be very weak. On the other hand, biased transmission would cause the population to track small changes in the environment accurately.

An aside: Biased modeling

So far in this chapter we have assumed that biased transmission results from conscious or unconscious choices made by an individual in the process of acquiring a cultural trait. Biased transmission could also result from choices made by the cultural parents about which variants to model for their cultural offspring. Consider a hypothetical example in which the trait of driving habits is culturally transmitted. Suppose that there are two variants: some individuals like to drive recklessly, while others do not. Naive individuals acquire the variant of liking to drive recklessly through observation of models driving recklessly. Further suppose that everyone in

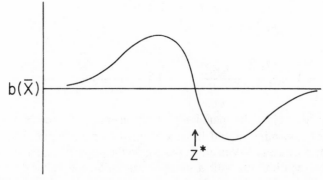

Fig. 5.3 The change during one generation in the mean of a quantitative character, $b(\overline{X})$, transmitted according to a directly biased cultural transmission rule, assuming a Gaussian bias function with a maximum at Z^*.

the population believes that reckless driving is dangerous but that the individuals who like to drive recklessly drive that way anyway. It seems plausible that the reckless drivers might want to avoid transmitting their driving habits to their offspring. They could do this by refraining from driving recklessly in the presence of their offspring, that is, by biasing their modeling. In general, we refer to any process in which experienced individuals selectively model different cultural variants as biased modeling.

Biased modeling results in a force that is similar to the force of guided variation. To see this consider the following simple model. Each offspring is exposed to two models who are characterized by one of two cultural variants, r for reckless and c for careful. Table 5.3 gives the linear transmission rule modified to represent the possibility of biased modeling. The parameters A_1 and A_2 give the weights of the two parents. The parameter $\mathcal{D}$ (for dissemble) gives the probability that a reckless parent will bias his or her behavior so that the offspring do not observe the reckless behavior. If nonselective mating is assumed, it is easy to show (see Box 5.2) that if p is the frequency of reckless individuals before transmission, then the frequency after transmission, p', is given by

$$p' = (1 - \mathcal{D})p \tag{5.13}$$

Unlike the force due to directly biased transmission, the force due to biased modeling does not depend on the amount of variability in the population, and in this way it is similar to guided variation. This is reasonable because from the point of view of the transmission process it is as if the parent had belatedly learned not to be reckless. Biased modeling will have different properties than guided variation if selection continues to act on the population, because selection will still be based on the phenotype that individuals inherited, not the one they model for their offspring.

Although it is possible to conceive of other kinds of biased teaching and modeling (Pulliam, 1983), we will not treat these in any detail in this or other chapters. We have chosen to do this simply because we must economize—the universe of potential models is far too large to exhaust. We believe that biased modeling and related processes will have properties that are very similar to those of guided variation and the various kinds of biased transmission with which we will deal. However, until such models are analyzed we cannot be sure. We can say, however, that empirical evidence suggests that the processes we have chosen to model are common, and the models indicate that these processes have novel and interesting dynamic properties.

Table 5.3 Transmission rule for an example of biased modeling

Variant of Parent 1	Variant of Parent 2	Probability That Offspring Acquires Cultural Variant	
		r	c
r	r	$1-\mathcal{D}$	$\mathcal{D}$
r	c	$A_1(1-\mathcal{D})$	$A_2+A_1\mathcal{D}$
c	r	$A_2(1-\mathcal{D})$	$A_1+A_2\mathcal{D}$
c	c	0	1

Box 5.2 Suppose that sets of cultural parents are formed at random. If p is the frequency of the "reckless" cultural variant before cultural transmission, then the frequency after transmission, p', is

$$p' = p^2(1 - \mathcal{D}) + p(1 - p)A_1(1 - \mathcal{D}) + (1 - p)pA_2(1 - \mathcal{D})$$

$$= (1 - \mathcal{D})\{p^2 + p(1 - p)(A_1 + A_2)\}$$

$$= (1 - \mathcal{D})p$$

Reprise

The three models of directly biased transmission analyzed in this section have several important qualitative properties in common:

1. Directly biased transmission creates a force that increases the frequency of the cultural variants that are favored by bias during the transmission process.

2. The magnitude of the force due to directly biased transmission depends on the amount of cultural variability that exists in the population. All other things being equal, the more variable the population, the greater the force.

3. Relatively weak biases that would be difficult to detect empirically can lead to rapid change in the frequency of different variants in the population, particularly when transmission has an important horizontal component.

4. A comparison of the models indicates that if one ignores the difference in generation time, vertical and horizontal transmission have very similar properties.

The Adaptive Consequences of Direct Bias

Bias is a derived force; to understand the evolution of a trait that is influenced by direct bias, we need to understand why cultural transmission has itself evolved to be biased in a particular way. Suppose that a particular cultural variant is common in a population. Further suppose that after some research we determine that it predominates as a result of the force of direct bias. At this point we might understand the dynamic processes that maintain the variant at high frequency, but we do not know why it is this variant and not some other that is favored by bias. To understand fully the evolution of the trait, we must also know why biased transmission has the particular direction and magnitude that it has in the population.

We will analyze the evolution of direct bias in much the same way that we did the evolution of guided variation in Chapter 4. We assume that the nature of the cultural transmission rule is genetically determined. Once again, we emphasize we make this assumption, not because we think that it necessarily pertains to contemporary humans, but because (1) it must have been true at some stage in the evolution of the human capacity for culture and (2) it formalizes the sociobiologists' use of the argument from natural origins. Even if the strength and direction of bias are traits like any other genetically transmitted trait, it turns out that unbiased transmission can evolve under plausible assumptions.

We will proceed in three steps. First we will describe a simple model in which alleles at a genetic locus determine the direction and magnitude of the force of direct bias. Next we will analyze the evolutionary properties of the model in a constant, homogeneous environment. In this kind of environment biased transmission will not be favored unless random variation is quite important. Finally, we will embed this model in a heterogeneous environment. In this case, it is very plausible that natural selection should favor biased transmission if the genetically transmitted character can favor the locally optimal variant in each of a variety of different habitats. Nevertheless, we also find that the conditions under which selection will cause neighboring populations to be genetically differentiated for cultural transmission biases are extremely restrictive.

A model of the genetic modification of direct bias

As before, assume that there are two cultural variants, c and d. Each naive individual is exposed to n cultural parents. The ith parent is characterized by a numerical value, X_i, equal to one if it has cultural variant c and equal to zero if it has variant d. Each individual is also characterized by one of three haploid genotypes, e, f, and h. It simplifies the notation to assign each individual a numerical genotypic value G, as follows:

$$G = \begin{cases} 0 \text{ if the individual is e} \\ 1 \text{ if the individual is f} \\ 2 \text{ if the individual is h} \end{cases}$$

Thus there are six possible combinations of cultural variant and genetic variant. It will become evident as we go along why we have chosen to keep track of three genotypes.

The assumed life cycles of genetic and cultural transmission are shown in Figure 5.4. The frequency of the individuals with genotype G and cultural variant X is F_{GX}. We use p to represent the frequency of variant c among models just before cultural transmission, and therefore $p = F_{01} + F_{11} + F_{21}$. q_G represents the frequency of genetic variant G at this stage in the life cycle; so $q_G = F_{G1} + F_{G0}$.

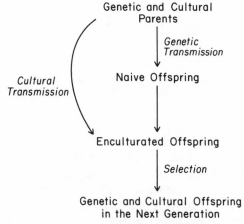

Fig. 5.4 The life cycle assumed in the model of the evolution of direct bias.

The probability that an offspring acquires the cultural variant c given that it (1) is exposed to parents with the cultural variants $X_1, \ldots, X_n$ and (2) has genotypic value G is given by

$$\text{Prob}(c|X_1, \ldots, X_n, G) = \frac{\sum_{i=1}^{n} \alpha_i X_i (1 + B_G)}{\sum_{i=1}^{n} \alpha_i (1 + B_G)} \tag{5.14}$$

This is the same model of biased transmission described in the previous section (see Eq. 5.9), except that the bias parameter, B_G, is indexed by G to indicate that offspring with different genotypes are characterized by different bias parameters. For example, offspring with genotypic value equal to one (i.e. genotype e) will have a cultural transmission rule characterized by the bias parameter B_1. We will always assume that $B_0 = 0$. This means that individuals with genotype 0 have an unbiased cultural transmission rule. We refer to genotype 0 as the unbiased allele. The values assigned to B_1 and B_2 will depend on the model. For example, to model what we call habitat-specific biases, we assume that B_1 and B_2 have the following values:

$$B_1 = B$$
$$B_2 = -B$$

This means that individuals with genotype 1 are characterized by a cultural transmission rule biased in favor of cultural variant c, and individuals with genotype 2 have a rule biased in favor of cultural variant d.

The effects of transmission. To derive the effect of transmission on the distribution of cultural and genetic variants, assume that genetic parents are drawn non-selectively from the pool of adults. Since genetic transmission leaves the frequency of each genotype unchanged, the frequency of genotype G among offspring is simply q_G'. Given that cultural parents and naive offspring associate randomly with regard to the offspring's genotype, and either (1) that there are just two cultural parents or (2) that biases are relatively weak, the frequency of individuals with genotype G and cultural variant X among offspring, F_{GX}', is given by

$$F_{G0}' = q_G[1 - p - b_G p(1 - p)]$$
$$F_{G1}' = q_G[p + b_G p(1 - p)] \tag{5.15}$$

The parameter b_G represents the effective strength of the force of direct bias when the offspring has the genotypic value G. The parameter b_G will be monotonically increasing with B_G, and when $B_G = 0$ it will always be true that $b_G = 0$. The exact relationship between the B_G and the b_G will depend on the number and weights of cultural parents (as for example in Eq. 5.6). The key feature of the model is that if the B_G are genetically controlled so are the b_G.

The six equations implied by Equation 5.15 have a simple intuitive interpretation. The population of naive offspring can be thought of as being divided into three subpopulations in which all individuals carry the same genotypic value. From the nature of genetic transmission we know that the subpopulation characterized by genotype G makes up a fraction q_G of the whole population. Individuals in all three subpopulations inherit their cultural variant from the same population of teachers. However, the subpopulation with genotype G is characterized by the bias parameter

b_G. Thus, a fraction $[p + b_G p(1 - p)]$ of the subpopulation with genotype G acquire cultural variant c and a fraction of the subpopulation $[1 - p - b_G p(1 - p)]$ acquire variant d.

The effects of selection. Now let us add natural selection to the model. As is conventional in population genetical models, differences in fitness are due to differences in probability of survival. Models with differences in fecundity can be much more complex. Let W_{GX} be the probability that individuals with cultural variant X ($X = 0,1$) and genotype G ($G = 0,1,2$) survive to become adults. Assume that the values of W_{GX} are as given in Table 5.4. The parameter s is a measure of the fitness of cultural variant 1 (c) in relation to cultural variant 0 (d). If s is positive, then individuals with cultural variant 1 are more likely to survive to adulthood than individuals with cultural variant 0. The parameter z is a measure of the cost of biased transmission. If z is positive, then, all other things being equal, the unbiased allele is favored over the biased alleles. This assumption is plausible because bias entails the evaluation of alternative variants just as in the learning models described in the last chapter. Thus, like learning, bias may entail costly experiments or additional neurophysiological machinery.

Table 5.4 The relative fitnesses of individuals with various combinations of genetically determined biases and cultural variants

Cultural Variant	Genotype		
	0	1	2
0	1	$1 - z$	$1 - z$
1	$1 + s$	$1 + s - z$	$1 + s - z$

With these assumptions, the frequency of individuals with the cultural variant X and genotype G among individuals who have survived to adulthood, F''_{GX}, is

$$F''_{GX} = \frac{W_{GX}F'_{GX}}{\sum_{G=0}^{2} (W_{G1}F'_{G1} + W_{G0}F'_{G0})} \qquad (5.16)$$

Equation 5.16 is exactly the same model of natural selection described in Chapter 4. The numerator gives the probability that an individual with cultural variant X survives, W_{GX}, multiplied by F'_{GX}, the frequency of individuals with cultural variant X and genetic variant G, and the denominator gives the average probability of survival for all individuals.

The evolution of direct bias in a homogeneous environment

Combining Equations 5.15 and 5.16 results in a set of three coupled recursions, one for the frequency of the cultural variant c and two for any pair of the genotypic frequencies. The nature of these recursions will depend on what is assumed about the bias and selection parameters. We begin our analysis by considering a model of the evolution of direct bias in a single homogeneous habitat in which cultural variant 1 (c) is always favored by natural selection and there are only two haploid genotypes, the unbiased allele and a genotype biased in favor of cultural variant 1 (c). We consider only cases in which the bias is costless ($z = 0$) or has a positive cost ($z > 0$). We represent this situation mathematically by assuming that the parameters take on the following values: $b_1 = b$, $s > 0$, $z \geqslant 0$, $q_2 = 0$.

Because one of the genotypes has been eliminated, we need only keep track of the frequency of the unbiased allele, q_0. To simplify the notation let $q_0 = q$. It can be shown that the recursions for these quantities are

$$q'' = q(1 + sp)/\overline{W}$$

$$p'' = p\left([1 + b(1 - q)(1 - p)](1 - z + s) + zq\right)/\overline{W}$$

(5.17)

where

$$\overline{W} = 1 + sp[1 + b(1 - p)(1 - q)] - z(1 - q)$$

and q'' and p'' are the frequencies of the unbiased allele and the cultural variant c in the next generation.

This system of recursions has very interesting behavior. (See Box 5.3 for mathematical details.) At equilibrium the frequency of the favored cultural variant is always one. If biased transmission has any direct effect on fitness ($z > 0$), then the only stable equilibrium frequency of the unbiased allele is also one. If biased transmission is completely costless ($z = 0$), then the equilibrium frequency of the two genotypes is indeterminate—all frequencies of the unbiased allele are neutrally stable equilibria.

To understand these results, consider the recursion for the frequency of q when selection is weak (i.e. z, $s \ll 1$) and p is fixed at some arbitrary value. Then

$$q'' = q + vq(1 - q)$$

(5.18)

where

$$v = b\{sp(1 - p)\} - z$$

This equation will be familiar to geneticists as the standard recursion for gene frequency at a haploid locus when selection is weak. The direction of change of the frequency of c depends on the sign of the parameter v, which is called the "selection differential" of the allele c. If the selection differential is positive, the frequency of the biased allele increases; otherwise it decreases. Notice that v depends on the frequency of the two cultural variants. The term in braces, $\{sp(1 - p)\}$, represents the intensity of selection on the cultural variants. Thus Equation 5.18 says that the strength of selection in favor of the bias allele is proportional to the intensity of selection on the cultural variants. Because variant c is always favored by selection (and by biased transmission as well if $q < 1$), this variant increases in frequency until the system reaches equilibrium at $p = 1$. At this equilibrium, there is no variation and thus the intensity of selection on the cultural variants is zero. This means that the fitness of the bias allele relative to the unbiased allele is $1 - z$, and therefore that the unbiased allele is always favored at equilibrium if $z > 0$. Put

Box 5.3 First consider the recursion for p. It is easy to show that $\hat{p} = 1$ and $\hat{p} = 0$ are equilibria for all values of q by simply substituting these values into both sides of the recursion. It is also easy to show that $\hat{q} = 0$ and $\hat{q} = 1$ are the only possibly equilibrium values of the recursion for q. Thus there are four possible equilibria of the form $(\hat{p}, \hat{q})$: (1, 1), (1, 0), (0, 1), (0, 0). To determine whether any particular equilibrium is stable, we need to evaluate the following matrix of partial derivatives at that equilibrium:

$$J = \begin{pmatrix} \dfrac{\partial p''}{\partial p} & \dfrac{\partial p''}{\partial q} \\ \dfrac{\partial q''}{\partial p} & \dfrac{\partial q''}{\partial q} \end{pmatrix}$$

If the absolute values of all of the eigenvalues of this matrix are less than one, then the equilibrium is stable.

The directional forces of selection and direct bias both act to increase p. This suggests that equilibria in which $\hat{p} = 0$ will be unstable. A rigorous analysis shows this intuition to be correct. The stability of the other equilibria is more subtle.

$$\frac{\partial q''}{\partial p} = \frac{sq\{\overline{W} - b(1 + sp)(1 - 2p)(1 - q)\}}{\overline{W}^2}$$

This derivative is equal to zero at both the possible stable equilibria (1,0) and (1,1). When one of the off-diagonal elements of a 2×2 matrix is zero the eigenvalues are just the diagonal elements of the matrix. Thus these equilibria will be stable if

$$\frac{\partial q''}{\partial q} = \frac{(1 + p)\{\overline{W} - q(z - sbp(1 - p))\}}{\overline{W}^2} < 1$$

At (1, 0) and (1, 1) this derivative has the values

$$\frac{\partial q''}{\partial q} = \frac{1 + s}{1 + s - z} \quad \text{and} \quad \frac{\partial q''}{\partial q} = 1 - z(1 + s)$$

Thus (1, 0) is unstable unless $z = 0$, and (1, 1) is stable unless $z = 0$. If $z = 0$, both equilibria are neutrally stable.

another way, in the absence of cultural variation, the cost of bias leads to its selective loss. Notice that this result is quite similar to the loss of guided variation in a constant environment, as we saw in Chapter 4.

The bias allele can only be favored if some force opposes natural selection and bias so that at equilibrium both cultural variants are maintained in the population. When this is the case, different cultural variants will have different fitnesses. Individuals with an appropriately biased transmission rule will have a higher probability of acquiring the cultural variant favored by selection, and genes leading to biased transmission may be favored by selection.

Several processes can maintain both variants in the population at equilibrium. The simplest is random variation. If the error rate of transmission is high enough (relative to the strengths of natural selection and biased transmission) to maintain both cultural variants at high frequency, then the bias allele may be favored.

Notice, however, that the maximum selection differential,

$$v_{max} = (bs/4) - z \qquad (5.19)$$

occurs when $p_1 = 1 - p_1 = 0.5$. Selection in favor of the biased allele depends on the product of b and s. Thus, if either selection or bias is weak, selection in favor of the bias allele will be weak also. However, if both bias and selection are strong, it seems unlikely that random variation will maintain sufficient variability to allow v to become large.

It should not be surprising that direct bias is unlikely to evolve in a population living in a constant, homogeneous environment. In such an environment, natural selection will tend to increase the frequency of the favored trait to a high frequency, whether there is any bias or not. An unbiased rule, for example "just copy mom," will result in a high probability of acquiring the most adaptive variant. Directly biased transmission will be favored only if there is a significant probability that naive individuals will be exposed to maladaptive variants, or, put another way, if they must choose among several different, potentially adaptive cultural variants.

Biased transmission in a spatially varying environment

Migration in a spatially varying environment is one force which plausibly might maintain enough variation to favor costly biases. Consider a population which is divided into two subpopulations which live in different habitats as in Figure 5.5. In subpopulation 1, the culturally transmitted variant c (i.e. cultural value, $X = 1$) is favored by natural selection relative to d (i.e. $X = 0$) by an amount $1+s:1$. In subpopulation 2, variant d is favored by an amount $1+s:1$. In each generation, after selection takes place, a fraction m of each subpopulation emigrates and is replaced by immigrants from the other subpopulation. In this model, some naive individuals will be exposed to cultural parents who have immigrated from the other sub-

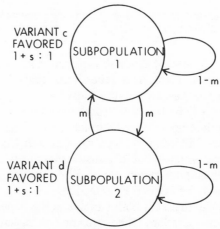

Fig. 5.5 The population structure assumed in the model of the evolution of direct bias in a spatially variable environment. The parameter m gives the fraction of each of the two populations that emigrates each generation.

population and are therefore more likely to be characterized by locally maladaptive cultural variants than are natal parents.

Because we are interested in the roles of genes and culture in determining the variation between human groups, we will consider two different models of the genetic control of bias. In the first, we will assume that a single allele causes cultural transmission to be biased in favor of the cultural variant that is favored in the local habitat. This model, the "general purpose bias" model, is a formalization of the view that humans are equipped with general purpose filters that cause them to select the cultural variant which is genetically adaptive in the local habitat (e.g. Alexander, 1979a; Irons, 1979a; Durham, 1976). In the second model, we will suppose that one allele biases cultural transmission in favor of variant c (and therefore against d), and the other allele biases cultural transmission in favor of variant d. This model, the "habitat-specific bias" model, is similar to the models of Lumsden and Wilson (1981), who argue that some of the cultural differences between human groups may result from genetic differences in the direction and magnitude of direct biases.

General purpose bias. Suppose that there are two genotypes. Individuals characterized by the unbiased genotype, $G = 0$, always have unbiased cultural transmission; the other genotype, $G = 1$, codes for a general purpose direct bias. Individuals with the bias allele have a cultural transmission rule that is directly biased by an amount B in favor of the cultural variant c in population 1 and cultural variant d in population 2. This means that individuals with the bias allele have a higher probability of acquiring the favored cultural variant than individuals with the unbiased allele in both habitats.

In the last chapter we saw that ordinary learning could lead to the development of the appropriate phenotype in a variety of habitats. Because directly biased transmission is the application of learning to preexisting culturally available variants, it may be reasonable to suppose that directly biased transmission may favor the locally adaptive variant in some range of habitats. For example, the cultural trait might be the mode of preparation of corn, one variant specifying an alkali treatment and the other not. In environments low in other sources of the amino acid mobilized by the alkali treatment, the treatment variant might be favored, while in other environments the no treatment variant might be favored. The bias might arise from two different guiding criteria: (1) an innate preference for balanced amino acid intake (e.g. rats come to prefer foods which contain nutrients in which their diet is deficient, and it is possible that a similar mechanism could evolve in humans), and (2) a preference for the least troublesome mode of preparing food. In environments low in lysine this combination of factors would lead to a preference for alkali treated corn. In other environments it would lead to a preference for the untreated corn. (This example is drawn from Katz et al., 1974.)

With these assumptions, we must keep track of four quantities: the frequency of one of the cultural variants and one of the genetic variants in each of the two subpopulations. Let p_i be the frequency of cultural variant c in subpopulation i, and let q_i be the frequency of the unbiased allele. (Notice that the meaning of the subscript on q has changed; it now indexes subpopulation.) As Box 5.4 shows, we derive recursions for these quantities by assuming that in each subpopulation the

Box 5.4 Let p_i'' be the frequency of cultural variant c before migration and q_i'' be the frequency of the general purpose bias allele before migration. Then the frequencies after migration, p_i''' and q_i''', are

$$p_1''' = p_1''(1 - m) + p_2''m$$

$$p_2''' = p_2''(1 - m) + p_1''m$$

$$q_1''' = q_1''(1 - m) + q_2''m$$

$$q_2''' = q_2''(1 - m) + q_1''m$$

Because of the symmetry of the model we know that the equilibrium frequency of the variant c in subpopulation 1 must equal the equilibrium value of variant d in subpopulation 2. Thus

$$\hat{p}_1 = 1 - \hat{p}_2$$

Similarly, the equilibrium frequency of the general purpose bias allele must be the same in both subpopulations. These facts greatly simplify finding the equilibria.
For example, consider the equilibrium value of p_1. Notice that

$$\hat{p}_1 = (1 - m)\hat{p}_1'' + m(1 - \hat{p}_1'')$$

$$= m + (1 - 2m)\hat{p}_1''$$

Then using Equation 5.17

$$\hat{p}_1 = m + (1 - 2m)\hat{p}_1\{[1 + b(1 - \hat{q}_1)(1 - \hat{p}_1)](1 - z + s) + z\hat{q}_1\}/\overline{W}$$

where $\overline{W}$ is as given in Equation 5.17. By rearranging this equation and applying the quadratic formula, one can show that the equilibrium value has the properties listed in the text.

---

model derived above applies and then adding an episode of migration. To analyze these recursions we first assume that the frequency of the unbiased allele is one, that is, there are no individuals in the population with biased transmission. The recursions lead to a stable equilibrium value of the locally favored cultural variant in each subpopulation (i.e. $\hat{p}_1$ in subpopulation 1 and $1 - \hat{p}_2$ in population 2) which is less than or equal to one and greater than or equal to one-half. Because of the symmetry of the model, the equilibrium frequency of the favored allele is the same in both subpopulations (i.e. $\hat{p}_1 = 1 - \hat{p}_2$). When there is no migration (m = 0) the equilibrium frequency of the favored allele is one. As the migration rate increases ($m \rightarrow \frac{1}{2}$), the equilibrium frequency of the locally favored allele moves close to one-half.

Under what conditions can the bias allele invade such a population? It can be shown that the frequency of the bias allele will increase whenever

$$\{(1 - \hat{p}_1)\hat{p}_1 s\}b > z \tag{5.20}$$

Because of the symmetry of the model the frequency of the favored cultural variant in either subpopulation can be used in Condition 5.20. This condition has two very important properties: first, it says that selection in favor of the bias allele depends on the product of s, the selection differential of the locally favored genotype, and b, the strength of biased transmission. Thus, if either s or b is small then selection in favor of the bias allele will be relatively weak. Second, selection in favor of the bias allele depends on the amount of variability for the cultural trait. This means that migration must be strong enough to maintain significant amounts of variation in the population.

It is also important to realize that as the bias allele becomes more common, the strength of selection in its favor will decrease. Directly biased transmission creates a force increasing the frequency of the locally favored variant. As the frequency of the bias allele increases, the equilibrium frequency of the locally favored variant will also increase, which will have the effect of decreasing the variability present (measured by $\hat{p}_i(1 - \hat{p}_i)$). This will weaken the selection in favor of the bias allele.

Condition 5.20 suggests that even if biased transmission has no cost (so that $z = 0$) the bias allele will increase slowly unless b and/or s is large. For example, suppose that $s = 0.1$, $b = 0.1$, $\hat{p}_1 = 1 - \hat{p}_2 = 0.9$ and that the initial frequency of the bias allele is 0.01. With these assumptions it will take about 5000 generations for the frequency of the bias allele to reach 0.5. If we assume that a human generation is about 20 years, 5000 generations corresponds to 100,000 years, roughly the age of the species "Homo sapiens" (Pilbeam, 1972: Chap. 8).

Habitat-specific bias. Next let us consider the evolution of two "special purpose" bias genotypes. Suppose that individuals characterized by genotype 1 always have a cultural transmission rule biased in favor of cultural variant c and that individuals characterized by genotype 2 always have a cultural transmission rule biased in favor of cultural variant d. This means that we must keep track of six quantities, the frequencies of one cultural variant and two genetic variants in each subpopulation. We have chosen to use the favored cultural variant in each subpopulation (i.e. c in subpopulation 1 and d in subpopulation 2), which we label p_i, and the two biased alleles $q_{1,i}$ and $q_{2,i}$ where in both cases i refers to the ith subpopulation.

With these assumptions, we can derive a system of six coupled recursions exactly as above. In this case we assume that the unbiased allele has an initial frequency of zero. This simplifies the calculations. It can be shown that at equilibrium both the frequency of the favored cultural variant and that of the allele that is biased in favor of the favored variant in each subpopulation are between one and one-half. Once again, the symmetry of the model causes the equilibrium frequency of the favored cultural variant and that of the allele biased in favor of that variant to be the same. As in the case of general purpose biases, increasing the migration rate moves the equilibrium values of the favored cultural variants closer to one-half.

Under what conditions can the unbiased allele invade such a population? It can be shown that it can invade whenever

$$[\hat{q}_1 - \hat{q}_2] \{(1 - \hat{p}_1)\hat{p}_1 s\} b < z \qquad (5.21)$$

where $\hat{q}_1$ and $\hat{q}_2$ are the frequencies of the alleles biased in favor of cultural variants c and d in population 1, the subpopulation in which cultural variant c is favored. For given values of s, b, and z, the fact that $\hat{q}_1$ and $\hat{q}_2$ are less than one guarantees it will be easier for the unbiased allele to invade a population with habitat-specific biases than one with general purpose biases. Just how much easier depends on the magnitude of the difference between the equilibrium frequencies of the two biased alleles. If this difference is small, then the unbiased allele will be able to invade a population with habitat-specific biases much more easily than a population with general purpose biases. If it is large, then there will be little difference between the two situations. Figure 5.6 shows critical values of the ratio z/s necessary for the unbiased allele to be able to invade a population with habitat-specific bias. Clearly, the habitat-specific bias must be very cheap if it is to evolve.

This result has a simple intuitive explanation. For directly biased transmission to be strongly favored by selection, migration must maintain enough variability to create a significant probability that offspring will be exposed to maladaptive variants. This means that migration must be a strong force relative to selection. Habitat-specific bias can be advantageous only if alleles for the bias appropriate to a particular habitat are more common in that habitat than other alleles. Natural selection acts to increase the frequency of such alleles because directly biased transmission generates an association between them and the locally favored cultural variant. Because the effect of selection on bias alleles is indirect, the intensity of selection on the alleles is always less than the intensity of selection on the cultural variants themselves. This means that migration is a strong force relative to the selection of the bias alleles, and therefore, we should not expect alleles that code for the appropriate habitat-specific bias to become very much more common than the other biased allele.

We expect this effect to be quite robust. It arises from two factors which do not depend on the details of the particular model presented above. If the environment is nearly constant and the force of random variation is weak compared to selection, biased transmission is not needed; selection alone will do the job. If environmental variation is great enough to make bias profitable, then, because selection on the

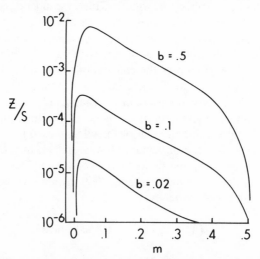

Fig. 5.6 The threshold values of the ratio of the cost of bias (z) to the selection advantage of the locally favored variant (s) as a function of the migration rate (m) for three values of the bias parameter, b. If the value of z/s exceeds this threshold value, the unbiased allele is favored relative to two habitat-specific bias alleles.

determinants of bias is indirect, it will always be weaker than the selection acting on the cultural variants themselves. The variations in the environment will also attenuate the genetic differentiation necessary for genetically transmitted habitat-specific biases to be effective. Pulliam (1983) has reached similar conclusions with a somewhat different model. We conjecture that these results are one instance of a more general phenomenon. Namely, natural selection (acting on genes) usually will not favor the cultural transmission of behavior unless cultural transmission can accomplish something that could not be achieved through genetic transmission alone. A population with habitat-specific bias is adapting to a spatially variable environment through the genetic differentiation of the population, a mode of response to varying environmental conditions that is available to noncultural species. In fact, ordinary genetic adaptation works better without the existence of the intervening process of cultural transmission. In contrast, a population with general purpose biases is adapting to the varying environment in a manner not available to noncultural organisms, and, we conjecture, therefore general purpose biases can be favored by selection.

An Evaluation of Sociobiological Hypotheses
Guided variation and direct bias are "sociobiological" forces

As we have noted, the forces of guided variation and directly biased transmission are derived forces; if they are the only forces that affect cultural evolution, then we should expect that the human sociobiologists will be successful in predicting human behavior using sociobiological theory. The force of guided variation tends to increase the frequency of the cultural variants that are favored by learning. Similarly, the force of biased transmission increases the frequency of the variant favored by bias. Ultimately, to explain the direction of each force, we must understand what has shaped the evolution of the direction and magnitude of guided variation and direct bias. We have taken pains to emphasize that the guiding criteria may be inherited culturally, and therefore that their evolution may be explained in terms of the forces that affect the frequency of cultural variants. However, if the only forces which shape cultural evolution are guided variation and directly biased transmission, this would seem of little consequence; in the end, the only organizing force in cultural evolution would be natural selection acting on genetically transmitted predispositions, and we would expect that, with the usual caveats, we would be able to predict cultural variation by asking what increases genetic fitness.

In the next three chapters, we will investigate several autonomous forces of cultural evolution, forces which do not derive their direction from guiding criteria in any simple way. Before doing this, however, it will be useful to consider whether the sociobiological models we have developed so far are adequate, at least in principle, to explain the evolution of the diversity of behaviors that characterizes different human groups. If the models are adequate as they stand, then we could conclude that human sociobiologists have developed a cogent hypothesis. As we shall see, even the limited range of models that we have analyzed so far can be interpreted in a variety of ways to explain human behavioral variation. We will conclude that some of these interpretations are plausible, while others are not.

Explanations for the differences between human groups

Compared with other animals, behavior in the human species is extremely varied. Individuals belonging to different human groups exploit a wide range of habitats using a variety of disparate subsistence techniques; they utilize widely different kinds of clothing and shelter, perform different rituals, depend on different kinds of social and political organization, and speak different languages. Although it could be argued that the social organization and adaptive strategy of most human groups are similar to those found in some other species, there is no other single animal species which exhibits the range of behaviors that characterize the human species.

The only two sources of the behavioral and morphological variation between populations of noncultural organisms are environmental variation and genetic variation. Two genetically identical populations may differ because they live in different environments, the same genetically transmitted developmental program giving rise to different phenotypes in the different environments. Or two populations in similar environments may differ because they have different genetic compositions, either because selection has favored different genotypes in the different environments or because of some historical accident, such as random genetic drift.

It is possible to explain the differences between human populations in terms of the same mechanisms that are at work in other species. In the human case, however, heritable cultural variation provides another potential source of variation. Two genetically identical human populations living in the same environment may behave differently because they have different culturally transmitted traditions. To take an obvious example, genetically similar individuals from different populations which live in similar environments might speak very different languages.

A large number of other proposals have been advanced to explain how learning, genetic transmission, and cultural transmission interact to determine human behavior (e.g. Ruyle, 1973; Durham, 1976; Boehm, 1978; Alexander, 1979a, b; Harris, 1979; Baldwin and Baldwin, 1981; Lumsden and Wilson, 1981; Plotkin and Odling-Smee, 1981). Virtually all of them rely on some combination of ordinary learning, guided variation, and directly biased transmission to explain human adaptations. We think it is useful to think of these views as varying in two dimensions: the first is the relative importance of environmental variation versus genetic variation, and the other is the importance of heritable cultural variation. From this perspective there are four polar hypotheses, as Table 5.5 shows.

Table 5.5 Four polar hypotheses regarding the relative importance of genetic and cultural variation in explaining behavioral variation in humans

	Heritable Cultural Variation Unimportant	Heritable Cultural Variation Important
Genetic Variation Unimportant	Pure environment	Environment + culture
Genetic Variation Important	Pure genes	Genes + culture

Proponents of the "environmental" hypotheses in the first row agree that the differences between human populations are due to responses to different environments and that the genetic differences between human groups are relatively trivial. Human behavior results from the interaction of a panhuman genetic program and a variable environment. The hypotheses differ in the emphasis given to heritable cultural variation. Proponents of a "pure environment" hypothesis would argue that the forces of guided variation and biased transmission are so strong that no understanding of the dynamics of cultural evolution is required. Richard Alexander's (e.g. 1979a) approach approximates this view. In contrast, adherents of a "culture plus environment" hypothesis would argue that these forces are relatively weak; in the short run most of the variation between groups is the result of different culturally transmitted traditions. In the longer run, however, the forces of guided variation and biased transmission are seen as ensuring that cultural variations are genetically adaptive. William Durham (1976, 1977, 1978, 1982) has defended a position close to this one in several papers.

Adherents of the "genetic" hypotheses of the second row agree that the differences between human populations are due primarily to genetic differences. They disagree on the extent to which these differences are mediated by cultural transmission. A proponent of the "pure genes" view would hold that most of the differences between human populations are simply due to genetic differences. One proponent of this view, C. D. Darlington (1969: 35), went so far as to ascribe the differences in language between human groups to genetically inherited differences in the morphology of the vocal tract. While not nearly so extreme, some of the models presented by Lumsden and Wilson (1981, see especially their Chap. 6) attribute differences between human groups to a combination of genetic differences and ordinary learning with little role for cultural transmission as we have defined it. Proponents of a "culture plus genes" view might concede that cultural transmission is important in determining human behavior, but there is genetic variation for the guiding criteria that govern the direction and magnitude of the forces of guided variation and biased transmission. Individuals in each local population have genetically transmitted biases that predispose them to acquire locally adaptive variants. In this way behavior can be culturally transmitted but at the same time the differences between populations are ultimately determined by genetic differences. The models presented in the early chapters of Lumsden and Wilson come close to this genes plus culture hypothesis.

In the remainder of this chapter we recast each of these four polar sociobiological hypotheses in the dual inheritance framework we have developed so far. We think that this is a fruitful exercise for two reasons. First, it can shed some light on what must be assumed to make each of the hypotheses plausible. Based on this exercise we will argue that the conditions necessary to support the pure genes and the genes plus culture views are extremely restricted. Second, there are good empirical reasons to suppose that the forces of guided variation and directly biased transmission are often quite weak, and therefore that the culture plus environment view is appropriate for at least some traits. This makes it more likely that other forces of cultural evolution are important and thus that the models of subsequent chapters are interesting.

The pure environment hypothesis

The pure environment hypothesis holds that human behavior results from the interaction between panhuman, genetically transmitted developmental rules and the local environment. Different human groups have different behaviors because individual humans quickly determine the best behavior in the local environment. The adherents of this hypothesis hold that there is little important genetic variation for behavior in the human species and that the transmission properties of culture are also unimportant. In the terms of the model of guided variation presented in Chapter 4, the most extreme version of this hypothesis requires that individuals be capable of acquiring enough information to be able to modify their behavior to maximize genetic fitness, no matter how much information must be acquired. In a less extreme version of the hypothesis, a flow of ideas among people living in different environments would allow some heritable cultural variation.

We believe that the views of Richard Alexander come close to the pure environment hypothesis. While Alexander does not think that learning is perfect, he clearly believes that bias and guided variation are strong enough to completely dominate the evolutionary dynamics of culture. Alexander (1979a: 78–79) writes:

> To whatever extent the use of culture by individuals is learned—and if this is not the rule then one is at a loss to explain how any special human capacity to use and transmit culture could have evolved—*regularity of learning situations or environmental consistency is the link between genetic instructions and cultural instructions which makes the latter not a replicator at all but, in historical terms, a vehicle of the genetic replicators.*

Cultural inertia, Alexander (1979a: 77) thinks,

> derives from the conflicts of interest among individuals and subgroups, from power distributions that result in stalemates, and from the incidental long-term persistence of some cultural institutions.

Thus Alexander does not view cultural transmission as a process that can preserve variation in the face of the forces of guided variation and direct bias.

In some respects, the pure environment hypothesis is a plausible one. Guided variation and directly biased transmission are powerful mechanisms for causing cultural evolution to generate behaviors that favor genetic fitness. Whenever it is easy to determine what is the best behavior in the local habitat, we might expect that the pure environment hypothesis will be approximately correct. Examined closely, the pure environment hypothesis boils down to the proposition that what we have defined as culture, the transmission of information via social learning, is relatively unimportant. A combination of ordinary genetic traits, a powerful system of ordinary learning, and very selective learning from others are sufficient to account for human behavior.

There are two reasons to suspect that, contrary to the pure environment hypothesis, culture has an important role in determining the differences between human groups. First, we think that the empirical evidence reviewed in Chapter 3 suggests that culture behaves as a fairly conservative transmission system. Second, it is plausible, on both theoretical and empirical grounds, that for many kinds of characters strong direct bias and guided variation would simply be too costly; they would require too much effort to evaluate the state of the environment and the payoffs to various strategies in such an environment.

To understand why we think learning generally may be quite costly, consider the example of the East African groups studied by Edgerton, which were discussed in Chapter 3. Consider a group of individuals who move from a moist region in which horticulture predominates to an arid region where they adopt pastoralism as an important part of their subsistence. It seems reasonable that many beliefs and values which were adaptive in a purely horticultural society would no longer be adaptive in the new habitat. What is the right mix of herding and farming? What are the relative values of land and cattle? How should one behave toward one's male kinsmen? Toward one's neighbors? How many children should a family have? The adherents of the pure environment hypothesis would imagine that the new pastoralists could easily determine the answers to these questions by themselves or, alternatively, observe a wide range of strategies employed by others and easily select the best ones for their own situation.

We are more impressed with the difficulties of most of these choices. When yield varies from year to year and from place to place, determining the optimal mix of herding and farming might be quite difficult. A useful trial of a particular strategy could occupy a substantial portion of a person's life. It seems even more difficult to determine the correct family size or the proper attitudes toward relatives. For these kinds of traits, copying the strategies of other individuals, perhaps making marginal improvements, seems a more practical course. This in turn would have the effect of weakening the forces of guided variation and biased transmission, and therefore of allowing substantial heritable cultural variation. As we noted in Chapter 3, Edgerton's data support this view.

All human choices may not be so difficult. Behaviors whose consequences are obvious or at least easy to learn should evolve rapidly when conditions change under the influence of direct bias and guided variation. For example, Edgerton (1971: 281) notes that cultural heritage explains little of the variation in behavior surrounding conflict among neighbors. The farming groups are all characterized by repressed hostility, suspicion, and the use of covert means of aggression such as witchcraft, while the pastoralist groups openly express their aggression. Edgerton argues that these differences result from the differences in individual mobility under the two subsistence modes. Farmers who quarrel with their neighbors incur a grave risk of a lengthy, costly feud because land ownership keeps neighbors in proximity to each other. Pastoralists who quarrel, by contrast, can simply move their camps to distant locations. It is easy to believe that pastoralists could recognize that their mobility permits free expression of discontent with their neighbors and that farmers could foresee the consequence of feuding.

The environment plus culture hypothesis

It is possible to include an important role for culturally transmitted traditions and still maintain that human behavior can, on average, be predicted by considerations of what maximizes genetic fitness. The key to this culture plus environment hypothesis is the fact that direct bias and guided variation do not have to be very strong forces in order to have important effects. For example, suppose that each naive offspring acquires one of two cultural variants according to a directly biased transmission rule such that b = 0.1. This means (from Table 5.2) that the probability that an offspring who is exposed to a set of cultural parents with different cultural variants will adopt the favored variant is only 0.55. Nonetheless, when the favored variant is rare it will increase at a compounded rate of 10 percent per generation! The model of cultural evolution by guided variation has similar properties.

This hypothesis is clearly consistent with the evidence that culture is a stable inheritance system. It is only supposed that direct bias and guided variation keep cultural variation on track in the long run. In the short run, most of the variation between groups can be explained in terms of cultural history. Such weak biases are also consistent with the hypothesis that it is costly for individuals to evaluate the merit of alternative cultural variants. Suppose that two alternative variants are tested in a series of trials. Thus, for example, one trial of each alternative might yield a 55 percent chance of choosing the superior one, two trials 59 percent, three trials 62.5 percent, and so on. If the cost of a single trial is significant, then weak biases may be relatively cheap compared with strong ones.

William Durham (1977, 1978, 1979, 1982) has defended a view of cultural evolution very close to the culture plus environment hypothesis. Durham clearly believes that culture is an inheritance system:

> An attribute may increase in frequency in a human population when it is spread by learning and maintained by tradition. Here the transmission of the attribute may be completely distinct from the biological processes of inheritance. Instead of differential reproduction, theories of cultural evolution propose that human attributes result from the differential replication by learning and imitation of variants introduced into a "cultural pool" by innovation and diffusion. [1979: 40]

Durham nonetheless believes that these culturally transmitted behaviors are usually biologically adaptive. Durham identifies four mechanisms which ensure that culturally transmitted behavior is adaptive. Three of these correspond to the mechanisms of direct bias or guided variation as we have defined them:

> People remain somehow selective in their receptivity to cultural innovation. . . . I believe that this ongoing selective retention is, and always has been, influenced by a number of human biases which tend to keep people from selectively retaining cultural attributes that run counter to their individual survival and reproduction. . . . Of these, perhaps the most important are learned biases. Robert LeVine (1973) has argued that the process of socialization teaches children from an early age not only adherence to social norms and traditional patterns of behavior but also selectivity in the adoption of new forms—a selectivity based on what is held to be adaptive and "for their own good."
>
> A second sort of bias might be called the bias of "satisfaction." Presumably throughout the organic evolution of hominids there was a persistent, genetic selective advantage for a neurophysiology which rewarded with sensory reinforcements and a feeling of 'satisfaction' those acts likely to enhance survival and reproduction. . . .

> There is potentially a third source of bias to be found in the learning structures and functions of the human brain. . . . [Durham, 1978: 431–432]

Durham's fourth mechanism is not a bias in our terms, but the natural selection of cultural variations. We will consider this topic in the next chapter.

The pure genes hypothesis

The pure genes hypothesis holds that the observed differences between different human groups have a significant genetic component. The most extreme version of this hypothesis would posit that human behavior is a highly canalized genetically controlled character, like finger number. In this view, most of the differences that are usually attributed to tradition are genetic. Very few contemporary scholars hold such an extreme hypothesis. However, there are many scholars who, while allowing an important role for environment, learning, and culture, believe that at least some significant portion of the differences between human groups has a genetic basis.

The simplest genetic hypothesis holds that only genetic and environmental differences are important and that the dynamic properties of cultural transmission can safely be ignored. The models of "cultural evolution" presented by Lumsden and Wilson (1981) in Chapters 5 and 6 fall into this category. Lumsden and Wilson imagine that there are two behavioral variants which they call "culturgens" and that every individual is aware of both variants. What varies between individuals in their model is the variant actually used. They suppose that, every so often, each individual evaluates its behavior and with some probability stops using the variant that it currently uses and adopts the alternative variant. This constitutes a simple model of learning. If individuals characterized by variant 1 are more likely to adopt variant 2 than individuals characterized by 2 are to adopt 1, then the learning process (or, as they put it, the "epigenetic rule") favors variant 2. Lumsden and Wilson do allow the frequency of usage of the two variants among an individual's peers or among members of the parental generation to affect the probabilities of switching behaviors. In our terminology, this constitutes a form of cultural transmission. However, in their actual analysis, transmission is assumed to be so weak in its effects that it has no qualitative impact (Lumsden and Wilson, 1981: 288).

It is important to understand that Lumsden and Wilson do not assert that transmission effects are always unimportant; in fact, they analyze other models in which such effects have an important role. However, their strongest claims about the general nature of human evolution are derived from the model described above (Lumsden and Wilson, 1981: 286–300). At the very least they appear to believe that it applies to some important portion of human behaviors.

Lumsden and Wilson introduce genetic variation into their model by assuming that a single diploid genetic locus (with two alleles) affects the probability of changing usage from one cultural variant to the other. Individuals who are homozygous for one of the alleles switch from one variant to the other with a constant probability of one-half. They refer to this homozygote as the "tabula rasa" genotype. Individuals who are homozygous for the other allele have a probability greater than one-half of switching from the deleterious cultural variant to the favored cultural variant, and a probability of remaining with the favored variant that is also greater than one-half. This homozygote, which they refer to as the bias genotype, has a genetic predisposition to learn to use the cultural variant favored by natural selection. Heterozygotes are assumed to be either tabula rasa or biased depending on the direction of dominance.

Based on this model, Lumsden and Wilson then go on to show that the biased allele will increase very rapidly in frequency. They argue for the adoption of a rule of thumb, which they call the "thousand year rule," to the effect that human populations which exist in the same environment for roughly 1000 years should have genes which cause individuals to preferentially acquire the locally favored phenotypic variants. Lumsden and Wilson do not explicitly apply this to the question of the differences between human groups. Their model deals with a single population in an unchanging environment. However, it is easy to interpret them (e.g. Maynard Smith and Warren, 1982) as implying that human populations that are separated for more than 1000 years should be expected to be genetically differentiated at loci which control the learning process.

Whatever Lumsden and Wilson might have intended, their model gives no justification for a general "thousand year rule." The rapid change in gene frequency in their model is due to two assumptions: First, they assume that selection on the phenotype is extremely strong; one variant has a fivefold advantage in the gathering of resources. This advantage translates into fitness in a complicated way which nonetheless maintains a substantial difference in fitness (Maynard Smith and Warren, 1982). Second, they assume that there is no migration between populations living in different habitats. We have seen that selection on the determinants of bias is weak unless selection is quite strong and learning quite effective. For this reason, generally a small amount of migration among groups will be sufficient to prevent the populations from differentiating genetically. From the viewpoint of our models, Lumsden and Wilson chose the only situation which would yield a significant amount of genetic differentiation between populations.

Lumsden and Wilson's model is curious in another way. In discussing the origin of human cognition (pp. 329–330), Lumsden and Wilson imagine that "cosmic good fortune" was required to overcome the initial costs of elaborate human cognitive abilities. In the particular model to which we have been referring, bad fortune seems a more apt description. The tabula rasa genotype is assumed to acquire one of the two phenotypic variants at random; in effect, tabula rasa individuals choose their phenotype by flipping a coin. The biased genotype which bears the cognitive costs does only slightly better. Since Lumsden and Wilson assume a constant environment, a fixed genetic specification of the appropriate behavior would clearly be an advantage, and so would an accurate but unbiased system of social learning. What Lumsden and Wilson have shown is that a genetically determined learning rule is superior to choosing behavior at random in an environment in which learning is of no utility. It seems to us that this result is not very surprising, and that the more interesting question is whether there are any circumstances in which accurate, weakly biased or unbiased social learning is superior to any combination of individual learning and genetic transmission. The models analyzed in this chapter and the last one suggest that such conditions do in fact exist (see also Pulliam, 1983).

The genes plus culture hypothesis

The final hypothesis we consider is the genes plus culture hypothesis. Proponents of this hypothesis hold that the transmission properties of culture are important, and that, in the short run, much of the behavioral variation both between and within human beings is attributable to heritable cultural variation. In the long run, however, this hypothesis holds that the direction of cultural evolution is determined by the forces of guided variation and directly biased transmission, and that the strength and direction of these forces vary among human populations because of genetic differences among them. For example, it might be supposed that one population has genes that predispose its members to adopt patrilineal social organization and a second population has genes that bias cultural transmission in favor of matrilineal ideology. In this way the lion's share of human behavior can be transmitted culturally, and at the same time the differences between human groups are ultimately attributable to genetic variation.

We know of no author who has explicitly defended a genes plus culture position. However, this hypothesis is implicit in the work of Lumsden and Wilson. In Chapter 4 of their book, *Genes, Mind, and Culture,* Lumsden and Wilson describe their most general model of the process of cultural transmission. In this model they allow the usage rate of a particular phenotypic variant in a population to affect the probability that individuals will adopt that variant. This introduces a combination of vertical, oblique, and horizontal cultural transmission into their model. They use this model to explain the historical inertia of cultural evolution and the shape of the frequency distribution usage rates among different societies or, in their terminology, "the ethnographic curve." When genetic determination of the rules of cultural transmission is added to their model, Lumsden and Wilson almost eliminate any cultural transmission from it. It seems clear from their discussion (p. 286) that this was done for mathematical convenience (i.e. the complete model was too difficult to solve), and that Lumsden and Wilson see the same basic evolutionary process governing both the genes that bias social learning and those that bias ordinary learning.

We think that the results of this chapter suggest that the genes plus culture hypothesis is unlikely to be correct. We considered two models of the evolution of genes that underlie direct bias in a spatially varying environment—one in which an allele for a general purpose bias competed against an allele for accurate and unbiased transmission (the unbiased allele) and a second in which two alleles, each biasing cultural transmission in favor of a specific variant, competed with an unbiased allele. We saw in the first model that alleles for general purpose biases could be favored by selection under a range of conditions. To the extent to which these conditions are plausible, this conclusion supports the culture plus environment hypothesis. In contrast, the second model suggests that it is very unlikely that alleles for habitat-specific biases could outcompete an unbiased allele. When migration between different habitats is weak, natural selection increases the frequency of the locally favored cultural variant so that biases can have little additional beneficial effect. When migration is strong it swamps the genetic differentiation that is necessary if genetically transmitted habitat-specific biases are going to be effective. A similar model can be constructed for the case of guided variation, and it yields the same qualitative result.

The Empirical Evidence

The four sociobiological hypotheses outlined above suggest a variety of important empirical questions. Are direct bias and guided variation typically strong or weak? Do direct bias and guided variation typically act to increase the frequency of fitness-enhancing cultural variants? Is there any evidence that there is genetic variation within or among groups for characters which affect direct bias and guided variation? These and other empirical questions must be answered before we can understand the role of culture in human evolution.

In this section we consider some of the empirical evidence that bears on the question, How strong are the forces of guided variation and direct bias? In the remainder of this book we will consider the effects of natural selection on asymmetrically transmitted cultural variation, frequency-dependent bias, and indirect bias. We will see that all of these three processes may act to increase the frequency of cultural variants that have lower genetic fitness than some other variants. We refer to these three processes as "maladaptive," recognizing that, while their effect on any particular trait may be maladaptive, it is still plausible that, taken over many cultural traits, they are adaptive. These maladaptive processes will be important only if direct bias and guided variation are weak enough to permit some characters to have substantial cultural heritability.

The other questions listed are also clearly of interest. We have chosen not to try to address them for several reasons. First, several of them are addressed at some length in the sociobiological literature. We have neglected some because we are less interested in which sociobiological hypothesis is most likely to be correct than we are in examining alternative models in which the "maladaptive" forces are important. Finally, the existing empirical evidence seems to us to be too flimsy to provide convincing answers to these general questions about the nature of guided variation and direct bias.

Evidence from the studies of the diffusion of innovations

Studies of the diffusion of innovations provide a useful body of data for judging the relative importance of strong versus weak direct bias. Modern science and technology have developed a cornucopia of useful techniques and products that present potential users of such technology with a wide variety of choices of new cultural behaviors. The individual decision to adopt or not adopt proffered innovations is a relatively simple one. Most of the innovations that have been studied involve economic or health advantages, and the great expense and complexity of developing the innovation have been borne by others. Often, cadres of specialists act as "change agents" to bring potentially useful innovation to the attention of potential users. The adopters need only assess the suitability of the innovation to their own situation and, if they choose to adopt, learn to adapt the innovation to local circumstances. These seem to us to be very favorable conditions for direct bias to be a strong force increasing the frequency of favorable innovations.

Rogers with Shoemaker (1971) reviewed over 1000 studies of the diffusion of innovations using the method of content analysis. (Also see Rogers, 1983, for a more recent discussion of these data.) The effect of direct bias is clearly evident in many of the cases they examine. The classic examples are the adoption of hybrid corn seed and 2,4-D weedkiller by farmers in the United States. Both these innovations were adopted by virtually all farmers within ten years of their introduction. Similar rates of adoption of steel cutting implements in place of stone tools by aboriginal cultivators have frequently been observed. Rogers and Shoemaker also discussed cases in which useless innovations were effectively avoided. They (Rogers with Shoemaker, 1971: 139) summarized: "Almost every one of these studies reports a positive relationship between relative advantage [of innovations compared to existing practices] and their rate of adoption. Perhaps this result is so self-evident as to be of little surprise." Clearly, direct bias can be a potent force.

However, much of their discussion focused on the difficulty of diffusing objectively useful innovations to potential users. These problems are illustrated by the difficulties encountered by a public health worker in Peru in an unsuccessful attempt to convince rural villagers to boil drinking water (Rogers, 1983: 1–5). As obvious as the benefits to health from this practice were to the professional change agent, she was unable to convince villagers because her theory of disease was in conflict with theirs, because producing boiled water takes some effort and people do not like its taste, and because many of the intended adopters distrusted government workers (an indirect bias effect). A common finding of studies of the diffusion of innovations is that a series of such impediments have to be removed before adoption occurs, even for highly useful innovations. Another common finding is that a small group of innovators and early adopters play a big role in the diffusion of most innovations even among relatively sophisticated people like farmers in the United States. Typically, early adopters are better educated, have wider social contacts, and are more prosperous than later adopters, who tend to acquire innovations simply by copying the early adopters (another indirect bias effect).

Rogers and Shoemaker's analysis of the diffusion of innovations is consistent with our interpretation of the models presented in the last two chapters. When it is easy for individuals to evaluate the utility of innovations, direct bias and guided variation can be powerful forces. Innovations tend to be adopted more slowly, on the other hand, when they are complex, difficult to try out on an experimental basis, or hard to observe (Rogers, 1983: 230–232). In the case of technical innovations, research and development institutions bear a large fraction of the cost of evaluating alternative variants. Early adopters are those individuals able to bear the remainder of the decision-making costs, having acquired the cognitive skills to make accurate evaluations (better education, wider experience) and the economic resources to bear the costs of trials that may fail. For those individuals for whom the costs of exercising bias or guided variation are higher, and for innovations that require more effort to evaluate, people adopt innovations, if they adopt at all, by copying the behavior of others they respect. Later adopters usually do not use an innovation on a trial basis or engage in learning to adapt the innovation to their peculiar circumstances. Very often existing tradition acts as a deterrent to innovation and only innovations carefully tailored for compatibility to traditional practices are successful (Rogers with Shoemaker, 1971: 143–154; Rogers, 1983: 223–230). The exceptional people who have a generally positive orientation to innovations include those with a wider circle of cosmopolitan acquaintances and quite considerable financial resources to absorb the costs of risky trials.

Evidence from behavioral decision theory

The conservative behavior of most people when confronted with innovations is comprehensible given our ability to make rational decisions. During the last decade a large literature has developed in psychology comparing actual human choice behavior to the normative expectations of formal theories of rationality. Recent reviews include Slovic et al. (1977), Nisbett and Ross (1980), and Einhorn and Hogarth (1981). The general conclusion of behavioral decision theory, as it is called, is that humans ordinarily make quite poor judgments, particularly when problems are novel or require statistical evaluation. Decisions are made using a series of rules of thumb, called heuristics, that cause individuals to form confident opinions based on inadequate or badly biased information and then hold to these opinions in the face of substantial disconfirming data.

Tversky and Kahneman's (1974) influential paper describes three general classes of judgment heuristics—representativeness, availability, and anchoring—discovered in the course of choice and judgment experiments. The representativeness heuristic is applied to a variety of problems in which one has to judge the probability of an event. Judgments of this type are often based on the resemblance of the event to the population from which it may have been drawn. For example, given a personality profile, people judge the probability that the person described belongs to various occupational groups on the basis of conventional stereotypes. People described as shy and withdrawn but helpful are judged much more likely to be librarians than surgeons, while for bold egotists the probabilities will be reversed. The representativeness heuristic is often effective in making judgments, but in the psychology laboratory it can be shown to lead to gross distortions relative to normatively appropriate techniques.

The representativeness heuristic leads to a variety of fallacies, including: (1) Because people expect samples to be representative of the population from which they are drawn, their inferences are erroneously insensitive to sample size and reliability of data. This causes people to make confident predictions on the basis of normatively insufficient data. (2) The representativeness heuristic causes the nature of chance events to be misconceived. If someone has a run of bad luck, most people think his luck is "due" to change because it must do so if the sample is to be representative of the population, even though normative theory holds that future trials are independent of past events. (3) The effect of regression to the mean is poorly appreciated because people expect each event to represent the process that gives rise to it.

People commonly use the ease with which instances or occurrences of an event can be brought to mind to estimate its probability. Kahneman and Tversky label this the "availability heuristic." Often effective, it gives rise to errors when the availability of information in memory does not correspond to the real frequency of events. Nisbett and Ross (1980) give many examples of this effect. Personal observations or reports of friends about products such as autos are given much more weight in decision making than pallid statistical information of much greater objective value. Correlations between events are often misjudged because co-occurrences are easily remembered, whereas other combinations, especially joint nonoccurrences, are hardly ever taken into account. Virtually any laboratory manipulation of attentional factors changes subjects' causal interpretations of experimental events, and so forth.

Anchoring heuristics involve the use of some starting point to think about a problem, followed by adjustments on the basis of further observations about the problem. Typically, the adjustments made are far too conservative. Nisbett and Ross (1980: Chap. 8) devote considerable attention to what is perhaps the most serious consequence of the anchoring heuristic, people's resistance to evidence discrediting their causal theories about particular processes. Having argued earlier that causal theories are often inappropriately mobilized by the availability and representativeness heuristics (Chap. 6), they discuss the striking tendency of judges to stick with inappropriate theories in the face of disconfirming evidence. They describe several experiments in which subjects were led to form causal hypotheses about some events, such as an occupational outcome (success as a firefighter), and some predictive variable (risk preference assessed on a written test). Typically two groups of subjects are encouraged to acquire opposite theories about the relationship in question. (It is easy to believe that the dangerous nature of a fireman's job requires either extra caution or a bold approach.) Then the experimenters discredit the information subjects received during a debriefing session. Typically, however, both groups of subjects show a marked tendency to cling to the erroneous belief they have formed, whatever it is, in the face of substantial efforts to discredit its evidential basis. More generally, people seem to form causal beliefs on slender evidence, and subsequently remember and use confirming instances to reinforce the belief while forgetting or discrediting disconfirming evidence.

The behavioral decision theory literature is now quite large, and paints a depressing picture of human decision-making abilities. Is there any possibility that this portrait is overdrawn? After all, most people in the real world do solve complex problems and behave competently in their everyday lives. Somehow the generally successful and appropriate actions people take in the real world must be reconciled with their failure in the laboratory. First, one wonders if the bias effects are a laboratory artifact not exhibited routinely in real-world decisions. This seems not to be the case. Nisbett and Ross (1980: 251) reply to this criticism by noting that laboratory experiments usually present simplified versions of real-life decision tasks. For example, data are usually supplied in a form that does not tax memory or require judgments about the pertinence or quality of the numbers given. They argue that laboratory tasks should show human decision making at its best. Slovic et al. (1977: 19) summarized field studies on predictive tasks: "(a) Experienced weather forecasters, when performing their customary tasks, are excellently calibrated. (b) Everybody else stinks." Second, it could be that the normative statistical models with which intuitive judgments are compared are themselves flawed with respect to the problems people actually have to solve. There is probably some truth to this proposition. Einhorn and Hogarth (1981) note that the tendency of decision makers to be insufficiently regressive by normative statistical standards is only a fair comparison if the statistics available are representative of a stationary process.

In a progressively changing world, extreme, nonregressive predictions may well be warranted. Still they summarize: "To consider human judgment as suboptimal without discussion of the limitations of optimal models is naive. On the other hand, we do not imply that inappropriate optimal models always, or even usually, account for observed discrepancies." (See also Nisbett and Ross, 1980: 265.)

It seems relatively clear that human decision making is ordinarily successful, not because we really follow sophisticated rules for making decisions, but because of other effects that impinge on realistic decisions. Nisbett and Ross (1980: Chap. 2) list three important ones: (1) Although judgment heuristics are quite fallible, they are far from useless and they are inexpensive. Given the number of decisions a person makes in a lifetime and the cost of following normatively appropriate strategies, it is unreasonable to expect a close approximation to formal scientific methods of judgment. (2) Many domain-specific cues and causal models are acquired culturally. Even when these theories or behavioral norms are inappropriately justified, they may often be quite utilitarian. Further, individuals often defer to experts who have acquired a body of culturally transmitted insights relevant to particular problems. (3) Many problems are solved collectively so that individual errors are reduced.

We think that behavioral decision theory provides several kinds of evidence about the strength of direct bias and guided variation.

1. The fact that individual human beings are not very good at solving novel problems, or ones requiring statistical evaluation, suggests that complex cultural adaptations are unlikely to be the result of individual learning alone. Many of the most interesting human adaptations have advantages that are only of a statistical nature. Consider how hard it is to evaluate whether a particular diet or mode of building construction is beneficial. Given the limits of human cognition described by behavioral decision theorists, it seems much more reasonable that individuals should, at most, make minor improvements to what they have acquired culturally.

2. The fact that strong beliefs are based on small and/or biased samples means that the decisions to adopt cultural variants will be very noisy; mere chance will cause different individuals to choose different variants in the same environment. This in turn suggests that guided variation and direct bias will often be weak.

3. The fact that beliefs are extremely resistant to change, even in the face of overwhelming evidence, also provides direct evidence that the forces due to direct bias and guided variation are weak.

We think these conclusions support our interpretation of the model results on direct bias and guided variation. For a broad class of behavioral alternatives, individual decision makers are unable or unwilling to make costly choice efforts. Rather, they combine low-cost bias and guided variation with a considerable reliance on culturally transmitted anchors for behavior. In theory, and apparently in practice, this is the rational way to take advantage of a cultural system of inheritance. When this is the case the dynamic properties of cultural transmission may be important.

Conclusion

The sociobiological hypotheses are of great importance because they provide a standard against which to judge other theories of cultural evolution. Any satisfactory account of culture in humans must tell us how posited structures of cultural inheritance arose during the course of organic evolution. Sociobiologists assume that, like other forms of phenotypic plasticity, social learning should generally act to increase genetic fitness. Within the framework of dual inheritance theory, this means that the guiding criteria which govern guided variation and direct bias have been (and are being) shaped by natural selection so that these forces favor genetically advantageous traits. To be sure, they aver, humans like other animals often make mistakes; bias and guided variation sometimes increase the frequency of deleterious cultural variants. However, there is no reason to suppose that understanding phenotypic variation in humans should present any fundamentally new problems. In particular, the dynamics of cultural transmission and evolution can safely be ignored.

We believe it is unlikely that this will be true for all or even most human behavioral variation. If the forces of bias and guided variation are strong, then there will be little heritable cultural variation and therefore cultural transmission will be of little importance. If they are not, the dynamics of cultural transmission will be important. In this chapter we have reviewed the evidence that native human decision-making inclinations and abilities, unaided by culturally inherited problem-solving techniques, are quite modest. In Chapter 3 we reviewed the evidence that many important cultural traits exhibit substantial cultural inertia in the face of substantial environmental change. These findings are hard to reconcile with the action of strong direct bias and guided variation.

When direct bias and guided variation are weak, other forces can come into play. We have already seen in the last two chapters that natural selection acting directly on cultural variation can play an important role in cultural evolution. Chapters 7 and 8 present evidence that the forces of frequency-dependent and indirect bias can have novel effects. It will not do to ignore the effects of cultural transmission until we understand how these subtler forces work. We turn to this task in the next three chapters.

6

The Natural Selection
of Cultural Variations:
Conflicts between Cultural
and Genetic Evolution

> I may take this opportunity of remarking that my critics frequently assume that I attribute all changes of corporeal structure and mental power exclusively to the natural selection of variations as are often called spontaneous; whereas, even in the first edition of the "Origin of Species," I distinctly stated that great weight must be attributed to the inherited effects of use and disuse, with respect both to the mind and body.
>
> Charles Darwin, *The Descent of Man* (1874),
> Preface to the Second Edition

Darwin's theory of evolution has survived the 100 or so years since his death remarkably intact. Darwin's view that the main driving force in evolution is the gradual accumulation of small changes by natural selection still dominates modern evolutionary thinking, and even many of Darwin's analyses of specific evolutionary problems, such as sexual selection, have been recently "rediscovered" after a period of confusion and neglect (see Ghiselin, 1969). From the modern perspective, Darwin was guilty of only one really major error: throughout his life he insisted that the inheritance of acquired variation commonly occurred in nature and was fully compatible with his theory of evolution by natural selection. We now know that with the exception of cultural species the inheritance of acquired variation does not occur in nature, and the modern neo-Darwinian theory of evolution takes this fact as one of its central premises. Nowadays, the view that the transmission of acquired characters does occur is usually associated with mystical or orthogenetic views of evolution which hold that forces other than natural selection are important in shaping the direction of evolutionary change (e.g. Koestler, 1971).

Only relatively recently has Darwin's idea of evolution by natural selection been associated with the genetics of Mendel and Weismann. During the first two decades of this century, evolutionary biology was divided into two warring camps. In one were the "biometricians," led by W. F. R. Weldon, and in the other were the "Mendelians," represented by William Bateson. The biometricians believed that evolution proceeded via the natural selection of very small phenotypic differences in quantitative characters. Pearson developed a mathematical theory of the effect of selection on multivariate quantitative characters (Pearson, 1902) that closely parallels the recent model of Lande (e.g. 1979), and an ingenious (although incorrect) theory of inheritance based on the notion that variation was maintained by the transmission of what modern biologists would call "environmental variation" (Pearson, 1901). The biometricians rejected Mendelism because they believed that it entailed large discontinuous changes in phenotype, and they considered this to be incompatible with the Darwinian theory of evolution by natural selection. In contrast, the Mendelians embraced the existence of Mendelian genetics in part because they (incorrectly) believed that it was impossible for natural selection to create major phenotypic change through the accumulation of small variations. For them evolution proceeded via a series of "hopeful monsters." It was not until Fisher (1918) and Wright (1921) showed how Mendelian inheritance and quantitative variation could be reconciled that Darwinism and Mendelism could be brought together in a single theory, and perhaps two more decades passed before this synthetic theory of evolution came to dominate in biology. (See Provine, 1971, for a discussion of this controversy.)

The natural selection of cultural variations

We have reviewed this bit of the history of biology because we think it illustrates that there is no necessary logical association between Darwin's idea of evolution by natural selection and the particular features of genetic inheritance. There are two necessary conditions in order for natural selection to operate: (1) There must be heritable variation in phenotype. (2) Phenotypic variation must be associated with variation in individual survival and reproduction.

Whenever these two conditions are satisfied the phenotypic variants that have the highest probability of being transmitted to the next generation will tend to increase in number. We showed in Chapter 3 that cultural transmission creates heritable phenotypic variation. To demonstrate that natural selection is a force in cultural evolution, we must still show that individuals characterized by alternative cultural variants differ in their probability of surviving and becoming effective models. Later in this chapter we will present empirical evidence that this is indeed the case.

The fact that both genetic and cultural variation are subject to natural selection does not mean that selection will favor the same phenotypic variants regardless of the mode of transmission. When two inheritance systems have asymmetric life cycles, selection may favor different phenotypic variants. We will see that for some cultural traits, for example, those transmitted at an early age from parents to offspring, the cultural variants that are favored by selection will be very similar to those that would be favored if the trait were transmitted genetically. For example, culturally transmitted food preferences may affect the survival and fecundity of individuals, and selection will favor the variants that provide the best nutrition in the local habitat. In this case the life cycle of cultural transmission is very similar to that of genetic inheritance. However, for other cultural traits the life cycles of cultural and genetic transmission may be quite asymmetric, and as a result, the kinds of traits that have the highest probability of being transmitted to the next generation may be quite different from those that maximize genetic fitness. For example, career goals acquired during professional training may interfere with raising a large family.

In this chapter we analyze the effect of natural selection on culturally inherited aspects of behavior. We begin by distinguishing selection from the force of guided variation and the forces that arise from biased transmission. Next, we review empirical evidence that suggests that individuals characterized by different variants of some cultural traits differ in their probability of successfully completing the life cycle necessary for the transmission of those traits. We analyze a model of the interaction of asymmetric cultural transmission and selection which will more clearly demonstrate the effect of asymmetry. Finally, we consider how genetically transmitted modifiers of the cultural life cycle might evolve. While there is a general tendency for selection to favor symmetric life cycles, it is easy to imagine plausible circumstances in which the evolutionary equilibrium is an asymmetric system of cultural transmission. We conclude the chapter with a possible empirical example of this effect.

Distinguishing natural selection from other forces

Biologists tend to apply the term "selection" to any process which (1) depends on heritable variation in phenotype and (2) leads to systematic, directional change in the frequency of different phenotypes in the population. A similarly inclusive terminology could be employed here for culture, and, indeed, Cavalli-Sforza and Feldman (1981) have applied the term "cultural selection" to what we have called directly biased transmission. We have elected to adopt a different terminology in which we distinguish three classes of directional forces: the force of guided variation, the forces due to biased transmission, and natural selection.

Distinguishing natural selection from the force of guided variation is relatively straightforward. The force of guided variation results from the cultural transmission of the results of learning and acts to increase the frequency of traits that best satisfy the learning criteria. Selection changes the frequency of different variants in the population by culling some variants but not others. This causes the strength of selection to depend on the amount of variation in the population. In contrast, because learning creates new variants, the effect of the force of guided variation on the mean phenotype in the population is independent of the amount of variation in the population. (See Eq. 4.11 and the preceding text for a more complete discussion.) Thus, the force of guided variation lies outside even the inclusive definition given above.

The distinction between selection and the forces due to biased transmission is more subtle. Like selection, biased transmission is a culling process that depends on the variation present in the population. Indeed, the closest biological analog to directly biased transmission is meiotic drive, a process which is usually categorized as a kind of natural selection operating at the gametic level. The distinction between selection and bias is based on the mechanism that is responsible for the culling process. We have defined biased transmission in terms of transmission probabilities. The culling of different cultural variants that occurs during biased cultural transmission results from the choices of individuals, particularly those made by naive individuals when exposed to modeling events. As we have emphasized, this means that biased transmission depends for its action on external criteria of desirability. We will use selection to refer to all the things that happen to an individual because it performs a given behavior, and that, in turn, affect the probability that the individual will be available as a model for naive individuals. No external criterion is required to produce the effects of selection. Rather, two alternative traits performed in the same environment need merely have differential effects on the life chances of the individuals that perform them.

We believe that it is worthwhile to make this distinction because natural selection and bias have different roles in the explanation of culturally transmitted adaptations. A model of cultural evolution which involves bias forces alone cannot account for the origin of an adaptation unless an explanation can be provided for how the biases themselves arose. In contrast, the natural selection of cultural variations is an autonomous force that does not depend on any external criteria. Given the existence of a system of social learning and a pattern of social life in which some individuals are more likely to be models than others, the natural selection of cultural variations will necessarily occur. As we shall see, under some circumstances this process can act to increase the frequency of variants that are maladaptive in terms of genetic fitness.

Empirical Examples

For natural selection to change the frequency of different cultural variants, individuals characterized by some cultural variants must be more likely to become cultural parents than individuals characterized by other variants. In this section, we examine three empirical examples. In each of these examples the data indicate that: (1) Individuals characterized by different variants of the culturally transmitted trait have different probabilities of becoming cultural parents; that is, there is selection of cultural variation. (2) There is reason to believe that forces of biased transmission and guided variation are weak compared to selection because the traits seem to be transmitted without much choice or because it is difficult to believe that people are aware of the consequences of their behavior.

We do not claim that these examples constitute proof of the importance of natural selection on cultural variation. However, we do believe they demonstrate that the natural selection of culturally transmitted variations could be an important force in cultural evolution, and that models which focus upon the effects of natural selection of culturally transmitted variations are as deserving of scientific attention as the ones which focus on guided variation and biased transmission.

Cultural variation for mortality and fecundity

Rates of mortality and fecundity are the basic stuff of ordinary Darwinian (genetic) fitness. When cultural transmission is symmetric, mortality and fecundity are also directly related to cultural fitness. However, since an individual must ordinarily survive long enough to occupy the social roles that are effective in horizontal and oblique transmission, mortality rates also affect cultural fitness when the cultural life cycle is asymmetric. For example, elderly people have important leadership roles in many human societies. All other things being equal, cultural variants that promote longevity are likely to be favored in such societies over variants that lead to early death.

Demographers have collected a considerable amount of data that indicate that culturally transmitted traits affect fecundity and mortality (for general reviews, see United Nations, 1973; Petersen, 1975; Weller and Bouvier, 1981). These data show fecundity and mortality vary as a function of nation, class, socioeconomic status, ethnic group, religious affiliation, and so forth, and that culturally transmitted traits affect many behaviors related to fecundity and mortality, including subsistence production and public health, the details of age at marriage, desired family size, and access to personal health care. Therefore, it seems very likely that different cultural variants frequently have different fitnesses.

The effect of religious beliefs on fecundity and mortality provides a particularly good example. Demographers have shown that measures of religious affiliation are strongly correlated with fecundity and mortality. The effects of religion on fecundity and mortality seem to be clearly linked to culturally transmitted information: religious beliefs frequently vary in their teachings about the desirability of children and about the use of health-impairing substances like alcohol, tobacco, and drugs. Some religions (e.g. The Church of Jesus Christ of Latter-Day Saints) preach both pronatalism and abstention. Others (e.g. the liberal Protestant churches of the United States) have no objection to birth control or moderate use of alcohol. As we saw in Chapter 3, parent-offspring similarities for religion are quite strong. Further, few religious conversion decisions are likely to be made in order to increase fertility or decrease mortality, at least ostensibly. Thus, there is a chance that a major component of the generation-to-generation increase or decrease in one religious doctrine relative to another is due to natural selection of vertically transmitted cultural variation, episodes of mass conversion or mass apostasy aside.

How strong are these effects? Janssen and Hauser (1981) conducted a reasonably well controlled study of fertility among Catholics and non-Catholics. They present longitudinal data from a large sample of men and women living in Wisconsin, in which the effects of current and background religion and various measures of education and socioeconomic status were analyzed using multiple regression techniques. Current religion had a stronger statistical effect than background religion. Catholic men and women could both be expected to have about 0.5 more children than non-Catholics, primarily because Catholics were more likely to have a third or fourth child than were non-Catholics. Since the mean number of children for males was 2.6 and for females 2.9 (in the total sample of roughly equal numbers of Catholics and non-Catholics), this fertility difference represents quite strong natural selection, assuming no countervailing effects on mortality. The data also indicate that the effect of bias was much weaker. Although 11.6 percent of the sample changed religions between high school and adulthood, the Catholics and non-Catholics gained and lost nearly equal amounts. The Catholic group increased slightly (2.5 percent) as a net result of conversions.

The effects of religious beliefs on mortality rates can be as striking as their effects on fertility. Middle-class Protestant sects with strongly abstemious doctrines like the Seventh-Day Adventists and the Latter-Day Saints show much lower age-specific death rates than comparable groups outside these sects. For example, McEvoy and Land (1981) report age-adjusted mortalities for members of the

Reformed Latter-Day Saints Church of Missouri about 20 percent below the rate expected from control populations. In their study, death rates for Latter-Day Saints members were especially low for lung cancer, pneumonia/influenza, and violent death (including automobile accidents), categories that might be expected to be lower if the clean-living doctrines of the Mormons were being followed.

There is also evidence that religious affiliation actually does affect behavior. Jensen and Erickson (1979) report data on juvenile delinquency from Tucson, Arizona. Their sample included Catholics, Protestants, and Mormons who filled out anonymous questionnaires regarding the number of delinquent acts committed. Religious belief, extent of religious activity, and attendance at services were negatively correlated with most types of delinquent behavior, but the most consistent correlations were for drinking and marijuana usage. There were also significant differences between the denominations. In particular, Mormon youths reported significantly less drinking and smoking, as might be expected from church doctrines. Interestingly enough, in this study the strongest effects observed between religious and nonreligious individuals, and among denominations, were for "victimless" delinquency. Crimes against people and property showed weaker effects of religion. McEvoy and Land infer that these and other findings indicate the specific doctrines preached by a given denomination are associated with specific behavioral outcomes.

Food preferences

Certain variations in food preferences between human groups may result from the natural selection of cultural variations. The evolution of human diets is almost certainly affected by genetically transmitted biases that make some foods taste good (Lumsden and Wilson, 1981: 38–43). In addition, it seems clear that people tend to base their cuisine on crops that are easily grown in the local environment. However, there are many dietary practices that are difficult to explain on the basis of these kinds of directly biased transmission. Many dietary variations, such as the highly variable addition of various pungent spices to food, seem to be acquired tastes that are incorporated into diets even though they are distasteful to the uninitiated. More important, some of these dietary practices seem to be beneficial adaptations; they have subtle, long-term effects that increase fitness. Because these beneficial effects are often not closely related to the way different foods taste and because they are often quite difficult to assess, even with the resources of modern science, it is not obvious that they are the result of biased transmission or guided variation. It seems at least as plausible to suppose that these items have reached high frequencies in some societies because they are favored by natural selection acting on cultural variation.

Solomon H. Katz and his associates have studied several traits affecting food consumption and preparation that plausibly occur because of selection rather than bias. The most convincing example is fava bean consumption in the circum-Mediterranean region (Katz and Schall, 1980). Fava beans are widely cultivated in this region, despite the fact that they cause a severe, often fatal disease called "favism" in certain sensitive individuals. The sensitive individuals are those who have the X-linked gene for glucose-6-phosphate dehydrogenase (G-6-PD) enzyme deficiency, which in turn is in high frequency in many circum-Mediterranean populations because it apparently confers resistance to malaria. Katz originally hypothesized that populations with high frequencies of G-6-PD deficiency would exhibit the lowest use of fava beans. However, fava bean consumption actually is highest in those populations with the highest frequencies of G-6-PD deficiency. A great variety of cultural beliefs have developed regarding fava beans during the long period of their use in this region. Despite some recognition that they can have harmful effects, fava beans continue to be eaten. This is especially curious since there is no evidence that fava beans are more nutritious or easier to cultivate than a number of alternate legume crops.

Katz and his colleagues present evidence that fava consumption is adaptive in malaria-prone regions because the bean contains compounds that confer resistance to malaria on individuals not protected by G-6-PD deficiency, and that this advantage compensates for the occurrence of favism in sensitive individuals. If this hypothesis is correct, it is difficult to imagine that the consumption of fava beans has been increased by direct bias or guided variation. There is no evidence that those who eat fava beans understand the biological complexities involved or have specific genetic biases (e.g. a distaste for the beans among G-6-PD deficient individuals). Indeed, Katz's hypothesis is not yet completely convincing, despite the application of considerable effort, a testimony to the difficulty of applying biases in complex cases.

A plausible hypothesis is that natural selection is acting on the cultural trait of fava bean consumption much as it is acting on the G-6-PD locus. Individuals characterized by beliefs that lead them to consume fava beans had a higher probability of surviving to adulthood and becoming cultural parents for the next generation than individuals who did not consume fava beans. The use of plant foods high in secondary compounds of presently unknown or poorly understood effects is widespread in human cuisines. Natural selection for such preferences could be an important phenomenon.

Selection and asymmetric transmission

Only parents can transmit genes. Individuals occupying a variety of other social roles—grandparents, siblings, heroes, teachers, people with high prestige—may be involved in cultural transmission. When this is the case, we say that transmission is asymmetric. Selection will act on asymmetrically transmitted cultural variation if (1) there is competition to occupy the roles that are effective in such transmission and (2) individuals characterized by some cultural variants are more often winners in this competition than individuals characterized by other variants. In the next section we will consider a model of the important effects of selection on asymmetrically transmitted variation in more detail.

We think that the spread of the skills and values characteristic of modern industrial society, first within the European West and now to the modernizing Third World, provides one example of the effects of selection on asymmetrically transmitted cultural variation. To make a case for this hypothesis we must show that (1) cultural variation for the traits involved in industrial roles exists and is, in part at least, transmitted asymmetrically and (2) some variants are disproportionately successful in competition for social roles effective in horizontal and oblique transmission.

To simplify what must in reality be an extremely complex example of cultural evolution, we will focus our discussion on a few traits. Let us first consider a trait which psychologists refer to as "cognitive style." Cognitive style is measured by a number of different tests. The embedded figures test is typical. Subjects are given a number of cards with complex geometrical forms which have simpler reference forms embedded in them. The task is to find the simple form concealed in the more complex one. A person's degree of "field independence" is scored by measuring the time required to complete a number of such tasks. The theory behind the measurement holds that the degree of field dependence is a measure of a fundamental attribute of cognition, the ability to analyze problems by dividing them into articulated parts (field independent) as opposed to the ability to interpret complex patterns as a whole (field dependent).

These measures of cognitive style are interesting in the context of modernization because traditional agricultural societies and Western industrial societies apparently differ in the average amount of field dependence. There is a large body of cross-cultural data about the occurrence of different variants and their correlates. (For reviews, see Berry, 1976; Witkin and Berry, 1975; Werner, 1979; and Witkin and Goodenough, 1981.) These data indicate that high field independence is found in two otherwise sharply contrasting groups: loosely organized, nomadic food-foraging peoples and the middle class of industrialized societies, including the modern elites of the Third World. Members of tightly organized, strongly authoritarian, hierarchical agricultural societies tend to score on the field-dependent end of the dimension. The members of the working class of industrial states exhibit lower field independence than members of the middle class.

Cognitive style, as measured by such tests, is correlated with a number of other psychological attributes. The most interesting correlate for our purposes is its relationship to social behavior. The data show that field-dependent individuals are more sensitive to social cues than field-independent ones. As a result, field-dependent people reach cooperative agreement with others more easily and are less individualistic and competitive in social situations than the field-independent individuals (Werner, 1979: 186).

Witkin and Berry argue that different ecological and sociological situations favor different cognitive styles. The tasks of food foragers and of the occupants of managerial and entrepreneurial roles in industrial societies require a good deal of independent, analytical evaluation of problems, while traditional agricultural societies require close cooperation and deference to authority. Studies quite outside the research tradition of Witkin and Berry give a similar picture of the relationship between role demands and values, at least among occupational classes in industrial societies (Kohn, 1981).

It is reasonable to infer from these data that the industrialization or modernization of an agricultural society of the pre-industrial West or of a contemporary Third World society involves, among other things, an increase in the proportion of the population scoring high on field independence. Could the hypothesis of asymmetrical transmission and selection fit the observed patterns?

1. Heritable cultural variation for cognitive style exists. The observed variation in cognitive style within societies is fairly substantial (Berry, 1976: 150). The fact that parental rearing practices are correlated with cognitive styles in children suggests that vertical transmission of cognitive style is important. Rearing styles that are warm and encourage children's independence are associated with field-independent cognitive styles, while styles which emphasize punishment and close conformance to social norms are associated with field dependence (Werner, 1979: 180–181). There is also good evidence that asymmetric transmission is effective in the transmission of cognitive style. Acculturation and, in particular, formal schooling have been shown to affect the degree of field independence (Berry, 1976; Werner, 1979: 184). School, work experience, and an exposure to mass media generally appear to be less important than parental influence but are nonetheless significant.

2. Variation for cognitive style is associated with differential success in achieving social roles effective in horizontal and oblique transmission. Cognitive style was first investigated in Western societies where high field independence is associated with middle-class status. Witkin and Berry's adaptation hypothesis has grown out of these and similar data from modernizing situations. The independent, analytical, competitive individualism of those who score high on field independence suits them for success in school, and school success is closely correlated with subsequent job status (Jencks et al., 1972).

These data suggest the following hypothesis to explain the increase in field independence with modernization: (1) A modernizing agricultural society begins with a population scoring low on field independence, but with considerable variation. (2) In the modernizing situation, the field-independent individuals are more likely to do well in school and subsequently to become teachers, business owners or managers, bureaucrats, and so on. Old elite roles favoring more field-dependent cognitive styles become, at least proportionately, less important. (3) The new field-independent elites transmit their values and skills to some extent horizontally and obliquely to their employees and pupils. Other traits, including disposition toward innovation and job aspirations, are also expected to be transmitted in the same way.

The models developed in the next section indicate that selection on asymmetrically transmitted variation can be a very powerful force, even when rates of horizontal and oblique transmission are modest, as long as the competition for access to the roles effective in this transmission is severe and selective. Thus it is plausible that the hypothesized mechanism could lead to rapid increase in the frequency of the variant of field independence.

Models of Natural Selection

The evidence cited in the previous section suggests that culturally transmitted traits may often be subject to natural selection. In order to understand how natural selection affects the frequency of different phenotypic variants in a population, we will analyze several simple models of the natural selection of cultural variation. When the life cycle of cultural transmission is symmetric to genetic transmission, these models can be borrowed directly from population genetics. We have already analyzed such models of the natural selection of culturally transmitted traits in Chapters 4 and 5. As we shall see, however, asymmetric cultural life cycles lead to effects that are not present in conventional genetic models.

A *dichotomous trait with a symmetric life cycle*

We will begin by adding selection to the very simple model of the vertical transmission of a dichotomous cultural trait introduced in Chapter 3. Suppose that a dichotomous trait is acquired culturally from the genetic parents at an early age. This trait takes on two variants, c and d. The frequency of the variant c in the pool of cultural parents is p. In Chapter 3, we showed that if the transmission rule is linear and if the formation of sets of cultural parents is nonselective, then the frequency of the cultural variant c is unaffected by cultural transmission. Let p' be the frequency of c in the population just after cultural transmission in the next generation. Then

$$p' = p \qquad (6.1)$$

Now we add an episode of natural selection. Suppose that individuals characterized by different cultural variants differ in the probability that they become parents. For example, the cultural trait might be one of the practices discussed above that affects individual survivorship, and individuals with one variant are more likely to survive to adulthood than individuals characterized by the other variant. It also might be that the cultural trait affects the ability of an individual to acquire the wealth and social position necessary to marry and have children. Let the probability that an individual with cultural variant c becomes a parent be W_c and that for individuals with variant d be W_d. We will refer to W_c and W_d as the "cultural fitnesses" of the variants c and d. In this case the cultural fitnesses of the variants are identical to their Darwinian or ordinary reproductive fitnesses, but this will not always be the case. (As in Chap. 5, we restrict attention to viability selection for simplicity.)

We now want to calculate the frequency of the variant c in the pool of parents, that is, after selection takes place. Suppose that the size of the entire population before selection is a large number, N'. Then the number of individuals with variant c in the pool of parents, N_c'', is

$$N_c'' = \begin{pmatrix} \text{Probability a c} \\ \text{individual} \\ \text{becomes a parent} \end{pmatrix} \times \begin{pmatrix} \text{Total number of c} \\ \text{individuals} \\ \text{before selection} \end{pmatrix}$$

or

$$N_c'' = (W_c) \times (p'N') \qquad (6.2)$$

Similarly, the number of individuals characterized by the variant d, N_d'', is

$$N_d'' = W_d(1 - p')N' \qquad (6.3)$$

The fraction of parents with the cultural variant c, p'', is simply

$$p'' = \frac{N_c''}{N_d'' + N_c''} \qquad (6.4)$$

Now we can use Equations 6.1, 6.2, 6.3, and 6.4 to write the frequency of the variant c during one generation, p'', as a function of the frequency of c among parents of the previous generation:

$$p'' = \frac{pW_c}{(1 - p)W_d + pW_c} \qquad (6.5)$$

To get an intuitive feeling for what this recursion means, consider Figure 6.1 where we have plotted the change in the frequency of c over one generation, $\Delta p = p'' - p$, as a function of p. First, notice that Δp is either positive for all values of p or negative for all values of p. Furthermore, it is positive if $W_c/W_d > 1$. This means that the frequency of c always increases if $W_c > W_d$ and decreases if $W_c < W_d$. In other words, the cultural variant with the highest cultural fitness increases. Also notice that the magnitude of Δp is largest for $p = \frac{1}{2}$ and approaches zero as p approaches zero or one. This illustrates the fact that the action of selection depends on there being variability in the population. The variance of the phenotypic values (assigning a phenotypic value 1 to c and 0 to d, as in Chap. 4) is $p(1 - p)$, which is a maximum at $p = \frac{1}{2}$ and zero at both of the boundaries.

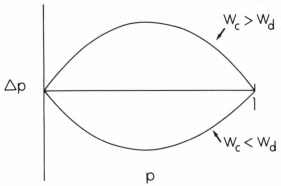

Fig. 6.1 The change in the frequency of cultural variant c, Δp, due to natural selection as a function of p. When the fitness of variant c, W_c, is greater than that of the alternative variant, W_d, Δp is positive for all values of p. When $W_c < W_d$, it is negative for all values of p.

The parent-teacher model

So far we have assumed that parents enculturate their children and that no other unrelated individuals are available to the naive child as models. Thus (as long as opportunities for extramarital reproduction are negligible), the phenotypic variants favored by selection acting on culturally transmitted variation are the same as those that would be favored if the trait were genetically transmitted. However, as we have seen, the empirical evidence suggests that for some traits, particularly those that typically are acquired at a later age, individuals other than the genetic parents are important in socialization. When this is true the effect of selection on the frequency of the different variants in the population is more complicated, and, under some circumstances, it can favor different phenotypic variants than would be favored if the trait were genetically transmitted.

To understand how this can happen we generalize the simple model analyzed above to include the possibility that individuals other than the genetic parents are important in enculturation. We accomplish this in two stages: first, we consider a very simple model in which children are enculturated by two kinds of individuals, their parents and teachers. The parent-teacher model allows us to understand the basic effect of asymmetric life cycles in the context of a very simple model. Then we analyze a more general multiple-parent model.

Once again we consider the evolution of a dichotomous cultural trait with two variants, c and d. In the parent-teacher model, we assume that for this trait each naive offspring is enculturated by two individuals, one of his genetic parents, say the mother, and a teacher. We suppose that cultural transmission proceeds according to the linear rule given in Table 6.1, that is, the parent has weight A and the teacher $1 - A$.

Table 6.1 The conditional probabilities of acquiring cultural variants c and d given the cultural variants that characterize the parent and the teacher

Parent	Teacher	Probability That Offspring Acquires Cultural Variant	
		c	d
c	c	1	0
c	d	A	$1 - A$
d	c	$1 - A$	A
d	d	0	1

As in the previous model, we suppose that individuals characterized by the two different cultural variants have different probabilities of becoming a parent. The probability for variant c is W_c and for variant d, W_d. We also suppose that individuals with different cultural variants have different probabilities of becoming teachers. Let Ω_c be the probability that an individual with the variant c becomes a teacher, and Ω_d the probability for individuals characterized by variant d. This means that there are two different, potentially conflicting, cultural selection processes. One process selects among individuals allowing some to become parents and thereby enculturate children, and a second process selects individuals who will become teachers and also be in a position to enculturate children.

To determine the kinds of phenotypes that result from this kind of selection process we will derive a recursion for the frequency of the cultural variant c. Let p be the frequency of c among offspring just after cultural transmission. First we want to compute the frequency of c among parents and teachers. From the symmetric model, the frequency of c among parents, p', is

$$p' = \frac{pW_c}{(1 - p)W_d + pW_c} \tag{6.6}$$

By analogy the frequency of the cultural variant c among teachers, p^*, must be

$$p^* = \frac{p\Omega_c}{(1 - p)\Omega_d + p\Omega_c} \tag{6.7}$$

The frequency of c after transmission in the next generation, p'', is given by the equation

$$p'' = p'p^* \begin{bmatrix} \text{Probability offspring is c given} \\ \text{both teacher and parent are c} \end{bmatrix} \tag{6.8}$$

$$+ \, p'(1 - p^*) \begin{bmatrix} \text{Probability offspring is c given} \\ \text{parent is c and teacher is d} \end{bmatrix}$$

$$+ \, (1 - p')p^* \begin{bmatrix} \text{Probability offspring is c given} \\ \text{parent is d and teacher is c} \end{bmatrix}$$

Assuming that sets of cultural parents are formed at random and that transmission is according to Table 6.1, this equation becomes

$$p'' = p'p^*[1] + p'(1 - p^*)[A] + (1 - p')p^*[1 - A] \tag{6.9}$$

By writing the [1] in the first term as $[A + (1 - A)]$, Equation 6.9 can be simplified to

$$p'' = A \, p' + (1 - A)p^* \tag{6.10}$$

Equation 6.10 is a very important result. It says that the frequency of the cultural variant c after transmission is the weighted average of the frequencies of c among parents and teachers, where the weights are the relative importances of parents and teachers in the transmission of the cultural trait in question. To see why this is important, suppose that individuals with cultural variant c are more likely to become teachers while those with the cultural variant d are more likely to become parents. Thus the frequency of c individuals will be higher among the pool of teachers and the frequency of d individuals will be higher among parents. Given Equation 6.10, it seems plausible that if teachers were important enough, then c could increase in the population even though d individuals are assumed to have higher genetic fitness.

We can make this intuitive argument more precise by using Equations 6.6 and 6.7 in combination with Equation 6.10 to derive a recursion for the frequency of the variant c. To simplify this process we will once again suppose that selection is weak. In the context of a dichotomous trait this means that $W_d \approx W_c$ and $\Omega_c \approx \Omega_d$. We can express this mathematically as follows. Let

$$\begin{aligned} W_c/W_d &= 1 + s \\ \Omega_c/\Omega_d &= 1 + \sigma \end{aligned} \tag{6.11}$$

where s and σ are small enough that we can ignore terms of order s^2 and σ^2. The parameters s and σ measure the selection advantage (or disadvantage) of c in the

---

Box 6.1 Combining Equations 6.6 and 6.11 results in the following expression for the frequency of c among parents, p′:

$$p' = \frac{p(1 + s)}{1 + sp}$$

If s is small enough that we can ignore terms of order s^2, then

$$p' = p(1 + s)\{1 - sp + (sp)^2 + \ldots\} = p + sp(1 - p)$$

Similarly, if σ is small enough to ignore terms of order σ^2 then

$$p^* = p(1 + \sigma)\{1 - \sigma p + (\sigma p)^2 + \ldots\} = p + \sigma p(1 - p)$$

Then combining these two expressions with Equation 6.10 yields

$$p'' = A[p + sp(1 - p)] + (1 - A)[p + \sigma p(1 - p)]$$
$$= p + p(1 - p)[As + (1 - A)\sigma]$$

---

two selection processes. So, for instance, if $\sigma > 0$ and $s < 0$, individuals with variant c are more likely to become teachers but less likely to become parents. It is shown in Box 6.1 that with this assumption the recursion for p is

$$p'' = p + p(1 - p)[As + (1 - A)\sigma] \tag{6.12}$$

As is illustrated in Figure 6.2, this recursion has a very simple interpretation. The term $[As + (1 - A)\sigma]$ is a sort of "effective selective advantage." It is the selective advantage of variant c in the selective processes that cull potential parents and teachers, weighted by the importance of parents and teacher in enculturation. If this term is positive the variant c always increases, and if it is negative the reverse

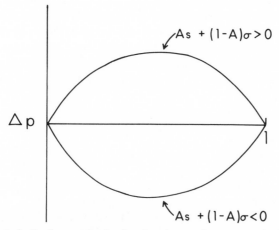

Fig. 6.2 The change in the frequency of cultural variant c, $\triangle p$, as a result of natural selection acting on both symmetric and asymmetric components of the cultural life cycle. When the effective selection advantage of variant c, $As + (1 - A)\sigma$, is greater than zero, variant c increases. When it is negative, variant c decreases.

occurs. This means that even if a cultural variant is maladaptive from the point of view of Darwinian fitness (i.e. $s < 0$), it can still increase in frequency.

A more complex model

Clearly this model is extremely stylized. Children are usually encultured by a variety of different kinds of individuals, and different children may be exposed to different numbers and kinds of parents. To show that these complications do not necessarily alter the qualitative effects of asymmetric life cycles that were explored with the parent-teacher model, we will analyze a more complex model of enculturation.

Suppose that each child has a set of cultural parents who occupy different "social roles." These social roles may include that of the "mother" and the "father," who, depending on the society, may or may not be the genetic parents of the offspring. Other important roles may be reserved for relatives, for example, grandparents in traditional Chinese society or the mother's brother in many matrilineal societies. Finally, totally unrelated individuals may play an important role, the shaman, the big man, or the leader of the secret society in traditional societies, or the priest, coach, or teacher in Western ones.

It seems unlikely that every child will be exposed to individuals occupying every possible social role. For instance, some children will have grandparents while others will not. To accommodate this situation within the model, we assume that a given naive individual is only exposed to a subset τ_j of all possible roles. Let Prob(τ_j) be the probability that an offspring is exposed to the subset τ_j. This probability can depend on the roles themselves. So, for example, it could specify that a child is exposed to the role of father or of stepfather, but not both. This probability cannot depend on the cultural variant of the individuals occupying the roles. This introduces indirect bias effects which we will treat in Chapter 8.

We suppose that individuals occupying different social roles have different importances in enculturation for any particular trait. For instance, for traits that are acquired at an early age, roles involved in primary child care are likely to be important. On the other hand, for skills that are acquired upon becoming adult, roles like teacher or military leader may be of primary importance. To model this in the context of a dichotomous character, we assume a linear cultural transmission rule as in Chapter 3. We assign the phenotypic value X_k to the kth parent where

$$X_k = \begin{cases} 1 \text{ if parent k is c} \\ 0 \text{ if parent k is d} \end{cases} \tag{6.13}$$

This means that in each set of cultural parents we assign a phenotypic value to each social role. Since, in general, there may be more social roles than there are parents, this means that we are assigning phenotypic values to nonexistent parents. We shall see, however, that this does not make any difference.

As with the linear model developed in Chapter 3, we assume that an individual occupying the kth social role has a *weight* A_k. Next we define a new quantity A_{kj} as follows:

$$A_{kj} = \begin{cases} A_k \text{ if k belongs to } \tau_j \\ 0 \text{ if k does not belong to } \tau_j \end{cases} \tag{6.14}$$

The probability that an offspring acquires cultural variant c given that it is exposed to cultural parents with the set of social roles τ_j and who have phenotypic values $X_1, \ldots, X_n$ is assumed to be

$$\text{Prob} \, (c \,|\, \tau_j, X_1, \ldots, X_n) = \frac{\Sigma_k A_{kj} X_k}{\Sigma_k A_{kj}} \tag{6.15}$$

This rule says that the actual weight of an individual occupying social role k in a particular set of cultural parents is the *raw* weight, A_k, normalized by the average weights of all the individuals in that set of cultural parents.

We suppose that the attainment of any of the social roles involves surviving a culling process analogous to natural selection. This means (1) that not everyone becomes a grandfather, a big man, or what have you, and (2) that different phenotypic variants have different probabilities of attaining any particular social role. Once again this may be because different variants have different probabilities of surviving to the age at which an individual can occupy a particular role, or it may be that particular skills or accomplishments are affected by culturally inherited factors. In both cases, the phenotypic variants that maximize the probability of attaining one role may not be the variants that have the best chance of attaining some different role. In the context of the simple dichotomous model we have analyzed, let Ω_{ck} be the probability that an individual with cultural variant c attains social role k, and let Ω_{dk} be the probability that an individual characterized by d attains social role k.

With these assumptions we can calculate a recursion for the frequency of the cultural variant c in the population. Suppose that the frequency of c just after cultural transmission is p. First, we calculate the frequency c in the pool of individuals who achieve social role k in adulthood, p_k':

$$p_k' = \frac{\Omega_{ck}p}{\Omega_{ck}p + \Omega_{dk}(1 - p)} \tag{6.16}$$

If sets of cultural parents are formed at random, the probability that a naive individual acquires variant c is given by

$$p' = \sum_j \text{Prob} \, (\tau_j) \sum_{X_1=0}^{1} \ldots \sum_{X_n=0}^{1} \text{Prob} \, (c \,|\, \tau_j, X_1, \ldots, X_n)$$
$$\times \left(\text{Prob} \, (X_1) \ldots \text{Prob} \, (X_n) \right) \tag{6.17}$$

By exchanging the order of summation, this can be rewritten as follows:

$$p' = \sum_{X_1=0}^{1} \ldots \sum_{X_n=0}^{1} \sum_k \overline{A}_k X_k (\text{Prob} \, (X_1) \ldots (X_n)) \tag{6.18}$$

where

$$\overline{A}_k = \sum_j \text{Prob}(\tau_j) \, (A_{kj}/\sum_l A_{lj}) \tag{6.19}$$

The parameter $\overline{A}_k$ represents the importance of parents in the kth social role averaged over all possible sets of cultural parents according to the frequency with which each set of cultural parents occurs. It is easy to show that Equation 6.18

becomes

$$p'' = \sum_{k=1}^{n} \overline{A}_k \, p'_k \tag{6.20}$$

Combining equations 6.16 and 6.20 gives us a recursion for the frequency of the cultural variant c in the population. This recursion has the same general properties as the parent-teacher model. In particular, if we define $\sigma_k = \Omega_{ck}/\Omega_{dk} - 1$ (in analogy with σ and s above) as the selection advantage of variant c in attaining role k and assume that selection is weak, then 6.20 becomes

$$p'' = p + p(1 - p) \left(\sum_{k=1}^{n} \overline{A}_k \sigma_k \right) \tag{6.21}$$

The sum is the selection advantage of variant c in role k averaged over all social roles, with each role being weighted by its importance in socialization. Equation 6.21 says that the variant c will increase in frequency if this quantity is positive and decrease if it is negative.

It is important to notice that the influence of a particular role on the overall selection advantage of a cultural variant depends on the strength of selection in attaining that role as well as the importance of the role. Given that the competition to attain some social roles like leader or big man may be very intense, it is possible that these roles may have a very important influence on the dynamics of the distribution of cultural variants.

The Evolution of Nonparental Transmission

The evolutionary origin and continued existence of asymmetric cultural transmission create a puzzle. The models analyzed in the last two sections suggest that natural selection acting on culturally transmitted variation will increase the frequency of variants which enhance cultural fitness. When cultural transmission is asymmetric, these variants may be different from those that maximize genetic fitness. Thus, all other things being equal, one would expect asymmetric cultural transmission often to be maladaptive. Nonetheless, the empirical evidence indicates that cultural transmission in humans is quite asymmetric, at least for some characters. This suggests that it might be fruitful to ask the question, Does asymmetric cultural transmission have some benefits that compensate for its intrinsic costs?

Indirect benefits of asymmetric cultural transmission

The most obvious answer to this question is that asymmetric transmission may be a by-product of many other adaptations. The kinds of individuals who will be available as models will depend on virtually all aspects of the social and economic system of the group in question. Groups specializing in trade or warfare may be characterized by the absence of males from the household, while in pastoral groups boys may spend long periods with their fathers following herds. Resource distribution and the political system will determine whether settlement is concentrated or dispersed, and hence the availability of models outside the family. Clearly, this list could be elaborated endlessly. In each case, the kinds of individuals that are available as models depend on other aspects of society which are important from an adaptive point of view; thus we would expect that the cultural life cycle cannot be made more symmetric without paying some penalty. For example, in a group specializing in trade a father might have to forgo lucrative trading opportunities in order to have a greater role in socialization.

Direct benefits of asymmetric cultural transmission

An individual's genetic parents represent a very small sample of the population from which they were drawn. Expanding the set of cultural parents may improve a naive individual's chances of acquiring the most favorable variant in two ways: If it is possible to identify favorable variants via direct or indirect bias, increasing the number of cultural parents may be adaptive insofar as it increases the chance that the set of cultural parents will include the most favorable variant. Expanding the set of cultural parents also enables the naive individual to get a better estimate of the distribution of variants in the population as a whole. This information is useful in choosing a variant under a wide variety of circumstances. In what follows we discuss each of these effects in more detail.

Increasing the number of cultural parents makes direct bias more effective. To see why, remember that direct bias can be thought of as a process in which individuals choose from among the variants to which they are exposed. Other things equal, one would expect that increasing the number of cultural parents would increase the number of different variants to which an offspring is exposed, and thus increase the chance of selecting the best variant.

This intuitive argument is supported by the models which were discussed in the last chapter. There we analyzed a model in which offspring acquired a quantitative cultural character from n cultural parents via the directly biased transmission rule. The effect of biased transmission was to move the mean cultural variant in the population toward the variant favored by the bias an amount $\Delta \overline{X}$, where

$$\Delta \overline{X} = (1 - 1/n_e)Cov(Z,\beta(Z)) \tag{6.22}$$

The covariance term represents the effects of the strength of the bias and the amount of variation in the population (see Eq. 5.10 and surrounding discussion for more details). The parameter n_e is the effective number of cultural parents. As n_e increases, the value of $\Delta \overline{X}$ also increases.

Now suppose that there are two genotypes in the population, one which causes its bearers to have an average effective number of cultural parents equal to n_e, and a second which causes its bearers to have a larger effective number of cultural parents, n_e^*. Equation 6.22 says that individuals with the second genotype will on average be closer to the variant favored by the bias than individuals with the first genotype. Assuming that the bias increases the frequency of adaptive variants, this means that individuals with more cultural parents will on average have higher genetic fitness. This is not an artifact of the quantitative model; an n parent dichotomous model yields a qualitatively similar result.

Increasing the number of cultural parents also makes indirect bias more effective. We will not examine indirect bias in detail until Chapter 8. However, it is easy to understand why asymmetric life cycles may be adaptive when there is indirect bias. Dad may be a lousy hunter; if cultural transmission is constrained to be symmetric, his sons either will be stuck with his techniques or will have to expend the effort to learn better ones. If transmission is not constrained to be symmetric, they can choose their models from among all the hunters in the village and thereby greatly increase their chances of acquiring the best variants of trap design and so on.

Asymmetric life cycles also may be adaptive because larger sets of cultural parents provide the naive individual with better information about the distribution of cultural variants in the population. For example, in the case of quantitative characters and blending inheritance, increasing the sample size decreases the variation in the offspring's estimate of the mean phenotype in the population. Since several forces tend to cause the mean phenotype in the population to be the optimal phenotype, increasing the number of cultural parents will increase fitness in these conditions.

Having more than two cultural parents also makes frequency-dependent bias possible. When there is frequency-dependent bias the naive individual uses the frequency with which different cultural variants occur as indicators of their merit. As we will see in Chapter 7, when transmission is biased in favor of the more common variant, it acts like what statisticians call "robust estimators" to reduce the chance that a naive individual will acquire badly maladaptive cultural variants from models who are drawn from the extremes of the distribution of cultural variants.

The Interaction of Selection with Direct Bias and Guided Variation

In this chapter we have been building an argument that natural selection acting on asymmetric cultural transmission can cause human behavior to diverge systematically from the predictions of sociobiological theory. So far the argument has had two parts: (1) Natural selection acting on culturally transmitted variation may increase the frequency of genetically maladaptive variants if the cultural life cycle is asymmetric. (2) There are good reasons to believe that natural selection acting on genes might favor cultural transmission with asymmetric life cycles.

It is important to emphasize that we are only arguing that it is possible that asymmetric cultural transmission has this effect. Even at that, the argument is still incomplete. The fact that natural selection acting on an asymmetric system of cultural inheritance may often favor maladaptive variants does not necessarily mean that these variants will increase in frequency; the effect of selection may be opposed by other forces like direct bias and guided variation. Indeed, as long as there is a genetic basis for the forces of guided variation and biased transmission, there will a tendency for some combination of these forces to evolve so as to correct distorting effects of asymmetric cultural life cycles. Some authors (e.g. Durham, 1976; Lumsden and Wilson, 1981) have argued that any important deviations of human behavior from what is genetically adaptive will eventually be eliminated in this way.

We think it is plausible, however, that in many situations direct bias and guided variation will not evolve to compensate for the effects of asymmetric transmission completely. In a spatially varying environment, migration can increase the frequency of maladaptive variants in each local habitat. In the last chapter we showed that in such an environment, selection in favor of biases which increased the frequency of locally favored variants was rather weak. If the cost of evaluating different cultural variants (necessary for the action of bias) was high enough, the bias would not evolve. A parallel argument can be made in the case of asymmetric transmission. Like migration, the combination of selection and an asymmetric life cycle can cause the frequency of maladaptive cultural variants to increase. We will shortly show that selection on the determinants of bias is also weak when the combination of asymmetric transmission and selection maintains maladaptive variants, and if bias is costly, correcting biases will not evolve.

Even if bias and guided variation do evolve so that they correct the effects of asymmetric transmission, there is no guarantee that they will be effective. Unlike maladaptive variants due to migration, the ones that result from asymmetric life cycles are coevolving with the genetic system. Under some circumstances, cultural evolution will tend to compensate for the effects of genetic evolution, and a kind of "arms race" will result. For example, suppose selection on cultural variation favors values and beliefs that lead to small families and selection on genetic variation favors desires that lead to large families. Then, selection on genes might increase the desire for children. In response, cultural selection might favor even more extreme beliefs about the appropriate family size. Genetic selection might again increase the desire for children, and so on.

In the remainder of this section we consider these two processes in the context of two simple models. First we consider the interaction of direct bias, natural selection, and asymmetric life cycles in a spatially varying environment. Then we analyze a model in which there is an arms race between cultural and genetic evolution.

Direct bias and asymmetric cultural life cycles

To investigate the interaction of bias and natural selection on asymmetrically transmitted cultural variation, we make use of the model of the genetic modification of bias discussed in the last chapter. There we assumed that (1) there were two culturally transmitted variants, c and d; (2) individuals with variant c were assumed to have a higher probability of becoming cultural parents in habitat 1 while individuals with variant d were more likely to become cultural parents in habitat 2; (3) there was a genetic locus that affected the magnitude and direction of the bias; and (4) the probability that any given individual became a genetic parent and the probability that the same individual became a cultural parent were equal, or, in other words, the cultural and genetic life cycles were symmetric. We then determined the conditions under which an allele which codes for unbiased cultural transmission (the unbiased allele) resists invasion by an allele which codes for bias in favor of genetically adaptive traits in each of the habitats (the general purpose bias allele).

In this section, we modify the model so that it represents a situation in which the cultural life cycle is asymmetric. Once again, assume that there are two culturally transmitted variants and two genetic variants. We adopt the notation used in Chapter 5, that is, cultural variants c and d are denoted by numerical value X, which equals 1 and 0, respectively, and genetic variants are denoted by the numerical value G, which can equal 0 (the unbiased allele) or 1 (the general purpose bias allele). Here we only consider the case of general purpose biases. It is assumed that individuals with the unbiased allele are characterized by unbiased transmission, while individuals with the bias allele have a transmission rule that is biased in favor of the cultural variant that maximizes the probability of becoming a genetic parent.

To model the effects of asymmetric life cycles we need only to change the pattern of cultural fitnesses in the way shown in Table 6.2. The top table gives the probability that different individuals characterized by various combinations of cultural and genetic variants become genetic parents. All other things equal, cultural variant c has higher genetic fitness in habitat 1 and cultural variant d has higher genetic fitness in habitat 2. However, as shown in the bottom table, we assume that the probabilities of becoming a cultural parent follow exactly the opposite pattern: individuals characterized by cultural variant c are more likely to become cultural parents in habitat 2, and individuals with cultural variant d are more likely to become cultural parents in habitat 1.

This is quite an extreme way to combine spatially varying environments with the effects of asymmetric life cycles because the forces of natural selection acting on genes and on culture are always opposed. This extreme model is useful because it represents the case in which bias is most likely to evolve. When selection on cultural and selection on genetic variation work together, then selection for biases would be weakened. This extreme model also is mathematically very similar to the model analyzed in Chapter 5 and therefore is very easy to analyze.

Once again, we want to know under what conditions a general purpose bias is favored relative to unbiased transmission. It can be shown that the frequency of the bias allele will increase whenever the following condition holds:

$$\{(1 - \hat{p})\hat{p}s\}b > z \tag{6.23}$$

where (as in Chap. 5) $\hat{p}$ is the frequency of the cultural variant with the highest genetic fitness in each habitat. The left-hand side of 6.23 represents the benefits of biased transmission and is the product of three terms: b, which measures the strength of the transmission bias; s, which measures the difference in genetic fitness of the two culturally transmitted variants; and $(1 - \hat{p})\hat{p}$, which measures the amount of cultural variation in the population. The right-hand side of 6.23 is the cost of biased transmission, z. If the benefits of biased transmission are greater than its costs, it will be favored by selection.

Notice that Condition 6.23 is exactly the same as the expression derived under the assumption that the genetic and cultural life cycles were symmetric (i.e. Condition 5.20, Chap. 5). The evolution of alleles controlling bias depends only on the magnitude of $(1 - \hat{p})\hat{p}$, the amount of cultural variation. For a given amount of cultural variation, its source is irrelevant. Of course, the nature of the selective forces will usually affect the amount of cultural variation. In the symmetric model selection and bias always acted in concert to increase the frequency of the cultural variant that had the higher genetic fitness, while in the asymmetric model they will

Table 6.2a Probability of becoming a genetic parent in habitat 1 (i.e. genetic fitness)

| Cultural | Genotype | |
Variant	0	1
0	1	$1 - z$
1	$1 + s$	$1 - z + s$

Table 6.2b Probability of becoming a cultural parent in habitat 1 (i.e. cultural fitness)

| Cultural | Genotype | |
Variant	0	1
0	$1 + \sigma$	$1 - z + \sigma$
1	1	$1 - z$

be opposed. Surprisingly, this difference can have the effect of making it easier or harder for the bias allele to increase in frequency.

To see this, consider the case of a population in which all individuals have the unbiased allele. In this case the equilibrium frequency of the favored variant will be determined only by the strength of selection on cultural variation, s in the symmetric model and σ in the asymmetric model. Recall that selection works with equal strength but in opposite directions in the two habitats in both models. This means that as selection becomes strong relative to migration, the frequency of variants with the higher cultural fitness approaches one. In the symmetric model this is also the variant with higher genetic fitness, while in the asymmetric model the variant with lower genetic fitness increases in frequency. The effects of this situation on the amount of cultural variation are shown graphically in Figure 6.3. Notice that the amount of cultural variation decreases as selection gets stronger; the direction of the selection does not matter. This means that the benefits of biased transmission will decrease as the strength of selection on cultural variation increases. In this simple model there is no relationship between the asymmetry of the life cycle and the strength of selection in favor of biased transmission.

Several caveats are in order, however. First, when selection on cultural variation favors maladaptive cultural variants, the evolution of biased transmission will usually increase the amount of cultural variation in the population, which in turn increases the strength of selection in favor of biased transmission. Thus, if the biased allele can increase when it is rare, it will always go to fixation. In contrast, when selection and bias work in the same direction, increasing the frequency of the bias allele weakens the selection in favor of bias, and a polymorphic equilibrium is possible. Second, in quantitative models there is a general tendency for selection on cultural asymmetrically transmitted variation to increase the strength of selection in favor of biased transmission. It is possible to construct models of quantitative characters in which asymmetric transmission reduces the selection in favor of biased transmission, but there is a general tendency for asymmetry to have an opposite effect. Finally, the strength of selection favoring guided variation will usually increase if the cultural life cycle is asymmetric, although, again, it is easy to construct models in which the opposite occurs.

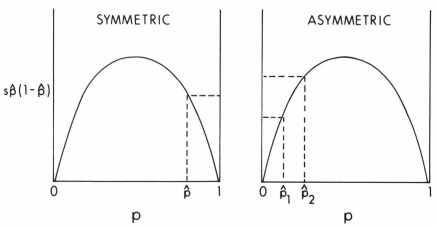

Fig. 6.3 Shows that asymmetric cultural transmission does not necessarily increase the strength of selection in favor of direct biases that favor genetically advantageous variants. The strength of selection favoring a general purpose bias allele is $s\hat{p}(1 - \hat{p})$. In both panels this quantity is plotted as a function of p. We also assumed that variant c has higher genetic fitness. In the left panel we assumed that cultural selection also acts to increase p in the local environment. Selection and immigration balance at the equilibrium value $\hat{p}$. The resulting strength of selection in favor of a general purpose bias is given by the height of the curve at $\hat{p}$. In the right panel we assumed that cultural selection acts to decrease p. If selection is weak so that the resulting equilibrium is $\hat{p}_2$, then the selection favoring direct bias is stronger than in the symmetric case. If, however, selection is strong so that the equilibrium is $\hat{p}_1$, then selection favoring direct biases is weaker than in the symmetric case.

A "Freudian" model

So far we have only considered the effect of genes which modify guided variation or directly biased transmission. It is also possible for genes to influence expressed behavior without creating or modifying the forces of cultural evolution. For example, suppose that family size is affected by culturally acquired beliefs about the correct or best family size and by a genetically transmitted trait which affects the frequency of sexual relations. It seems plausible that such a genetic character might not have any effect on the cultural transmission of beliefs about family size. When this situation exists, it is possible for the coevolution of genes and culture to become a sort of arms race in which cultural and genetic traits evolve in opposite directions, but with behavior remaining at an intermediate value.

To make this argument more concrete we use the following simple model. As usual we begin building the model by conceptually following a cohort of individuals through a single generation. Suppose that each individual inherits a quantitative genetic character from his genetic parents. The value of this character in a particular individual will be denoted G; the mean value among genetic parents is $\overline{G}$. Further suppose that each individual inherits a quantitative cultural variant from n teachers according to the linear rule described in Chapter 3. The value of this character in a particular individual will be labeled X, and the mean value among cultural parents is $\overline{X}$. Finally, we suppose that an individual's behavioral phenotype, Y, is a simple summing of the genetic and cultural influences:

$$Y = X + G \qquad (6.24)$$

To fully describe this population, we need to keep track of the joint distribution of genetic and cultural variants. We will denote this distribution among offspring as $F'(X,G)$. From the results of Chapter 3, we know that the mean values of the cultural $(\overline{X}')$ and genetic $(\overline{G}')$ variants in the population are unchanged by transmission (i.e. $\overline{G}' = \overline{G}$ and $\overline{X}' = \overline{X}$).

Next, we assume that the probability that an individual becomes a genetic parent, $W(Y)$, depends on its phenotype in the following way:

$$W(Y) = \exp\left\{\frac{-(Y - H_g)^2}{2S_g}\right\} \tag{6.25}$$

The parameter H_g is the phenotypic value that has the highest probability of becoming a genetic parent, and the parameter $1/S_g$ is a measure of the intensity of selection. Similarly, the probability of becoming a teacher, $\Omega(Y)$, is given by

$$\Omega(Y) = \exp\left\{\frac{-(Y - H_c)^2}{2S_c}\right\} \tag{6.26}$$

The parameter H_c is the phenotypic value that has the highest cultural fitness, and $1/S_c$ is a measure of the intensity of selection on teachers. Generally we expect that $H_g \neq H_c$, which means that selection on culture favors a different phenotypic value than selection on genes. For convenience we will establish the convention that $H_c > H_g$. This situation is shown graphically in Figure 6.4.

With these assumptions, we can calculate the mean value of G among genetic parents and the mean value of X among cultural parents in the next generation. These calculations are very similar to those shown in Chapters 4 and 5. They result in the following system of recursions:

$$\overline{X}' = \overline{X} + \frac{U}{S_c + V + U}\{(H_c - \overline{G}) - \overline{X}\}$$
$$\overline{G}' = \overline{G} + \frac{V}{S_g + V + U}\{(H_g - \overline{X}) - \overline{G}\} \tag{6.27}$$

where V is the equilibrium variance of the genetic character and U is the equilibrium variance of the cultural character.

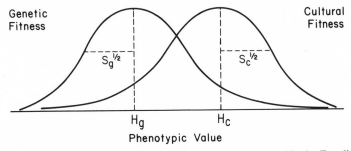

Fig. 6.4 The fitness functions for genetic and cultural selection assumed in the Freudian model. The phenotypic value that maximizes genetic fitness is H_g, and the value that maximizes cultural fitness is H_c. The intensities of the two selection processes are measured by $S_g^{1/2}$ and $S_c^{1/2}$.

Our usual strategy at this point in the analysis is to solve the recursion and find the equilibria. However, as is illustrated in Figure 6.5, these recursions do not have an equilibrium; there is no combination of $\overline{G}$ and $\overline{X}$ that simultaneously satisfies both recursions. Instead the mean values of the genetic character and the cultural character evolve in opposite directions indefinitely. Since it has been assumed that $H_c > H_g$, $\overline{X}$ increases and $\overline{G}$ decreases. However, by combining the two recursions it is possible to show that the mean phenotype in the population (i.e. $\overline{X} + \overline{G}$) does reach a steady state that is intermediate between the genetic and cultural optima.

This behavior makes sense given the assumptions of the model. On average the cultural variant X will be paired with the average genetic variant, $\overline{G}$, and, therefore, the average cultural fitness of individuals with cultural variant X depends on $X + \overline{G}$. Thus as long as $\overline{G}$ is intermediate between H_g and H_c, larger than average cultural variants will always be favored by the selection process that acts on potential teachers. The converse is true for the genetic trait. Put metaphorically, each inheritance system is motivated to continuously "up the ante" in an attempt to move the resulting phenotypes nearer their respective optima.

This is not a completely reasonable result; something must intervene to prevent infinite values of $\overline{G}$ and $\overline{X}$. One possibility is that extreme differences between genetic and cultural influences are maladaptive. The outcome of this model is analogous to regulating the speed of an automobile to 30 miles per hour by simultaneously pushing the accelerator and the brake to the floor. This seems like an undesirable state of affairs. One would expect that individuals with strongly conflicting genetic and cultural variants would have reduced fitness with respect to both kinds of transmission when compared with individuals whose genetic and

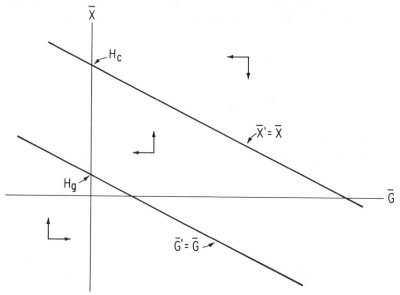

Fig. 6.5 Shows that the recursions given in 6.27 do not have an equilibrium. The line labeled $\overline{X}' = \overline{X}$ gives the combinations of values of $\overline{X}$ and $\overline{G}$ which lead to no change in $\overline{X}$. Similarly, the line $\overline{G}' = \overline{G}$ gives the combinations that lead to no change in $\overline{G}$. Since these lines do not intersect, there can be no equilibrium.

cultural variants combined harmoniously to achieve the same phenotypic value. It is easy to modify the model to allow for this possibility by multiplying both the genetic and cultural fitness of an individual by the term

$$K(G,X) = \exp\left\{\frac{-(G - X)^2}{2S_k}\right\} \tag{6.28}$$

This reduces both the cultural and the genetic fitness of an individual as the difference between the genetic and cultural variants increases. The strength of this effect is proportional to $(1/S_k)^{1/2}$.

We have analyzed this model with the following simplifying assumptions: (1) the intensities of cultural and genetic selection are equal (i.e. $S_g = S_c = S$), and (2) selection is weak (i.e. $S,S_k \gg V,U$). In this case, the mean values of the genetic and cultural characters reach a stable equilibrium as long as $S_k < S$—that is, if the effect of conflicting genetic and cultural specifications on fitness is greater than the direct effects of the characters themselves. The equilibrium value of $\overline{Y}$ is always intermediate between the genetic and cultural optima, but the equilibrium values of $\overline{G}$ and $\overline{X}$ can be widely disparate, especially if S is nearly equal to S_k.

A variety of other processes could be invoked to cause the cultural and genetic means to reach a stable equilibrium. We expect that most of these mechanisms will share the qualitative behavior of the specific model analyzed here; namely, an intermediate equilibrium phenotype may often be achieved through a balance of strong opposing forces—genetically inherited propensities pulling the individual in one direction and culturally inherited beliefs pulling in the other. The model analyzed above shows that this can be the result even if such intrapsychic conflict is directly selected against.

This model evokes a familiar picture of the human psyche. Many authors (see Campbell, 1975, for a review) have portrayed humans as torn between the conflicting demands of an animal id and a socially acquired superego. One is tempted to conclude that because so many observers have found this picture of the human psyche plausible there must be something to it. It is intriguing that this view of human behavior is a natural outcome of a dual inheritance model of human evolution. However, the fact that different thinkers within the Western tradition have found such a model plausible may be more a testament to cultural transmission than to empirical reality. Moreover, the dual inheritance models give us no reason to suppose that there should only be two conflicting behavioral principles. It seems reasonable that there are many different mutually asymmetric channels of cultural transmission. If this is so, one of the obvious predictions is that humans should have many conflicting goals.

Reprise

In this chapter we hope to have convinced the reader that natural selection acting on culturally transmitted variation will tend to create evolutionary forces that conflict with the dictates of ordinary natural selection acting on genetically transmitted variation. Indeed, we suspect that this effect will occur anytime an organism is characterized by two or more asymmetric systems of inheritance. It will be useful to review the key points of the argument:

1. Natural selection acting on asymmetrically transmitted variation may favor cultural variants that are genetically maladaptive. Individuals characterized by a particular cultural variant may be more or less likely to achieve a given social role than individuals with other cultural variants. This means that the attainment of many different social roles entails surviving a selection process. The variant that maximizes the probability of attaining social roles other than that of parent may often be different from the variant that maximizes the probability of becoming a genetic parent. If individuals occupying social roles other than parents are involved in cultural transmission, then many of the selection processes that act on cultural variation may increase the frequency of genetically maladaptive cultural variants.

2. Selection on asymmetrically transmitted variation may be very strong. The competition for many social roles, especially those with high prestige, is likely to be much more intense than the competition to become a parent. For example, only a single individual may be able to be mayor or headman at any given time. If these roles are even moderately important in socialization, there will be very strong selection on asymmetrically transmitted cultural variation.

3. It is easy to imagine that asymmetric cultural life cycles may themselves be genetically adaptive. First, the nature of the cultural life cycle has a multitude of effects on individual genetic fitness. Virtually every aspect of behavior affects what kinds of individuals are available as models for other individuals. Thus modifying the cultural life cycle may have indirect costs. Second, in heterogeneous environments, asymmetric life cycles may make biased transmission more effective, and therefore make it more likely that individuals acquire locally adaptive cultural variants. For many of these traits the cultural and genetic optima will be similar. Thus, it seems very plausible that asymmetric cultural life cycles may be adaptive when averaged over all the traits that are transmitted.

4. It is plausible that direct bias and guided variation will often fail to correct for the effects of selection acting on asymmetrically transmitted cultural variation. In Chapter 5, we argued that for directly biased transmission to be favored by selection, the bias must increase the probability of acquiring the locally adaptive cultural variant in a wide range of habitats. For some traits this may be readily accomplished because either (a) the locally adaptive variant does not vary much from habitat to habitat or (b) it is easy to evaluate the different variants that one is exposed to and determine which is most adaptive. However, for other traits, particularly basic beliefs and attitudes that affect many aspects of an individual's life, it may be very difficult for individuals to determine which is the best variant. For these traits, we expect that direct bias and guided variation will be weak. In this chapter, we showed that these conclusions may also hold even when natural selection acting on asymmetrically transmitted cultural variation increases the frequency of maladaptive variants.

Taken together, these points suggest that cultural transmission may often lead to the evolution of behavior that is qualitatively different from that predicted by socio-biological theory. Cultural transmission creates persistent, heritable variation between individuals. The existence of such variation allows a multitude of biological, social, and economic selective processes to affect the frequency of different culturally transmitted variants in the population. Given the variety of roles in human societies, it seems virtually certain that in some cases these selective processes will favor behavioral variants that are genetically maladaptive. Nonetheless, cultural inheritance can persist if, averaged over all traits, cultural organisms have significant advantages over noncultural organisms.

We believe that this reasoning is sufficiently plausible to refute the argument that human behavior must conform to the predictions of sociobiological theory. The human capacity for culture could have evolved in the way that we have suggested; the capacity for cultural transmission may be adaptive, and at the same time whole suites of characters may not enhance the inclusive fitness of individuals. Moreover, as we shall see in the next two chapters, there are processes other than natural selection that can lead to a similar conclusion.

On the other hand, humans could inherit virtually all of their behavior culturally and, at the same time, most important aspects of human behavior could be understood in terms of sociobiological principles. All that is required is (1) that the forces of biased transmission and guided variation ultimately have a genetic basis, (2) that these forces act to increase genetic fitness, and (3) that they are much stronger than natural selection on asymmetric cultural variation. The models presented in this chapter suggest that asymmetric cultural transmission may cause human evolution to diverge from the predictions of sociobiological theory. Whether and to what degree it actually does is an empirical problem.

The Demographic Transition

Earlier in this chapter we argued that the evolution of the culturally transmitted trait of field independence and associated child-rearing styles in industrializing societies may provide an example of the effects of selection acting on asymmetrically transmitted cultural traits. The evolution of this complex of traits may also illustrate how selection on asymmetrically transmitted variation can act to reduce ordinary Darwinian fitness. From a sociobiological perspective the demographic history of industrialization is a puzzle. One would expect that bias, guided variation, and selection on the vertical components of cultural transmission as well as on genetic traits should all act to increase fertility up to some optimum determined by the availability of resources to raise the resulting offspring. The per capita resources available in industrial and modernizing societies have expanded enormously, and death rates have fallen substantially. But fertility and completed family size drop in the "demographic transitions" that accompany industrialization.

A human sociobiologist might explain the demographic transition by arguing that during modernization environments change more rapidly than do the criteria controlling guided variation and direct bias. According to this view, fertility limitation is a by-product of outmoded vestigial tendencies to choose the wrong number of children. This hypothesis is certainly plausible. Burley (1979) presents a cogent argument that the cryptic estrous cycle of human females evolved as a mechanism to prevent the spread of fertility-minimizing measures by cultural transmission early in human evolution. She hypothesizes that the pain and discomfort of bearing, rearing, and raising children would act as powerful reinforcers favoring cultural variants leading to low fertility. Evolution, by making human females unaware of when they ovulate, combined with a powerful sex urge, made fertility control more difficult. Modern birth control methods might cause the demographic transition by finessing this mechanism. Other hypotheses of this general type could undoubtedly be constructed, perhaps based on Alexander's (1979: 77–78) notion that culture embodies the history of past reproductive conflicts.

It is also possible to explain the demographic transition as resulting from selection on asymmetrically transmitted variation. Recall that we argued that people like teachers and managers are disproportionately important in horizontal and oblique transmission in modernizing societies. In these circumstances, natural selection should act to increase the frequency of norms and values that stress the importance and value of these roles. Conflict with ordinary fitness will occur if one's success or that of one's children in professional roles is negatively correlated with family size. This is plausible since individuals with small families will have more time, money, and other resources to devote to the attainment of these social roles.

This hypothesis has the weight of common experience behind it. Modern young adults with professional aspirations delay marriage and child rearing and limit family size in order to acquire an education and establish a career. Professional success is viewed as a goal which conflicts with large families, partly because of the direct effect of children on one's own success and partly because individuals who desire professional success are likely to want professional success for their children. The latter implies each child must acquire a costly education; few parents can hope to pay for a college education for all the children in a large family. People may also feel that children conflict with the goal of maintaining an appropriate life-style, the right kind of house, car, leisure time activities, and so forth. In the interest of simplifying the discussion, we will ignore the effects of "conspicuous consumption" until Chapter 8, except to say that costly displays of status could be an important indirect bias effect favoring horizontal and oblique transmission.

We think that a good empirical case can be made that the causes of the demographic transition include natural selection operating on asymmetrically transmitted cultural variation. To establish the plausibility of this hypothesis we need to find evidence that (1) having large families inhibits upward mobility in industrial societies and (2) those who achieve higher status in such societies spread ideas such as norms of family size, the desirability of education and professional achievement, and child-rearing styles via asymmetric transmission.

There is evidence that large families do impose burdens on those who desire professional success for themselves or their children. Hill and Stafford (1974) report that the time parents allocate to their preschool children has a positive correlation with their education. The authoritative child-rearing patterns necessary to develop field-independent children seem on the face of it to be more demanding of parental time. This is certainly true for fathers, since the active participation of fathers in child rearing appears to be necessary to develop high levels of field independence, especially in sons (Werner, 1979: 181–182). Similar evidence comes from the study of family size and birth order effects on IQ (Zajonc and

Markus, 1975; Zajonc, 1976). Large families appear to show reduced IQs among the children, even when controlling for social class, due to a dilution of parental attention to each child. Mason and Palan (1981) report data from Malaysia which show that a major motivation for fertility reduction is to send children to school. Traditionally, mothers trained older children to look after younger ones, a family labor mobilizing device that is lost when children are sent to school. Statistical studies support the hypothesis that large families are negatively correlated with educational achievement, and therefore probably also with movement into occupations effective in horizontal and oblique transmission under modern or modernizing conditions (Terhune, 1974; Watson et al., 1979). For a general review of the effects of costly investments in children in the Third World, see Schultz (1979).

There is also evidence that asymmetrically transmitted cultural traits are involved in the demographic transition. Very likely the idea that small families are desirable is one of the important traits transmitted by successful professionals. Stevens (1981) analyzed the statistical effects of upward mobility on fertility. His objective was to solve the puzzle presented by the fact that past studies had found quite variable effects of mobility on fertility. He interpreted his findings as showing that the extra economic resources gained by mobility had a positive effect on fertility, but that upwardly mobile individuals also tended to adopt the attitudes and behaviors of their newly achieved class, including lower fertility. The net effects of mobility thus vary according to how far and into what class an individual moves. Similarly, Jain (1981) found that the apparently complex effect of education of women on fertility could be interpreted as women's moving toward fertility norms expected from a given degree of education from quite different starting points, depending on the nation studied.

On a larger scale, Caldwell (1976) and Freedman (1979) have argued that it is impossible to explain the timing of demographic transition either historically in the West or in the Third World today without positing a role for the asymmetrical transmission of values. The key fact is that, although the demographic transition is usually associated with industrial development, different societies have begun their transition at different points in the development process, and the transition has proceeded at quite different rates in different societies. For example, Caldwell gives data from the urban Yoruba of Nigeria, who have been exposed to considerable modernizing influence but who still overwhelmingly have high fertility. Caldwell attributes the inhibited demographic transition of the Yoruba to their success in adapting their traditional extended family system to urban life. (Recall here LeVine, 1966, which showed an intermediate level of need for achievement among Yoruba.)

Caldwell views the economic independence of the nuclear household as the key variable in the demographic transition. As industrialization proceeds, asymmetric transmission will eventually make the nuclear household the norm and lead to decisions to reduce family size. This shift will be more or less rapid, however, depending on the cultural inertia exerted by the preexisting family norms. In Caldwell's view, the overwhelming economic strength of the West has caused it to dominate international communication to the extent that the demographic transition is now spreading in advance of industrialization, rather than as a consequence of it. In Freedman's (1979: 9) more conservative view,

> In addition to the direct effect of actual changes on life conditions, changing
> perceptions of what is desirable and possible can affect motivations about
> family size. This results from literacy and communication and transportation
> links to the cumulating world storehouse of models, ideas and things.

Conclusion

It is possible to cite many other empirical examples which plausibly support the
notion that natural selection acting on culturally transmitted variation may act to
increase the frequency of genetically deleterious variants. For example, several
authors (Richerson and Boyd, 1978; Pulliam and Dunford, 1980; Werren and
Pulliam, 1981; Pulliam, 1982) have independently argued that the predominance of
unilineal kinship systems among human societies is an example of the effect of
selection acting on asymmetrically transmitted cultural variation. Hamilton (1964)
showed that natural selection acting on genes could favor self-sacrificial altruistic
behavior by individuals toward their genetic relatives. It is possible to show that a
similar principle holds for cultural transmission, except now the altruism is toward
an individual's cultural relatives. When subsistence technology favors a pattern of
unilocal postmarital residence (e.g. newlyweds always live with the bride's parents), it is plausible that the resulting patterns of cultural kinship will favor unilineal
social organization. Another example is the existence of celibate religious orders.
It seems plausible that by avoiding the costs of bearing or supporting children,
celibates could devote more time and resources to spreading their beliefs horizontally.

The fact that these hypotheses are plausible does not mean that they are correct.
In virtually every case it is possible to construct a hypothesis that indicates that the
seemingly maladaptive behaviors in question are, in fact, genetically adaptive.
Greene (1978), Alexander (1979a), and Kurland (1979) have independently proposed ways in which matrilineality can be genetically adaptive, and Hartung (1976)
has suggested an adaptive rationale for patrilineal social organization. Alexander
(1979a: 80) has suggested that celibate priests may increase their inclusive fitness
by helping their relatives to reproduce. He has also suggested that the parishioners
may coerce priests into being celibate so that they cannot use their influential
position to increase their own reproductive success.

Determining which of these two classes of hypotheses is correct in any particular
circumstance requires much more information than is typically available. It is
important to note, however, that this argument cuts both ways. There is no a priori
reason to accept either kind of hypothesis: Dual inheritance models and conventional sociobiological models are both consistent with the origin of the human
species through the processes of ordinary organic evolution. Which hypothesis is
correct in any given situation is an empirical question. For some behaviors, for
example those involving sexual jealousy, we think that it is very plausible that the
sociobiological hypothesis is correct. For others, like celibate religious orders and

the limitation of family size among the modern middle classes, it seems more plausible to us that other mechanisms are at work.

We think that the results of this chapter are very important because they mean that, under the circumstances outlined earlier in this chapter, the natural selection of culturally transmitted variations can cause human behavior to diverge systematically from the predictions of conventional sociobiological theory. In the next two chapters we will investigate two other processes which have the same effect.

7

Frequency-dependent Bias and the Evolution of Cooperation

> To us at the time, a suicide air force was a very natural thing, nothing more than a means of self-defense toward the end of the war. True, the war ended and saved me 28 years ago, but if I had to be a Kamikaze pilot again, I would.
>
> Sei Watanabe, Lt. Gen., Japan Defense Force, Ret., quoted in *The Cherry Blossom Squadrons,* Hagomoro Society (1973: 52)

Why did men like Sei Watanabe choose to become Kamikazes when death was the nearly certain result? Coercion does not seem to have been an important factor. Like most of the thousands of Kamikaze pilots, Watanabe was a volunteer. A shortage of suitable airplanes forced the Japanese navy to turn down volunteers until the very last days of the war. Indeed, according to Millot's (1970) history of the Kamikazes, the idea of suicide attacks originated among ordinary pilots who were frustrated by their inability to damage American ships in the face of faster and better armored American fighter planes. Only later was it adopted as a legitimate tactic by the Japanese navy. Nor can we attribute all the willingness to volunteer to a combination of youthful patriotism and ignorance about the realities of war, although these factors were undoubtedly important. Many of the volunteers were experienced combat pilots. One of the difficulties that faced the commanders of Kamikaze squadrons was that experienced pilots were required to escort the Kamikazes to their targets, and these pilots wanted to be Kamikazes (Millot, 1970). For many volunteers, the answer seems to be that they believed such extraordinary measures were necessary for Japan to escape defeat. Given that suicide tactics were much more effective than conventional attacks, these men felt obligated to implement them, even if it meant their own deaths.

And how did men come to have such self-destructive beliefs? Millot argues that the complex of beliefs that gave rise to the Kamikaze tactic can be traced back to the Samurai military code of feudal Japan which called for heroic self-sacrifice and put death before dishonor. When the Japanese military modernized in the nineteenth century, the officer corps was drawn from the Samurai class. These men brought their values and transmitted them to subsequent generations of officers who in turn inculcated these values in their men.

We find this kind of historical explanation unsatisfying for two reasons. First, it is incomplete. It tells us why a particular generation of Japanese came to believe in heroic self-sacrifice for the common good; it does not tell us how these beliefs came to predominate in the warrior class of feudal Japan. Second, it is not general enough. The beliefs that led the Kamikazes to die for their country are just an especially stark example of a much more general tendency of humans to behave altruistically toward members of various groups of which they are members.

We would like an explanation which tells us how the mechanisms of cultural transmission can cause altruistic beliefs to increase in frequency and eventually to predominate in a society. Such an explanation must overcome two difficulties.

1. It must tell us how the tendency to acquire self-sacrificial beliefs and values could have evolved. The central tenet of sociobiological theory is that behavior of humans (and all other organisms) should maximize genetic fitness. A corollary of this principle is that natural selection can lead to cooperation among large numbers of individuals only if they are genetically closely related, as for example in the social insects. For the ecological and demographic parameters that characterize most mammals, cooperation will be limited to relatively small groups of related individuals. With the exception of humans, this result seems consistent with the available data (Wilson, 1975). Thus we should expect that biased transmission and guided variation should act to reduce the frequency of self-sacrificial beliefs and values.

2. It must tell us why altruisic cooperation is directed toward some individuals and not others. In most societies, individuals belong to more than one social grouping, for example, a clan, an ethnic group, a social class, or a state. The interests of these groups often conflict with each other and with the individual's own interests. In making choices, how much weight should the individual give to his own interests and the interests of each of the groups to which he belongs? For sociobiologists, the theory of kin selection gives relatively clear answers to these questions. Alternative theories explaining the extensive non-kin cooperation in the human species need to be similarly specific.

Donald Campbell (1975) has argued that the altruistic nature of most systems of moral teaching suggests that these cultural traits have been shaped by some kind of group selection process; according to Campbell's argument, groups with belief systems that cause individuals within the group to cooperate effectively survive longer and produce more cultural propagules. Eventually this process would cause self-sacrificial belief systems to predominate. There are two difficulties with this explanation. First, it seems likely that directly biased transmission, guided variation, and natural selection should act within groups to decrease the frequency of self-sacrificial cultural variants. Experience with genetic models suggests that such within-population forces will tend to be stronger than selection among groups. Second, any mode of cultural transmission which allowed group selection to predominate would itself be selected against.

In this chapter we show that the kind of cultural group selection envisioned by Campbell can be the by-product of an otherwise adaptive mode of biased cultural transmission. We begin by analyzing a model of cultural transmission in which naive individuals have a tendency to acquire the variant that is more common among the individuals available to them as models. This "conformist" transmission rule is one example of a more general class of rules we label "frequency-dependent bias." Conformist frequency-dependent bias has two interesting effects: first, in a spatially varying environment, it can provide a simple general rule that improves the chance of acquiring the locally favored cultural variant, and second, it increases the amount of cultural variation among groups relative to the amount of cultural variation within groups. This in turn can cause selection between groups to favor cultural variants which enhance the success of the group at the expense of the individual. We will conclude by considering evidence on ethnocentrism in the context of these models.

Models of Frequency-dependent Bias

According to our definition, frequency-dependent bias occurs whenever a naive individual uses the frequency of a variant among his models to evaluate the merit of the variant. It is important to understand this does not mean that frequency-dependent transmission occurs whenever the probability that an individual acquires a particular variant depends on the frequency of the variant among its models. Indeed, the latter will be true almost any time there is cultural transmission. Our definition of frequency-dependent bias requires that naive individuals be *disproportionately* likely to acquire the more (or less) common variant.

To understand this distinction better, consider the following simple example: suppose a cultural trait with two variants, c and d, is transmitted vertically by n models with equal intrinsic weights. Even if transmission is completely unbiased, the probability that a naive individual acquires trait c still depends on the frequency of c among his models in the way shown in Figure 7.1a. When transmission is unbiased, this relationship is a straight line because unbiased transmission is analogous to naive individuals' randomly choosing a model. The probability of getting a particular variant is just the frequency of the variant among the set of models. Figure 7.1b graphs the relationship between the frequency of c and the probability that a naive individual acquires c assuming that transmission is directly biased in favor of c. The probability that a naive individual acquires c is always greater than if he had selected a model at random. We presume that this results from the fact that naive individuals evaluate alternative variants and tend to choose variant c over variant d.

Suppose that naive individuals use the commonness of a variant among their models as an indirect measure of its merit. This will result in an increase in the probability of acquiring the more common variant *relative to unbiased transmission* as is shown in Figure 7.1c. When the frequency of c in the set of models is greater than one-half, the probability that a naive individual acquires c with frequency-dependent transmission is greater than at the same frequency with unbiased transmission. When the frequency of c among models is less than one-half, the probability of acquiring c is reduced relative to unbiased transmission. Obviously, frequency-dependent bias could also favor the rarer variant. More complex kinds of frequency dependence are also possible (Lumsden and Wilson, 1980).

Frequency-dependent bias should also be distinguished from direct bias in which the strength and direction of bias depend on the frequency of the variant in the population. It may often be that the merit of a variant depends on the frequency of the variant in the population. For example, the attractiveness of an occupation may

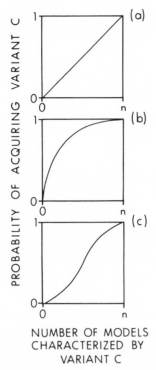

Fig. 7.1 The probability that a naive individual acquires a cultural variant depends on the frequency of that variant among that individual's models assuming (a) unbiased transmission, (b) directly biased transmission, and (c) frequency-dependent biased transmission.

depend on how many individuals in the population pursue it. If the number of university professors is large relative to the demand, becoming a university professor may be unattractive; if there is a shortage of engineers, becoming an engineer may be quite appealing. In these cases the magnitude and direction of direct bias acting on the transmission of cultural variants that affect occupational choice depend on the frequency of these variants in the population. We want to distinguish this "frequency-dependent direct bias" from frequency-dependent bias because the former requires the naive individual to evaluate the merit of different variants. Effective evaluation of the alternatives may be costly in the same way as ordinary direct bias. In contrast, in frequency-dependent bias the naive individual does not directly evaluate the merit of the variants to which he is exposed; rather, he simply uses the frequency of a variant among his models (not the population) as an indirect measure of its merit.

A simple model of frequency-dependent bias

To see how frequency-dependent bias affects the frequency of alternative cultural variants in a population, consider the very simple case of vertical transmission of a dichotomous trait by sets of three models. We begin with three models because this is the smallest set of models in which frequency-dependent bias is possible. As before, assume that each individual can be characterized by one of two culturally

Table 7.1 The effect of a simple example of frequency-dependent cultural transmission

Cultural Variant of			Probability That Offspring Acquires Cultural Variant	
Model 1	Model 2	Model 3	c	d
c	c	c	1	0
c	c	d		
c	d	c	$2/3 + D/3$	$1/3 - D/3$
d	c	c		
d	d	c		
d	c	d	$1/3 - D/3$	$2/3 + D/3$
c	d	d		
d	d	d	0	1

transmitted variants, c and d. The probability that an individual acquires variant c, given that he is exposed to a particular set of models, is shown in Table 7.1. This cultural transmission rule is particularly simple because each of the models is assumed to have the same role. It does not matter which models are characterized by variant c, only how many are so characterized. Let p be the frequency of c in the population of models.

If one assumes that each set of models is a random sample of the population, then it is shown in Box 7.1 that the frequency of c among naive individuals after transmission, p', is given by

$$p' = p + Dp(1 - p)(2p - 1) \tag{7.1}$$

There are several things to note about Equation 7.1. First, if the frequency-dependent bias parameter, D, equals zero, cultural transmission is unbiased and, as one would expect, transmission leaves the frequency of traits unchanged. Second, the direction of force depends on both the sign of D and the frequency of c: if

---

Box 7.1 With random mating the probability of forming a set of parents with i c individuals given that the frequency of c is p, $M(i|p)$, is

$$M(i|p) = \binom{3}{i} p^i (1 - p)^{3-i}$$

The frequency of c after transmission, p', is

$$p' = (1)M(3|p) + (2/3 + D/3)M(2|p) + (1/3 - D/3)M(1|p)$$
$$= p^3 + (2/3 + D/3)\{3p^2(1 - p)\} + (1/3 - D/3)\{3p(1 - p)^2\}$$
$$= p\{p^2 + 2p(1 - p) + (1 - p)^2\} + D\{p^2(1 - p) - p(1 - p)^2\}$$
$$= p + Dp(1 - p)(2p - 1)$$

$D > 0$, cultural transmission creates a force increasing the frequency of the more common variant in the population. That is, if $p > 0.5$, then $p' > p$, and if $p < 0.5$, then $p' < p$. If $D < 0$, transmission increases the frequency of the rarer variant in the population.

The relationship between direct and frequency-dependent bias will be clearer if Equation 7.1 is rewritten as follows:

$$p' = p + [D(2p - 1)]\text{Var}(p) \qquad (7.2)$$

Thus the magnitude of the force depends on two factors: the variance of the trait in the population just as in the case of direct bias, and the term $D(2p - 1)$ which is like a bias parameter that depends on the frequency of the variant in the population. When $p = \frac{1}{2}$, the frequency-dependent bias parameter is zero; as $p \to 0$ or 1 the absolute magnitude of the parameter increases; its sign depends on the sign of D.

Making the model more complicated

Clearly this is a very simple model. One would like to know if making the model more realistic leads to any qualitative changes in the results. In this section we add several complications to the model, one at a time. First, suppose that models in different social roles have different linear weights. To allow for unequal weights suppose that the ith model has a basic weight α_i ($\Sigma\alpha_i = 1$). Then, as is shown in Table 7.2, we suppose that the actual weight of the ith model, A_i, depends on (1)

Table 7.2 The probability of offspring acquiring trait c or d given a particular set of models when the parents have different intrinsic weights, α_1, α_2, and α_3

Cultural Variant of			Probability That Offspring Acquires Cultural Variant	
Model 1	Model 2	Model 3	c	d
c	c	c	1	0
c	c	d	$\dfrac{(\alpha_1 + \alpha_2)(1 + D/2)}{1 + (D/2)(1 - 2\alpha_3)}$	$\dfrac{\alpha_3(1 - D/2)}{1 + (D/2)(1 - 2\alpha_3)}$
c	d	c	$\dfrac{(\alpha_1 + \alpha_3)(1 + D/2)}{1 + (D/2)(1 - 2\alpha_2)}$	$\dfrac{\alpha_2(1 - D/2)}{1 + (D/2)(1 - 2\alpha_2)}$
d	c	c	$\dfrac{(\alpha_3 + \alpha_2)(1 + D/2)}{1 + (D/2)(1 - 2\alpha_1)}$	$\dfrac{\alpha_1(1 - D/2)}{1 + (D/2)(1 - 2\alpha_1)}$
d	d	c	$\dfrac{\alpha_3(1 - D/2)}{1 + (D/2)(1 - 2\alpha_3)}$	$\dfrac{(\alpha_1 + \alpha_2)(1 + D/2)}{1 + (D/2)(1 - 2\alpha_3)}$
d	c	d	$\dfrac{\alpha_2(1 - D/2)}{1 + (D/2)(1 - 2\alpha_2)}$	$\dfrac{(\alpha_1 + \alpha_3)(1 + D/2)}{1 + (D/2)(1 - 2\alpha_2)}$
c	d	d	$\dfrac{\alpha_1(1 - D/2)}{1 + (D/2)(1 - 2\alpha_1)}$	$\dfrac{(\alpha_3 + \alpha_2)(1 + D/2)}{1 + (D/2)(1 - 2\alpha_1)}$
d	d	d	0	1

his basic weight and (2) the commonness of his cultural variant in the set of models to which he belongs. It is shown in Box 7.2 that this transmission rule results in the following change in the frequency of c:

$$p' = p + D_e p(1 - p)(2p - 1) \tag{7.3}$$

where

$$D_e = D\left(1 - \sum_{i=1}^{3} \alpha_i^2\right) = D(1 - 1/n_e)$$

where n_e is the effective number of models as defined in Chapter 5. Equation 7.3 says that increasing the effective number of models (while holding the actual number constant) increases the strength of the frequency-dependent bias. We derived a similar result in the case of direct bias.

This result is interesting in the context of horizontal transmission. Suppose that a particular individual encounters two other individuals, and then, given his own behavior and that of the others, acquires (or remains) type c with a given proba-

---

Box 7.2 Let $P(c\,|\,ccd)$ denote the conditional probability that an offspring acquires variant c given that it is exposed to models with variants c, c, and d. Then from the table

$$P(c\,|\,ccd) = \frac{(1 - \alpha_3)(1 + D/2)}{1 + (D/2)(1 - 2\alpha_3)}$$

If D is small enough to ignore terms of order D^2, then

$$P(c\,|\,ccd) \approx (1 - \alpha_3)[1 + (D/2) - (D/2)(1 - 2\alpha_3)]$$

which can be simplified to become

$$P(c\,|\,ccd) \approx 1 - \alpha_3 + D\alpha_3 - D\alpha_3^2$$

Analogous derivations yield expressions for $P(c\,|\,cdc)$ and $P(c\,|\,dcc)$. The sum of these three terms is

$$P(c\,|\,ccd) + P(c\,|\,cdc) + P(c\,|\,dcc) = 2 + D\left(1 - \sum_{i=1}^{3} \alpha_i^2\right)$$

Due to the symmetry of the model, $P(c\,|\,ddc) = 1 - P(c\,|\,ccd)$. Thus

$$P(c\,|\,ddc) + P(c\,|\,dcd) + P(c\,|\,cdd) = 1 - D\left(1 - \sum_{i=1}^{3} \alpha_i^2,\right)$$

The frequency of c after transmission, p', given that it was p before transmission, is

$$p' = p^3 + p^2(1 - p)\{P(c\,|\,ccd) + P(c\,|\,cdc) + P(c\,|\,dcc)\}$$
$$+ \, p(1 - p)^2\{P(c\,|\,ddc) + P(c\,|\,dcd) + P(c\,|\,cdd)\}$$

Combining these expressions yields Equation 7.3 in the text.

bility. As we showed in Chapter 3, this model is identical to a vertical model in which different social roles have different weightings except that the generation time is now the time it takes to encounter two other individuals. The result just derived suggests that if individuals give great weight to their own behavior or to that of individuals occupying one social role, the effect of frequency-dependent bias will be weakened.

These results can also be extended to include nonrandom formation of sets of models. It seems likely that in many cases sets of models will not be formed at random; rather, similar individuals will tend to aggregate. For example, among husbands and wives in the United States, many characters such as political party and religious affiliation are highly correlated. In population genetics, the analogous phenomenon is called "assortative mating." To model assortative formation of sets of three models, we assume that there is a constant correlation, r, between the cultural variants of two of the models and that the third model is chosen at random. For example, the political beliefs of a child's mother and father might be highly correlated with each other but uncorrelated with beliefs of the child's teachers. With this assumption the probability that each set is formed is as given in Table 7.3. It is shown in Box 7.3 that the frequency of variant c after frequency-dependent transmission is given by

$$p' = p + D(1 - r)p(1 - p)(2p - 1) \tag{7.4}$$

Table 7.3 The probability that each of the possible sets of models form when the sets may form nonrandomly

Correlated Models		Uncorrelated	Probability of Formation
Model 1	Model 2	Model	of Set of Models
c	c	c	$\{q^2(1 - r) + qr\} q$
c	c	d	$\{q^2(1 - r) + qr\} (1 - q)$
c	d	c	$\{q(1 - q) (1 - r)\} q$
d	c	c	$\{q(1 - q) (1 - r)\} q$
c	d	d	$\{q(1 - q) (1 - r)\} (1 - q)$
d	c	d	$\{q(1 - q) (1 - r)\} (1 - q)$
d	d	c	$\{(1 - q)^2 (1 - r) + (1 - q)r\} q$
d	d	d	$\{(1 - q)^2 (1 - r) + (1 - q)r\} (1 - q)$

Box 7.3 According to our assumptions, a fraction $1 - r$ of the sets of models are formed at random. Thus

$$p' = (1 - r)[p + Dp(1 - p)(2p - 1)]$$
$$\quad + r\{p^2 + p(1 - p)[(2/3 + D/3) + (1/3 - D/3)]\}$$
$$= (1 - r)[p + Dp(1 - p)(2p - 1)] + rp[p + (1 - p)]$$
$$= p + (1 - r)Dp(1 - p)(2p - 1)$$

Equation 7.4 says that positive assortative formation of sets of models weakens the force due to frequency-dependent bias. This makes sense since assortative mating decreases the probability that the correlated models will be characterized by different cultural variants. In the extreme case when r = 1, the correlated models are exactly the same. This means that sets of models can have at most two different models, and frequency-dependent transmission can have no effect. In general the more variability that exists in sets of models the stronger the force of frequency-dependent bias. Positive assortment weakens frequency-dependent bias, and negative assortment strengthens it.

Finally, these results can be generalized to allow more than three models. Assume that there are n models and that each model has an equal weight, 1/n. As usual, we assign the ith model a numerical value, X_i, which is equal to one if he is characterized by cultural variant c and is equal to zero if he is characterized by d. Finally, we assume that the frequency-dependent bias depends only on the number of models that are characterized by a particular cultural variant. With these assumptions we can write the transmission rule algebraically as follows:

$$\text{Prob(naive individual} = c \mid j) = j/n + D(j) \qquad (7.5)$$

where

$$j = \sum_{i=1}^{n} X_i$$

The function $D(j)$ gives the effect of frequency-dependent bias in a set of cultural parents with j c individuals.

It is easy to conceive of a wide variety of different kinds of frequency-dependent bias when there are more than three models. For example, naive individuals might be predisposed to imitate traits which characterize an odd number of their models. More plausibly, naive individuals might be predisposed to imitate the most common type as long as it is not too common, but beyond a certain frequency, they imitate the rare type. Here we want to restrict attention to the two simplest cases, common type favored, or "conformist transmission," and rare type favored, or "nonconformist transmission." Lumsden and Wilson (1981) consider models which include more complex frequency-dependent effects. Conformist transmission requires that $D(j) \geq 0$ for $j \geq n/2$ and $D(j) \leq 0$ for $j \leq n/2$, and nonconformist transmission requires the reverse. To focus on the effects of frequency-dependent bias we also assume (1) that there is no random variation, so that $D(n) = D(0) = 0$, and (2) that there is no direct bias, so that $D(j) = D(1 - j)$.

With these assumptions it is shown in Box 7.4 that n-model frequency-dependent bias has properties that are very similar to the three-model case. Conformist transmission increases the frequency of the variant with the higher frequency, and nonconformist transmission increases the frequency of the variant that is in lower frequency. In both cases the magnitude of the force approaches zero as p approaches 1, $\frac{1}{2}$, or 0.

Box 7.4 With random mating the probability of forming a set of parents with j c individuals, given that the frequency of c is p, M(j|p), is

$$M(j|P) = \binom{n}{j}p^j(1 - p)^{n-j}$$

Thus the frequency of c after transmission, p', is

$$p' = \sum_{j=1}^{n} \{j/n + D(j)\}\binom{n}{j}p^j(1 - p)^{n-j}$$

Because M(j|p) is the binomial distribution

$$p' = p + \sum_{j=1}^{n} D(j)\binom{n}{j}p^j(1 - p)^{n-j}$$

Let k = n/2 + 1 if n is even and k = (n + 1)/2 if n is odd. Then we can rewrite this equation as follows:

$$p' = p + \sum_{j=k}^{n} D(j)\binom{n}{j}p^j(1 - p)^{n-j} + D(n - j)\binom{n}{n - j}p^{n-j}(1 - p)^j$$

And since D(j) = −D(n − j) < 0, it follows that

$$p' = p + \sum_{j=k}^{n} D(j)\binom{n}{j}[p^j(1 - p)^{n-j} - p^{n-j}(1 - p)^j]$$

First consider conformist transmission. Then D(j) > 0 for j > k. Thus the frequency of c will increase whenever 1 > p > 1/2 and will decrease whenever 1/2 > p > 0. If transmission is nonconformist, the reverse will occur.

The Adaptive Advantages of Conformist Transmission

It would be interesting to know if there are any circumstances in which individuals who acquire their behavior via frequency-dependent bias will have higher fitness on the average than individuals who utilize a cultural transmission rule without the conformist effect. One such situation may exist when a population is subdivided into a number of subpopulations in which different behaviors are favored by selection. In such subdivided populations, migration between subpopulations will often maintain cultural variation in each subpopulation. In many cases, however, the variant favored by selection, guided variation, or direct bias in a particular subpopulation will also be the most common variant. Under these conditions, conformist transmission is a simple general rule that increases the probability that an individual will acquire the locally favored variant.

In this section we analyze the evolution of frequency-dependent bias in a spatially varying habitat, proceeding much as in earlier chapters. First, we describe and analyze a simple model in which alleles at a genetic locus influence the extent to which cultural transmission is characterized by frequency-dependent bias. Then this model is embedded in a spatially varying environment. We will see that there are a range of plausible environments in which alleles causing cultural transmission to be subject to frequency-dependent bias will replace alleles leading to unbiased transmission.

A model of the genetic modification of frequency-dependent bias

Consider a large population of individuals, each of whom is characterized by one of two cultural variants, c and d. We assume that this trait is acquired via oblique cultural transmission from three models and that the members of the set of models for each naive offspring are drawn randomly from the individuals present in each subpopulation. As indicated earlier in this chapter, we believe that much more general models will have the same qualitative properties. Also, suppose that each individual is characterized by one of two genotypes, e and f. Individuals with genotype e are characterized by an unbiased transmission rule. Individuals with genotype f are characterized by a rule with frequency-dependent bias as shown in Table 7.1. Genetic parents are also drawn at random from the population as a whole.

With these assumptions there are four kinds of individuals, ec, fc, ed, and fd. The frequencies of each of these kinds of individuals in the pool of cultural parents are F_{ec}, F_{fc}, F_{ed}, and F_{fd}. The frequency of the cultural variant c among models $(F_{ec} + F_{fc})$ is p, and the frequency of the genotype e among parents $(F_{ec} + F_{ed})$ is q. The frequency of each of these kinds of individuals after transmission is

$$F'_{ec} = q[p + Dp(1 - p)(2p - 1)]$$

$$F'_{fc} = (1 - q)p$$

$$F'_{ed} = q[1 - p - Dp(1 - p)(2p - 1)]$$ (7.6)

$$F'_{fd} = (1 - q)(1 - p)$$

Next, suppose that the probability that c individuals become parents (either genetic or cultural) is W_c, and the probability that d individuals become parents is W_d. It will be useful to let the ratio $W_c/W_d = 1 + s$. Then, the frequency of c among cultural parents, p'', is

$$p'' = (1 + s)[p + qDp(1 - p)(2p - 1)]/\overline{W}$$ (7.7)

where

$$\overline{W} = 1 + s[p + qDp(1 - p)(2p - 1)]$$

The properties of this recursion will be clearer if we assume that selection and biased transmission are so weak that terms of order s^2, sD, and D^2 can be ignored. Under this assumption

$$p'' \approx p + p(1 - p)[s + qD(2p - 1)]$$ (7.8)

The net effect of frequency-dependent transmission and selection depends on the sign of the term, $s + qD(2p - 1)$. By hypothesis, selection favors variant c, which means that $s > 0$. The effect of frequency-dependent bias depends on the signs of D and $(2p - 1)$. If transmission is conformist ($D > 0$), then transmission tends to increase p if $p > \frac{1}{2}$ and decrease it if $p < \frac{1}{2}$. This means that if $p > \frac{1}{2}$, the net effect of selection and conformist transmission always is to increase p. On the other hand, if $p < \frac{1}{2}$, the net effect of the two forces depends on the relative magnitudes of qD and s. If transmission is nonconformist ($D < 0$), then the net effect of the two forces always increases p if $p < \frac{1}{2}$. When $p > \frac{1}{2}$, the direction of the force again depends on the relative magnitudes of qD and s. For a given nonzero value of q, this recursion has three equilibria, $p = 0$, $p = 1$, and $p = \frac{1}{2}(1 - s/qD)$. The internal equilibrium can be stable only if $D < 0$.

The frequency of the bias genotype e among genetic parents is

$$q'' = q[1 + sp + sDp(1 - p)(2p - 1)]/\overline{W} \qquad (7.9)$$

To better interpret Equation 7.9, assume that selection is weak. Then 7.9 simplifies to

$$q'' = q + q(1 - q)s_e(p) \qquad (7.10)$$

where

$$s_e = sDp(1 - p)(2p - 1)$$

The term s_e is the effective selective advantage of the bias genotype as a function of the frequency of the cultural variants. The form of s_e is shown graphically in Figure 7.2. The bias genotype will increase if (a) $D > 0$ and $\frac{1}{2} < p < 1$ or (b) $D < 0$ and $0 < p < \frac{1}{2}$. In other words, conformist transmission is always favored by selection if the favored cultural variant is more common than the alternative variant; nonconformist transmission is favored if the favored cultural variant is rarer than the alternative variant.

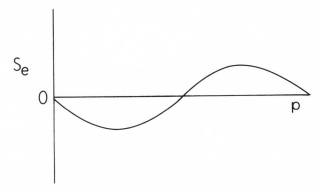

Fig. 7.2 The effective selective advantage (s_e) of a genotype exercising frequency-dependent bias relative to an unbiased genotype as a function of the frequency of the favored cultural variant in the population (p).

In a temporally and spatially uniform environment, frequency-dependent bias cannot be important in the long run. If $D > 0$, the only possible stable equilibrium values of p are zero and one, and at these values frequency-dependent bias can have no effect, beneficial or deleterious. If $D < 0$, then a stable internal equilibrium value for p is possible. However, consideration of the complete set of two recursions shows that the bias genotype will decrease in frequency. These facts suggest that we consider a spatially varying environment.

Frequency-dependent bias in a spatially varying environment

Suppose that a very large population of individuals is subdivided into n large subpopulations. As in the previous section, each individual is characterized by one of two culturally transmitted behaviors, c and d, and one of two genotypes, e and f. The frequency of c individuals among models just before cultural transmission in the ith subpopulation is labeled p_i, and the frequency of the bias genotype, e, among parents in the ith subpopulation is q_i. We suppose that in the ith subpopulation $W_c/W_d = 1 + s_i$, where s_i can be either negative or positive. This means that the cultural variant c is favored in some habitats but not in others. We have gone to the trouble of using a model with more than two subpopulations because it will be useful when we come to investigate the effect of selection among subpopulations later in this chapter.

Let p_i be the frequency of the cultural variant c in the ith habitat. Then, using the results of the last section, the frequency of c after transmission and selection in the ith subpopulation is

$$p_i'' = (1 + s_i)[p_i + q_iDp_i(1 - p_i)(2p_i - 1)]/\overline{W_i} \qquad (7.11)$$

where

$$\overline{W_i} = 1 + s_i[p_i + q_iDp_i(1 - p_i)(2p_i - 1)]$$

The frequency of genetic variant e in the ith subpopulation is

$$q_i'' = q_i[1 + s_ip_i + s_iDp_i(1 - p_i)(2p_i - 1)]/\overline{W_i} \qquad (7.12)$$

After selection some individuals emigrate. Each individual has a probability $(1 - m)$ of remaining in his natal subpopulation to reproduce and a probability m of emigrating. The individuals who emigrate have an equal probability of settling in each of the n subpopulations, including the one they just left. Some density-dependent process regulates the size of each subpopulation so that each subpopulation contributes an equal number of individuals to the pool of migrants each generation. Given these assumptions, the frequency of c individuals in the ith subpopulation after migration, but before transmission, p_i''', is

$$p_i''' = (1 - m)p_i'' + (m/n)\sum_{j=1}^{n} p_j'' \qquad (7.13)$$

for $i = 1,\ldots,n$.

In Box 7.5, we show that the equilibrium frequency of c individuals in the ith subpopulation, $\hat{p}_i$, must satisfy the following conditions:

$$\bar{p} = \hat{p}_i - \frac{(1 - m)}{m} \left(\frac{\hat{p}_i(1 - \hat{p}_i)\{s_i + \hat{q}_i D (2p_i - 1)[1 + s_i(1 - \hat{p}_i)]\}}{\overline{W}_i} \right) \qquad (7.14)$$

where $\bar{p}$ is defined as the average frequency of c individuals in the whole population at equilibrium, that is,

$$\bar{p} = (1/n) \sum_{i=1}^{n} \hat{p}_i \qquad (7.15)$$

Similarly, the frequency of the conformist genotype in the ith subpopulation after migration is

$$q_i''' = (1 - m)q_i'' + (m/n) \sum_{j=1}^{n} q_j'' \qquad (7.16)$$

and the equilibrium frequencies of the genotype e, q_i, must satisfy

$$\bar{q} = \hat{q}_i - \frac{(1 - m)}{m} \left(\frac{\hat{q}_i(1 - \hat{q}_i)s_i[D\hat{p}_i(1 - \hat{p}_i)(2\hat{p}_i - 1)]}{\overline{W}_i} \right) \qquad (7.17)$$

Now, suppose that the population is fixed for the unbiased genotype. (This is an equilibrium since the second term on the right-hand side of 7.17 is zero in every

---

Box 7.5 For convenience let

$$p_i'' = p_i + F(p_i)$$

where the function $F(p_i)$ is defined implicitly by Equation 7.11. Then from Equation 7.13

$$p_i''' = \{p_i + F(p_i)\}(1 - m) + m/n \sum_{j=1}^{n} \{p_j + F(p_j)\}$$

for $i = 1, \ldots, n$. Thus at equilibrium

$$0 = -m\hat{p}_i + F(\hat{p}_i)(1 - m) + m/n \sum_{j=1}^{n} \{\hat{p}_j + F(\hat{p}_j)\} \qquad (1)$$

again for $i = 1, \ldots, n$. Now we sum both sides over i, which yields

$$0 = -m \sum_{i=1}^{n} \hat{p}_i + (1 - m) \sum_{i=1}^{n} F(\hat{p}_i) + m/n \sum_{i=1}^{n} \sum_{j=1}^{n} \{\hat{p}_j + F(\hat{p}_j)\}$$

$$= -m \sum_{i=1}^{n} \hat{p}_i + (1 - m) \sum_{i=1}^{n} F(\hat{p}_i) + m \sum_{j=1}^{n} \hat{p}_j + m \sum_{j=1}^{n} F(\hat{p}_j)$$

$$= \sum_{i=1}^{n} F(\hat{p}_i)$$

Thus at equilibrium the changes in the frequency of c before dispersal must sum to zero. With this result Equation 1 above becomes Equation 7.14 in the text.

subpopulation.) To determine whether the conformist genotype can increase, we need to calculate the equilibrium frequency of c in the various subpopulations, $\hat{p}_1, \ldots, \hat{p}_n$. The right-hand side of 7.14 defines a function of $\hat{p}_i$, $f(\hat{p}_i)$ which is plotted in Figure 7.3. Equation 7.14 says that the ith subpopulation will be in equilibrium if $\bar{p} = f(\hat{p}_i)$. In general, $\bar{p}$ will also be a function of $\hat{p}_i$. If, however, we assume that there are a large number of subpopulations, then the average frequency of c individuals in the whole population, $\bar{p}$, will be approximately independent of the changes in the frequency in any subpopulation. Thus, for any given value of $\bar{p}$, say P_0, the equilibrium frequency of c in the ith subpopulation, $\hat{p}_i$, can be determined graphically by finding the intersection of $f(\hat{p}_i)$ and the line $\bar{p} = P_0$.

So far the presentation has been fairly general. Now we make the special assumption that $\bar{p} = 0.5$. (This would occur if on average c and d are equally likely to be favored by selection and if the distribution of initial frequencies of c in the subpopulations satisfies certain conditions.) With this special assumption, it is easy to show that conformist transmission is adaptive. In Figure 7.3a the form of $f(\hat{p}_i)$ is plotted assuming that $D = 0$ and that $s_i < 0$. The latter assumption means that d individuals are favored by selection in subpopulation i. Notice that $\hat{p}_i < 0.5$, that is, at equilibrium the favored trait is more frequent. Moreover, this must be true in every subpopulation. Thus, according to Equation 7.11, the conformist genotype will increase in every subpopulation. This makes sense since offspring who acquire their behavior via a conformist cultural inheritance rule have a higher probability of acquiring the trait favored by selection than offspring who utilize a linear rule. Thus selection should act to increase D.

(a)

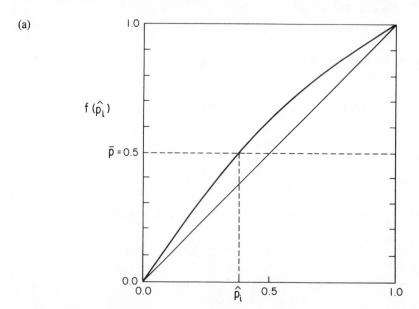

Fig. 7.3 Graphs of the function $f(\hat{p}_i)$ for three values of D, assuming that the frequency of variant c in the metapopulation, $\bar{p}$, is 0.5. Equilibria occur whenever $f(\hat{p}_i) = 0.5$. Thus, when $D = 0$ (a), or when D is small (b), there is only one possible equilibrium in each subpopulation. When D is large enough (c), there are three equilibria, p_c, p_t, and p_d.

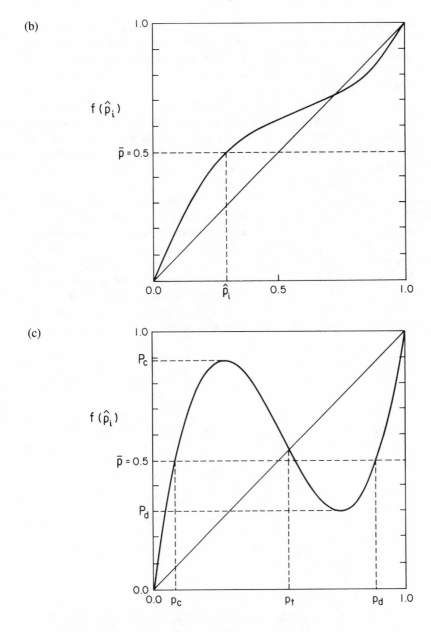

In Figure 7.3b, $f(\hat{p}_i)$ is also plotted assuming that the conformist genotype is fixed in each subpopulation (i.e. $\hat{p}_i = 1$ for $i = 1,\ldots,n$). Once again the equilibrium frequency of the favored cultural variant is greater than one-half and therefore the conformist genotype can resist invasion by the unbiased genotype. It will also favor invasion by a genotype with an even stronger conformist effect. This suggests that selection will continue to increase D until $D = 1$ or a situation like that pictured in Figure 7.3c is reached. Now there are three equilibrium values of

$\hat{p}_i$, which we will label p_c, p_d, and p_t. The central equilibrium, p_t, is unstable, and the other two equilibria are stable. In subpopulations at equilibrium, at p_c selection will continue to favor increased values of D; however, in subpopulations at equilibrium at p_d, selection will favor decreased values of D. It is unclear under what conditions selection will continue to increase D.

It would be of interest to see if selection would continue to favor frequency-dependent bias when $\bar{p} \neq \frac{1}{2}$ and when there are three equilibria. To investigate these questions we have performed a number of computer simulations of the recursions defined by 7.11 and 7.12. These simulations suggest that the results derived above generalize to these more general cases (see Fig. 7.4). Selection continues to increase D when $\bar{p} \neq \frac{1}{2}$ and when D is large.

This model illustrates what we believe is an important general property of conformist transmission. In spatially varying environments, it can serve as a simple, generally applicable rule that increases the probability that individuals acquire traits that are favored in the local habitat. The forces of guided variation, directly biased transmission, and natural selection will act to increase the frequency of the favored cultural variant. However, migration from habitats in which other variants are favored will tend to reduce the frequency of the locally favored variant. These forces may often result in an equilibrium in which the locally favored variant is the most common variant. When this is true, individuals who have a tendency to

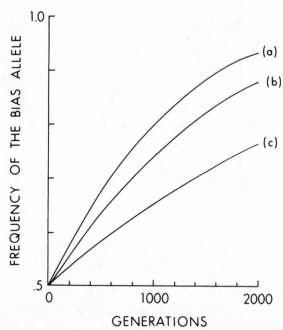

Fig. 7.4 The frequency of the frequency-dependent bias allele is plotted against time for three sets of parameter values. In each case m = 0.05, s = 0.1, and D = 0.25. In (a), cultural variant c was favored in half of the subpopulations and d in the other half. In (b), cultural variant c was favored in one-fourth of the subpopulations and d in the other three-fourths. In (c), c was favored in one-eighth of the subpopulations. In each case the frequency of the bias allele eventually converged to one.

acquire the most common variant would also have an improved chance of acquiring the locally favored variant.

Frequency-dependent bias and quantitative characters: An analogy with robust estimators

We believe that this advantage of conformist transmission is likely to generalize to a wide variety of other models. A consideration of a quantitative model of conformist cultural transmission provides two different kinds of evidence supporting this claim. First, we show that conformist transmission of a quantitative character is also adaptive in a spatially varying environment. Second, the quantitative model demonstrates that conformist transmission is analogous to the use of what statisticians call "robust estimators." Robust estimators are widely useful in statistics when data are "contaminated," that is, when some of the observations have been generated by processes other than the one of interest. We think it plausible that conformist transmission is useful in a wide range of variable environments for similar reasons.

Two models are very unlikely to be characterized by exactly the same cultural variant of a quantitative character, and therefore naive individuals cannot literally adopt the more common variant. This means that we must generalize our notion of conformist transmission. Suppose that the distribution of the cultural variant in the population is unimodal as is shown in Figure 7.5a. Then, as is shown in 7.5b, in a typical set of models, those models with the biggest and smallest cultural variants will tend to be drawn from the tails of the distribution, while those with intermediate variants will tend to be drawn from its center. This suggests that in the case of quantitative characters, a conformist transmission rule should be biased against those models whose trait values are the most extreme and in favor of models whose trait values are intermediate.

A wide variety of such transmission rules are conceivable. Here we will consider one very simple example, a "trimmed mean" rule. Suppose each naive offspring is

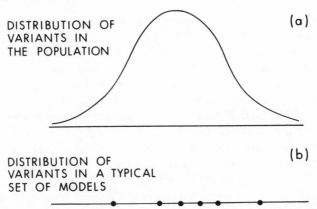

Fig. 7.5 (a) The distribution of individuals in a large population as a function of values of a quantitative cultural trait. (b) A representative example of a set of six models drawn from such a large population.

exposed to five models with equal intrinsic weights. As before, the ith model is characterized by a cultural variant with value X_i. The naive individual estimates the cultural variant of the ith model to be Z_i. With blending inheritance, we assumed that a naive individual simply adopted the average of the Z_i as his own cultural variant. We now suppose that the naive individual ranks the models according to their values Z_i, "throws out" the models he estimates have the smallest and the largest cultural variants, and then adopts the average of the remaining three models as his own cultural variant. Naive individuals, in effect, adopt the 20 percent trimmed mean of the Z_i as their own cultural variant.

First, let us consider the force generated by this transmission rule, assuming that the distribution of cultural variants in the population is normal with mean $\overline{X}$ and variance V. Because the trimmed mean is a widely used statistical estimator, its properties are known in this case (Tukey and Mosteller, 1977). The mean value is not changed by transmission, and the variance after transmission is reduced by a factor of approximately $(1/n)[2/\pi + (1 - 2(0.2))(1 - 2/\pi)]$. Notice that the reduction in the variance is not quite as great as in the blending case. Finally, as the number of parents increases, the distribution of cultural variants in the population becomes approximately normal. If we assume that (1) random variation, measured on some scale, is approximately normally distributed, (2) there is no migration from other habitats, and (3) there are a modest number of models, say 5–10, then it is reasonable that the culturally transmitted trait will be distributed normally at equilibrium. Under these conditions simple blending inheritance should be favored over the trimmed mean rule because it will have a smaller variance at equilibrium.

Next, suppose that models are drawn from two normal distributions with the same variance, V, but different means, $\overline{X}_1$ and $\overline{X}_2$. Models are drawn with probability m from distribution 2 and probability $1 - m$ from distribution 1, where $m < \frac{1}{2}$. Notice that the mean of this compound distribution, $\overline{X}'$, is simply

$$\overline{X}' = \overline{X}_1(1 - m) + \overline{X}_2 m \tag{7.18}$$

These assumptions are meant to approximate the case in which a fraction m of the models are immigrants from another habitat. We have computed the effect of conformist transmission using Monte Carlo methods, and the results are shown in Figure 7.6. They indicate that (1) the mean of the population after transmission is intermediate between $\overline{X}_1$ and $\overline{X}'$, (2) the variance is reduced, and (3) the third moment of the distribution is quite small. These results suggest that the trimmed mean rule should be favored relative to a blending rule in a variable environment because naive individuals with the trimmed mean rule would on average acquire a cultural variant closer to the local optimum than offspring who used a blending rule.

The trimmed mean is but one of many robust estimators of central tendency (Andrews et al., 1972; Tukey and Mosteller, 1977). All of these estimators are less sensitive to outlying observations than is the ordinary arithmetic mean. This property of robust estimators is useful when (1) data are drawn from a "thick-tailed" distribution, such as the chi-squared distribution, or (2) data are drawn from a normal distribution that is contaminated by data drawn from another distribution with a different mean or a larger variance.

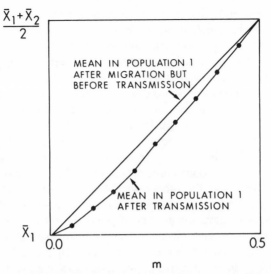

Fig. 7.6 The effects of conformist transmission exercised on a quantitative trait by a 20 percent trimmed mean rule. m is the migration rate. In the case of complete mixing (m = 0.5), the mean after transmission moves population 1 to the mean of populations 1 and 2, and the conformity rule has no effect. At intermediate migration rates, the rule tends to return population 1 back toward its premigration value, $\overline{X}_1$.

It is reasonable to suppose that the combination of migration and a spatially variable habitat will often cause the distribution of cultural variants in a population to be a contaminated normal distribution. When this is true, both the theory of robust estimators and our Monte Carlo result suggest that some kind of conformist rule will be favored. On the other hand, it is also reasonable to suppose that the distribution of cultural variants will often be approximately normal. In this case, a blending rule will be favored. However, simulation studies of the properties of various estimators (Andrews et al., 1972) have shown that robust estimators like the trimmed mean are only slightly inferior to the arithmetic mean for normal populations, and they are much better for contaminated or thick-tailed distributions. This suggests that averaged over a wide variety of situations, a conformist rule like the trimmed mean would be superior to a linear blending rule.

Empirical Research on Conformity

We have argued that conformist transmission, a form of frequency-dependent bias, is adaptive in spatially varying habitats because it provides a simple and generally applicable rule that increases the chance of acquiring locally adaptive behaviors. Is there any evidence that human cultural transmission is actually characterized by a conformist effect? Social psychologists have devoted much effort to studying the effect of conformity on the acquisition of beliefs and attitudes. (See Keisler and Keisler, 1969, for a review.) Unfortunately, most of this research does not clearly distinguish between the homogenizing effects of any kind of cultural transmission and the special effects of conformist transmission as we have defined it. Nonetheless, it will be useful to briefly review this work for several reasons. First, it is important to understand why what psychologists have called conformity is not identical to what we have defined as conformist transmission. Second, some of this research suggests that conformist transmission exists. Finally, we think that these experimental methods could easily be modified to determine whether human social learning is regularly characterized by a conformist effect.

The seminal experiments of Sherif (1935) provide a good example of the experimental method that psychologists have used to study conformity. Sherif's experimental protocol uses an optical illusion known as the "autokinetic effect." When people are placed in a darkened room and shown a stationary pinpoint of light, the light usually appears to be moving. In Sherif's experiments, several individuals were placed in a darkened room and shown a spot of light. One of these individuals was the real subject, and the others were Sherif's confederates. The real and counterfeit "subjects" were asked to estimate the distance that the light had traveled. The real subject gave his answer after all the confederates, who were instructed to give estimates very different from the usual estimates. Sherif, and other researchers after him, found that the estimate given by the real subject tends to be very close to that of the confederates, no matter how inaccurate theirs might be. That is, the subjects' opinions conform to those of the majority.

Sherif's technique is unusual in that he used a fairly ambiguous estimation task. In most of the work in this area, the naive subject is put in a situation in which there is a sharp contrast between his own perceptions and the stated estimates of the confederates. For example, Asch (1951) asked individuals to judge which of three obviously different lines matched a fourth line which was exactly the same size as one of the first three. The confederates chose one of the lines that did not match. A sizable fraction of the subjects conformed to the opinion of the majority in this experiment as well.

There are two different ways to understand these kinds of results. Some psychologists have argued that the subject is merely publicly complying with the opinion of the majority, while privately maintaining his own opinion (Keisler and Keisler, 1969). Others think that the subject is genuinely unsure and uses the opinion of others as a guide. In the second view, the results of Sherif and others are evidence of the importance of social learning in adults (Thelen et al., 1979). It seems likely that both effects are important. We would hypothesize that experiments like those of Asch, in which the choice of confederates is obviously at variance with the experience of the subject, probably represent public compliance, while experiments like those of Sherif, in which the judgment task is ambiguous, are more likely to represent the effects of cultural transmission.

Some of the best evidence that Sherif's results represent the effects of cultural transmission comes from an experiment conducted by Roher et al. (1954). The members of two groups of subjects were individually placed in darkened rooms and shown a moving light. In one group the light actually moved 2 inches; in the other it moved 8 inches. On average, individuals in the first group estimated a substantially smaller distance than individuals in the second group. Then pairs of individuals, one drawn from each group, were placed together in a room with a stationary light and asked to repeatedly estimate the distance that the light traveled. As Table 7.4 shows, the mean values estimated by the two groups converged toward the mean of the two values—exactly what one would expect if the process were

Table 7.4 Results of an experiment by Roher et al. (1954) showing the mutual socialization of individuals drawn from different training regimes for an ambiguous task

| | Mean Estimates of Individuals with | |
	2 in. Training	8 in. Training
Alone	3.08	8.74
Together	6.29	6.41
1 Year Later	5.50	5.09

governed by linear horizontal transmission. One year after the original experiment, subjects were retested individually; as is shown by the table, the estimates formed by the cultural transmission process seemed quite stable.

In this experiment there is no "majority" to conform to—individuals modify their estimates when exposed to others and then retain the modified judgments for at least one year.

These experiments on conformity do not provide good evidence that conformist cultural transmission exists. To demonstrate it, one would need to show that there is a nonlinear effect of numbers of confederates on the acquisition of belief. The numbers of confederates have been varied in several of the studies, but the results are quite ambiguous. Moreover, in most cases the experimental protocol was like Asch's. In such experiments it is easy to imagine that what is being observed is public compliance rather than the acquisition of a new belief through cultural transmission.

The only evidence we know of that conformist transmission exists comes from an experiment performed by Jacobs and Campbell (1961). They formed "micro-societies" of two, three, or four individuals. During the first "generation" there were one or two real subjects in each society, and the remainder were confederates. Each society was subjected to the Sherif protocol described above. Then, during the next generation, one of the confederates was removed and re-placed by a real subject. This process was repeated until all of the confederates were removed; from then on, in each generation a subject was removed and replaced with another subject. The experiment continued for eleven "generations."

Jacobs and Campbell began with the hypothesis that arbitrary traditions could be perpetuated by social transmission. Their results (see Fig. 7.7) did not support their hypothesis. In each experiment the mean estimate of the distance traveled by the light decreases from the initial estimate given by the confederates to a stable, constant value. Most of these results seem consistent with a model of transmission plus relatively weak guided variation. For some reason, individuals left alone tend to estimate the distance traveled at a stable value of 4 inches. In the micro-societies, they inherit the views of their cultural parents and then modify them according to their own judgments. Thus, the mean estimate moves a small distance toward the value favored by individual decision making, 4 inches. Repeated over many gener-ations, this process causes the mean to converge to a stable value of 4 inches.

One of the experimental treatments used by Jacobs and Campbell suggests the existence of conformist transmission. Compare the results shown in Figure 7.7a

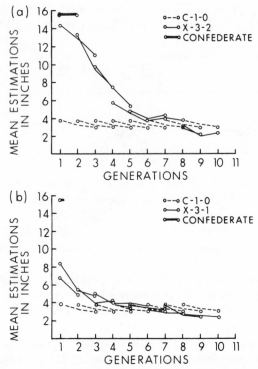

Fig. 7.7 The histories of individuals' estimates of the distance traveled by a small light in a dark room. Each line represents the estimates of a single individual during each generation that the individual was present. The lines labeled C-1-0 represent the estimates of solitary control individuals. Confederates always estimated 16 inches. The lines labeled X-3-2 in (a) are the estimates of subjects in three-person groups initiated by two confederates and one subject. The lines labeled X-3-1 in (b) are the estimates of subjects in three-person groups initiated by one confederate and two subjects. (From Jacobs, R. C. and D. T. Campbell. 1961. The perpetuation of an arbitrary tradition through several generations of laboratory microculture. *J. Abn. Soc. Psychol.* 62: 649–658, figures 3 and 5. Copyright © 1961 the American Psychological Association.)

with those in Figure 7.7b. In the former the micro-society was begun with two confederates and one naive subject. The real subjects' average estimate of the distance that the light moved was 14–15 inches, very close to that of the confederates. This result contrasts with that shown in Figure 7.7b. Here the group was begun with a single confederate and two subjects. In this case, the subjects' initial estimate averaged about 8 inches, substantially below that of the confederate. One way to interpret this result is that there is a nonlinear effect of numbers; subjects are disproportionately influenced by a majority of two compared to a minority of one.

Clearly this single result is inconclusive. It is possible to provide other sensible interpretations. However, this experimental protocol could easily be used to determine whether conformist transmission is acting in this situation. One would need to begin societies with a wider range of combinations of subjects and confederates. For example, using societies of five and six individuals, the experimenter could vary the initial number of confederates from zero to four and zero to five. The effect of the confederates on the estimates of the subjects could be estimated and the existence of a nonlinear effect of numbers confirmed or rejected. Jacobs and Campbell's protocol is especially useful because the use of several generations amplifies the effect of weak forces, making them easier to detect.

Conformist Transmission and Cultural Group Selection

In this section we argue that the models of frequency-dependent bias developed so far in this chapter provide an attractive explanation of the otherwise puzzling fact that humans engage in self-sacrificial cooperation in large groups. We begin by defining the problem cooperation presents to theories that posit a selfish human nature. Next, we briefly outline why many biologists believe that evolution should have led to a selfish human nature. Then, we show that one of the by-products of conformist frequency-dependent bias is an increase in the strength of the group selection of cultural variation so that it may be a strong force relative to forces acting within groups, such as direct bias and natural selection. Since selection between groups may favor beliefs and attitudes which benefit the group at the expense of the individual, this provides an explanation for human cooperation. Conformist transmission may be favored by natural selection even though it has this deleterious effect for individuals, because it increases the chance of acquiring locally adaptive cultural variants in a heterogeneous environment.

Cooperation and public goods

Throughout this chapter, we assume that social cooperation entails the production of what economists call "public goods" and that in large groups, rational selfish individuals will not voluntarily cooperate to produce public goods. A rational, self-interested individual seeks to maximize his own personal welfare and is indifferent to changes in the welfare of others (except perhaps his genetic relatives). Public goods are characterized by two features: "jointness of supply" and lack of "exclusiveness." Jointness of supply means that the consumption of a unit of the good by one individual does not reduce the amount of the good remaining for others to consume a full unit. This is not true of an ordinary good such as gasoline. When someone burns a gallon of gasoline, that reduces the supply of gasoline available for others by one gallon. In contrast, someone's "consumption" of a public good like clean air or public safety does not affect the amount of this good available to others. Lack of exclusiveness means that once a public good is produced it is difficult to prevent other members of the group from benefiting by it.

Many of the fruits of social cooperation are public goods. The modern state provides law and order within its boundaries and protection from attacks by other countries; labor unions provide higher wages and cartels higher prices. In each case, large groups of unrelated individuals cooperate to pursue a common goal. The achievement of these goals leads to benefits that flow to all members of the group without regard to their contribution.

Cooperation and the paradoxical nature of self-interest

Most economists believe that rational, selfish individuals will not voluntarily invest in the provision of public goods in large groups, except in special circumstances (Buchanan, 1968; Olson, 1971; for a contrary view see Taylor, 1976). To see why, consider the following hypothetical example. First, suppose that two pastoralists, Pete and Rob, quarter their identically sized herds together each night in a given meadow. The animals must be guarded to prevent losses to predators. We suppose each pastoralist has two alternatives: either he guards the herd (labeled c, for cooperate) or he does not (labeled d, for defect). The reduction in losses to the entire herd due to a single pastoralist's efforts at guarding are assumed to be $\mathcal{R}$, and the cost of guarding I. The payoffs to Pete are shown in Table 7.5. Suppose that the benefits of guarding the herd exceed the cost; this means that $\mathcal{R} > I$. Even if this is true, Pete will not be motivated to guard the herd unless $\mathcal{R}/2 > I$. If $\mathcal{R}/2 < I$, Pete is better off not guarding whether or not Rob guards (since $\mathcal{R}/2 < I$ implies that $\mathcal{R}/2 - I < 0$). Rob faces a similar matrix of payoffs. He will not guard if $\mathcal{R}/2 < I$, and the result is that both will achieve a payoff of zero. This is true even though both would be better off if they both guarded. Readers acquainted with game theory will recognize this situation as the Prisoner's Dilemma.

Table 7.5 Payoffs for two pastoralists who may guard (c) or not guard (d) their jointly pastured herd

	Rob's Behavior	
Pete's Behavior	d	c
d	0	$\mathcal{R}/2$
c	$\mathcal{R}/2 - I$	$\mathcal{R} - I$

Now let us generalize this model to a group of N pastoralists. Each pastoralist who chooses c reduces the predation losses of the entire herd an amount $\mathcal{R}$ and pays a cost I. The payoffs to Pete assuming that $\mathcal{M}$ pastoralists choose to guard the herd are given in Table 7.6. Pete's choice in the N-person case is similar to the two-person case. As long as $\mathcal{R}/N < I$, Pete achieves a higher payoff by defecting no matter what the other members of the group choose. Since each member of the group faces the same choice, the outcome will be that no one will guard the herd. Notice that if N is large, this may occur even though the aggregate benefits that result from guarding the herd could be many times higher than the aggregate costs. Because of this logic, groups of rational, selfish individuals may forgo actions that would be extremely beneficial to every member of the group. The fact that the

Table 7.6 Payoff schedule for a pastoralist who may guard (c) or not guard (d) a joint herd when $\mathcal{M}$ of the N other owners guard

Pete's Choice	Payoff to Pete if $\mathcal{M}$ Others Guard
d	$\mathcal{R}(\mathcal{M}/N)$
c	$\mathcal{R}(\mathcal{M} + 1)/N - I$

temptation to defect will tend to increase as the size of the group increases makes it especially difficult to explain patriotism or ethnocentrism as the result of rational self-interest.

This very simple model has been extended in a variety of ways by political scientists and economists interested in public choice. (For a recent survey of this literature see Hardin, 1982.) Perhaps because voluntary provision of public goods is so widely observed, many of these authors have searched for, and found, special conditions that can lead to cooperation (e.g. Hirshleifer, 1983). Nonetheless, on balance the public choice literature suggests that voluntary provision of public goods should be rare. Here we will consider only two of these extensions, the punishment of noncooperators and repeated interactions.

The effect of coercion. It might be argued that individuals cooperate in order to avoid punishment by other members of their own group. This notion seems plausible based on common experience. However, it does not solve the theoretical problem; it only raises the new problem of why individuals should cooperate to punish other individuals. To see this, suppose that the pastoralists have the opportunity to punish others who did not guard the herd. Suppose that each punisher punishes one defector and that the cost of being punished is $\mathcal{D}$. Then, on average, punishment will reduce the payoffs of defectors an amount $\mathcal{K}\mathcal{D}/(N - \mathcal{M})$, where $\mathcal{K}$ is the number of punishers and $N - \mathcal{M}$ the number of defectors. Finally, assume that the cost of punishing is $\mathcal{F}$. Then the payoffs for each of Pete's possible choices of behavior are given in Table 7.7.

Table 7.7 Payoff schedule for a pastoralist with the possibility of punishment for not guarding

Pete's Choice		Payoff to Pete Assuming $\mathcal{M}$ Others Guard and $\mathcal{K}$ Others Punish
Guard but don't punish	c/n	$\mathcal{R}(\mathcal{M}+1)/N - I$
Guard and punish	c/p	$\mathcal{R}(\mathcal{M}+1)/N - I - \mathcal{F}$
Don't guard and don't punish	d/n	$\mathcal{R}(\mathcal{M}/N) - \mathcal{D}\mathcal{K}/(N-\mathcal{M})$
Don't guard but punish	d/p	$\mathcal{R}(\mathcal{M}/N) - \mathcal{D}(\mathcal{K}+1)/(N-\mathcal{M}) - \mathcal{F}$

There are two things to notice about these expressions. First, it is clear that if enough members of the group choose to punish, Pete will be better off if he cooperates. However, Pete is always worse off if he chooses to punish. Thus, it is irrational to punish. Since all the members of the group face the same choice, no one will punish, but this means that there is no reason to cooperate. In essence, punishment itself is an investment in the production of another public good, the amount of cooperation in the group. Each potential punisher can have only a small incremental effect on the number of cooperators, and again, the cost to the individual participating in the punishment of another could be substantial. The rational, selfish individual would let the other guy do the punishing.

Repeated interactions and reciprocity. Some authors (e.g. Trivers, 1971; Flinn and Alexander, 1982) have asserted that repeated interactions among a large but finite group of rational, selfish individuals may lead to voluntary cooperation via reciprocity. This assertion is not supported by existing theoretical results. The theory of the repeated interaction of pairs of individuals is fairly well developed (Shubik, 1970; Taylor, 1976; Axelrod, 1980, 1984; Axelrod and Hamilton, 1981). These studies indicate that selection can favor the evolution of reciprocal strategies which lead to cooperation. The theory of repeated interactions in larger groups is much less fully developed. The best study (Taylor, 1976) indicates that repeated interactions can lead to cooperation, but that the reciprocal arrangements are complex and seemingly quite delicate, and that these difficulties increase as group size increases. Given that humans often do cooperate in very large groups, it would seem useful to pursue other possible explanations.

Group selection and the evolution of cooperation

One way to explain the evolution of altruistic cooperation in the human species is to imagine that group selection (acting on genes which affect behavioral propensities) is an important force in human evolution. Group selection occurs whenever the fitness of an individual depends on the behaviors of other individuals in a local group. In the case of cooperative production of a public good, the fitness of an individual depends on the number of cooperators in the group. If the incremental benefit of investing in the public good exceeds its incremental cost (e.g. $\Re > I$ in the example of the last section), then groups with more than the average number of cooperators have higher average fitness. Such groups contribute disproportionately to the next generation, and thus selection among groups increases the frequency of cooperation. However, because cooperators have lower fitness than other members of their own group, selection within groups decreases the frequency of cooperators within each group. Cooperation will increase in the whole population only if selection among groups is a stronger force than selection within groups.

The strength of selection among groups depends (among other things) on the amount of genetic variation that exists among groups; the more genetic variation among groups, the stronger the force of group selection. If all groups have the same frequency of cooperators, or if the differences do not have a genetic basis, selection cannot act to increase the frequency of cooperative genotypes. Genetic variation among groups is created by sampling error caused by finite populations (genetic drift) and the process of creation of new groups. Variation is destroyed by selection within groups, selection between groups, and migration among them.

Models of group selection can be conveniently divided into two classes (Wade, 1978b) based on the processes which create and maintain variation among groups.

1. In "intrademic" group selection models, groups are assumed to be quite small and the amount of migration among groups to be quite large; thus, a large amount of variation among groups is created and destroyed every generation. A variety of theoretical studies have shown that intrademic group selection can be effective in increasing the frequency of cooperative behaviors if (1) groups are small or (2) the process by which groups are formed causes cooperators to be more likely to interact with each other than chance alone would dictate (Wilson, 1975, 1977, 1980, 1983; Hamilton, 1975; Matessi and Jayakar, 1976; Uyenoyama, 1979; Wade, 1978a; Michod, 1982).

2. In "interdemic" group selection it is assumed that groups are relatively large and that migration among groups is quite small; thus, only a small amount of variation is created and destroyed each generation. A number of theoretical studies suggest that interdemic group selection can be effective only if the process of creation of new groups creates substantial variation, there are large differences in the mean fitness of subpopulations, and migration rates are very low (e.g. Eshel, 1972; Levin and Kilmer, 1974; Maynard Smith, 1976; Slatkin and Wade, 1978; Boorman and Levitt, 1980; Aoki, 1982a, 1982b; Crow and Aoki, 1982; see Wade, 1978, and Uyenoyama and Feldman, 1980, for reviews).

Taken together these results suggest that altruistic cooperation in large groups of genetically unrelated individuals is unlikely to evolve. This deduction is supported by the fact that altruistic cooperation among large groups of unrelated individuals has not been observed except in the human species (Williams, 1966). If this deduction is correct, much of human cooperative behavior is not genetically adaptive under contemporary conditions. Modern humans cooperate in very large groups with extensive gene flow between them, despite the fact that in theory neither intrademic nor interdemic group selection can favor altruistic cooperation under these conditions.

Several authors have argued that group selection was a more important influence on human evolution in the past. For example, W. D. Hamilton (1975) argues that the population structure that probably characterized food-foraging hominids during the middle and late Pleistocene (small, partly isolated groups who exchanged mates with their nearest neighbors) was ideally suited to maximizing selection between groups. Pierre van den Berghe (1981) makes a similar argument. Richard Alexander (1971, 1979a; also see Alexander and Tinkle, 1968) argues that the human ability to make weapons greatly increased the amount of intergroup conflict, and that such conflict is an especially effective agent of selection at the group level. These authors imagine that contemporary humans retain a genetically transmitted predisposition to cooperate, even though contemporary human population structures would not permit either mode of group selection to favor the cooperative behavior.

While these hypotheses are certainly plausible, they are very unattractive (Alexander, 1979a: 222). Since we cannot observe human behavior under late Pleistocene food-foraging conditions, we have very little way of knowing what the population structure was like or if it was sufficient to permit the evolution of the altruism that these authors envision. Moreover, if the hypothesis is correct it greatly weakens the explanatory power of sociobiological theory because we can no longer assume that behavior observed in different societies can be predicted by what maximizes fitness in the local environment. Given these problems it seems reasonable to consider an alternative hypothesis based on the dynamics of cultural transmission.

Conformist transmission and group selection

The theoretical argument against group selection is based on models which assume genetic inheritance. The same conclusions may not hold for culturally transmitted traits. We have already seen that conformist transmission can act to amplify differences in the frequency of cultural variants in different subpopulations. This suggests that selection among subpopulations might be more effective in the presence of conformist transmission. In this section we will analyze a model of interdemic group selection acting on a cultural trait which shows that this intuition is correct; when there is conformist transmission, interdemic group selection can be a strong force in determining the eventual equilibrium of the population, even when subpopulations are arbitrarily large, extinction rates are small, and migration rates are substantial.

We make two modifications to the model of conformist cultural transmission presented in a previous section. First, we assume that s_i, the selection differential of the cultural variant c, equals s and is negative in every subpopulation. This means that noncooperators (d individuals) are favored by natural selection in every subpopulation. Second, we assume that occasionally one of the subpopulations becomes extinct, leaving an empty habitat which is then recolonized by individuals from the surviving subpopulations. The probability that the ith subpopulation becomes extinct during any given generation is assumed to be a monotonically decreasing function of the frequency of c during that generation p_i, labeled $\mathscr{E}(p_i)$. This means that increasing the proportion of defectors in a subpopulation increases the probability that the subpopulation becomes extinct. For the present, this extinction may be thought of as involving the actual deaths of the individuals in the extinct population. Later in the chapter, however, we will argue that "cultural extinction" need not involve any actual mortality.

Equilibrium in a single subpopulation. Under what conditions will selection among subpopulations be stronger than selection within subpopulations? To answer this question we first determine the equilibrium of the population in the absence of any extinctions, and then assume that extinctions occur so infrequently that the population as a whole reaches equilibrium before the next extinction occurs. The assumed combination of very large subpopulations and very infrequent extinctions weakens the action of group selection, and in genetic models would result in group selection's being of negligible importance. Next, we determine if an equilibrium composed exclusively of defectors is unstable, so that cooperation can increase when rare.

Suppose that the values of the frequency-dependent bias parameter, D, the selection coefficient, s, and the migration rate, m, are such that the equilibrium of the ith population can be determined using Equation 7.14. Further, imagine that all of the subpopulations except subpopulation i are at equilibrium, and that the frequency in the whole population is $\bar{p}$. In this case, the equilibrium of the ith subpopulation depends on its initial frequency. If the initial frequency is greater than p_t, the unstable "threshold equilibrium," the subpopulation will reach a stable equilibrium with cooperators at a high frequency, p_c. We will refer to such subpopulations as "cooperator equilibria." If the initial frequency of cooperators is less than p_t, the subpopulation will achieve a stable "defector equilibrium" with a low frequency of cooperators, p_d.

Equilibrium of the entire population. These results about the equilibrium of a single subpopulation can be used heuristically to determine the equilibrium for the entire population. First, note that conditions in each of the subpopulations are identical. Thus all of the subpopulations must be in one or two equilibrium states. The function $f(p_i)$ has an internal minimum labeled P_d and an internal maximum labeled P_c. If the mean frequency of cooperators, $\bar{p}$, in the whole population is greater than P_c or less than P_d, then only one stable subpopulation equilibrium exists, and therefore all subpopulations must be at the same frequency. Label this frequency p^*. Since all subpopulations are identical, the entire population can be in equilibrium only if $f(p^*) = p^*$. This occurs only for $p^* = 1$ and $p^* = 0$. Thus, for $P_d > \bar{p}$ the only possible stable equilibrium occurs when the entire population is composed entirely of defectors. If $P_c > \bar{p} > P_d$, then two stable equilibria are possible. We will denote the frequency of variant c at these equilibria as $p_c(\bar{p})$ and $p_d(\bar{p})$ to emphasize the fact that the equilibrium frequency of c in any subpopulation depends on the mean frequency of c in the population as a whole. See Figure 7.3c for a graphical illustration of this situation. Let ϕ be the fraction of the subpopulations that are at the cooperative equilibrium, $p_c(\bar{p})$. An internal equilibrium for the entire population will exist if

$$\phi p_c(\bar{p}) + (1 - \phi)p_d(\bar{p}) = \bar{p} \qquad (7.19)$$

Satisfying Condition 7.19 does not assure that an equilibrium is stable or that it can be reached from any particular initial condition. Computer simulations indicate, however, that such equilibria are stable once they are reached, and that most initial configurations for which $P_c > (1/n)\Sigma_{i=1}^n p_i > P_d$ result in an internal equilibrium of the kind described by Equation 7.19. These simulations also indicate that the graphical method outlined in a previous section gives very good approximations for the values of p_c and p_d, even when the number of subpopulations is as small as ten.

Adding extinctions. Now consider the effect of an occasional rare extinction on a population that has achieved an internal equilibrium. A proportion ϕ of the subpopulations are assumed to be at an internal equilibrium p_c and a fraction $(1 - \phi)$ are at p_d. The internal unstable equilibrium is p_t. The extinction of a subpopulation leaves an empty habitat that is colonized by individuals from the other subpopulations. After extinction and colonization, both the subpopulation and the population as a whole will return toward a stable equilibrium. This equilibrium may not be identical to the one that existed before the extinction. Suppose a cooperator subpopulation goes extinct and is replaced at the new equilibrium by a defector subpopulation. This changes the mean frequency of cooperators from $\bar{p}$ to a slightly smaller value. This in turn changes the possible stable equilibria to slightly lower values and reduces the frequency of cooperative subpopulations after extinction. If a defector subpopulation goes extinct and is replaced by a cooperative one, then a new equilibrium is reached, characterized by slightly increased values of these quantities.

The conditions under which cooperation may increase. What is the long-run net effect of changes caused by extinctions on the evolution of the entire population? The eventual equilibrium in the subpopulation undergoing colonization is determined by the frequency of cooperators among the colonizers, p_e. Let $\Lambda(x)$ be the probability that p_e is greater than x. If $p_e < p_t$, then the population will move toward a defector equilibrium. If $p_e > p_t$, the new equilibrium will be cooperative. Let ϕ' be the proportion of cooperative subpopulations after the extinction. The expected value of ϕ', $E\{\phi'\}$, is given by

$$E\{\phi'\} = \phi[1 - \mathscr{E}(p_c)] + \phi\mathscr{E}(p_c)\Lambda(p_t) + (1 - \phi)\mathscr{E}(p_d)\Lambda(p_t) \quad (7.20)$$

The fraction of cooperative subpopulations may be expected to increase if

$$\Lambda(p_t) > \frac{\phi\mathscr{E}(p_c)}{\phi\mathscr{E}(p_c) + (1 - \phi)\mathscr{E}(p_d)} \quad (7.21)$$

The right-hand side of 7.21 gives the fraction of all extinctions that occur in subpopulations in equilibrium at a value p_c. Since we assume that the extinction rate is a monotonically decreasing function of the frequency of cooperators, this quantity is always less than ϕ. The left-hand side of 7.21 is the probability that a habitat recently vacated by extinction will achieve a cooperative equilibrium after recolonization. Thus, if the probability that a cooperative subpopulation will be formed after an extinction exceeds the probability that cooperative subpopulations become extinct (for a given value of ϕ), then the frequency of cooperators in the whole population will increase.

The evolution of the population as a whole depends critically on the magnitude of $\Lambda(p_t)$, which in turn depends on the mode of colonization. Recently vacated habitats could conceivably be recolonized in a variety of ways. The number of subpopulations contributing colonizers may vary. The absolute number of colonizers might also be small and variable, and colonizers might not represent an unbiased sample of the population. We will assume the following model. Let g(j) give the probability that a large number of colonizers are drawn at random from j subpopulations (j = 1,. . .,n). Then for small values of ϕ,

$$\Lambda(p_t) \approx g(1)\phi \quad (7.22)$$

In this case, 7.21 reduces to the following expression:

$$g(1) > \frac{\mathscr{E}(p_c)}{\mathscr{E}(p_d)} \quad (7.23)$$

Inequality 7.23 says that cooperators can increase in the population when rare if the ratio of the extinction rate of cooperative subpopulations to that of defector subpopulations is less than the probability that colonizers are drawn from a single subpopulation. It can also be shown that whenever extinction and recolonization make $\phi = 0$ an unstable equilibrium, $\phi = 1$ is a stable equilibrium.

It is important to remember that Condition 7.23 requires that D, s, and m be such that both cooperative and noncooperative equilibria exist for all values of $\bar{p}$. Given that this is the case, however, these conditions are nearly independent of the relative magnitudes of s and $\mathcal{E}(p_i)$. Conformist transmission "decouples" the processes of individual and group selection near the boundaries $\phi = 0$ and $\phi = 1$. This will not be true for other values of ϕ. Here Λ will depend on p_t, which in turn depends on the relative magnitudes of s, D, and m.

Another remarkable feature about Condition 7.23 is that it depends on the ratio of the extinction rates. In conventional models, the strengths of both group and individual selection depend on the ratios of survival rates of groups and individuals. This difference is important because the probabilities of extinction might be very low, and at the same time the ratio $\mathcal{E}(p_c)/\mathcal{E}(p_d)$ might be much less than one. For example, suppose that the survival rate of cooperative subpopulations is 0.9999 and that of noncooperative subpopulations is 0.99. The ratio of the extinction rates is 0.01, and therefore cooperation will increase if only 1 percent of the empty habitats are colonized by a single subpopulation.

We have been unable to derive general conditions under which the combination of conformist transmission and group selection would favor the increase of cooperators. The heuristic argument outlined above suggests, however, that the following conditions favor the establishment of cooperators in a population:

1. The parameters D, s, and m must be such that both cooperator and defector equilibria can coexist when cooperators are rare. This requires that the conformist effect be substantially stronger than selection and migration. The formal condition is $(1 - D/s)^2/8(D/s) > (m/s)$.

2. The mode of colonization should lead to a significant probability that colonizers are drawn from a single subpopulation.

3. The ratio of the extinction rates of cooperator and defector subpopulations should be significantly less than one, but the extinction rates themselves need not be large.

If conformist transmission is a significant force acting on the frequency of traits within subpopulations, and if the mode of colonization is favorable, group selection can increase the frequency of cooperators. This can occur even if extinction rates are very low, migration rates are substantial, and subpopulations are very large. Without conformist transmission, selection and migration constantly erode the variation between subpopulations. We have also shown elsewhere that conformist transmission can protect variation between groups against direct biases that favor the defector variant (Boyd and Richerson, 1982). Extinction must be frequent enough to balance these processes. Strong conformist transmission creates the possibility that subpopulations may be maintained indefinitely with a high frequency of cooperators. Whether cooperators then increase depends on the relative extinction rates of cooperator and defector subpopulations and the probability that recolonized subpopulations achieve a cooperative equilibrium.

A qualitative interpretation of the model

The empirical facts of human cooperation do not seem easily reconciled with the view that human nature is egoistic. Any alternative view that holds that humans are by nature cooperative must overcome two related difficulties. First, it must be able to account for the evolution of humans who cooperate on a large scale with genetically unrelated individuals. Second, given that individuals belong to many different groups with potentially conflicting goals, it must specify with which group (or groups) an individual will identify. The model of cultural group selection provides one explanation that overcomes both these problems.

The main requirement of the model is that humans inherit at least some portion of the values, goals, and beliefs that determine their choices by way of conformist cultural transmission. To explain the evolution of human cooperation, we need to account for the evolution of a human capacity for culture which is characterized by the conformist effect. We have seen that conformist transmission may be favored in spatially variable environments because it provides a simple, general rule that increases the probability of acquiring behaviors favored in the local habitat. It is plausible that averaged over many traits and many societies this effect could compensate for what is, from the genes' "point of view," the excessive cooperation that also may result from conformist transmission.

Cultural endogamy. To deal with the question of conflicting goals, we must interpret the results of our very simple model in terms of the complexity of social reality. Under specified conditions, group selection acting on cultural variation favors cooperators, individuals whose behavior reduces their own welfare but increases the probability that their subpopulation will escape extinction. The key defining characteristic of the subpopulation is that it is completely mixed; sets of parents are drawn at random from the pool of individuals within it. In contrast, the flow of cultural traits between subpopulations is restricted, since migration rates are less than one. We shall say that the subpopulation is "culturally endogamous." In human societies, individuals can belong to many social groupings, of varying sizes and purposes, and with varying criteria for membership. Our model suggests that humans will engage in behaviors that promote the interests of a particular group as a whole only if (1) they acquire behaviors culturally from other members of the group via conformist cultural transmission and (2) the group is culturally endogamous. These characteristics, taken together, specify the group with which individuals should identify.

Different social groupings may be culturally endogamous for some traits but not for others. For traits that are acquired by young children from members of their family, the culturally endogamous group might be very similar to the genetic deme. That is, an individual's cultural parents would be drawn from the same social grouping as its genetic parents. The culturally endogamous group for a trait acquired disproportionately from parents of one sex may be different from the culturally endogamous group for traits acquired from parents of both sexes. For example, suppose that beliefs about what constitutes acceptable behavior during warfare are acquired exclusively from males. In patrilocal societies, the culturally endogamous group for these beliefs could be very small (so small as to require substantial amendments to the model). In the same societies, the culturally endogamous group for behaviors acquired from both sexes—for example, language or religious beliefs—could be very large. In contrast, in matrilocal societies, the culturally endogamous group might be the same for warfare, language, and religion. For traits acquired as an adult, the culturally endogamous group may be different again. For example, many aspects of individual behavior in modern corporations, including professional goals, work norms, and beliefs about the nature of the product and the marketplace, are acquired culturally from individuals who precede them in the firm (Van Maanen and Schein, 1979). For these behaviors, the culturally endogamous group may be the firm. Other examples of groups that may be culturally endogamous for certain traits include fraternal organizations, craft guilds, and, of course, academic disciplines.

Cultural extinction does not require mortality. When there is conformist transmission, the extinction of a group need not entail the physical death of individuals; the breakup of the group as a coherent social unit and the dispersal of its members to other groups will suffice. Imagine that the members of an "extinct" subpopulation are dispersed randomly to all the other subpopulations. Because the members of a subpopulation are either mostly cooperators or mostly defectors, this will change the frequency of cooperators in the pool of migrants during the generation in which the extinction takes place. This will perturb each of the subpopulations from its equilibrium value, but since each subpopulation is small compared to the whole, the perturbation will be small. Each subpopulation will reach the same equilibrium that it would have reached if the members of the extinct group had never entered it. Intuitively, the dispersal of a group is equivalent to extinction because conformist transmission favors the more common variant. Cooperators persist in cooperative groups because they are common in those groups. If they are dispersed, their numbers will usually be insufficient to cause the frequency of cooperators in defector groups to exceed the threshold necessary to cause a change to a cooperative equilibrium, and vice versa.

To put this in more concrete terms, consider the following hypothetical example. Suppose that the cultural trait in question affects the rotation period in a swidden agricultural system. Defectors have a cultural variant that causes them to have a shorter rotation period. Occasionally, when coupled with especially unfavorable weather, this causes a temporary failure of the agricultural system in the entire subpopulation. It is unlikely that this would lead to the actual extinction of the group. Rather, members would disperse, different families attempting to join other groups. In any particular new group, the immigrants form only a small proportion of the group, so that, if conformist transmission is important, they will have little effect on the subsequent agricultural practices in the group. Clearly, this is only one of many patterns of dispersal that might actually take place. Different patterns will lead to different outcomes. For another example, involving a reinterpretation of Rappaport's (1968) study of the Maring, see Peoples (1982).

The model suggests that group selection is more effective when vacant habitats are recolonized by individuals drawn from a single subpopulation. This model of colonization seems plausible in the human case for several reasons: first, in a social species in which division of labor and cooperative subsistence activities are important, it seems likely that a cohesive social unit drawn from a single parent population will typically emigrate to colonize empty habitats. Second, even if a vacant habitat is colonized by groups that originated in more than one subpopulation, behavioral isolating mechanisms may prevent them from fusing to form a new culturally endogamous group. Finally, warfare may play an important role in determining group survival. Defeated groups may be dispersed and replaced by individuals from the victorious group.

Evolution of ethnic cooperation

One human grouping that seems to satisfy the requirements of the model is the ethnic group. The flow of cultural traits within the ethnic group is often much greater than the flow between ethnic groups. The model predicts that group selection acting on culturally transmitted traits will favor cooperative behavior within ethnic groups and noncooperative behavior toward members of other groups. Table 7.8 lists the traits identified with the syndrome of ethnocentrism in LeVine and Campbell (1972). In their book, LeVine and Campbell review the evidence that this syndrome is a very common characteristic of human ethnic groups and the theories that have been advanced to explain it. The list of behaviors in Table 7.8 seems consistent with the predictions of the model. Sanctions against theft and murder within the group provide civil order, a public good benefiting group members. This contrasts with the lack of sanctions protecting outgroup members. Moreover, cooperative behavior typifies interactions between group members, and lack of cooperation typifies interactions between members of different groups. Finally, individuals are willing to fight and die for their own group in warfare against other groups. In recent times, actions on behalf of the ethnic group have often been taken in direct opposition to the authority and power of the modern state—witness movements for ethnic autonomy in many parts of the world today. It also must be kept in mind that the groups in question are often very large. In such large groups, it is hard to imagine that any kind of reciprocal arrangement is responsible for the observed behavior. These generalizations about human ethnocentrism suggest that the ethnic group is one locus of altruistic behavior.

The variation in behavior toward ethnic group members also provides some support for the hypothesis that group selection acting on culturally transmitted behavior has shaped human behavior. LeVine and Campbell categorized social structures as "socially divisive" and "socially integrative":

> The former type of society has structural features such as *patrilocality or local group endogamy* that foster the development of a parochial loyalty structure. . . . In the socially integrated type, the dispersion of males . . . fosters the development of loyalties to wider groupings. . . . Since the socially divisive societies have warfare among segments of the ethnic community, and the socially integrated societies do not, the social structures are seen as favoring different norms of conduct concerning social intercourse within the ethnic community. [P. 53, emphasis ours]

They go on to argue that while socially divisive societies are characterized by extensive feuding and violence, they are infrequently involved in large-scale warfare, and when they are involved in warfare, alliances are formed opportunistically on the basis of immediate military contingencies. In contrast, while socially integrative societies have much less violence within groups, they readily cooperate in large-scale conflict. LeVine and Campbell cite Noberini's (1966) cross-cultural

Table 7.8 Traits identified with the syndrome of ethnocentrism by LeVine and Campbell (1972)

Attitudes and Behaviors toward Ingroup	Attitudes and Behaviors toward Outgroup
See selves as virtuous and superior.	See outgroup as contemptible, immoral, and inferior.
See own standards of value as universal, intrinsically true. See own customs as original, centrally human.	
See selves as strong.	See outgroup as weak.
	Social distance.
	Outgroup hate.
Sanctions against ingroup theft.	Sanctions for outgroup theft or absence of sanctions against.
Sanctions against ingroup murder.	Sanctions for outgroup murder or absence of sanctions against outgroup member.
Cooperative relations with ingroup members.	Absence of cooperation with outgroup members.
Obedience to ingroup authorities.	Absence of obedience to outgroup authorities.
Willingness to remain an ingroup member.	Absence of conversion to outgroup membership.
Willingness to fight and die for ingroup.	Absence of willingness to fight and die for outgroups.
	Virtue in killing outgroup members in warfare.
	Use of outgroups as bad examples in the training of children.
	Blaming of outgroup for ingroup troubles.
	Distrust and fear of the outgroup.

study of warfare as supporting this view. Again, it appears that the unit upon which group selection has worked is the culturally endogamous groups. If this unit is small, as in the case of socially divisive societies, then so is the unit within which social cooperation takes place. In socially integrated societies, the culturally endogamous unit is larger (at least with regard to traits transmitted by men) and so is the scale of violent conflict.

Conclusion

The simple model of cultural group selection outlined here clearly is not verified by the data concerning ethnic cooperation. Nor is it a complete hypothesis to account for cooperative behavior in humans. The real world is undoubtedly much more complex than our representation of it. However, the model does illustrate what we believe is a crucial property of the evolution of cultural species: if the rules of cultural transmission are different from the rules of genetic transmission, similar selective regimes may result in very different equilibria. The model also provides a qualitative prediction about the kind of transmission rules that might explain human cooperative behavior; that is, a cultural transmission rule that increases the frequency of the more common variant can cause group selection to be a strong force in determining the kinds of behaviors that characterize different human societies.

8

Indirect Bias and the
Evolution of Symbolic Traits

> . . .what are the advantages which we propose by that great purpose of human life which we call bettering our condition? To be observed, to be attended to, to be taken notice of with sympathy, complacency and approbation, are all the advantages we can propose to derive from it.
> Adam Smith, 1790, *The Theory of Moral Sentiments* (p. 121, 6th ed.)

The utilitarian view of human society propounded by Adam Smith in the *Wealth of Nations* is still important in the social sciences. It forms the basis of much of Western economic theory which, according to its practitioners, successfully explains much of human behavior in economic contexts. It has also been used by economists (e.g. Posner, 1980; Becker, 1981), political scientists (e.g. Hardin, 1982), sociologists (e.g. Goode, 1978), and anthropologists (e.g. Schneider, 1974) to explain human behavior in many noneconomic contexts.

As many authors have pointed out (e.g. Rosenberg, 1980b), however, utilitarian theories typically are incomplete because (1) they do not specify people's preferences in sufficient detail and (2) they do not explain why people have the preferences they do. These are very serious shortcomings. Without some constraint on the nature of preferences, virtually any observed behavior can be rationalized. Economists, for example, usually assume that individuals strive for material well-being, for wealth and leisure (e.g. Stigler and Becker, 1977). Many of the things people do seem to contradict this view of human nature. Why should someone risk his or her life to reach the summit of Mount Everest or to save an unknown stranger drowning in a frozen river? Other things people do, while not directly deleterious, do not seem very closely related to material well-being. Why should some people spend a third of their income to own a classic Porsche or to collect period furniture? Can these behaviors be explained within the economist's paradigm without simply defining people's preferences in terms of their behavior?

One approach is to suppose that, as Adam Smith (1790) suggested, people want those things that cause them "to be observed, to be attended to with sympathy, complacency and approbation. . ." In short, people value prestige, and they do things like climbing mountains and buying fancy cars because such behaviors are effective in gaining prestige. The problem with this approach is that it solves one problem by creating two more. First, we do not know why some things are prestigious and others not. Why should we admire people who risk their lives climbing mountains but not people who risk their lives running across freeways?

Second, we do not have any explanations, other than introspection, why people should value prestige. Clearly, what is really required is a theory of preferences that predicts what people will value.

As Jack Hirshleifer (1977) has noted, sociobiological theory provides one attractive basis for such a theory; humans are hypothesized to strive to maximize their inclusive fitness because this tendency has evolved through natural selection. If sociobiological theory is correct, we should be able to predict people's choices (at least on the average) by asking what maximizes their reproductive success. This will often be difficult, and therefore actual predictions may be ambiguous. But at least sociobiology does provide a complete utilitarian theory.

In the context of the current problem, however, it seems difficult to see how climbing Mount Everest or owning a Porsche increases an individual's reproductive success. In fact, it seems likely that the resources consumed in these endeavors could be put to much better uses. One could argue that these kinds of behavior are the result of sexual selection; perhaps these behaviors enhance a male's reproductive success because females prefer men who do such things. There are several difficulties with this kind of explanation. The most obvious is that some women like to climb mountains and many like to drive fancy cars. It is also doubtful that in many cases (like mountain climbing) there is any correlation between the prestige gained and mating success. Finally, why should females prefer males who do stupid things? Would they not be better off choosing males who demonstrate their prowess at productive endeavors like making money or caring for children?

In his book *Culture and Practical Reason,* Marshall Sahlins (1976a) argues that cultural processes define preferences and that any form of utilitarian analysis must be derived, therefore, from cultural processes rather than vice versa. Moreover, he asserts that culture is constituted of conventional symbols, so humans are very largely free to develop meaningful systems of culture, only broadly constrained by the imperatives of the natural world expressed through natural selection or other utilitarian principles. In his words,

> [T]he practical interest of men in production is symbolically constituted. The finalities as well as the modalities of production come from the cultural side: the material means of the cultural organization as well as the organization of the material means. We have seen that nothing in the way of their capacity to satisfy a material (biological) requirement can explain why pants are produced for men and skirts for women, or why dogs are inedible but the hindquarters of the steer are supremely satisfying of the need to eat. [P. 207]

However, Sahlins does not give a satisfactory account of the cultural processes that generate particular patterns of preferences in different societies.

In this chapter we will analyze a model of cultural transmission with indirect bias. This model can explain why people value prestige and why certain traits are effective in garnering prestige. Under some assumptions, the model is consistent with the sociobiological expectation that human culture is adaptive, but under others it allows cultural processes a causal autonomy similar to that envisioned by Sahlins. Often it seems that culture can be autonomous *and* adaptive. We begin by setting up the model of indirect bias and deducing the kinds of cultural forces that result. We then go on to argue that indirect bias, like frequency-dependent bias, provides a simple, general rule by which a naive individual can increase the chance of acquiring a locally favored cultural variant without directly evaluating the merit of alternative variants. This result allows us to understand both the evolution of the desire for prestige and why certain characters come to be prestigious. We will then show that under some conditions indirectly biased cultural transmission leads to a dynamic analogous in some ways to the process of "runaway" sexual selection first elucidated by R. A. Fisher (1958). This can cause the characters that act as markers of prestige to become exaggerated and "maladaptive." The runaway process is a mechanism that may roughly correspond to the autonomous causal force postulated by Sahlins and other symbolic anthropologists.

Defining indirect bias

In defining indirect bias, it will be useful to distinguish three classes of characters.

1. Indicator traits. Some characters affect the importance of individuals as models. For example, suppose that naive individuals are more inclined to imitate successful individuals and that an individual's success is measured by observing a particular character—number of cows, number of children, or number of publications. We call this trait the "indicator trait."

2. Indirectly biased traits. Individuals' values of the indicator trait may affect their importance in the cultural transmission of other characters, the indirectly biased traits. For example, individuals might tend to acquire the clothing styles, pronunciation, and beliefs about the world that characterize the most successful individuals among potential models.

3. Preference traits. The naive individuals must have some criterion by which to determine the values of the indicator trait that are preferable. In the case of traits such as wealth, the criterion probably would be "more is better," but in other cases there might be some intermediate value that is admired. For example, contemporary Americans tend to admire people whose families are of intermediate size, not the childless or the prolific. We will call this trait the "preference trait."

We will say that transmission is indirectly biased if naive individuals prefer some models over others based on an indicator trait and use such preferences to determine the attractiveness of that model for other characters (the indirectly biased traits).

It is easy to see why indirect bias might be adaptive. In Chapter 5, we argued that it may often be very difficult or costly to evaluate the relative merit of different cultural variants, especially when they have long-lasting effects. In many cases, a single trial of a trial-and-error evaluation of the alternative variants may take a lifetime. One obvious way around this problem is to adopt the variants used by successful people, as Flinn and Alexander (1982) suggested. It may be difficult to evaluate the best hunting practices from among the myriad of possibilities, so just copy the most successful hunter. Since it is difficult to determine exactly which of his techniques makes him successful, one might imitate everything that is plausibly connected with his hunting success, from the way he sets his traps to the chant he says every day before going off to hunt. Later in this chapter, we will see that this intuitive argument can be made more precise.

Evidence for Indirect Bias

Evidence from social learning experiments

What we call indirectly biased transmission is related to the Freudian concept of identification. (See Rancour-Laferriere, 1981, for an extended discussion of the relationship between identification and imitation.) Freudians believe that children form strong affective attachments to particular persons, especially their parents, that lead the child to have a generalized desire to be like those persons. Certain characteristics in the parents or other models are hypothesized to affect the degree of identification. Strong identification causes children to acquire cultural traits quite distinct from the traits giving rise to the original identification.

Since identification has been a controversial subject in psychology, students of social learning have conducted a number of useful experiments to investigate its effect on social learning (Yando et al., 1978: 62–65). Unfortunately, most of these studies have focused on how indicator traits (in our terminology) affect the amount of attention that is paid to different models, and relatively few studies actually demonstrated that indicator traits affect the probability that different modeled variants are actually acquired. It seems reasonable to infer that characteristics of models that attract attention will also stimulate acquisition (Rosenthal and Zimmerman, 1978: 251–254). However, because symbols of prestige and other traits that act as stimuli of affect and attention play so many other roles in social life, the amount of attention paid to others and the extent of social learning from them may be poorly correlated. For example, Landy and Segall (1974) showed that essays supposedly written by attractive women received higher evaluations from males than those supposedly written by unattractive ones. Males may use female attractiveness as an indicator trait in indirectly biased social learning, but other reasons for this behavior are easily imagined.

A few studies, however, do suggest that social learning is sometimes characterized by indirect bias, at least in the laboratory. Bandura, Ross, and Ross (1963) tested three theories of parent-offspring identification in a laboratory setting. Experimental families composed of a preschool or third-grade child and two "parental" models were constructed. One model mimicked a powerful, controlling parent, and the other a more passive, consuming parent. Sexes of "parents" and children were varied independently of the model attributes. The models also displayed a variety of incidental behaviors while playing games with the children. The test of imitation was the number of these incidental behaviors displayed by the children. The main effect was a disproportionate modeling of the powerful, controlling parent. The interacting sex variables had some effect, but most treatments showed a 50–100 percent greater number of imitations of incidental behaviors modeled by the controlling parent. Many studies have been made of the effect of nurturant versus nonnurturant models on children's imitation (Yando et al., 1978: 64–65). For example, Yussen and Levy (1975) exposed preschoolers and third graders to warm and neutral adult models. Warm models increased attention, reduced susceptibility to distraction, and enhanced recall of modeled events.

These results are only suggestive. Observers do appear to react to some traits of others in a way that affects the general attention given to a person and hence the modeling of traits not involved in attracting attention. However, the data available from social learning studies are not yet sufficiently extensive to give a general picture of the phenomenon. The range of indicator characters studied is small, the potential variation in the responses among naive individuals little studied, and most studies have treated only transmission from adult to child.

Evidence from the diffusion of innovations

The study of the diffusion of innovations has produced a considerable body of observational data that suggests that indirect bias is important. Some individuals play a much greater role in the spread of innovations than do others; those who, once persuaded to adopt an innovation, are very likely to be imitated by their fellows are called opinion leaders. Rogers with Shoemaker (1971: Chap. 6) devote a chapter to reviewing the patterns of information flow during the adoption of an innovation as a function of the social statuses and other sociological attributes of earlier and later adopters. The most general effect discovered in the study of the diffusion of innovations is that opinion leaders are usually of somewhat higher social status than followers, but that the difference is relatively slight compared to the total extent of the status hierarchy in the whole social system. Opinion leaders are usually respectable solid citizens of the community who conform to community norms but have more contact with the larger world and more social participation in local affairs. Opinion leaders may or may not have a positive attitude toward innovation. Some evidence suggests that traditional and modern societies have different patterns of opinion leadership. Traditional societies seem to have more general purpose leaders, and the social distance between leaders and followers seems less, compared to modern or modernizing communities.

Rogers suggests that these patterns of imitation result from the use of a basically sound choice criterion on the part of potential adopters. On the one hand, the apparent success of high-status individuals is an indirect indication that they know valuable techniques that might be profitably adopted. On the other, individuals who are too different in status are likely to be different in other ways from potential adopters. For example, they may be large rather than small landowners. He cites cases of two types of errors that are possible in choices of opinion leaders, depending on the details of the situation. One can choose leaders who are too similar to oneself in a situation where higher status individuals have adopted traits that would be useful, or one can imitate those whose techniques are unsuited to one's own situation. Choosing an opinion leader drastically different in status is likely to result in the latter problem. In our terms, an adaptive indirect bias is one in which there is a strong relationship between the potential model's indicator character (e.g. social status) and the utility of the other traits that are to be imitated. It appears that effective indirect biases of this type are often found to be operating in diffusion-of-innovation studies.

Rogers with Shoemaker (1971: 221) illustrate the way indicator traits are used to define opinion leadership with an example from East Pakistan. Village leaders were enrolled in a training program with the expectation that they would act as opinion leaders in the diffusion of agricultural innovations in their home communities. The local followers appeared to use mode of dress as an indicator trait. As long as village leaders tied their long shirts above their knees when they worked, they retained their status as opinion leaders and were influential in the diffusion of the agricultural innovations. When they allowed them to drop below their knees in imitation of the training program leaders, villagers switched allegiance to new opinion leaders and the flow of innovations stopped. Rogers hypothesizes that the followers felt that their former leaders had become too much like the higher-class teachers.

Evidence from sociolinguistics

Sociolinguists have been able to show that dialect evolution occurs fairly rapidly (Fishman, 1972; Labov, 1972). In typical speech communities, measurable changes occur over a few decades, and the differences in speech patterns between older and younger speakers can be used to map their trajectory. The changes are strongly correlated with sociological variables, especially social class, and intermediate social classes are usually the leading group. In the United States dialects are evolving rapidly, despite the use of a standardized dialect of English by the broadcast media. Dialect change is usually initiated in those subgroups within a larger speech community whose identity as a group is threatened. A distinctive regional or class dialect thus becomes a symbol of social status and group solidarity.

Labov (1980) illustrates these generalizations with a study from Philadelphia. Among Philadelphia whites, the immigration of large numbers of rural blacks in recent decades has stimulated a strenuous reassertion of local rights and privileges and a parallel development of a local Philadelphia white dialect. The dialect pattern thus reflects the deep social and political divisions between the city's ethnic groups.

The leaders of the Philadelphia dialect changes are upper-working-class women. The speakers who show the most "advanced" sound changes are those with the highest status in their *local* community, and with wide-ranging contacts inside and outside of it. From these centrally located individuals, dialect innovations spread outward to lower status and eventually to higher status speakers. The importance of locally relevant prestige as the key trait of effective models is similar to that found for opinion leaders in the diffusion of technical innovations. In dialect evolution, however, the innovations themselves originate with this group. The use of a few opinion leaders as models for dialect transmission, the indirect bias effect, plus the importance of horizontal transmission in language learning probably account for the speed of dialect evolution.

The evidence that dialect change results from the action of indirect bias is fairly convincing. Much small-scale linguistic variation, especially dialect, is not consciously recognized by speakers. Labov (1972: 308) reports that speakers of a distinctive dialect on Martha's Vineyard are not aware of most of the differences between their dialect and that of mainlanders. Vineyarders are conscious of using a certain amount of archaic nautical jargon, but this is only indirectly related to the phonological aspects of their dialect studied by Labov. This suggests that it is unlikely that they have deliberately chosen to adopt the advanced forms of the dialect. Rather, they appear to have granted a considerable social status to fishermen who best exemplify a spirit of resistance to the encroachment of higher status summer visitors. Their admiration of the fishermen's independent ways and scornful distaste for the visitors, on whom most islanders are uncomfortably dependent economically, leads to the inadvertent copying of the fishermen's dialect. Interestingly enough, those young people who plan to leave the island, and have switched their prestige norms to favor mainlanders, show much less of the distinctive Martha's Vineyard dialect (Labov, 1972: 32).

Models of Indirect Bias

In this section we build a model of indirect bias in two steps:

1. So far we have only considered models in which there was a single culturally transmitted character. To model indirect bias, it is necessary to keep track of at least two different culturally transmitted characters, the indicator trait and the indirectly biased trait. We begin by generalizing the blending model discussed in Chapter 3 to the case of more than one culturally transmitted characters.

2. In Chapter 5 we analyzed a model of direct bias in which there was a single culturally transmitted quantitative character. It was assumed that an individual's phenotypic value for the character affected his attractiveness as model for that character. Here, we simply add a second quantitative character and assume that the value of the first character also affects the attractiveness of the individual for the second character.

Cultural transmission with multiple characters

To model indirect bias we need models of cultural transmission in which individuals are characterized by values of several different cultural traits. In Chapter 3, we introduced quantitative cultural characters with the example of an individual's position along a single left-right political continuum. As we all know, the beliefs of many people are not easily placed on this continuum. In such cases it is better to characterize individuals in terms of their positions along several different dimensions—fiscal conservatism versus fiscal liberalism, morally conservative versus libertarian, pro defense versus anti defense, and so on. Thus the beliefs of people like the so-called neoliberals (fiscally conservative, pro defense, but libertarian on moral issues) who do not fit on the usual left to right scale can be represented.

The existence of interacting multiple traits in the same individual is described mathematically by supposing that each individual's cultural repertoire can be characterized by k numbers, $X_1, \ldots, X_k$. Each number represents a particular aspect of an individual's cultural repertoire. For example, X_1 might represent the individual's attitude toward fiscal issues, X_2 the individual's attitude toward defense, and so on. Such an ordered sequence of numbers is called a vector. We distinguish vectors by printing them in boldface, for example $\mathbf{X} = (X_1, \ldots, X_k)$. We also assume that an individual's overt behavior, for example in terms of public statements, on each of the various issues can also be characterized by a vector of values $\mathbf{Y} = (Y_1, \ldots, Y_k)$. We assume that the relationship between the cultural variant and the behavior in each dimension is exactly as in the one-dimensional case (see Chap. 3, pp. 70–71).

The population is thus characterized by the joint distribution of cultural variants. This distribution tells us what fraction of the population has each combination of cultural variants. For quantitative characters this distribution takes the mathematical form of a k-dimensional joint probability density function, which we will label $P(X_1, \ldots, X_k)$ or sometimes to save space, $P(\mathbf{X})$. It is easiest to see what this means in the two-dimensional case. Suppose dX_i is a small increment in X_i, where $i = 1,2$. Then the value of $P(X_1, X_2)\, dX_1\, dX_2$ approximately gives the probability that an individual chosen at random from the population has a cultural variant that lies in the small (dX_1, dX_2) rectangle as is shown in Figure 8.1. This figure also illustrates why it is not always possible to simply treat each different trait independently. When the two characters are not independent, evolutionary forces acting on one character will affect the frequency of the other character. This effect will be very important in the remainder of this chapter.

It is often possible to choose a scale of measurement for each of the characters such that the joint distribution of phenotypes in the population has approximately a multivariate normal distribution. When this is true, it is possible to characterize the population by (1) the mean value in the population of each character, $\overline{X}_i$, (2) a variance for each character, V_i, and (3) the covariance between each pair of characters, C_{ij}. The means and the variances have exactly the same meaning as in the one-dimensional case. The covariances measure the extent to which the different traits co-occur. If the covariance for a pair of characters is positive, then individuals with a larger than average value of one trait also tend to have a larger than average value for the second trait. For example, there probably is some tendency in the United States for people who are fiscally conservative also to be pro defense. If we have chosen our scale of measurement so that more conservative opinions are represented by a larger number (consistent with the usual left to right representation), then these two characters will have a positive covariance. When this is true the characters are said to covary.

In the next two sections we will generalize the blending model of cultural transmission of quantitative characters described in Chapter 3 to the case of two characters. We will see that the major novelty introduced is the way that transmission affects the covariance between characters in the population.

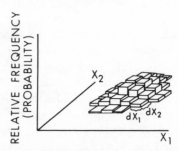

Fig. 8.1 Visualization of a two-dimensional joint probability distribution of quantitative characters. The height of each column is proportional to the frequency of individuals that are characterized by a narrow range of values of traits X_1 and X_2.

A bivariate blending model

Let us begin by describing a blending model of the cultural transmission of two quantitative characters. Suppose that each naive individual is enculturated by n models. The jth model is characterized by a two-dimensional vector of cultural variants $X_j = (X_{1j}, X_{2j})$. The naive individual observes the behavior of each model and forms an estimate of his or her vector of cultural variants $Z_j = (Z_{1j}, Z_{2j})$. In analogy with the one-dimensional case, we will assume that

$$Z_{1j} = X_{1j} + e_{1j}$$

$$Z_{2j} = X_{2j} + e_{2j}$$

(8.1)

where e_{1j} and e_{2j} are random variables with a bivariate normal distribution, $N_j(e_{1j}, e_{2j})$, with means equal to zero, variances E_{1j} and E_{2j}, and a covariance E_{12j}. This means that, as before, we assume that the naive individual's estimate of the jth model's cultural rule may diverge from his or her actual rule. Since the behavior that characterizes models will depend on the environment, it is plausible that the errors in the naive individual's estimate of the two traits (i.e. e_{1j} and e_{2j}) in a particular model will covary. For example, the two traits might be political beliefs about fiscal policy and about foreign policy. If the model is in an environment that tends to elicit conservative behavior whatever his beliefs might be, then naive individuals may overestimate the conservativeness of the model's actual beliefs for both characters. We represent this idea mathematically with the assumption that e_{1j} and e_{2j} are not necessarily independent. It is plausible that the performances of different parents will also covary. However, for simplicity we will assume that the errors made in estimating one model's rule are independent of the errors made in estimating the rule of some other model.

We will suppose that each character is transmitted according to the blending rule used in Chapter 3. Suppose that a naive individual has been exposed to a set of models and formed the following estimates of their cultural variants $Z_1, \ldots, Z_n$. Then the naive individual's cultural variants for each of the two characters (X_{10}, X_{20}) will be

$$X_{10} = \sum_{j=1}^{n} A_{1j} Z_{1j}$$

(8.2)

$$X_{20} = \sum_{j=1}^{n} A_{2j} Z_{2j}$$

Because we have assumed that A_{1j} does not necessarily equal A_{2j}, a particular model may have a different weight in the transmission of character 1 than in the transmission of character 2. This is meant to reflect the notion that individuals occupying different social roles may be more or less important in the transmission of different traits.

As usual we want to determine how transmission changes the distribution of cultural variants in the population. This means we need to determine the effect of transmission on the mean value and the variance of each character, and on the covariance between the characters. Let $M(\mathbf{X}_1, \ldots, \mathbf{X}_n)$ be the probability that a set of models with the combination of vectors of cultural variants $(\mathbf{X}_1, \ldots, \mathbf{X}_n)$ is formed. Then the mean value of the character X_i after transmission, $\overline{X}'_i$, is given by

$$\overline{X}_i = \int \ldots \int N_1 \, (e_{11}, e_{21}) \ldots N_n \, (e_{1n}, e_{2n}) M(\mathbf{X}_1, \ldots, \mathbf{X}_n)$$

$$\sum_{j=1}^{n} A_{ij}(X_{ij}+e_{ij}) \, d\mathbf{X}_1 \ldots d\mathbf{X}_n \, de_{11} \ldots de_{2n} \tag{8.3}$$

where $i = 1, 2$. This equation is very similar to Equation 3.22, the expression for the mean after transmission in the one-dimensional case. If the formation of sets of models is nonselective, derivations virtually identical to the one given in Box 3.2 yield

$$\overline{X}'_i = \overline{X}_i \tag{8.4}$$

and a similar derivation yields the following expressions for the variances after transmission:

$$V'_i = \sum_{j=1}^{n} A_{ij}^2 \, (V_i + \overline{E}_i) \tag{8.5}$$

where $i = 1$ or 2 and

$$\overline{E}_i = \frac{\sum_{j=1}^{n} A_{ij}^2 \, E_{ij}}{\sum_{j=1}^{n} A_{ij}^2}$$

$\overline{E}_1$ and $\overline{E}_2$ are weighted averages of the errors introduced in the imitation of each class of model. Equations 8.4 and 8.5 are equivalent to the expressions for transmission of one character given in Chapter 3. Thus, adding a second character does not alter the effect of blending inheritance on the means or variances of the characters transmitted.

However, to completely specify the distribution of cultural variants in the population after transmission we need to determine the effect of transmission on the covariance between the characters. The covariance between any two random variables u and v is defined as $E(uv) - E(u)E(v)$ where $E(\cdot)$ denotes the expectation. In the present case, we want to compute covariance between the values of trait 1 and trait 2 after transmission, C_{12}, given the distribution of cultural variants before transmission. It can be shown that

$$C_{12}, = (R/\overline{n}_e) \, (C_{12} + \overline{E}_{12}) \tag{8.6}$$

where

$$\overline{E}_{12} = \frac{\sum_{j=1}^{n} A_{1j} A_{2j} E_{12j}}{\sum_{j=1}^{n} A_{1j} A_{2j}}$$

(8.7)

and

$$\overline{n}_e = \left(\sum_{j=1}^{n} A_{1j}^2 \sum_{j=1}^{n} A_{2j}^2 \right)^{-1/2}$$

and

$$R = \frac{\sum_{j=1}^{n} A_{1j} A_{2j}}{(\sum_{j=1}^{n} A_{1j}^2 \sum_{j=1}^{n} A_{2j}^2)^{1/2}}$$

(8.8)

Equation 8.6 says that the effect of blending inheritance on the covariance between two characters is similar in some ways to its effect on the variance. The covariance is increased each generation by the new covariation that is introduced by correlated errors, measured by $\overline{E}_{12}$. It is decreased each generation by an amount that is proportional to $1/\overline{n}_e$, the geometric mean of the effective numbers of models for each trait. This is the same blending effect that reduces the variances. However, unlike the effects of blending inheritance on the variance, the reduction in the covariance also depends on the parameter R. This parameter, which has the form of a correlation coefficient, measures the extent to which the sets of models are the same for the two traits. To see this consider two extreme cases:

1. $A_{1j} = A_{2j}$. This means that each of the models has exactly the same importance in the transmission of both traits. Then $R = 1$, $\overline{n}_e = n_e$, and blending inheritance has the effect of reducing the variances of each of the characters and the covariance between them by the same factor, $1/n_e$.

2. $A_{1j} > 0$ implies $A_{2j} = 0$, and $A_{2j} > 0$ implies $A_{1j} = 0$. This means that the sets of models for the two characters do not overlap. One set of individuals serve as models for trait 1 and a different set for trait 2. In this case $R = 0$, and any covariance that existed in the population before transmission is completely eradicated by the transmission process.

The effect of blending inheritance on the covariance between characters depends on the extent to which the sets of models for the two traits are composed of the same individuals. As the sets of models transmitting two traits become different, transmission exerts a force reducing the covariance between characters even more strongly than it does the variances. As we will see, this is important because it is the ratio of the covariance to the variance that determines the strength of indirect bias.

We have also generalized the multifactor model presented in Chapter 3 to allow for multiple characters. This model is of interest for two reasons. First, the amount of overlap in the set of models has the same qualitative effect on the covariance between characters in the multifactorial model as in the blending model, which suggests that this result is robust. Second, this model also allows for another mechanism that can act to preserve the covariance between characters. Recall that in Chapter 3 we imagined that each observable behavioral character was based on a number of culturally transmitted factors. In the context of a two-character model, this means that there can be a significant covariance between two characters even if there is no covariance between the underlying factors as long as at least one factor influences both characters. This makes sense intuitively. For example, people who believe in the perfectibility of man may have liberal attitudes about many issues, while those who believe that men are irremediably troublesome may tend to hold conservative views.

The effects of indirect bias on the mean phenotype

In this section we combine the model of cultural transmission of two characters with the model of directly biased transmission introduced in Chapter 5 to determine the effect of indirect bias on the joint distribution of the two traits in the population. First, assume that each naive individual is exposed to n models. The importance of the jth model for the ith trait is given by a constant linear weight labeled A_{ij}. In Chapter 5, direct bias was modeled by allowing an individual's cultural variant to affect its linear weight. Suppose that trait 1 is the indicator trait and trait 2 is an indirectly biased trait. Then, according to our definition of indirect bias, the importance of the jth model for the indirectly biased trait depends on the variant of the indicator trait that characterizes the jth model. We will say that the variants of the indicator trait that make an individual most likely to be imitated are the "admired" variants. Consideration of why indirect bias might be adaptive, and even superior to direct bias, is explored in the next section.

Consider a particular naive individual exposed to n models. To make the equations easier to follow, we modify the notation used in the last section. We denote the value of the indicator trait of the jth model as X_{Ij} and the value of the indirectly biased trait of the jth model as X_{Pj}. The naive individual's estimates of the jth model's indicator trait and indirectly biased trait are Z_{Ij} and Z_{Pj}, respectively. Then, according to the blending model, the naive individual's cultural variants for the indicator trait, X_{I0}, and the indirectly biased trait, X_{P0}, are

$$X_{I0} = \sum_{j=1}^{n} A_{Ij} Z_{Ij} \qquad (8.9)$$

and

$$X_{P0} = \sum_{j=1}^{n} A_{Pj} Z_{Pj} \qquad (8.10)$$

where A_{Ij} and A_{Pj} are the importances of the jth model in the transmission of the indicator and indirectly biased traits. We assume that the transmission of the indicator trait is subject to direct bias exactly as in Chapter 5. This means that the weight of the jth model is a function of his or her variant of the indicator trait, that is,

$$A_{Ij} = \frac{\alpha_{Ij}(1 + \beta(Z_{Ij}))}{\sum_{k=1}^{n} \alpha_{Ik}(1 + \beta(Z_{Ik}))} \tag{8.11}$$

Equation 8.11 says that the importance of the jth model in the transmission of the indicator trait is given by a basic weight, α_{Ij}, that depends on the jth model's social role and a modifying term that depends on his cultural variant.

To represent indirect bias we assume that the weight of the jth·model for the indirectly biased trait, A_{Pj}, is a similar function of his indicator trait Z_{Ij}, that is,

$$A_{Pj} = \frac{\alpha_{Pj}(1 + \Theta(Z_{Ij}))}{\sum_{k=1}^{n} \alpha_{Pk}(1 + \Theta(Z_{Ik}))} \tag{8.12}$$

Equation 8.12 says that the importance of the jth model in the transmission of the indirectly biased trait also depends on a basic weight. We write this α_{Pj} to emphasize that the basic weight of the jth model may be different for the two traits. However, α_{Pj} is modified by function $\Theta(Z_{Ij})$, the indirect bias function, which gives the effect of the indicator trait's value on the weight of a model in the transmission of the indirectly biased trait. We will assume that the form of the indirect bias function, $\Theta(\cdot)$, is generally similar to that of the direct bias function, $\beta(\cdot)$, but that the strengths of the two processes may be different. The value of the indicator trait that maximizes $\Theta(\cdot)$ is the most admired variant of the indicator trait, and individuals with this value will, on average, have the greatest weight in the transmission of the indirectly biased trait.

We want to determine how transmission affects the mean values of the two characters in the population. Once again assume that (1) sets of models are formed at random and (2) the effect of bias in any single generation is small. The transmission rule for the indicator trait is directly biased, and thus from Equation 5.10 the mean of the indicator trait in the population after transmission, $\overline{X}'_I$, is equal to

$$\overline{X}'_I = \overline{X}_I + (1 - \sum_{j=1}^{n} \alpha_{Ij}^2) \text{Cov}(Z_I, \beta(Z_I)) \tag{8.13}$$

where $1/\Sigma\alpha_{Ij}^2$ is the effective number of models for the indicator trait and $\text{Cov}(Z_I, \beta(Z_I))$ is the covariance of the indicator trait and the bias function. The covariance is a measure of the strength of directly biased transmission.

An exactly parallel derivation shows that the mean of the indirectly biased trait after transmission is given by

$$\overline{X}'_P = \overline{X}_P + (1 - \sum_{j=1}^{n} \alpha_{Pj}^2) \text{Cov}(Z_P, \Theta(Z_I)) \tag{8.14}$$

Notice that the strength of indirect bias depends on the covariance of the value of the indirectly biased trait Z_P and on the value of the indirect bias function $\Theta(Z_I)$, which is a function of the indicator trait. Thus variants of the indirectly biased trait that are positively correlated with the admired variants of the indicator trait will increase in frequency.

We can understand better what this means by rewriting the covariance term in the following form:

$$\mathrm{Cov}(Z_P, \Theta(Z_I)) = \mathrm{Corr}(Z_I, Z_P)\left(\frac{\mathrm{Var}(Z_P)}{\mathrm{Var}(Z_I)}\right)^{1/2} \mathrm{Cov}(Z_I, \Theta(Z_I)) \qquad (8.15)$$

This way of writing Equation 8.14 emphasizes the fact that the strength of indirect bias depends on the extent to which the indicator trait and the indirectly biased traits are correlated. If the correlation is increased, then, all other things equal, the force of indirect bias will also be increased. Equation 8.15 also indicates that the strength of indirect bias depends on the amount of variation that exists for the indirectly biased trait. In this way, indirect bias is similar to direct bias and natural selection.

It is also clear from Equation 8.15 that even if $\beta(\cdot) = \Theta(\cdot)$, the strength of indirect bias can be greater than the force of direct bias as long as

$$|\mathrm{Corr}(Z_I, Z_P)| > \left(\mathrm{Var}(Z_I)/\mathrm{Var}(Z_P)\right)^{1/2} \qquad (8.16)$$

This means that indirect bias can be stronger than direct bias based on the same criterion if the amount of variation in the indirectly biased trait is sufficiently greater than that of the directly biased trait to compensate for the less than perfect correlation between the two. For example, in a poor village the variation in wealth displayed might be very small, but the correlated variation in some useful skill might be quite large. Indirect bias using wealth displayed might cause a substantial increase in skills, while the change in the indicator due to direct bias might be quite small.

Forces affecting the covariance between characters

The correlation between the indicator trait and the indirectly biased trait affects the strength of indirect bias. To fully understand indirect bias, we must understand the forces that affect the covariance between the two characters. We have been able to think of four kinds of forces that affect the covariance:

1. We have already seen that transmission itself affects the covariance. Non-overlapping sets of models for the two traits act to reduce the covariance, while covarying estimation errors act to increase it.

2. We have also argued that in the multifactorial model of the transmission of more than one character, the existence of factors which affect more than one character act to preserve covariation.

3. Natural selection can affect the covariance between characters when the two characters interact to determine fitness.

4. Indirectly biased transmission itself can increase the covariance between the indicator trait and the indirectly biased trait. This effect is especially pronounced when the preference trait is also an indirectly biased trait.

In order to consider the effects of natural selection on the covariance between two culturally transmitted characters, the model of natural selection used in Chapter 4 must be generalized to allow for more than two characters. To do this we assume that an individual's cultural fitness is a function of both of its cultural variants, $W(X_I, X_P)$. This function gives the probability that an individual with the combination of cultural variants X_I and X_P becomes a model. Then the joint distribution of cultural variants after transmission, $P'(X_I, X_P)$, is given by

$$P'(X_I, X_P) = \frac{P(X_I, X_P)W(X_I, X_P)}{\int\int P(X_I, X_P)W(X_I, X_P)dX_I dX_P} \qquad (8.17)$$

We assume that the distribution of cultural variants before selection is bivariate normal. To evaluate the distribution of cultural variants after selection we must choose a fitness function.

One plausible way to generalize the one-dimensional model of selection used in Chapter 4 is to assume that $W(\cdot)$ has a bivariate Gaussian form, as pictured in Figure 8.2a. In this example individuals whose vector of cultural variants departs from the optimum vector of cultural variants (H_I, H_P) are less likely to become models. Notice that individuals who deviate from the optimum by having values of X_I and X_P that are either both too large or both too small suffer a much smaller decline in fitness than individuals who have one large value and one small value. In this example, the two characters interact in their effects on fitness. The fitness

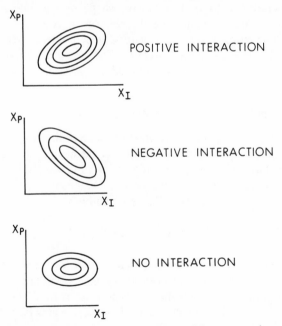

Fig. 8.2 Bivariate Gaussian fitness functions as contours of fitness on a plane whose dimensions are values of traits X_1 and X_2.

function shown in Figure 8.2b illustrates the opposite kinds of interaction between the traits; now individuals with a large value of X_I and a small value of X_P are favored relative to individuals with small or large values for both traits. Figure 8.2c shows an example of a fitness function in which there is no interaction between the two traits.

Positive interactions between traits are believed to be common in genetic evolution because of allometric relationships. For example, animals with forelegs and hind legs that are both too short may be better off than others who have forelegs that are too long and hind legs that are too short. It seems likely that analogous phenomena exist in the case of many culturally transmitted characters. To take a complex example, social acceptance is often thought to be contingent on matching display traits with skills. Lawyers who talk and dress like farmers are likely to be thought of and treated as oddities by their fellows. Even in academia, where standards of dress are quite relaxed, an ecologist who regularly wore a three-piece suit would excite quizzical comment (we have never met one), whereas an economist who did the same (and many do) would not attract any notice. To the extent that violating such expectations causes unfavorable judgments about people, selection (and perhaps biased cultural transmission) will act to increase covariation.

When two characters have interactive effects on fitness, natural selection will create a force that affects the correlation between the characters. This is most easily proved if it is assumed that the fitness function is a bivariate Gaussian function. Unfortunately, it is cumbersome to analyze even this simple case without using matrix notation. The interested reader can find complete analyses in Lande (1979) and Karlin (1979). These authors conclude that the equilibrium distribution of the two variants in the population is a compromise between two forces. Selection tends to cause the population to conform to the shape of the fitness function, while random variation tends to cause the distribution to conform to the probability distribution of the random errors. Thus natural selection tends to cause variants that interact positively to be positively correlated. The strength of this effect will depend on the relative strength of selection and random variation.

The correlation between fitness and other characters

So far we have only considered correlation between ordinary culturally transmitted characters. When we investigate the adaptive consequences of indirect bias, it will also be of interest to know whether the regression of fitness itself on a character that affects fitness can be nonzero at equilibrium. The change in the mean value of a character due to natural selection, $\Delta \overline{X}$, is given by

$$\Delta \overline{X} = \text{Var}(X)\text{Reg}(W(X),X) \qquad (8.18)$$

If we assume that random variation maintains a finite variance in the character and that there are no other directional forces acting on a population, then the mean will come to equilibrium only when the regression of an individual's fitness on his cultural variant is zero. This makes sense; if some variants have higher fitness on average, selection should increase their frequency.

However, if the equilibrium results from a balance of selection and other forces, then the regression of fitness on a character can be nonzero. For example, in a spatially varying environment the mean phenotype at equilibrium will be determined by a balance between the forces of selection and migration. To see how this affects the covariance between a character and fitness, consider the following very simple model of the evolution of a quantitative character in a spatially varying habitat. Suppose a large metapopulation is composed of a large number of subpopulations living in different habitats. There is a single quantitative character which is transmitted according to a linear transmission rule. In each subpopulation this character is subjected to stabilizing natural selection. Now consider a single subpopulation in which the optimal value of the character is H and the width of the fitness function is S. After selection, a fraction, m, of the subpopulation emigrates and is replaced by immigrants from the metapopulation. We assume that the local population is small enough relative to the metapopulation that we can neglect the effects of the local population on the metapopulation. For simplicity, we assume that the mean cultural variant in the metapopulation, and thus among the immigrants, is zero. With these assumptions it can be shown that the equilibrium mean of the character among models in the local population, $\overline{X}$, is approximately

$$\overline{X} = \frac{VH}{mS + V} \tag{8.19}$$

where V is the equilibrium variance of the character. When migration is weak compared to selection, the equilibrium mean is near H. When selection is weak compared to migration, it is near zero, the metapopulation mean. At the equilibrium described by 8.19 there will be a positive regression of fitness individuals on the values of their cultural variants. When selection and migration are both weak, it can be shown that this has the following simple form:

$$\text{Reg}(W(X),X) = (H - \overline{X})/S \tag{8.20}$$

Equation 8.20 says that regression of fitness on a character is proportional to the mean character's distance from the equilibrium.

The adaptive consequences of indirect bias

In Chapter 5, we argued that only direct biases that are adaptive in a wide variety of habitats are likely to evolve. For some characters, the same variants may be adaptive in many different habitats, and a simple invariant bias may be favored. For other characters, quite different variants may be favored in different habitats. If it is not too difficult for each individual to try each variant and evaluate it according to some generally applicable criteria of satisfaction, then the evolution of a general purpose direct bias is plausible. However, for many characters, it may be very difficult to evaluate the merit of different variants. For the most basic beliefs and values each trial might occupy a lifetime.

Rather than attempt to determine which variants of each trait lead to success, an alternative approach is to simply imitate the successful, as suggested by Flinn and Alexander (1982). If adopting a particular variant causes individuals to have higher fitness than the average individual, then it follows that the adaptive variant should occur in higher frequency among individuals with high fitness. Thus it seems plausible that the strategy of imitating the successful, a form of indirect bias, might provide an alternative to direct bias, one that increases an individual's chances of acquiring locally adaptive cultural variants, is applicable in a wide variety of environments, and does not require costly evaluation of the different variants.

The results that have been derived so far in this chapter can be used to make this argument in more detail. Consider the model of a population in the spatially variable habitat discussed in the previous section, supposing that there are two quantitative traits. The indicator trait is a proxy for fitness. It could be any trait which has a high, positive correlation with genetic fitness in most of the habitats. Number of offspring, wealth, and political power are likely candidates, at least in nonindustrial societies. For example, Irons (1979b) showed that a number of economic and political traits connoting high prestige were correlated with fitness among the Turkoman. The indirectly biased trait is an ordinary culturally transmitted character; the optimum value of the indirectly biased trait is different in different habitats. As before, consider evolution in one of the habitats in which the optimum value of the indirectly biased trait is H. From the previous section, we know that at equilibrium the regression of fitness on the indirectly biased trait has the value given in Equation 8.20.

Now suppose there are a few rare naive individuals who tend to choose models with large values of the indicator trait according to the indirectly biased transmission rule outlined above. If the indicator trait is highly correlated with fitness and the distribution of the indicator and indirectly biased traits is approximately bivariate normal, then according to Equation 8.14 the mean value of X_P among these naive individuals will be

$$\overline{X}'_P = \overline{X}_P + \underbrace{(1 - \sum_{j=1}^{n} \alpha_{Pj}^2) \, \text{Cov}(Z_I, \Theta(Z_I))}_{\text{strength of bias}} \times \underbrace{(H - \overline{X}_P)/S}_{\text{strength of selection}} \qquad (8.21)$$

Equation 8.21 shows that on average the mean phenotype of naive individuals who utilize indirect bias will be closer to the optimal phenotype than will that of naive individuals who utilize a linear, unbiased rule. The strength of indirect bias is proportional to the product of the strength of the bias and the strength of selection. Moreover, we have made no assumptions about the value of H; the same simple decision rule will increase the probability that naive individuals adopt favored variants in every habitat.

Given that there are easily observable characters that are correlated with fitness in a wide variety of habitats, it seems, to us at least, that indirect bias provides a good general purpose cultural acquisition rule. It should generally require less effort to apply than direct bias. Essentially, with indirect bias the individual uses the lives of others as experiments to evaluate different cultural variants. Because of this, indirect bias may be much cheaper than direct bias, particularly for traits which may have multiple effects over an individual's lifetime. It also means that indirect bias will increase the probability of acquiring a favored cultural variant in many different environments. If there are no characters which are strongly correlated with fitness in most habitats, then all these conclusions are suspect. We consider some aspects of this issue in the next section.

The Runaway Process

Thus far we have assumed that every individual in the population admires the same variant of the indicator trait—that is, the cultural transmission rule of every individual is governed by the same indirect bias function. This means that the criteria of indirect bias cannot evolve. They cannot be affected by selection, direct bias, or guided variation. If there are truly characters which are positively correlated with fitness in the entire range of habitats that characterize the human species, this would not be too important. However, it seems to us that few such characters are likely to exist. Biologists have found it very difficult to measure the fitness of noncultural animals in the field, and it is probably at least as difficult to assay fitness in the human case. The relationship between numbers of offspring and fitness is often quite ambiguous, since offspring must survive and reproduce themselves to count. Wealth and power are problematic because different characters may denote wealth and power in different societies, and because wealth and power are not necessarily correlated with fitness. The relationship between prestige and fitness is even more ambiguous; indicators of prestige are often almost incomprehensible to those not raised in a particular culture. If indirect bias is to provide a means of acquiring adaptive behaviors in a variety of environments, the criteria that determine what is admired probably will be transmitted culturally and will respond to the forces of cultural evolution.

In this section, we generalize the model of indirect bias so that the criteria that determine which variants of the indicator trait are admired are allowed to vary. We will see that under some circumstances these criteria will evolve so that indirect bias increases the frequency of genetically adaptive variants. However, we will also see that an unstable runaway process, analogous to runaway sexual selection in ordinary genetic evolution, is possible. This process can cause the indicator trait to coevolve with the preference trait so as to cause the indicator trait to become extremely exaggerated. In a later section we review data that suggest that humans frequently engage in exaggerated, maladaptive displays of prestige, and that this behavior is understandable in terms of indirect bias.

To get an intuitive understanding of why indirect bias can lead to an unstable runaway process, it is helpful to review R. A. Fisher's (1958) explanation for the evolution of exaggerated male characters, such as the tails of peacocks and birds of paradise. Imagine a species in which females choose males for their mates based on a sex-limited morphological character, the size of their tails. Further, suppose that females, on average, prefer males with tails that are too large. That is, males with smaller tails would be more likely to survive than males with the tails that most females prefer. Never mind, for the moment, why females make such odd choices. There are two competing selective forces acting on male tail size: sexual selection due to female choice acts to increase the frequency of males with large tails, and ordinary viability selection acts to increase the frequency of males with small tails. In polygynous species, in which a small proportion of males are responsible for a large proportion of matings, sexual selection can be much stronger than viability selection. When this is the case, males with large tails will be favored and tail size will increase. Fisher's insight was to see that under some conditions, the same process of sexual selection that increased the frequency of males with large tails could also increase the frequency of females who preferred large tails. Females who mate with males who have large tails will tend to have sons who also have large tails, and will tend to transmit a preference for large tails to their daughters and their sons' daughters. In other words, female choice will cause the preference for large tails and large tails themselves to become correlated. If the net effect of individual and sexual selection is to favor large tails, selection will also lead to a correlated response in female preferences. Put anthropomorphically, selection may favor females who prefer males who will produce "sexy" sons. As has been recently shown by Lande (1981) and Kirkpatrick (1982), under the right conditions this can lead to a self-reinforcing process in which both tail size and the tail size most preferred by females increase indefinitely.

A closely analogous process can cause a cultural runaway process when transmission is indirectly biased. Rather than females choosing mates based on a male character, the cultural process is driven by naive individuals choosing models based on the value of the indicator trait. Again consider a hypothetical example in which individuals choose models based on the value of a character marking prestige, for example, their style of dress. Further suppose that for still unspecified reasons the majority of the population admire a colorful but otherwise maladaptive mode of dress. Individuals who dress practically are better protected from the weather and spend less on clothes, but are less admired and therefore less likely to be imitated. In other words, we assume that natural selection acting on cultural variation favors practical dress and indirect bias favors colorful dress. It is easy to see in this case how the net effect of these two forces could act to increase the frequency of colorful dressers. It is somewhat less obvious that indirect bias can increase the frequency of individuals who admire and tend to imitate colorful dressers. Individuals who admire colorful dress will tend to acquire colorful dress. If individuals tend to acquire their beliefs about what styles of dress make a person admirable and their own style of dress from the same individuals, then forces that increase the frequency of colorful dress will also act to increase the frequency of individuals who tend to imitate colorfully dressed people. It is as if people choose models from whom they will acquire traits that will subsequently make them more likely to be imitated.

A model with variable biases

To model the evolution of the criteria which determine the strength and direction of indirect bias, we assume that there is a culturally transmitted quantitative character, the preference trait, that affects which variants of the indicator trait an individual finds attractive. Two naive individuals exposed to the same set of models but characterized by different values of the preference trait will, on average, adopt different cultural variants of other traits affected by indirect bias. Using the term "preference trait" does not imply that the naive individuals necessarily make conscious choices, only that they tend disproportionately to imitate models with some variants of the indicator trait. To allow for the possibility that the preference trait will be affected by the force of indirect bias, it is necessary to consider the simultaneous evolution of an indicator character. In the most interesting cases of indirect bias, there will also be a number of indirectly biased traits whose evolution was also affected by the same indicator and preference traits. However, to keep the model manageable we will treat only the evolution of an indicator and a preference trait. We do not believe that adding more indirectly biased traits will have important qualitative effects on the results of the model.

Real situations undoubtedly are more complex. For example, consider dialect evolution on Martha's Vineyard, studied by Labov (1972). An example of an indicator trait is the extent to which an individual uses nautical jargon in everyday speech. The use of a rich, "salty" vocabulary is thought by Vineyarders to be a marker of status as an old stock Vineyarder. A preference trait is the extent to which an individual desires to imitate other individuals who exemplify the rugged independence of the old Islanders. In addition to these two traits, the evolving trait complex on Martha's Vineyard includes phonological aspects of their dialect and a number of other traits related to social organization, status, and group identity. Some of the traits in this complex, for example, dialect phonology, may indicate status as an old stock Islander. Although dialect phonology is not easy for people to perceive consciously, people do seem to form judgments of others based on this character (Labov, 1972: Chap. 6). It also seems likely the evolution of dialect is embedded in a large system of indirect bias involving many other traits. The two-trait model presented here is an attempt to obtain a qualitative glimpse into the dynamics of systems like this one in which there are many traits that indicate status and many others that are affected through their correlation with the indicator traits.

Assume that individuals undergo the following life cycle. First, naive individuals acquire values of both the indicator trait and the preference trait vertically according to an unbiased transmission rule. This is followed by an episode of oblique transmission which is affected by both direct and indirect bias according to the model described in the last section, in which the preference trait is also the indirectly biased trait. Cultural transmission is followed by an episode of natural selection in which an individual's fitness is determined by the value of his indicator trait. We will assume that the preference trait has no direct effect on the cultural or genetic fitness of an individual; its only effects on fitness are through its effects on cultural transmission.

If the joint distribution of cultural variants is approximately bivariate normal, we only need to keep track of the means and variances of each of the characters and their covariance. It turns out that, given the assumptions of the model, the variances and the covariances reach a stable equilibrium independent of the values of the means. To derive recursions for the mean values of the two traits we assume (1) that the variances are at equilibrium at values V_I and V_P and the covariance is also at an equilibrium value C, and (2) that the forces of biased transmission and selection are weak enough that we can regard these values as approximately constant during a single generation.

Recursions for the means

In order to derive recursions for the mean values of the indicator and preference traits in the population, we begin with the effects of oblique transmission. Let $\overline{X}_I$ and $\overline{X}_P$ be the means of the indicator and the preference traits in the population just before oblique transmission. Each naive individual is exposed to n models. Consider a particular naive individual, Peter, who is characterized by the preference trait value, X_{P0}. We assume that Peter's value of the indicator trait after oblique transmission, X'_{I0}, is given by the following blending rule:

$$X'_{I0} = \frac{\sum_{k=1}^{n} Z_{Ik}\alpha_{Ik}\left(1 + \beta(Z_{Ik},X_{P0})\right)}{\sum_{k=1}^{n}\alpha_{Ik}\left(1 + \beta(Z_{Ik},X_{P0})\right)} \tag{8.22}$$

where Z_{Ik} is Peter's estimate of the value of indicator trait of the kth model computed exactly as above. Equation 8.22 is the same transmission rule discussed in the last section, except that now the shape of the bias function depends on the value of the preference trait in the naive individual, X_{P0}. We assume that each individual also modifies his or her preference trait during oblique transmission. Then Peter's value of the preference trait after oblique transmission is given by

$$X'_{P0} = \frac{\sum_{k=1}^{n} Z_{Pk}\alpha_{Pk}\left(1 + \Theta(Z_{Ik},X_{P0})\right)}{\sum_{k=1}^{n}\alpha_{Pk}\left(1 + \Theta(Z_{Ik},X_{P0})\right)} \tag{8.23}$$

where Z_{Pk} is Peter's estimate of the preference trait of the kth model.

Based on the results derived above, we know that if sets of models are formed at random, then the mean of the indicator trait after transmission is

$$\overline{X}'_I = \overline{X}_I + (1 - \sum_{j=1}^{n}\alpha_{Ij}^2)\text{Cov}\left(Z_I,\beta(Z_I,X_{P0})\right) \tag{8.24}$$

and the mean value of the preference trait after oblique transmission is given by the analogous expression

$$\overline{X}'_P = \overline{X}_P + (1 - \sum_{j=1}^{n}\alpha_{Pj}^2)\,\text{Cov}\left(Z_P,\Theta(Z_I,X_{P0})\right) \tag{8.25}$$

To evaluate the covariance terms we need to assume some particular functional form for the direct and indirect bias functions. We will assume that the direct bias function has the form

$$\beta(Z_{Ij},X_{P0}) = b\,\exp\left(\frac{-(Z_{Ij} - X_{P0})^2}{2B}\right) \tag{8.26}$$

and that the indirect bias function has the similar form

$$\Theta(Z_{Ij}, X_{P0}) = u \exp\left(\frac{-(Z_{Ij} - X_{P0})^2}{2\theta}\right) \tag{8.27}$$

These functions have the same Gaussian form as the bias function that was introduced in Chapter 5. Now, however, the value of the preference trait in the naive individual (X_{P0}) determines which value of the indicator trait maximizes the weight of a model in oblique transmission of both the traits. Notice that the intensity of the direct bias acting on the indicator trait, measured by $1/B$, may differ from the intensity of indirect bias acting on the preference trait, measured by $1/\theta$.

It can be shown that if bias is weak (i.e. $B, \theta \gg V_I, C$) the means after transmission are

$$\overline{X}_I' = \overline{X}_I + V_I B'(\overline{X}_P - \overline{X}_I)$$
$$\overline{X}_P' = \overline{X}_P + C\theta'(\overline{X}_P - \overline{X}_I) \tag{8.28}$$

where

$$B' = (1 - \sum_{j=1}^{n} \alpha_{Ij}^2)(b/B)$$

and

$$\theta' = (1 - \sum_{j=1}^{n} \alpha_{Pj}^2)(u/\theta)$$

The parameter B' measures the effective intensity of biased transmission acting on the indicator trait and θ' measures the effective intensity of indirect bias acting on the preference trait. The variances and covariances refer to the population of models who participate in oblique transmission.

To model the effects of selection we assume that the probability that an individual characterized by the cultural variant X_I becomes a model, $W(X_I)$, is given by Gaussian fitness function

$$W(X_I) = \exp\left(\frac{-(X_I - H)^2}{2S}\right) \tag{8.29}$$

It can be shown with a derivation similar to that in Box 4.5 that if selection is weak (i.e. $S \gg V_I$) the mean values of the two traits in the population after selection are

$$\overline{X}_I'' = \overline{X}_I + V_I[B'(\overline{X}_P - \overline{X}_I) + (1/S)(H - \overline{X}_I)]$$
$$\overline{X}_P'' = \overline{X}_P + C[\theta'(\overline{X}_P - \overline{X}_I) + (1/S)(H - \overline{X}_I)] \tag{8.30}$$

Since unbiased transmission does not affect the mean of either character, these recursions also give the means of the two characters during the next generation.

Mathematical properties of the recursions

These recursions have very interesting properties that may explain the evolution of some human behaviors that are puzzling from a sociobiological point of view. Let us begin by determining the equilibrium values of the mean value of each of the two characters in the population. By setting $\overline{X}_P'' = \overline{X}_P$ and $\overline{X}_I'' = \overline{X}_I$, we can see that the population will be in equilibrium if the following conditions are satisfied:

$$0 = (1/S)(1/B' - 1/\theta')(H - \overline{X}_I) \tag{8.31}$$

$$\overline{X}_P = \overline{X}_I + (1/S)(1/B')(H - \overline{X}_I) \tag{8.32}$$

The right-hand side of Equation 8.31 is the product of three terms. The equation will be satisfied whenever any one of these terms is zero. One of three qualitatively different kinds of equilibrium outcomes will result depending on which of these terms is zero. We first outline the mathematical properties of each of the three kinds of equilibria and then provide a qualitative interpretation of all three.

First, let us consider the case $(1/S) = 0$, which means that there is no selection. The only forces acting on the population are direct and indirect bias. If we set $(1/S) = 0$ in Equation 8.30 or 8.32, it is easy to see that the system will be in equilibrium any time that the mean values of the trait are equal. Thus any point on the line $\overline{X}_I = \overline{X}_P$ is an equilibrium. It can be shown that this line of equilibria will be stable whenever

$$B'V_I > \theta'C \tag{8.33}$$

Equation 8.33 says that the line of equilibria is stable whenever the strength of directly biased transmission acting on the indicator trait is stronger than the force of indirect bias on the preference trait. To see why this is so, consider Figure 8.3. The equilibria lie on the 45-degree line that goes through the origin. Consider a population that has an initial distribution of cultural variants so that $\overline{X}_P > \overline{X}_I$. Such a population is characterized as a point lying above the line. This means that the average individual prefers variants of the indicator trait that are larger than the average value of the indicator trait in the population so the mean value of the indicator trait increases. However, the effect of indirect bias also causes the value of the preference trait to increase because the correlation of preference traits and indicator traits causes imitators of admired models to acquire even more extreme preferences than they had before. If the indirect effect is larger than the direct effect, then the mean of the preference trait is increasing faster than the mean of the indicator trait and both traits "run away." If the indirect effect is weaker, then they eventually come to rest at some point along the line of equilibria. However, all points along the line are neutrally stable with respect to each other. Thus, when populations are finite, random sampling error will cause the population to "drift away."

Let us consider dialect evolution on Martha's Vineyard in the context of this model. While the real situation is undoubtedly too complex to be represented exactly by this simple model, this exercise will help make the results of the model more concrete, and perhaps give some insight into the nature of the dynamic

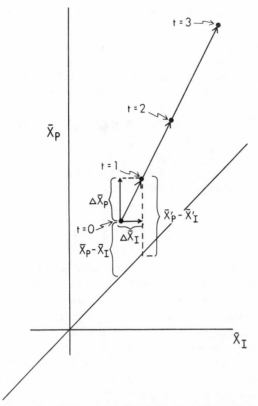

Fig. 8.3 Illustrates the case of unstable indirect bias with a line of equilibria. A one-generation step of the system is shown in detail. Under the condition given in the text, the increase of the preference trait in the population ($\Delta\bar{X}_P$) is greater than the increase in the indicator trait ($\Delta\bar{X}_I$). As shown, this causes the distance the population means are away from the unstable equilibrium line to increase from one generation to the next ($\bar{X}'_P - \bar{X}'_I \geq \bar{X}_P - \bar{X}_I$). Because the per-generation changes are proportional to the difference by which mean preferences exceed mean values of the indicator trait, as illustrated, the system will run away from the line at an accelerating rate once displaced.

processes which govern dialect evolution. Let us suppose again that the extent to which individuals use salty talk is the indicator trait and the extent to which individuals admire salty talk is the preference trait. The point above the line in Figure 8.3 represents a situation in which the average teenage Vineyarder prefers more salty talk in his or her models than the average adult Vineyarder actually speaks. Thus teenage Vineyarders will tend to imitate models whose dialect is more "salty" than the general population, and the average Vineyarder in the next cultural generation will use more salty talk. It seems reasonable that the teenage imitators will tend to acquire their preferences regarding the most admirable amount of salty talk from the same models from whom they acquired their dialect. If individuals who use a lot of salty talk also admire salty talk, the amount of salty talk preferred by the average individual will also increase due to the effect of indirect bias. If this effect is stronger than the direct effect on the amount of salty talk, the average amount of salty talk and the preference for salty talk will run away. We believe that if another trait like phonological dialect were added to this model, it would be carried away as well.

Next, let us consider the case $(1/B' - 1/\theta') = 0$. This means that the relative strengths of directly biased transmission on the indicator trait and indirectly biased transmission on the preference trait depend only on V_I and C. In this case there is also a line of equilibria, but now it is defined by the equation

$$\overline{X}_P = [1 + (1/(B'S))]\overline{X}_I + [1/(\theta'S)]H \tag{8.34}$$

At any point along this line the forces of bias and selection exactly balance each other. The line is stable whenever the forces of selection and direct bias that act on the indicator trait are greater than the force of indirect bias that acts on the preference trait or

$$\theta'C < V_I(B' + 1/S) \tag{8.35}$$

If this condition is not satisfied, the mean value of both traits will increase or decrease indefinitely depending on the initial state of the population. Still more interesting, even if the condition is satisfied and despite the fact that natural selection is acting on the preference trait, the population is free to drift along the line of equilibrium. The reason for this is that any amount of selection can be balanced by the appropriate amount of indirect bias. In the case of language evolution, a group might evolve a new dialect even though the more extreme speakers faced substantial selective penalties, perhaps because they were unable to communicate with a larger parent group.

Finally, consider the case $\overline{X}_I = H$. This means that the mean value of the indicator trait is the value with the highest fitness. From Equation 8.32 we know that the mean of the preference trait must also be equal to H. Thus, unless there is no selection $(1/S = 0)$ or the intensities of direct and indirect bias are equal $(B' = \theta')$, selection will cause cultural transmission to be biased in favor of the cultural variant that maximizes cultural fitness. However, it can be shown that this equilibrium is unstable if Condition 8.35 is violated.

Condition 8.35 says that the fitness-maximizing equilibrium is unstable if the strength of selection and direct bias on the indicator trait together are less than the strength of indirect bias on the preference trait. When the equilibrium is stable the indicator trait may converge to the optimum from any initial condition, and at this equilibrium, the average individual finds individuals with the optimum value of the indicator trait most attractive. If Condition 8.35 is not satisfied, however, the mean values of both traits will not remain at the optimum even if they begin there. Instead they will "run away" indefinitely toward larger or smaller values.

A qualitative interpretation of the results

The preceding analysis suggests that the evolution of the criteria determining indirect bias has three qualitatively distinct modes:

1. Stable fitness maximization. If the strength of indirect bias acting on the preference character is weak compared to the combined forces of selection and direct bias on the indicator character, then the preference character will eventually reach a stable equilibrium at the value that maximizes fitness. In other words, both direct and indirect bias will evolve so that naive individuals tend to imitate models with the optimum value of the indicator trait. The reason this result makes sense is most clear in the case in which transmission of the preference trait is unbiased. Here, the only evolutionary forces acting on the mean value of the preference trait are the effects of selection and direct bias acting through the indicator trait. Naive individuals who prefer to imitate models with the optimum value of the indicator trait will be more likely to acquire that value than individuals who prefer some less adaptive value, and selection favors this preference. This process eventually will cause the optimum value of the preference trait to predominate in the population.

2. The runaway process. If the strength of indirect bias acting on the preference character is strong compared to the combined forces of selection and direct bias acting on the indicator character, then according to the model the values of both the indicator trait and the preference trait will run away, becoming indefinitely larger or smaller depending on the initial condition. Clearly, this cannot really occur; nothing can grow or shrink indefinitely. Some process not accounted for in the model will eventually restrain the population. The correct lesson to be drawn from the model is that when the evolution of a preference trait is affected by indirect bias, the resulting process may be inherently unstable. Where it exists, such instability is likely to result in one of two outcomes, either an equilibrium in which both the preference character and the indicator character are quite distant from the optimum, or permanent oscillations. The outcome depends upon whether the runaway process is inherently oscillatory and on the nature of the processes which ultimately come to restrain the population.

3. The "drift-away" process. If no natural selection is acting on the indicator trait and/or if the effective intensities of direct and indirect bias are equal, then the model has a line of equilibria. The line may be unstable, which leads to a runaway process that is qualitatively similar to the case already described. The line may also be stable, in which case every point on the line is neutrally stable with regard to every other point on the line. When this is the case, cultural drift will cause finite populations to drift randomly along the line. (See Cavalli-Sforza and Feldman, 1981: 109–124, for an extensive discussion of such random effects.) Stevan Arnold (personal communication) calls this the "drift-away" process. This case is interesting because it allows any value of the indicator trait to become common, even if it is selected against. The mean value of the indicator trait in different populations living in the same environment will drift apart, even though the indicator trait is subject to strong natural selection and direct bias. This may occur because these forces are exactly balanced along the line by the force of indirect bias.

It is improbable that the conditions necessary for a line of equilibria to exist will often be fulfilled exactly. That there would be no selection on the indicator trait, or that the intensities of indirect and direct bias would be precisely equal, seems unlikely. However, in many cases of interest, selection may be weak relative to bias, or difference in the intensities may be small compared to the magnitudes of selection and bias. There will be a single equilibrium point, but it will be only very weakly stable in the direction of what would have been the line of equilibria had the conditions been exactly fulfilled. Thus, the forces resisting drift will be weak, and we would expect a large variance in the mean values of the indicator trait in different populations.

The last two of these three modes of the evolution of indirect bias are likely to increase the frequency of maladaptive culturally transmitted variants. Can this behavior be consistent with the origin of the capacity for cultural transmission via ordinary Darwinian processes? We think that the theory of sexual selection once again provides some insight. Like indirect bias, runaway (or drift-away) sexual selection can lead to maladaptive characters, particularly in males. Moreover, the exaggerated male characters observed in many species seem to be evidence that the runaway process described by Fisher actually occurs in nature. Fisher reasoned that this could occur because the male character was originally correlated with fitness. For example, tails that are larger or showier than average might have been correlated with male fitness in the proto-peacock in a variety of habitats. If a character is correlated with fitness, then females may benefit by using it to choose their mates. However, once female choice has evolved, the potential for the runaway process exists. It is easy to imagine that many species evolve female choice, and in most of these female choice remains adaptive. However, in a few the necessary conditions for the runaway process exist, and female choice ultimately leads to maladaptive male characters.

A similar argument can be made for the evolution of indirect bias. As we have argued earlier in this chapter, indirect bias may provide a good general rule of thumb for choosing among different cultural variants. As long as the indicator trait is correlated with fitness, an individual can increase his or her chance of acquiring adaptive cultural variants using indirect bias, particularly in variable environments. However, just as it may be difficult to know which cultural variants are adaptive in the local environment, it may also be difficult to determine which variants are sufficiently correlated with fitness to be useful as indicator traits. In this case, it may be useful to use indirect bias to modify one's preference trait. As we have seen, this can cause the preference trait to evolve to the most adaptive value (case 1 above), but it can also lead to the evolution of maladaptive variants of the preference and indicator traits by either the runaway or the drift-away process (cases 2 and 3). We imagine that indirect bias is adaptive when averaged over many characters and many societies, but that in some societies, for some characters, the necessary conditions for the runaway or drift-away processes exist. In these cases, indicator traits that were initially correlated with fitness become exaggerated.

Possible Examples of the Runaway Process

Do the runaway or drift-away processes actually occur in human societies? Ideally, data to answer this question would allow us both to trace the trajectory of an indicator trait from an initially adaptive state to an exaggerated state and to demonstrate that indirect bias was the agent responsible for the exaggeration of the trait. As far as we know, no such data exist. For the present, we must be satisfied with circumstantial evidence: the existence of traits that seem consistent with an origin and maintenance by the runaway process. Such traits should have the following properties: (1) More exaggerated variants should be associated with greater prestige. (2) The values of the trait observed should not make sense from an adaptive point of view. (3) The observed variant should be plausibly interpreted as an exaggerated version of a sensible indicator trait. Here we will discuss two such empirical examples, the practice of growing enormous yams on the island of Ponapae and the practice of extensive tattooing which was widespread in Polynesia until recently.

Yams as markers of prestige on Ponapae

According to William Bascom (1948), on the Micronesian island of Ponapae a man's prestige is partially determined by his ability to contribute very large yams to periodic feasts. Each year several feasts are given by the chief of each district. In addition to staple foods like fresh breadfruit, coconut, and seafood, the head of each farmstead contributes a "prize" yam, or yams. Everyone at the feast examines the yams and praises the contributor of the largest single yam for his generosity and his skill and ability as a farmer. Moreover, as Bascom reports, "Success in prestige competition is regarded as evidence of not only a man's ability, industry, and generosity, but also of his love and respect for superiors" (p. 215). The chiefs raise men who are consistent contributors of large yams to titled positions.

Several lines of evidence suggest that this practice is not simply a good way to provide food for a party, but instead represents an exaggerated marker of prestige. First, prestige is not correlated with a man's real contribution to the feast. The contributions of other important foodstuffs like fresh breadfruit or seafood are irrelevant to the prestige competition. So too is the total amount of yams that a man contributes; all that counts is the size and, to a lesser extent, the shape of the largest individual yam. Moreover, these yams are truly huge; they sometimes exceed 9 feet in length and 3 feet in diameter, and up to twelve men must carry them. The yams used by families in their everyday diet are much smaller. Individual farmers go to great effort to raise large yams. Appropriate varieties must be found and maintained, special, laborious cultivation techniques are used, and great care must be taken to prevent neighbors from spying out the size of a man's yams. Bascom concludes that "the labor expended in growing prize yams is far greater than would be necessary to produce the same quantity of foodstuff from a larger number of smaller yams of the same variety" (p. 217). Nor should it be thought this extravagance is possible because there are never shortages of food on Ponapae as, "Not infrequently families go hungry at home when they have large yams in their farms ready for harvest" (p. 212).

It is also easy to construct a plausible scenario to explain the evolution of the practice of growing very large yams based on a runaway process. Suppose that at some earlier time Ponapaens did not devote any special effort to growing large yams. It seems reasonable that under such conditions more skillful or industrious farmers might have tended to bring larger yams to feasts, and thus that the size of a man's yams would provide a useful indicator trait for all kinds of skills and beliefs associated with farming. By imitating the people who grew large yams, naive individuals could increase the chance that they would acquire the cultural variants they needed to be successful farmers. Once the size of yams became an indicator trait, beliefs or practices that lead to larger yams would increase. Individuals with a stronger tendency to admire large yams will be more likely to acquire these beliefs. This will cause the two traits to be correlated—and therefore, when the practices that lead to larger yams increase, so too will the admiration for the ability to grow large yams.

Tattooing in Polynesia

The practice of tattooing was widespread in Polynesia until recent times (e.g. Brown, 1910; Handy and Handy, 1924; Gifford, 1929; Hiroa, 1930). Boys, and to a lesser extent girls, received their initial tattooing as they approached adulthood. Later in life some individuals would periodically add embellishments to their tattoos. In the most elaborate cases, virtually the entire body was covered with intricate tattoos. While the evidence is somewhat anecdotal, it suggests that this practice can be understood as a result of the runaway process.

The extent and nature of an individual's tattoos seem to have been related to his (or her) prestige. For example, in Samoa

> The amount of tattooing an individual possesses is attached significance in the fashionable Samoan world. Half a suit is of no importance, but if a man can show an *aso tali tu,* which begins the second half of the work, he is considered "all right." [Handy and Handy, 1924: 21]

and on Mangareva

> Tattooing was a necessary adornment in Mangareva. . . . The amount of tattooing that a person underwent depended on his rank and ability to pay. . .the correct association of extensive tattooing is with successful warriors. [Hiroa, 1938: 176–177]

The evidence also suggests people admire and respect the tattooed. Once again on Samoa,

> custom, personal status, and the approbation of men and women were the incentives to undergoing the operation. . . . The fear of pain is overcome by the keen desire to bear the marks of manhood and to be able to hitch the kilts a little higher at the evening dances and so demonstrate superiority over the untattooed. [Hiroa, 1930: 661]

Being tattooed was painful and somewhat dangerous. When a boy reached maturity, his father would hire a tattoo artist if he had the means. Handy (1922: 12) reports that, "The operation, as may be imagined, was extremely painful, and the patient cried and screamed without restraint." Because the process was so painful, only about a square foot of the body could be tattooed at one sitting, and then three to five days were allowed before the next session (Handy, 1922; Linton, 1939). Sometimes boys could not stand the pain and made do with less elaborate markings (Hiroa, 1930). Then, "[A]fter each sitting, there were from eight to twelve days of local inflammation, followed by fever and sometimes swellings, which were at times fatal" (Handy, 1922: 12), although this was apparently rare (Hiroa, 1930).

Tattooing was also expensive. The initial tattooing of a youth required roughly at least six months to complete. During this time the father had to supply food and shelter for the artist and his family. In addition, the tattoo artist required a considerable payment in the form of mats, waistcloths, and decorations (Handy and Handy, 1924). More difficult or elaborate figures required more time and a more skillful tattoo artist.

> Every enhancement within a ban, or on the dark spaces, takes extra time and care and the artist has to be paid accordingly; not only has to be paid more but he also eats more food. Hence enhanced designs may only be secured by those who can pay. [Hiroa, 1930: 654]

Embellishment of existing designs was also costly. As a result only the wealthy could afford an extensive and elaborate tattooing (Handy, 1922; Hiroa, 1938).

To understand how tattoos could have evolved as markers of prestige, we must imagine that the extent of a person's tattooing indicated his usefulness as a model. The most elaborate tattooing would certainly indicate wealth. It is less clear why more modest tattooing would be a good indicator trait. Perhaps tattoos once indicated courage and ability to withstand pain, or perhaps they were useful during warfare to intimidate one's enemies. Whatever the reason, once tattoos became associated with prestige, the runaway process could lead to the seemingly maladaptive extremes that were observed in Polynesia.

We believe that many other traits in both simple and complex societies are plausibly the result of the runaway or drift-away processes that indirect bias can create. Indeed, we find it difficult to walk through a downtown shopping district or attend university functions without thinking about indirect bias.

Symbolic Culture and the Runaway and Drift-Away Processes

Some of the most strenuous objections to human sociobiology have come from symbolic anthropologists, especially from Marshall Sahlins (1976a, 1976b). The members of this subdiscipline of anthropology believe that symbols are the essential feature of human culture. In fact, they often define culture as a set of symbols whose meanings are shared by members of a human society. To varying degrees, symbolic anthropologists believe that the meanings associated with a set of symbols evolve according to an internal, cultural logic that is at least partially independent of adaptive considerations. Because the set of meanings shared by a group shapes the way members of the group perceive the physical and social world in which they live, culture can strongly affect individual behavior. It can define what is edible and what is not; to whom an individual owes obligations and to whom he does not. Thus, according to symbolic views of culture, historical processes which assign meanings to symbols are at least as important in determining the social organization or subsistence technology of a group as the nature of its environment.

From the point of view of a human sociobiologist, this argument is unsatisfactory unless it can be made consistent with the argument from natural origins. Symbol systems are learned, and the hypothesis that learning is structured to enhance fitness is fundamental to sociobiology. The symbols that encode meanings may be arbitrary, but the meanings themselves are expected to enhance fitness. We are not aware of any symbolic anthropologist who has provided a cogent account of how a system of symbolic culture which promotes maladaptive behavior might have evolved. Sahlins (1976b) supports his claims with an unconvincing attack on the argument from natural origins and an equally dubious series of empirical examples that he believes cannot be reconciled with a sociobiological hypothesis. (His key example of Polynesian adoption practices has been shown by Silk, 1980, to be consistent with sociobiological expectations.)

In this section, we will argue that dual inheritance models, particularly those including indirect bias, show how the autonomous symbol systems envisioned by symbolic anthropologists might have evolved. We will consider three cases: (1) Under some circumstances, the evolution of symbols may be autonomous without conflicting with a genetic-fitness-maximizing hypothesis. We call this the "weak interaction" hypothesis. (2) In still other cases, the runaway or drift-away dynamic may result in group selection on symbolic traits, so a "group functional" hypothesis of symbolic evolution must also be entertained. (3) Finally, we will argue that the runaway and drift-away cases of indirect bias provide an evolutionary basis for Sahlins's postulated cultural reason, or something very like it, without violating the criterion of a plausible natural origin for nonadaptive or maladaptive cultural traits. Here this hypothesis is labeled "afunctionalism." Because we often have had considerable difficulty understanding symbolic anthropologists, our attempt to reinterpret their views is based on rather free interpretations of the original texts. We are emboldened to offer the following analysis only by the equally frank admission of practitioners of this subdiscipline that considerable debate over such fundamental issues divides them, as well (Basso and Selby, 1976; Schwimmer, 1978).

What are symbols?

The key defining feature of symbols is that they are arbitrary. A sign is something that stands for something else. According to semiotic theory three basic varieties of signs can be recognized (Jakobson, 1971: 345ff., 697ff.), icons, indices, and symbols. More properly each of these concepts can be thought of as a quantitative dimension; any particular sign can be described in terms of the degree to which it exemplifies the pure type: icon, index, or symbol. Icons are signs that are factually similar to the thing or process signified. For example, a technical drawing describing farming technique is an icon. An index has a factual connection with the thing signified. For example, a bulging storage bin and fat cattle are indices of a farmer's skill and energy because they are correlated with farming talent. A symbol is a sign that stands for the thing symbolized by conventional agreement. In language, it usually does not matter what sound pattern or series of letters are used to signify a particular thing or concept, it only matters that the members of a speech community agree on some convention.

Other cultural symbol systems are similar to language, although how similar is debatable (Silverstein, 1976). The Stars and Stripes serve as a symbol of the U.S.A. and the Tricolor symbolizes France, but if history had been different and the flags' associations were reversed, no problem would arise. The giant yams of Ponapae are at least partly symbols. Since special skills are needed to grow them, a giant yam is not necessarily an iconic sign of farming skill or even a good index of general horticultural talent. Convention could specify quite other means of signifying prestige in such a horticultural society—the growing of small, perfectly shaped "bonsai" yams, or spherical yams, or most anything else imaginable.

Nevertheless, the Ponapaens take giant yams quite seriously as icons, or at least indices, of prestige. Perhaps the ability to grow giant yams even *is* prestige on Ponapae, not just a sign of it. However arbitrarily symbolic giant yams appear to us, they are important to their growers, while bonsai yams and spherical yams would be irrelevant or perhaps humorous. Thus Sahlins would say that giant yams are meaningful to Ponapaens, much as steak and the Stars and Stripes are to Americans. The problems that symbolic anthropologists pose for us are how behaviors that are objectively mere symbols can come to be taken by the native as central to his existence, and whether such behaviors can be functional.

The weak interaction hypothesis

The evolutionary dynamics of a symbolic system are quite different from those of ordinary adaptations. The variant words for "cat" in different languages and patterns for flags in different nations are all functionally equivalent. It is very difficult to see how natural selection, or direct bias, or guided variation can be used to explain the evolution of such symbols in the same way that is possible for ordinary phenotypic traits. For each symbolic trait we observe, a very large number of alternatives are equivalent in terms of fitness. The simplest hypothesis we might have for the evolution of symbol systems is that the forces involved are only random variation, drift, and some kind of frequency dependence. In other words, symbol systems could evolve by the random jiggling of mean usage, combined with selection or bias against variants that were so distant from the mean as to cause problems in communication. To the extent that symbol systems function simply for communication within a culture, these forces might be sufficient.

However, variations in dialect and grammar, for example, can themselves be used as signs of people's place in a social system (Labov, 1972; Ervin-Tripp, 1976). Thus symbolic traits often vary as a function of status and prestige, and are likely to be used as a basis for indirect biases. Even if indirect biases are an important force in the evolution of symbol systems, such a mechanism may do no more than speed up the proliferation of symbols or signs to reflect more subtle social differences. Exactly which dialect variant, costume, or ritual characterizes a group has no adaptive consequences so long as it does its differentiating job. Any of a large variety of alternatives would have worked just as well.

Direct bias may also affect the evolution of symbol systems. David Schneider (1976: 205) writes:

> Social life is meaningful; new meanings are established with reference to old meanings and grow out of them and must be made, in some degree, congruent with them; and exchange, whenever and wherever it occurs, must be articulated with the existing system of meanings.

In other words, people prefer to adopt new symbols that bear some comprehensible relationship to old ones, if only to keep the whole system comprehensible and easy to remember. Dialect changes spread from core forms to correlated ones (Labov, 1972: 174–175). One of the functions of language appears to be to organize memory (Simon, 1957; Bandura, 1977: 25–26) so the internal logical organization of the cultural system may be functionally important. However, the requirement that a symbol system be a reasonably coherent logical system does not mean that there are not many equally functional systems. In a system of arbitrary symbols, a bias rule enforcing consistency and logical order within the system will not cause convergence to similar forms in similar environments, as we might expect in the case of a bias affecting an ordinary trait.

We call this the "weak interaction hypothesis" because relationships between the content of the symbolic system and the ultimate adaptation-producing force of natural selection are quite tenuous. (See Cohen, 1974, for a similar hypothesis, but without a selection-based theory of function. Also see Durham, 1976.) We can easily explain by a sociobiological hypothesis why humans have symbolic capacities for culture. The main adaptive functions include interpersonal communication and memory organization. Both of these functions may contribute to more efficient social learning and hence to more effective use of the various advantages of cultural transmission. However, since these functions are served equally well by any well-organized symbolic system, we cannot explain much of the difference between the structures of different cultural systems by adaptive arguments. Language is the prototypical case; Chinese is not an adaptation to life on the Yellow River Plain, nor is English an adaptation to living in the British Isles, except in the very limited sense that it is useful to speak the language that happens to be common in a given place. Adaptation in principle puts only the very broadest constraints on the form of symbolic structures.

The weak interaction hypothesis thus requires a nonfunctional theory to explain what specific symbols come to have a particular function, but it does not allow symbolic evolutionary processes to affect functional ones strongly. What symbol is used for a given meaning may be arbitrary with respect to function, but the underlying meaning itself is not. As Abner Cohen (1974: 86) puts it:

> The analysis of symbolic forms in relation to symbolic functions which is the central problem of social anthropology can be greatly enhanced through comparing different cultural forms that are carried by different groups. Thus one aspect of our work is to reduce cultural heterogeneity to functional uniformities.

In terms of the sociobiological theory of function, so long as alternative symbolic traits differ little in fitness, their evolution will be subject to random variation, drift, frequency-dependent bias, indirect bias, and internal logical biases without causing any fitness variation upon which natural selection could operate. The functional equivalence that results from the arbitrary association of symbols with their referents could result in almost complete autonomy for evolution of the symbol systems without much disturbing their functional properties.

Symbolic functionalism

A symbolic hypothesis presents a sharp alternative to sociobiological ones if it proposes an alternative to the standard neo-Darwinian interpretation of function in terms of genetic fitness. If symbolic traits are especially prone to runaway or drift-away evolution as a consequence of indirect bias, the between-group cultural variation generated by this process may be subject to group selection. This in turn would favor cultural variants which enhance the cultural success of the group, even at the expense of harming that of the individual. This hypothesis is distinct from those proposed by Alexander (1974, 1979a) and Hamilton (1975) in which culture is imagined to facilitate genetic group selection through warfare. The issue here is not whether humans are group selected or not, but whether the mechanism is selection on genetic or cultural variation.

In Chapter 7, we showed that frequency-dependent bias could increase the amount of cultural variation between groups relative to that within groups. This, in turn, had the effect of increasing the strength of selection between groups relative to the strength of selection and direct bias within groups. The runaway or drift-away dynamics that result from indirect bias can also increase the relative strength of selection between groups. In the drift-away process there is a line of equilibria; each value on the line is neutrally stable with respect to every other point on the line. Even a small amount of selection among groups will completely determine where along the line a population will be at equilibrium. In the runaway process small differences in initial conditions result in very different unstable trajectories. If, as we have assumed earlier, some process not accounted for in the model ultimately causes the population to reach a stable equilibrium, then it may be that such small initial differences also generate large amounts of equilibrium variation between groups. This variation could lead to strong group selection.

In the case of the drift-away process we can make these arguments somewhat more rigorously. Suppose that a population is divided into a large number of finite subpopulations. Let the mean of the indicator and preference traits in the jth sub-population be $\overline{X}_{I,j}$ and $\overline{X}_{P,j}$, respectively. Further suppose that the values of $\overline{X}_{I,j}$ and $\overline{X}_{P,j}$ are distributed according to a bivariate normal distribution with the vector of means $(\tilde{X}_I, \tilde{X}_P)$ and the covariance matrix

$$\begin{pmatrix} \tilde{V}_I & \tilde{C} \\ \tilde{C} & \tilde{V}_P \end{pmatrix}$$

The mean value of the indicator trait in the ith subpopulation is assumed to affect the size of the jth subpopulation, N_j, in the following way:

$$N_j = N \exp\{-(\overline{X}_{I,j} - X^*)^2/2\tilde{S}\} \tag{8.36}$$

Subpopulations with different mean values of the indicator trait achieve different sizes. The nearer the mean value of the indicator trait in a subpopulation is to X^*, the larger it is. The strength of this group selection effect is measured by $1/\tilde{S}$.

Let us now consider the forces that affect the distribution of subpopulation means. The finite subpopulations will vary each generation due to sampling error. This will have the effect of increasing each of the terms in the covariance matrix by an amount $(1 + 1/N_j)$. It has no average effect on the average values of the subpopulation means. Next, suppose a fraction m of each subpopulation emigrates each generation and migrates to a randomly chosen subpopulation. If m is small and the populations are not too different, this has the effect of reducing each of the terms in the covariance matrix by a factor of $(1 - m)$. Because larger subpopulations contribute disproportionately to the pool of migrants, migration has the effect of moving the average value of the indicator trait in the entire population, $\tilde{X}_I$, toward X^*. Because the values of $\tilde{X}_I$ and $\tilde{X}_P$ are correlated, this between-group selection will also move the value of $\tilde{X}_P$ toward X^*. If $\tilde{S}$ is large compared to $\tilde{V}_I$, this becomes

$$\Delta \tilde{X}_I = (m\tilde{V}_I/\tilde{S})(X^* - \tilde{X}_I)$$

$$\Delta \tilde{X}_P = (m\tilde{C}/\tilde{S})(X^* - \tilde{X}_P)$$

(8.37)

Finally, the subpopulation means respond to the within-population forces of selection and direct and indirect bias. If we combine all of these forces, we get recursions for the overall population means, variances, and the covariance. It is possible to show that these recursions will always reach a stable equilibrium in which the equilibrium values of $\tilde{X}_I$ and $\tilde{X}_P$ are equal to X^*, the value of the indicator trait that maximizes group size.

This result supports the conjecture that group selection on cultural variation may be easier when the variants are also subject to indirect bias. In essence, the drift-away process (and presumably the runaway process too) creates group-level variation that is protected from selection at the individual level. It is attractive because it may explain why the altruistic, group functional behavior of humans seems to be so commonly embedded in systems of supernatural sanctions and costly rituals. Campbell (1975) has alluded to this problem by noting that religion may provide a stronger source of adaptive wisdom for people living in modern societies than sciences like psychology have yet developed. Rappaport (1979: 100) writes of his proposed functions of Tsembaga ritualized warfare:

> I have argued, however, that there may be no simple, direct relationship between the amount of testable empirical knowledge included in a cognized model and the appropriateness of the behavior it elicits. It is by no means certain that the representations of nature provided us by science are more adaptive than those images of the world, inhabited by spirits whom men respect, that guide the action of the Maring and other "primitives." To drape nature in supernatural veils may be to provide her with some protection against human folly and extravagance.

Similarly, Freilich (1980) argues that the most symbolic culturally transmitted traits code for "proper," group functional behavior and are opposed by less symbolic "smart" traits that are related to individual advantage. Perhaps it is necessary to remove cognized models from easy attack by individual calculation in order to achieve group-level functions. Otherwise direct bias, guided variation, and other forces derived from selection for individual cultural and genetic success may destroy them. The runaway and drift-away processes derived from the indirect bias force may provide such protected variants. Finally, Goode (1978) has interpreted prestige itself as a means of social control. In his functional view of prestige, status and recognition are normally accorded to those who are most altruistic and effective at promoting the welfare of the group as a whole.

In its most extreme version, this hypothesis would invert the usual sociobiological interpretation of prestige. Irons (1979b), Dickemann (1979), and others have argued that the fact that in many societies prestigious males are also polygynous is strong confirmation of the hypothesis that cultural traits enhance genetic fitness. However, if prestige is accorded mainly for group functional behavior, then it is possible that group selection acting on cultural variation has favored patterns of mating that act to increase the frequency of genes which increase the success of the group but would reduce individual fitness in the absence of the culturally acquired mate preference. Throughout this book, we have assumed that genetically transmitted biases could act to shape the direction of cultural evolution. Cultural traits which affect mating preference could similarly affect genetic evolution through the action of sexual selection. In effect, the human genome could be "domesticated" by culturally transmitted traits. Much as a prize bull has high genetic fitness because he contributes to a farmer's profit, a prestigious figure may be allowed extra opportunities to reproduce because his genotype produces individuals that tend to be active on behalf of their culture.

Afunctionalism

Marshall Sahlins's "cultural reason" hypothesis envisions a more radical departure from sociobiological hypotheses than the weak interaction or cultural group selection proposals. Ultimately, the latter two leave function to be explained by some form of natural selection, even if selection on culture rather than genes. Sahlins (1976a: 102) objects:

> All these types of practical reason have also in common an impoverished conception of human symboling. For all of them, the cultural scheme is the *sign* of other "realities," hence in the end obeisant in its own arrangement to other laws and logics.

While we hesitate to claim that any version of dual inheritance theory directly translates into Sahlins's cultural reason, the runaway process does resemble it.

To show that the runaway process conforms to the views of symbolic anthropologists like Sahlins we need to show that it has two properties. First, it must lead to the evolution of symbols. Second, the dynamics of the evolution of symbols by the runaway process should, in some sense, be driven by cultural factors, not genetic or environmental ones.

How does the runaway process create meaningful symbols? The runaway process creates symbolic indicator traits, beginning with icons and indices, in the following sense: We assumed that initially the admired variant was a good indicator of adaptive superiority. All other things being equal, it is plausible that the best farmers would tend to grow the largest yams. Thus at the outset the indicator trait is an index of farming skill, not yet a symbol of prestige. If the runaway process ensues, the most admired variant of the indicator trait will not be the most useful index of an individual's adaptive traits—it will confer prestige, but only because the rest of the population believes that it is prestigious. It is likely that farmers could devote the time and energy necessary to grow gigantic yams to better purposes. It is true that we can explain the connection between the indicator trait and prestige by understanding the dynamics of the runaway process, so the connection between the symbol (giant yams) and the meaning (prestige) is not completely arbitrary. However, it is in the nature of the runaway process that very small differences in initial conditions can give rise to very different results. In a different population starting under almost identical conditions the process might result in a different indicator of prestige. It might be the color or shape of the yam that would be important, or another aspect of farming altogether.

The runaway process can also be thought of as deriving its dynamics from cultural factors. Once the runaway process has been initiated, the main force acting on the indicator trait results from the choices made by naive individuals, choices which are based on their values of the preference trait. Thus we imagine that the mean amount of time and effort devoted to raising giant yams increases because people admire and imitate those who grow large yams. The main force acting on the preference character is due to the same cultural preference. The size of yams that people find most admirable increases because they have a tendency to acquire their attitudes about yams from people who grow large yams. Adaptive factors are necessary to explain the evolution of the indirect bias mechanism, and why some characters are initially associated with success. But once initiated, a runaway process follows its own internal logic.

If many different traits have been entrained in this runaway process, each culture may contain a more or less equal number of afunctional or counterfunctional traits. Group selection, individual selection, and the other functional forces derived from them may eliminate the most extreme counterfunctional traits and whole cultures with an excessive concentration of deleterious traits. However, at equilibrium a large amount of costly cultural variation might remain in most cultures. If each culture has approximately the same sum total of functional and counterfunctional traits, variance in group fitness could be very small even if the mix of functional and counterfunctional traits is very different in different cultures.

Symbol systems generated in this way would tend to retain a strong internal logical relationship between the various traits in the system. The runaway process will generate variation which is random with respect to fitness because small variations in the initial conditions with respect to the indicator and preference traits will lead to quite different outcomes. However, the trajectory generated by the runaway process is smooth, and the traits involved maintain an organized correlation to one another. If this hypothesis is correct, a large amount of cultural variation might be comprehensible only in terms of the internal logic that drove the runaway process in each culture. This logic will, however, have more in common with esthetic than functional design. Much as peacock tails and bowerbird houses are thought to result from runaway sexual selection, the indirect bias runaway process will generate traits with an exaggerated, interrelated, aesthetically pleasing but afunctional form. The functional forces may thus constitute merely "a range of tolerance in the exploitation of the environment or the satisfaction of biological requirements beyond which the system as constituted can no longer function—is 'selected against'" (Sahlins, 1976a: 208).

The range of tolerance might be extremely broad if cultural mechanisms control genetic reproduction as in the previous hypothesis. If the cultural runaway process entrains actual mate choice, people may come to have genes that cause them to prefer mates who display a gaudy repertoire of cultural symbols. Perhaps the elaborate esthetic sense of modern *Homo sapiens* is as much a consequence as a cause of cultural evolution.

Notice that in the case of the cultural runaway process colorful displays are not as likely to be limited to the male sex as they are with the genetic analog. A prestigious male or female can have an unlimited number of cultural offspring by nonparental transmission, whereas in the genetic case only males can take advantage of multiple matings to increase their fitness enough to compensate for costly displays. The fact that women as well as men participate in elaborate symbolic behaviors is more consistent with a cultural than with a genetic runaway explanation.

Even this version of the symbolic hypothesis can be consistent with the notion that the human cultural inheritance system is adaptive. We have seen that indirect bias provides a good general inheritance rule because it allows an efficient shortcut to directly evaluating alternative cultural variants. Thus it is possible that, averaged over many different traits and many different human groups, indirect bias is adaptive, even though for some traits in some groups it leads to the elaboration of maladaptive markers of prestige. As in the cases of selection on asymmetrically transmitted cultural variants and frequency-dependent bias, the cost of individual evaluation of traits may favor indirect bias even if cultural traits are frequently entrained in the maladaptive runaway process.

Even if cultural evolution has so completely entrained genetic evolution in the runaway dynamic that ordinary adaptation exerts only the weakest constraints on the evolution of symbolic traits, it could have done so without violating the assumption of natural origins. We need only imagine that natural selection favored symbolic capacities and the use of indirect bias during the period when the potential for the runaway and drift-away arose. Once this potential evolved, even for perfectly good adaptive reasons, adaptive forces might not be strong enough to prevent grossly maladaptive outcomes.

Conclusion

It it is often argued that Darwinian theories of evolution must result in adaptive or functional hypotheses about human behavior (Sahlins 1976a, 1976b). The results of this chapter demonstrate that this argument is incorrect. Nonadaptive, or even frankly maladaptive, cultural variants can spread in a population under the influence of indirect bias, even in the face of selection and direct bias favoring more adaptive variants. Furthermore, the runaway or drift-away situation arises naturally from the genetically adaptive uses of indirect bias. Hypotheses derived from models of indirect bias may or may not correspond closely to those sought by symbolic anthropologists to explain symbolic behavior, or some alternative hypothesis based on individual self-interest may ultimately be shown to best explain the data. However, we do believe that the models of this chapter demonstrate that dual inheritance models offer a wide variety of systematically linked hypotheses about the nature of human behavior.

9
Conclusion

> All resemblances of *social origin* in society are the direct or indirect fruit of the
> various forms of imitation,—custom-imitation or fashion-imitation, sympathy-
> imitation or obedience-imitation, precept-imitation or education-imitation, na-
> ive imitation, deliberate imitation, etc. In this lies the excellence of the contem-
> poraneous method of explaining doctrines and institutions through their history.
> It is a method that is certain to come into more general use.
>
> Gabriel Tarde, *The Laws of Imitation* (1903, p. 14)

The turn-of-the-century French sociologist Gabriel Tarde believed that invention
and imitation were the crucial distinguishing features of human life. In *The Laws
of Imitation,* he described his attempt to build a theory of "pure sociology" based
on the dynamics of these two processes. He thought that the historical development
of "doctrines and institutions" was driven by a "logical duel." Doctrines and
institutions arise by invention and spread by imitation. People are often exposed to
two similar ideas that conflict with each other. In the end the conflict must be
resolved by the overthrow of one idea by the other, or by some reconciliation
between them.

Fateful decisions by the late nineteenth- and early twentieth-century founders of
the disciplines that constitute the biological and social sciences created the logical
duels that we still struggle to resolve by triumphs or compromises. The unified
character of a previous generation of scientific theorizing, perhaps best exemplified
by Darwin's attempts to include humans in the compass of evolutionary theory and
at its worst by Spencer's speculative analogizing, broke down. A detailed examination of the reasons for this development is best left to professional historians of
science. However, it is interesting to examine the rationales given by Tarde's
generation, who did so much to create the form of modern science.

Tarde made two important choices in the elaboration of his theory: (1) he set
aside all biological considerations in an effort to develop a "sociology pure and
abstract" and (2) he rejected the notion of "the adaptation of living or social types
to external phenomena" as a legitimate mode of explanation (Tarde, 1903 [1962]:
xxi–xxii; 141). He defended the rejection of biological considerations mostly as a
practical matter of disciplinary specialization; these were important but better left
to other, more competent specialists. But he also argued that biological explanations of human differences had been overemphasized and that the laws of imitation gave a truer and more hopeful account of human progress than racist theories.
Tarde rejected adaptation to external conditions as a prelude to his development of
a scheme of internal, logical, and extralogical laws of imitation.

These choices, and similar ones made by Tarde's contemporaries, defined the major issues in the scientific study of the human species; we still debate them in much the same terms today. Here there is a certain appeal to Tarde's model of the "logical duel." Once invented and diffused, contradictory ideas struggle for supremacy until one is triumphant or until a resolution is invented. The invention and initial spread of different ideas might have led to different disciplinary structures and scientific debates.

Many of the principals in the current debate about the roles of culture and biology in human behavior argue for the triumphant overthrow of views in conflict with their own. With regard to the importance of biology and adaptation, all of the logically possible combinations are stoutly defended by one group of scholars or another. Like Tarde, Marshall Sahlins (1976a, 1976b) argues that both the effects of genes and adaptation to economic or ecological circumstances can be safely ignored in explanations of culture in favor of factors internal to the logic of culture. By contrast, Marvin Harris (1968, 1979) proposes that adaptation to material conditions by cultural mechanisms is paramount but asserts that the effects of genes on this process are of little or no importance. Human sociobiologists (such as Irons, 1979a) take a third position: that genetic adaptation is paramount and that there are various mechanisms by which imitation might be constrained to enhance biological fitness. Finally, ethologists, some sociobiologists, and perhaps classical social Darwinists (Bannister, 1979) have often argued that biology plays a large role in human behavior but that these traits were selected under past environments and are often quite pathological under contemporary conditions.

We think a reconciliation of these views is more likely than the triumph of one. Human beings are both biological *and* cultural organisms. Systems of inheritance have internal structure *and* relationships to the external world. Individuals are the products of gene pools *and* cultures; they are loci of natural selection *and* decision making. Clifford Geertz's (1973: 44) plea expresses our feelings almost exactly: "we need to replace the 'stratigraphic' conception of the relations between the various aspects of human existence with a synthetic one; that is, one in which biological, psychological, sociological, and cultural factors can be treated as variables within unitary systems of analysis." It is certainly likely that in isolated instances certain explanations of human behavior will be triumphantly rejected. For example, we do not think that genetic differences between races for behavioral traits will prove important. However, most proposals regarding the causes of human behavior seem to have some merit, at least as interesting hypotheses. A synthetic rather than stratigraphic conception of the aspects of human behavior studied by the disciplines in the social and biological sciences seems to us to be more fruitful.

That genes and culture, individuals and populations, and adaptation and symbols all play a role in human evolution is a truism, yet the twentieth-century scientific debates about human behavior result from giving causal priority to one element or another. In the absence of models which explicitly link the elements, say genes and culture, the commonsensical middle position has nothing to offer except the truism, while the extreme positions are at least provocative and interesting.

In this chapter we do three things. First, we summarize the main results of the book. This is not an easy task since it seems that the presence of two systems of inheritance leads to complex evolutionary problems and possibilities. Second, we try to show that some of these diverse possibilities correspond to the hypotheses that figure in traditional scientific debates over the causes of human behavior. This discussion is designed to emphasize the role that dual inheritance theory might play in unifying the human sciences. It summarizes our argument that the theory can be used to construct many different plausible hypotheses in a common framework that allow us to understand, if not the real world, at least how our various theories of it are related to each other. Finally, we outline what we think are the most important theoretical and empirical gaps in our present understanding of human evolution and behavior. On the theoretical side, the set of sample theories and general models we and others have constructed obviously need to be extended. On the empirical side, more information is necessary to constrain the selection of appropriate sample theories and to test the predictions of general models.

Summary of Main Results

The main virtue of the Darwinian approach to the study of cultural evolution is that it provides a natural framework for expressing the relationship between the causal elements that combine to produce human behavior. It often allows apparently conflicting, opposed hypotheses to be formulated as special cases of more general models and gives logical structure to mixed or intermediate hypotheses. For example, the degree of the coupling of cultural traits to genes can be expressed by the strength of genetically transmitted determinants of the guided variation and bias forces. According to Rapoport (1967), many seemingly irreconcilable scientific conflicts have been resolved by theories of this kind.

Mechanisms and origins

We have tried to build models to answer two related kinds of questions: First, given assumptions about the structure of cultural transmission, how might evolution proceed? If the assumptions of the analysis are empirically correct and the model a reasonable one, we obtain some understanding of how evolution works. Second, we want to understand under what circumstances a particular structure of cultural transmission is likely to be adaptive: why do particular structures or behaviors exist? Answers to such "why" questions are more fundamental, but necessarily more speculative and problematical, than answers to "how" questions.

Some biologists are critical of the "adaptationist program" in evolutionary biology, and especially of attempts to apply it to the human case (Gould and Lewontin, 1979). Abuses of adaptive arguments are fairly common. Functional "just-so" stories are easy to construct, the side effects of changes in one character on other characters are sometimes ignored, and assumptions of equilibrium may often be incorrect. Evolutionary accidents and random events, even on a grand scale, may play a role in evolution (Stanley, 1979).

It is important to keep in mind, however, that hypotheses invoking accidents or disequilibrium are equally prone to abuse. Such hypotheses are difficult to test empirically because they are intrinsically more complex and because they involve dimly understood events of the past. If ordinary adaptive explanations are prone to the just-so problem, so are these alternatives. Moreover, such hypotheses provide too convenient a way to rescue the assumption that humans have transcended nature. Humans seem to be predisposed to believe that culture provides a fundamentally superior mode of adaptation. Our understandable desire to see humans elevated somehow above the common run of beasts ought to be taken into account before we accept explanations entailing accidental evolutionary "breakthroughs."

The cultural inheritance system

In Chapter 3 we defined culture as the information affecting phenotype acquired by individuals by imitation or teaching. The crucial problem addressed in that chapter was whether or not culture can usefully be described as a system of inheritance. We concluded that a number of lines of evidence, ranging from the psychological properties of social learning to the existence of the cultural analog of phylogenetic inertia, support this assumption. The most important source of ambiguity is the difficulty in estimating the relative importance of cultural variation, genetic variation, and the effects of correlated environments. All three factors can cause behavioral similarities in families, among whom data are most easily collected. The data do not contradict the common assumption that the bulk of human behavioral variation is cultural, but neither do they rule out an important role for genes or for the effects of correlated environments.

We believe that the evidence is sufficient to justify theoretical analyses that depend upon the assumption of large amounts of heritable cultural variation. In Chapter 3, we introduced very simple models in which naive individuals accurately copied their cultural parents. We supposed that errors occurred but that they were random and unsystematic. Not surprisingly, such models show that unbiased copying leaves the mean variant in the population unchanged. This, in turn, suggests that we look for processes which systematically affect the frequency of different variants in the population.

Inheritance of acquired variation

Cultural transmission differs from genetic transmission because it includes the inheritance of acquired variation. Errors in social learning, other random environmental effects on behavior, and systematic, nonrandom variations acquired by learning may be transmitted. The effects of random errors, the cultural analog of mutation, were included in many of the models in the book. For example, in Chapter 3 we noted their possible role in maintaining variation in the face of blending inheritance. Usually, however, we chose to concentrate on forces that affect mean trait values and frequencies.

In Chapter 4, we analyzed a model in which a simple model of learning was coupled with cultural transmission. A naive individual first learned its parent's behavior, and then modified what it acquired according to a learning rule that was assumed to result in behavior which, on average, more closely approximates a goal that is contingent on the individual's environment. The result is an evolutionary force, labeled the force of "guided variation," that moves the mean behavior of the population toward the goal of learning. The strength of this force depends on the amount of learning, but even quite weak learning can lead to a potent evolutionary force. Unlike the forces that result from biased transmission and natural selection, the force of guided variation is independent of the amount of variation in the trait in the population.

It might seem that such a capacity to transmit the results of parents' learning to children acts as an unmitigated adaptive advantage by cutting the children's cost of learning. We saw in Chapter 4 that this reasoning is incorrect. Even when cultural transmission itself imposes no costs, it is most likely to be favored, relative to genetic transmission plus ordinary learning, only in environments that are not too variable.

Sequential transmission and the bias forces

Although we have often spoken of naive individuals imitating experienced models, the distinction between the two is only relative. Even an infant engaging in its first episodes of social learning is an active, sentient organism. In general, we do not expect imitation to be a passive process. Individuals are likely to evaluate alternative traits and alternative models and adopt some traits disproportionately on the basis of such evaluations. We termed the series of evolutionary forces that result from these processes biased transmission and distinguished three types: (1) direct biases exercised by evaluating the traits to be adopted by their own properties, (2) frequency-dependent biases in which the commonness or rarity of traits is used as the criterion for adoption, and (3) indirect biases which result from choosing models on the basis of index traits, after which other traits are imitated without further evaluation.

The psychological mechanisms responsible for direct bias overlap substantially with those that underlie guided variation. One can think of direct bias as a kind of trial-and-error learning in which modeled behaviors, instead of self-generated ones, are used as trials to be tested against the guiding criteria. Like guided variation, even weak biases can move the population toward the optimum trait value (or toward high frequencies of the variant favored by the bias, at any rate) fairly rapidly. Unlike the force of guided variation, all of the bias forces depend on the existence of cultural variation; rates of evolution are maximal when variation is a maximum.

Direct bias and guided variation are also similar because they are derived "decision-making" forces. Understanding their adaptive significance requires us to examine the guiding criteria that control how alternative cultural variants are evaluated. Ultimately, we must understand these derivative forces in terms of natural selection and random effects operating on either genetic or cultural variation in the rules that govern how choices are made. In Chapter 5, we attempted to deduce what kinds of genetic determinants of biases might be favored by selection on genes, concluding that general biases have an advantage in spatially variable environments. As with guided variation, the adaptive advantages of culture appeared to be greatest when culture provides a way of adapting to a variable environment that is not available to genes directly. General-purpose direct biases are a mode of adaptation to spatial variation useful in situations where migration rates are too high to allow a really effective genetic response. As a corollary, the models suggested that genetic differentiation between human populations for determinants of biases is unlikely. The intensity of selection on the determinants of biases is always weaker than selection on genes determining phenotypes more directly. If genetic adaptation to variable environments is favored, it is more likely to be via direct genetic specification of behavior than indirectly through biases.

The crucial determinant of the strength of direct bias and guided variation is the cost of estimating which cultural variant is favored in the local environment. If this cost is high, our model predicts that direct bias and guided variation will be weak or even nonexistent. Weak learning will allow cultural variation to be preserved. On the other hand, if costs are low, strong biases or guided variation might evolve. In the case of guided variation, strong learning implies that little use is made of culture at all. Strong bias implies little *heritable* cultural variation; people might choose ideas from a large common pool, as suits their circumstances, rather than from a small sample of models whom they come to measurably resemble.

The available empirical data do not support any sweeping generalizations about the strength of guided variation and directly biased transmission. However, some evidence suggests that direct bias and guided variation may be weak for at least some classes of traits. The evidence from social learning theory (reviewed in Chap. 3) indicates that many traits are acquired by imitation and are only weakly influenced by trial-and-error learning. Psychometric data appear to show substantial heritability of cultural traits, and the existence of cultural inertia indicates that cultural trait frequencies change relatively slowly. The evidence from behavioral decision theory suggests that humans' ability to make accurate choices is quite modest. Often, people acquire cultural theories about the world based on weak or nonexistent evidence (this will lead to weak biases) and then are resistant to disconfirming experience. Finally, decision-making costs are likely to be especially high for many common choices that have low "trialability"—whom to marry, what occupation to choose, what major capital investments to make, whether to convert to another religion, and so forth. For such behaviors, an individual can try only one to a few alternatives in a lifetime, and mistakes are generally costly.

Asymmetric transmission and the natural selection of cultural variations

If we are correct, the forces of guided variation and direct bias are often weak enough to lead to substantial cultural variation, and therefore natural selection will be an important force acting to change the frequency of different cultural variants. It seems likely that individuals characterized by some cultural variants will be more likely to survive or attain social positions that cause them to be imitated than individuals characterized by other variants. When this is true, natural selection will increase the frequency of those variants. However, when the cultural and genetic transmission systems are asymmetric, the variants favored by selection on cultural variants need not be those which would optimize genetic fitness.

Two inheritance systems are asymmetric when their patterns of transmission differ. In many diploid sexually reproducing organisms, the inheritance of sex and autosomal chromosomes is asymmetric. Cultural and autosomal genetic transmission are asymmetric to the extent that models other than genetic parents are effective in cultural transmission or when the two biological parents have unequal weights. Since virtually every society allocates roles in socialization of children to adults other than genetic parents, and because peers can learn from one another, cultural and genetic transmission are often asymmetric. Different elements of the cultural repertoire are also commonly transmitted asymmetrically with respect to each other.

Asymmetric transmission may commonly be genetically adaptive, and hence a capacity for this form of cultural inheritance may be favored. Since cultural transmission is sequential and occurs over a long span of time, the capacity for asymmetric transmission acts as insurance against the death or absence of genetic parents. Increasing the effective number of cultural parents via asymmetric transmission also increases the effectiveness of direct, frequency-dependent, and indirect biases. Indeed, frequency-dependent bias is not possible unless cultural transmission is asymmetric; if, as we have argued, these forms of biased transmission provide a good general purpose way of increasing the chance of acquiring locally favored variants, then this must favor asymmetric transmission.

In our view, the most interesting potential effect of asymmetric transmission is the way natural selection can act on asymmetrically transmitted variants. If models occupying social roles other than that of genetic parent are important in cultural transmission, and if cultural variation affects which people attain these roles, then selection can increase the frequency of cultural variants that reduce ordinary genetic fitness. (Analogous results obtain in the case of asymmetries within the genetic system, Hamilton, 1967.) In metaphorical terms, if opportunities for asymmetric transmission exist, individuals may be forced to "decide" between increasing their genetic and their cultural fitness. For example, modern middle-class young adults seem to reduce the number of children they have, and to direct resources to the achievement of professional success, in order to have an effective role in horizontal or oblique transmission. Similarly, in big-man-dominated horticultural societies, those who compete for high-status roles seem to depend on the exploitation of relatives to achieve influence. In agricultural societies, parents often manipulate their children in order to live a comfortable old age. When age confers high status, elders could be sacrificing their genetic interest in their children and grandchildren for the chance to be active in oblique transmission.

Frequency-dependent bias

Frequency-dependent bias occurs whenever individuals who are exposed to more than two models are disproportionately likely to imitate the common types (conformist transmission) or the rare types (nonconformist transmission). In Chapter 7, we showed that conformist frequency-dependent bias creates a force which acts to increase the frequency of the more common cultural variant in the population. This means that, in a heterogeneous environment, it also has the effect of greatly reducing the importance of a given degree of migration into a semi-isolated subpopulation from surrounding ones.

"When in Rome, do as the Romans do" expresses the simplest adaptive consequence of a frequency-dependent bias. The prevailing behavior of the inhabitants of a local area may be superior to that of immigrants and visitors if local conditions are special. A frequency-dependent bias is likely to be advantageous in spatially heterogeneous habitats because this decision rule is probably inexpensive compared to a detailed evaluation of various alternatives.

Frequency-dependent bias also has the effect of decreasing variation within groups and increasing and preserving variation between groups. In Chapter 7 we modeled how cultural group selection might work and argued that some of the patterns of human altruism can be explained by this mechanism. We also argued that the evidence regarding the scale of cooperation, for example within ethnic groups, is difficult to reconcile with any model, including sociobiological models, which portrays human behavior as self-interested in the inclusive fitness sense.

Indirect bias

Indirectly biased transmission occurs when some traits—we called them indicator traits—affect an individual's attractiveness as a model for other traits. For example, being characterized by a dialect that indicates prestige may cause an individual to be an attractive model for beliefs about innovations or attitudes toward political issues. The possibility of imitating models other than genetic parents, and of imitating different models for different traits, means that indirect bias is potentially a very important force. It acts to increase the frequency of traits that are correlated with the indicator trait on which the choice or preference trait operates. Several transmission effects and forces tend to build and preserve the covariation between indicator traits and incidental ones.

Indirect bias can be an effective decision rule for acquiring adaptive information. As Flinn and Alexander (1982) argue, imitating those who appear to be successful in a particular habitat is a commonsensical rule, and we showed in Chapter 8 that this intuition is indeed correct. In a spatially or temporally varying environment some characters, such as wealth, may be correlated with fitness in a variety of habitats. When this is the case, indirect bias provides an economical way of increasing one's chance of acquiring locally adaptive cultural variants.

On the other hand, indirect bias can lead to unstable runaway or drift-away dynamics analogous to those that may operate in some cases of sexual selection. We suppose that indirect bias becomes established because of its adaptive advantages and that under most circumstances this may be the only result. However, if certain conditions are met, the system evolves by the dynamic of indirect bias alone. If the average person prefers to accord high prestige to (and imitate the behavior of) people with above-average values of the indicator trait, the preferences can continue to evolve, dragging the indicator trait up another notch as well. We know this process as "keeping up with the Joneses." In imitating the Joneses' new car purchase, we may also have acquired the Joneses' heightened sensitivity to cars as markers of status, doing our bit to feed the further evolution of the system.

The runaway and drift-away cases may also create between-group variation that can be affected by group selection. For example, in the runaway case, an accident of initial conditions might have caused evolution to run in the direction of pious self-denial instead of conspicuous consumption. The average person might tend to admire somewhat older or less expensive cars than people on average own. If variation between groups is not destroyed by the flow of ideas between groups, then selection among groups will favor those groups in which the runaway (or drift-away) process has increased the frequency of variants that enhance their success in competition with other groups. This argument may explain why the ethical systems that bind complex societies together are deeply embedded in complex systems of meaningful symbols; the norms that regulate individual conduct for the good of the group might originally have been produced as accidental by-products of the evolution of the symbol system.

Culture, costly information, and the argument from natural origins

A central concern of this book has been to assess the human sociobiologists' claim that human behavior can be understood in the same way as the behavior of other animals—by investigating how alternative behaviors affect genetic fitness. This claim is based on what we called the argument from natural origins: since humans evolved from acultural ancestors, and since selection can only favor traits that increase the fitness of their bearers, it is likely that the human capacity for cultural inheritance enhances genetic fitness. Human sociobiologists interpret this argument to mean that we can understand particular behaviors of people in particular societies, or classes within societies, by analyzing how alternative variants of those behaviors affect genetic fitness.

The argument from natural origins itself is compelling, but the human sociobiologists' interpretation is not because they fail to account for the fact that individual learning sometimes is costly and error prone. When this is the case, it may be more efficient to copy the behavior of others than to make an elaborate individual search for the optimal behavior. In many circumstances the behavior of experienced conspecifics is closer, on the average, to the optimal behavior than the behavior that a naive individual could discover by itself. If imitation is also easier than trial-and-error learning, then it seems plausible that social learning would be favored by selection. The models in Chapters 4 and 5 show that this argument is cogent; a strong dependence on social (as opposed to individual) learning can be favored by selection in many kinds of variable environments. Once cultural transmission is established, selection on the capacity for culture can use the properties of cultural transmission to reduce the cost of individual decision making still further. Rules of thumb for acquiring culture, such as indirect and frequency-dependent biases, can substitute for trial-and-error learning. There often appear to be genetic fitness advantages to asymmetric transmission, if only to make better use of the bias forces. However, asymmetric transmission can create patterns of cultural variation on which natural selection can act to favor variants which do not maximize genetic fitness, such as limitations on family size to increase individuals' abilities to transmit culture to individuals other than offspring. Cultural behaviors that are irrelevant or counter to genetic fitness can also evolve in the runaway and drift-away cases of indirect bias.

Even if many cultural traits have evolved away from genetic fitness maximizing values, the cultural transmission system as a whole can be fitness maximizing. It need only be the case that the costs of stronger individual learning, more accurate biases, and more symmetrical transmission are higher than the costs imposed by the evolution of nonoptimal cultural traits. Selection for genetic capacities for culture should favor those with maximum total benefits averaged over many individuals and many generations, even if reducing information costs means that most individuals carry many nonoptimal cultural traits, considered one trait at a time. The available evidence is consistent with the assumption that people do depend extensively on weakly biased cultural transmission to acquire the bulk of their behavioral repertoires. In evolving a reliance on cultural transmission, the human species may well have "traded" high rates of random error caused by individual learning in variable environments for a lower rate of systematic error (with respect to genetic fitness) due to the partial autonomy of cultural evolution.

By taking account of the cost of acquiring information, we were able to construct a variety of hypotheses about the origin of culture and the mechanisms by which genes and culture interact, all of which are consistent with the argument from natural origins. These range from sociobiological hypotheses in which human behavior tends strongly to maximize genetic fitness to hypotheses in which the runaway case of indirect bias has entrained genetic evolution by setting up criteria for mate choice. Moreover, it is easy to formulate intermediate hypotheses and to imagine that the extent to which human behavior maximizes genetic fitness depends on the kind of trait, the structure of cultural transmission in particular societies, the environmental situation, and other details.

The Utility of Dual Inheritance Theory

The skeptical reader who has come this far with us (or the impatient one who has turned to this chapter in order to peek at our summary) may be disturbed by the qualified nature of our conclusions. Constructing an acceptable science of human behavior has always been confusing, complex, and controversial. Does dual inheritance theory offer a way out of these traditional difficulties, or does it merely express them in new words? The answer is that dual inheritance theory is useful because it allows us to view opposing arguments as variants of a single theory that differ in their assumptions about the structure of cultural inheritance and the relative magnitude of the various forces affecting cultural evolution. Traditional controversies can ultimately be resolved by measuring the properties of cultural transmission and thereby determining which variant of the more general model is appropriate. In other words, we believe that the Darwinian models of cultural evolution that we and others have constructed can often clarify the issues involved in explaining human behavior so that steady progress can be made by further empirical and theoretical work.

If this claim is correct, a Darwinian theory of cultural evolution can play the same unifying role that its analog does in biology. It could be argued that Darwin's main contribution to biology was not his theory of natural selection but rather his recognition that the key to understanding organic evolution is the close study of heritable variation; if we can account for how heritable variation is transmitted, expressed in organisms, and modified with descent from ancestors, we understand evolution. To be sure, Darwinian biology triumphed over natural theology and earned an important place in nineteenth- and early twentieth-century science because natural selection offered a sound, materialistic basis for a theory of organic evolution. However, Darwinian theory owes part of its ongoing vitality to the fact that it acts as a framework for progressive empirical investigation and theory building. The Darwinian framework has unified biologists, even when they have disagreed violently about the nature of the forces governing evolution. For example, none of the principals in the fierce debate that rocked biology after the rediscovery of Mendel's laws (Provine, 1971) disagreed that evolutionary problems should be framed in terms of the dynamics of heritable variation, only about how the forces of evolution actually worked. Once the genetical theory of natural selection of Fisher and Wright was understood, it could be used together with measured selection and mutation rates to provide a unified understanding of evolutionary processes satisfactory to Mendelians and Darwinians. Nor do any of those engaged in the contemporary debate over the relevance of the microevolutionary processes to the macroevolutionary events, as seen in the fossil record, disagree with this fundamental postulate (Stebbins and Ayala, 1981; Gould, 1982). By his correct choice of the essence of the problem, Darwin began the construction of a general theory that structured scientific debate, spurred experiments, and hence permitted scientific progress.

In the social sciences, no such framework has gained wide acceptance. This has led to the "cyclical and repetitive opposition" of theoretical explanation described by Sahlins (1976a: 102). In order to illustrate the contribution we think our theory makes, we will review our results in terms of three problems in the social sciences that have led to long-continued unproductive debates. The first of these problems is the relationship between synchronic (ecological) and diachronic (historical) processes in explaining human behavior. Explanations based on one or the other often are treated as competing whereas in dual inheritance theory they are complementary. Second, the relationship between individuals and cultures or societies has been the locus of repeated debate between theorists who begin with one unit of analysis or the other. Our models suggest that the relationship between individuals and groups is indeed problematical but that the answer to the puzzle rests in solving certain reasonably well defined empirical problems. Finally, there are longstanding conflicts over the role of the symbolic attributes of human culture and cognition. Can symbols affect cultural evolution in some fundamental way?

The relationship between ecological and evolutionary processes

By and large, social scientists have not attempted to link the day to day events in the lives of individuals (ecological or synchronic processes) and the long-term or large scale patterns of human societies (historical or diachronic processes). Until quite recently, theorists of cultural evolution showed little interest in underlying mechanisms of evolution (Campbell, 1965, 1975). For example, in anthropology, Julian Steward's (1955) method of cultural ecology was not satisfactorily linked to his descriptive theory of multilinear evolution, though he obviously assumed that some link must exist. Contemporary human ecologists like Vayda and Rappaport (1968) seem to view historical and ecological explanations as either competing or separate but complementary.

In biology, Darwinian theory is a unified theory of evolution and ecology. Evolutionary processes affect ecological ones because the physiology and behavior of individuals are affected by the genetic composition of the population. At the same time, the processes of evolution, and hence the ultimate causes of what genes individuals inherit, are ecological in character. Ecologists end up with a theory of what adaptations to expect in given environmental circumstances, and evolutionists have a satisfactory theory of organic history.

The central presupposition of dual inheritance theory is that a similar causal relationship between ecological and evolutionary processes governs cultural evolution. Processes on an evolutionary time scale affect contemporary behavior because they determine the nature of the cultural traditions that characterize any society. On the other hand, to understand evolutionary processes we must understand the forces that act on an ecological time scale to affect cultural variation as it is carried through time by a succession of individuals.

To see how this connection is made, imagine that two groups with independent cultural histories move into a new, unfamiliar ecological zone. The new zone is, let us say, especially well suited to nomadic pastoralism, but one of the original groups is agricultural by tradition, the other hunts and gathers. If learning were costless, both groups would adopt pastoral nomadism immediately. A synchronic ecological theory would explain behavior quite well. If cultural traditions were extremely stable, both groups would retain their traditional modes of life indefinitely in the new zone even in the face of severe penalties for doing so. The ecological theory would be useless, and a diachronic historical explanation would be necessary. More likely, neither model would work well. In Chapter 3 we reviewed evidence that much of the behavior observed in any one generation must be explained by cultural transmission from the previous generation, and in later chapters we analyzed the forces that will make more or less strong, environmentally contingent changes in culture each generation. For example, in Chapter 4 we analyzed models of guided variation that suggest that an exclusive dependence on either individual learning or tradition is unlikely in general. To continue our example, both societies will acquire new traits by invention and diffusion over a period of several generations as new adaptations are developed. Some techniques and values will spread more rapidly than others, and the rates will likely be different in the two societies. Evolutionary forces imposed by the environment will be strong for some behaviors, such as basic subsistence techniques, weaker for others, such as modes of social organization, and virtually absent for still others, such as grammar and syntax. Historical differences may lead the two societies to develop quite different ultimate adjustments to the new zone, particularly if they compete. Perhaps the original hunting group might develop a pure pastoralism in poorer parts of the zone, whereas the original farming group might preempt a few oases and combine herding and agriculture. After many generations, each society will contain some traits that are recognizably related to those of its distant past, some that have developed and spread in the recent past, some that are still developing and spreading, and some that have been borrowed from other groups.

Cultural transmission leads to persistence of behavioral traits through time, but generation by generation, even day by day if our measurements were fine enough to detect it, traditions are modified by accident, individual choices, and natural selection. The causes of historical change, the forces of cultural evolution in our terms, are processes that occur synchronically, but typically take many generations to complete their work. If this view is correct, synchronic and diachronic explanations of human behavior are merely different ways of looking at the same suite of causal processes, the action of evolutionary forces on the genetic and cultural systems of inheritance.

The relationship between individuals and populations

Social scientists typically have viewed the society (or population) and the individual as antithetical starting points for theory. Social scientists who have adopted a methodological individualism, for example economists, paint a different picture of human behavior from those social scientists who take the society as the basic unit of analysis, like the followers of Durkheim. Marxists and others who select classes or interest groups as the basic unit reach still different conclusions. It seems likely that much of this diversity of opinion stems from the complexity of human social systems. For example, human social behavior is sometimes characterized by remarkable levels of coordination and cooperation but other times by extreme self-interest. Both the proponents of group-level functionalism and those who argue that individual self-interest predominates can easily find many empirical facts that are consistent with their respective interpretations.

Dual inheritance theory provides a natural way to link processes at the individual level with those at the level of the group. If any of the transmission models we developed in Chapter 3 and applied in the rest of the book are at all faithful to reality, cultural evolution, like genetic evolution in a sexual species, is always a group or population phenomenon. This is so because social learning is a process by which individuals acquire samples (often quite biased samples, to be sure) of their society's total collection of cultural variants. The cultural traditions of society are, in this minimal sense, imposed on individuals. However, this fact alone does not allow us to deduce whether evolutionary processes will favor individually advantageous or group functional traits. To understand why a group is characterized by a particular distribution of variants, we must understand how the forces of cultural evolution act on the group. Some of these forces have their origin in the psychology of individuals. Learning and rational calculation will affect the frequency of different cultural variants through the action of the forces of guided variation and biased transmission. Other forces are the result of larger scale social processes. Cultural transmission creates heritable variation between individuals and groups. Many social processes can increase the frequency or salience of some kinds of individuals or groups through the force of natural selection. To understand the cultural traditions that characterize a particular society, we need to estimate the net effects of these various forces.

In Chapters 7 and 8 we considered the evolution of moral systems which require altruistic self-sacrifice. We assumed that the forces rooted in individual psychology would generally tend to favor selfish moral beliefs. On the other hand, it also seems plausible that human groups whose members hold self-sacrificial beliefs, which in turn lead to effective cooperation and a larger supply of public goods, would be more successful associations than groups whose members were solely self-interested. Given these assumptions, direct bias and guided variation would act to increase the frequency of individually advantageous beliefs within groups, while selection between groups would act to decrease the frequency of such beliefs to the extent to which self-interest conflicts with cooperative activities. The relative strength of these two processes will depend on the relative amounts of culturally transmitted variation within and between groups. In Chapter 7 we showed that if people are predisposed to imitate locally more common cultural variants (a form of frequency-dependent bias), group selection may predominate. In Chapter 8 we analyzed models of indirect bias in which drift-away and runaway dynamics similarly might lead to substantial group variation on which selection could act. In general, such models make it possible to explain the curious mixture of selfishness and cooperation that seems to characterize human social systems.

Symbolic reasoning and communication

It is a common argument that human mental capacities associated with culture somehow allow humans to transcend the ordinary imperatives of nature. A. R. Wallace (1905), the co-discoverer of the theory of natural selection, believed that humans became exempt from its operation. More recently, Marshall Sahlins (1976a, 1976b) has argued that no adaptive or functional theory can be a complete explanation of human behavior. In Chapter 8 we described his view of human behavior: the use of arbitrary symbol systems leads cultural evolution to follow the internal cultural logic of meaningful systems of fundamentally arbitrary cultural symbols; humans construct, and impose upon nature, a symbolic order of their own devising. Natural processes as diverse as gravity and natural selection merely constrain such constructions, engineering constraints in the case of gravity and the need to survive and reproduce in the case of natural selection.

The critical issue is not whether humans use meaningful symbol systems but how the dynamics of the evolution of such systems can come to conflict with functional imperatives imposed by the decision-making forces and natural selection. The difficulty is that the evidence that symbolic traits are nonfunctional is not compelling; functional theorists of various colorations can give adaptive explanations for even the most bizarre cultural traits. The anti-sociobiological cultural materialist Marvin Harris (1974, 1977, 1979) has been notably inventive in this regard.

Dual inheritance theory is useful here because it shifts attention away from interpretation of macroscopic patterns of culture to the microscopic mechanisms by which the properties of symbols might drive cultural evolution in directions irrelevant, or even counter, to adaptive demands. In Chapter 8 we described a microscopic causal mechanism, indirect bias, that can systematically elaborate the subjective meaning of cultural traits, even in the face of selective penalties for doing so. When a naive individual selects models on the basis of one trait and then imitates other traits without further bias, the indicator traits on which the bias is based are immediately indexical in character. The foods people eat signal their prestige and hence their general suitability as models for traits quite apart from diet. Once indirect bias is used, even if for perfectly good adaptive reasons, such as using prestige traits correlated with the possession of superior resource gathering skills to bias model choice, the resulting evolutionary dynamic is unstable under some conditions.

The model is formally very similar to models of female choice sexual selection used by biologists (Lande, 1981). In fact, we were attracted to models of sexual selection for this problem by a certain esthetic resemblance of elaborate male secondary sexual characters to the similarly elaborate artifacts that are often a part of cultural symbol systems and by the resemblance of the underlying mechanism of female choice to indirect bias. In the case of female choice sexual selection, females are supposed to use display traits of males to choose those males which will endow offspring with the greatest reproductive success. In the cultural analog, cultural offspring choose their own cultural parents, but the structure of the situation is otherwise quite similar. Both unstable sexual selection and unstable indirect bias cause evolution to proceed in orderly but nonfunctional directions. Eventually, the traits on which the selection of models is based can become quite irrelevant to ordinary adaptive advantages. Thus indirect bias can explain how arbitrary but subjectively meaningful cultural symbols evolve from functional indices, as in the elaborate, highly variable dress and diet markers of prestige.

Again, if this model is a reasonable one, the repetitive and cyclical debates between functionalist and nonfunctionalist can be brought to the point of an ordinary scientific problem, progressively resolvable by further empirical and theoretical work. Do humans actually make extensive use of indirect bias in cultural transmission, using arbitrary cultural symbols as the basis of choice? If the answer is yes, then many symbolic cultural traits may have to be explained as nonadaptive or maladaptive consequences of runaway or drift-away evolution.

Future Work

We are acutely aware that the dual inheritance model of human evolution rests on less than completely compelling arguments. The present theoretical machinery and empirical evidence are insufficient to resolve most of the interesting outstanding problems. However, we do think that the diversity of plausible models that can be developed by applying this approach to cultural evolution makes a very strong case for its utility. The logical duels of twentieth-century social science have sometimes descended to burlesque imitations of the real thing, fought with much loud invective but rubber swords. Unfortunately, some of the most important and basic questions have been treated with the lowest comedy. By providing a framework in which opposing theories can be expressed, dual inheritance theory provides a set of rules for a sharper, cleaner, more productive logical duel.

If we have done an adequate job in the body of this book, the best directions for future work will be as clear to our readers as they are to us, far clearer in many technical areas no doubt. Nevertheless, our own ideas on the point will complete this, the most important argument we have attempted to make.

Theoretical models

The complexity of the dual inheritance system offers a rich field for formal modeling. Although a respectable amount of analytical work has been done on this problem by Karlin (1979), Lumsden and Wilson (1980a, 1980b, 1981), Cavalli-Sforza and Feldman (1981 and references therein), and Cloninger and his colleagues (Cloninger et al., 1979a, 1979b; Rice et al., 1978, 1980), many interesting questions remain unaddressed. Few sample theories are available to represent various processes, and the number of robust theoretical results is small. Especially important theoretical problems are:

More complex models of biased transmission. Most decisions about whether or not to adopt a cultural variant may involve the application of several biases, and once acquired, a cultural trait can act to bias subsequent transmission events. Multiple biases and chains of biases may have substantially different properties than the simpler types we have examined. Pulliam and Dunford (1980) have argued that cognitive consistency, the pleasure felt when a new cultural variant fits well with a person's existing repertoire, is an important type of complex bias. These effects may exemplify only the need to keep decisions simple, or they may permit effective and complex, but inexpensive, decisions by coupling them to a few primary guiding criteria. The latter result might enhance the plausibility of the stronger versions of the sociobiology hypothesis. Can such complex biases operate effectively?

Better models of the evolution of altruism. The scale of human social organization, we argued in Chapter 7, is hard to explain without group selection. Although conventional models of general reciprocal altruism in large groups are not a good alternative to group selection, it is possible that networks of pairwise reciprocal altruism may have interesting properties. Similarly, hierarchical models with mixtures of reciprocity and exploitation could be a viable alternative to group selection.

Models of age-structured cultural transmission. A considerable amount of recent empirical work has been devoted to studies of the human life cycle (e.g. Baltes and Brim, 1979; Elder, 1974; Brim and Kagan, 1980). The acquisition and transmission of culture is distributed throughout the human life cycle; this is one of its main structural disanalogies with genes. Although we and others have made some models indirectly based on this phenomenon, the effects of age structure have not been explicitly investigated. As a cohort ages, the various forces of cultural evolution may cause the frequencies of some traits to change substantially. Changes in the pattern of intergenerational transmission could have important evolutionary effects in such a system. For example, changes in the average age at which parents have children could change the frequency of traits the children acquire. Thus environmental conditions that affect cohort behavior of the type hypothesized by Easterlin (1976) and studied by Elder (1974) could have much stronger effects than would be possible in a genetic system.

Models which incorporate a transmissible environment. Models of cultural transmission show that correlated environments are easily confounded with cultural and genetic transmission (Cavalli-Sforza and Feldman, 1973b, 1978; Eaves et al., 1978; Cloninger et al., 1979a, 1979b). This problem is especially difficult when environmental effects have dynamical properties of their own. Examples include the inheritance of money and artifacts of various kinds, especially the persistence of expensive capital facilities such as improved agricultural land, transportation infrastructure, and so forth. Becker (1981) and Schelling (1978) analyze several models of related processes. Nelson and Winter (1982) have developed an interesting series of models of the evolution of firms in which capital is important as well as the knowledge that conceptually resides in individuals. Understanding the institutional complexity of modern societies will require the mating of a micro-level theory like the one we have developed here with the more aggregated one of Nelson and Winter.

These effects, or parts of them, fall into the categories of social learning we carefully excluded from our definition of culture in Chapter 3. Information is not being directly transmitted to the next generation, but environmental modifications made by one generation do constrain the decisions, or condition the ordinary learning, of the next. Thus, unlike ordinary environmental effects, they are endogenous to the evolving system of behavior. Almost any cultural explanation for a given pattern of behavior can be countered by a hypothesis involving transmitted environment plus individual decisions. For example, underdevelopment can be explained as a lack of the culturally transmitted skills and attitudes necessary for industrial production or by consequences of having to compete with the historically industrial nations whose inheritance of a functioning industrial system (ownership of capital) gives them advantages quite independently of culture. Probably both effects play a role in underdevelopment, but it is easy to imagine that either could be the primary controlling effect. The lack of models in which both are explicitly included makes even primitive speculation difficult. Such models would mimic Alexander's (1979a: 77) version of cultural inertia, and perhaps the Marxist notion of historical forces.

Empirical studies

Formal theoretical analysis is a useful tool for clarifying logic but an arid exercise in the absence of well-designed empirical studies. A great deal of the existing information from the social sciences (and human biology) can be used to guide the development of dual inheritance theory, as we hope our various illustrative examples have shown. However, there is often no substitute for data collected with the solution of a particular theoretical problem in mind. Even at the level of sophistication of existing models, such theoretically refined data are necessary right across the spectrum of the social science disciplines. Micro-level data are needed to understand the properties of cultural transmission and to make estimates of the population-level consequences of these properties, especially the strengths of the various forces imposed on cultural variation. More critical macro-level data on patterns of variation between cultures and over long spans of time within cultures are required to estimate what range of basic hypotheses are plausible (and which hypotheses for which traits in which circumstances). A few examples of experimental and observational studies that we think would be especially useful are as follows:

Experimental studies of the "laws" of cultural transmission. The evidence reviewed in Chapter 3, we argued, is sufficient to indicate that culture does behave as an inheritance system, but it is certainly inadequate to answer many questions about the mechanics of cultural transmission. Is transmission particulate, blending, or multifactorial? Does the analog of genetic linkage exist? That is, when a naive person is exposed to several models, and controlling for bias effects, is there a tendency for blocks of traits to be acquired from different models, or are repertoires assembled independently for each trait? One approach to this problem is to fit theoretical models to data on family resemblances (e.g. Eaves et al., 1978; Cloninger et al., 1979a, 1979b; Cavalli-Sforza et al., 1982). The difficulty with this design is that many complex processes interact to produce the observed correlations. As was the case with biological inheritance, the use of experimental designs to isolate the transmission processes from other sources of variation is a promising approach. Full scale socialization experiments are, of course, impractical, but the social learning experiments pioneered by Albert Bandura and his co-workers could be extended to these problems.

Experimental studies of the dynamics of cultural evolution. Jacobs and Campbell (1961) pioneered the use of multi-"generation" social learning experiments. The basic design is to start a small laboratory society with a specified culture by the use of confederates, and then replace the confederates one by one with naive subjects who use first the confederates, then each other, for models. The change in cultural traits is measured as a function of "generation." Jacobs and Campbell used this design to test the rate of approach to naively preferred judgment on an ambiguous perception test as a function of personality type (authoritarian versus nonauthoritarian). In our terms, they were measuring the strength of guided variation.

Only a few subsequent studies have used this technique. For example, Insko et al. (1980, 1982, 1983) used it to test hypotheses about the evolution of social stratification. Zucker (1977) used it to test the effects of institutionalization on fidelity of cultural transmission. The hypothesis (confirmed) was that attributing a position in a formal organization to models caused naive individuals to imitate them more faithfully. The Insko et al. (1980) study showed a guided variation effect, and the Zucker study the influence of indirect bias.

This experimental design could be modified so that the effects of all the forces could be investigated. Selection could be modeled by removing variant individuals or groups from the experimental population, migration by exchanging individuals between groups, and random errors by measuring the divergence between replicated groups. The experimenter can also manipulate the environment by giving individuals or groups tasks to perform, the payoffs of which are manipulated. Subjects from different cultures or subcultures could be used to investigate the effects of natural cultural variation on the various forces.

Quantitative field studies. The drawbacks to field studies are the complexity of real situations and the consequent difficulty of isolating causal factors. Still, the ultimate test of the micro-assumptions and macro-predictions of evolutionary hypotheses must be made using field data. The human case is particularly vexing in this regard because of the impossibility of conducting field experiments to bridge the gap between highly artificial laboratory manipulations and natural observations. However, the range of ethnographic variation in humans is large, and even within societies the range of variation in such important things as family structure and educational institutions is commonly quite considerable.

In our opinion, the development of good theoretical tools is the main requirement for making good use of observational data. Without sharply opposed hypotheses or key variables to measure, almost any interpretation can be imposed on a necessarily rather ambiguous set of field data. The recent movement in ecological anthropology to develop and test quantitative models of human foraging behavior derived from general ecological theory is a promising example (Smith, 1983). The virtue of the models used, like those from sociobiology applied by Chagnon and Irons (1979), Irons (1979b), Dickemann (1981), and others, is that field measurements can be made to support or contradict the models. Alternatives to models drawn from biology can and should be made similarly specific and applied to field conditions.

Reasonably sharp field tests of some of the macro-level predictions of the various models developed here should prove practical. For example, if group selection on cultural variation is important, it will result in detectable flows of resources outside networks of kinship and reciprocal altruism. It should make possible reciprocal relations of mutual trust in situations where cheating or evasion of responsibilities is easy. In many situations, a detectable fraction of successful "cheaters" ought to exist. The models also predict a sharp boundary between those insiders suitable for altruism and trust and outsiders who may be cheated fairly freely (extramural sanctions aside). The ethnic group data reviewed in Chapter 7 support the group selection hypothesis, but they are far short of the actual measurement of patterns of cooperation and conflict. The effect may very well turn out to be weak or absent in the face of quantitative data.

New types of micro-level field studies are needed to understand the structural properties of cultural transmission and the action and interactions of forces. The most difficult problem in such studies is the separation of genetic, cultural, and correlated environment effects on phenotype. In isolation, conventional psychometric, socialization, and life cycle studies are unlikely to make more than modest contributions to our understanding of the complex problems we outlined in Chapter 3. In the absence of detailed information about how socialization actually proceeds in families (and outside of them), one is reduced to highly abstract guesses about the structure of models, in a situation where many alternatives are equally plausible. For example, it is not possible to judge whether the high correlations between parents observed for many traits in psychometric and sociometric studies are due to assortative mating or cultural transmission after marriage (Cavalli-Sforza et al., 1982). Students of human development have the techniques to assess the putative pathways of cultural and environmental influences but do not collect the quantitative data on parent-offspring and other resemblances necessary for psychometric analysis.

A better approach would be to combine psychometric analysis with long-term longitudinal studies of socialization—cultural trait acquisition and transmission— throughout the complete life cycle. The most practical design for a study of this type might be to build a psychometric study around an existing large scale longitudinal study such as that of Werner and Smith (1982). Or, alternatively, longitudinal studies could be initiated on a subset of a sample on which psychometric data exist, like that of Horn et al. (1979). The advantage of the former strategy is that good longitudinal studies of humans require many decades to complete and it would be useful to incorporate existing ones.

Quantitative longitudinal studies are also useful to obtain fine-grained data on the forces that affect cultural variation. Werner and Smith (1982), for example, have shown how variation in child-rearing practices affects the life chances of economically deprived children on Kawai. However, simple cross-sectional studies of forces like natural selection and indirect bias would be extremely valuable. The trade-offs hypothesized in Chapter 6 between genetic and cultural fitness are critically measurable with data only modestly more elaborate than those reviewed. Does the socialization of professionals lead to reduced norms for family size and an enhanced opportunity to participate in horizontal and oblique transmission? Can similar effects be demonstrated in non-Western prestige systems? Similarly, the dynamics of the spread (or failure) of abstemious religious doctrines in the face of biases against their practices offer a rich field for the study of a variety of evolutionary forces.

Another important advance would be to measure traits which indicate cultural "coancestry" in different individuals. Genetic relatedness is a reasonable surrogate for genetic influences, and is the basis of biometrical models of the patterns of variation attributable to genetic effects. Comparable indices of cultural "parentage" are necessary to provide quantitative guides for transmission models. Dialect variation and similar symbolic traits might be used as indices of cultural similarity; genetic and environmental effects on them are negligible. Such traits would be the cultural analog of eye color and blood type.

Conclusion

We have taken as our task the construction of simple models for as many of the basic mechanisms of cultural evolution as we could find suitable detailed suggestions for and for which we could make a plausible empirical case. If these models collectively represent a reasonably complete theory, albeit a highly simplified one, they ought to be a useful guide for further exploration. Like a sixteenth-century map of the world, the scale is small, distortions undoubtedly exist, some of the processes included are likely to prove apocryphal, and large areas are blank. The purpose of theory at this juncture is, we believe, to summarize a state of quite imperfect knowledge about the causes of human behavior in a way which makes further refinement as simple as possible. The polemicist's conceit that we know enough to solve basic questions in this field makes for lively controversies, but it is misleading if taken too seriously. Too much hard work remains to be done.

References and Author Index

Bracketed numbers denote page numbers in the present volume on which the works are cited

Ahlstrom, W. M. and R. J. Havighurst. 1971. *400 Losers*. San Francisco: Jossey-Bass. [47]

Alexander, R. D. 1971. The search for an evolutionary philosophy of man. *Proc. R. Soc. Victoria* 84: 99–119. [231]

Alexander, R. D. 1974. The evolution of social behavior. *Ann. Rev. Ecol. Syst.* 5: 325–383. [46, 275]

Alexander, R. D. 1979a. *Darwinism and Human Affairs*. Seattle: Univ. Washington Press. [12, 13, 34, 46, 56, 81, 133, 153–160, 200, 202, 231, 275, 296]

Alexander, R. D. 1979b. Evolution and culture. In: *Evolutionary Biology and Human Social Behavior: An Anthropological Perspective*, N. A. Chagnon and W. Irons, eds., pp. 59–88. North Scituate, Mass.: Duxbury. [46, 158]

Alexander, R. D. and D. W. Tinkle. 1968. Review of *On Aggression* by K. Lorenz and *The Territorial Imperative* by R. Ardrey. *Bioscience* 18: 245–248. [231]

Andrews, D. F., P. J. Pickel, F. R. Hampel, P. J. Huber, W. H. Rogers, and J. W. Tukey. 1972. *Robust Estimates of Location: Survey and Advances*. Princeton: Princeton Univ. Press. [222–223]

Aoki, K. 1982a. Polygenic altruism and extinction group selection. *Jap. J. Genet.* 57: 297–300. [231]

Aoki, K. 1982b. A condition for group selection to prevail over counteracting individual selection. *Evolution* 36: 832–842. [231]

Arnold, S. 1978. The evolution of a special class of modifiable behaviors in relationship to environmental pattern. *Am. Nat.* 112: 415–427. [93]

Arnold, S. 1981. Behavioral variation in natural populations. I. Phenotypic, genetic and environmental correlations between chemoreceptive responses to prey in the garter snake, *Thamnophis elegans*. *Evolution* 35: 489–509. [55]

Aronfreed, J. 1969. The problem of imitation. In: *Advances in Child Development and Behavior*, L. P. Lipsitt and H. W. Reese, eds., 4: 209–319. [45]

Asch, S. E. 1951. Effects of group pressure upon the modification and distortion of judgments. In: *Groups, Leadership and Men*, H. Guetzkow, ed., pp. 177–190. Pittsburgh: Carnegie. [224]

Atkinson, R. C., G. H. Bower, and E. J. Crothers. 1965. *An Introduction to Mathematical Learning Theory*. New York: Wiley. [84, 85]

Axelrod, R. 1980. Effective choice in the prisoner's dilemma. *J. Conflict Resolution* 24: 3–25. [230]

Axelrod, R. 1984. *The Evolution of Cooperation*. New York: Basic Books. [230]

Axelrod, R. and W. D. Hamilton. 1981. The evolution of cooperation. *Science* 211: 1390–1396. [230]

Bachman, J. G. 1970. *Youth in Transition*. Vol. 2. *The Impacts of Family Background and Intelligence on Tenth Grade Boys*. Ann Arbor: Survey Research Center, Univ. Michigan. [50]

Bachman, J. G., J. M. O'Malley, and J. Johnston. 1978. *Youth in Transition*. Vol. 6. *Adolescent to Adulthood—Change and Stability in the Lives of Young Men*. Ann Arbor: Survey Research Center, Univ. Michigan. [50]

Bacon, M. K., I. L. Child, and H. Barry III. 1963. A cross-cultural study of correlates of crime. *J. Abn. Soc. Psychol.* 66: 291–300. [47]

Baldwin, J. D. and J. I. Baldwin. 1981. *Beyond Sociobiology*. New York: Elsevier. [158]

Baltes, P. B. and O. G. Brim. 1979. *Life Span and Behavior*. New York: Academic Press. [295]

Bandura, A. 1977. *Social Learning Theory*. Englewood Cliffs, N.J.: Prentice-Hall. [42, 43, 273, 297]

Bandura, A., D. Ross, and S. A. Ross. 1963. A comparative test of the status envy, social power, and the secondary reinforcement theories of identificatory learning. *J. Abn. Soc. Psychol.* 67: 527–534. [44, 244]

Bandura, A. and R. Walters. 1963. *Social Learning and Personality Development*. New York: Holt, Rinehart & Winston. [38, 41]

Bannister, R. 1979. *Social Darwinism: Science and Myth in Anglo-American Social Thought*. Philadelphia: Temple Univ. Press. [281]

Barker, L. M., M. R. Best, and M. L. Domjon, eds. 1977. *Learning Mechanisms in Food Selection*. Waco, Tex.: Baylor Univ. Press. [86]

Barnett, S. A. 1975. *The Rat: A Study in Behavior*. Rev. ed. Chicago: Univ. Chicago Press. [86]

Bascom, W. R. 1948. Ponapae prestige economy. *Southwestern J. Anthropol.* 4: 211–221. [269–270]

Basso, K. H. and H. A. Selby. 1976. *Meaning in Anthropology*. Albuquerque: Univ. New Mexico Press. [272]

Baumrind, D. 1967. Child care practices anteceding three patterns of preschool behavior. *Genet. Psychol. Monogr.* 75: 43–83. [46, 47]

Becker, G. S. 1981. *A Treatise on the Family*. Cambridge, Mass.: Harvard Univ. Press. [241, 295]

Bell, A. P. 1969. Role modeling of fathers in adolescence and young adulthood. *J. Counseling Psychol.* 16: 30–35. [53, 54]

Bell, G. D. 1963. Processes in the formation of adolescents' aspirations. *Social Forces* 42: 179–186. [54]

Berry, J. W. 1976. *Human Ecology and Cognitive Style: Comparative Studies in Cultural and Psychological Style*. New York: Wiley. [179–180]

Blau, P. M. 1965. The flow of occupational supply and recruitment. *Am. Sociol. Rev.* 30: 475–490. [39, 50]

Block, J. H. 1973. Conceptions of sex role: Some cross-cultural and longitudinal perspectives. *Am. Psychol.* 28: 512–526. [50]

Boas, F. 1940 (1966). *Race, Language and Culture*. Paperback ed. New York: Free Press. [132]

Boehm, C. 1978. Rational pre-selection from Hamadryas to Homo sapiens: The place of decisions in adaptive process. *Am. Anthropol.* 80: 265–296. [4, 132, 158]

Bonner, J. T. 1980. *The Evolution of Culture in Animals*. Princeton: Princeton Univ. Press. [81, 82, 83, 130]

Boorman, S. A. and P. R. Levitt. 1980. *The Genetics of Altruism*. New York: Academic Press. [231]

Boyd, R. and P. J. Richerson. 1982. Cultural transmission and the evolution of cooperative behavior. *Hum. Ecol.* 10: 325–351. [235]

Boyd, R. and P. J. Richerson. 1983. The cultural transmission of acquired variation: Effects on genetic fitness. *J. Theoret. Biol.* 100: 567–596. [113]

Boyle, R. P. 1966. The effects of the high school on student's aspirations. *Am. J. Sociol.* 71: 628–639. [54]

Bradshaw, A. D. 1965. Evolutionary significance of phenotypic plasticity in plants. *Adv. Genet.* 13: 115–155. New York: Academic Press. [4, 83]

Brent, P. 1981. *Charles Darwin: A Man of Enlarged Curiosity*. New York: Harper & Row. [19]

Brim, O. G. 1958. Family structure and sex role learning by children: A further analysis of Helen Koch's data. *Sociometry* 21: 1–16. [54]

Brim, O. G. and J. Kagan, eds. 1980. *Constancy and Change in Human Development*. Cambridge, Mass.: Harvard Univ. Press. [295]

Brittain, C. V. 1963. Adolescent choices and parent-peer cross-pressures. *Am. Sociol. Rev.* 28: 385–391. [54]

Bronfenbrenner, U. 1970. *Two Worlds of Childhood: U.S. and U.S.S.R.* New York: Russell Sage Foundation. [54]

Brown, G. B. 1910. *Melanesians and Polynesians: Their Life Histories Compared*. London: Macmillan. [270]

Buchanan, J. M. 1968. *The Demand and Supply of Public Goods*. Chicago: Rand McNally. [228]

Bulmer, M. G. 1980. *The Mathematical Theory of Quantitative Genetics*. Oxford: Clarendon. [121]

Burley, N. 1979. The evolution of concealed ovulation. *Am. Nat.* 114: 835–858. [199]

Bush, R. R. and F. Mosteller. 1955. *Stochastic Models for Learning*. New York: Wiley. [83, 84]

Caldwell, J. C. 1976. Toward a restatement of demographic transition theory. *Pop. Dev. Rev.* 2: 321–366. [201–202]

Campbell, D. T. 1960. Blind variation and selective retention in creative thought as in other knowledge processes. *Psychol. Rev.* 67: 380–400. [132]

Campbell, D. T. 1965. Variation and selective retention in sociocultural evolution. In: *Social Change in Developing Areas: A Reinterpretation of Evolutionary Theory*, H. R. Barringer, G. I. Blanksten, and R. W. Mack, eds., pp. 19–49. Cambridge, Mass.: Schenkman. [11, 290]

Campbell, D. T. 1975. On the conflicts between biological and social evolution and between psychology and moral tradition. *Am. Psychol.* 30: 1103–1126. [11, 197, 205, 276, 290]

Cattel, R. B. 1960. The multiple abstract variance analysis equations and solutions: For nature-nurture research on continuous variables. *Psychol. Rev.* 67: 353–372. [52]

Cavalli-Sforza, L. L. and M. W. Feldman. 1973a. Models for cultural inheritance. I. Group mean and within group variation. *Theoret. Pop. Biol.* 4: 42–55. [69]

Cavalli-Sforza, L. L. and M. W. Feldman. 1973b. Cultural versus biological inheritance: Phenotypic transmission from parents to children (A theory of the effect of parental phenotypes on children's phenotypes). *Am. J. Hum. Genet.* 25: 618–637. [51, 295]

Cavalli-Sforza, L. L. and M. W. Feldman. 1978. The evolution of continuous variation. III. Joint transmission of genotypes, phenotypes and environment. *Genetics* 90: 391–425. [52, 295]

Cavalli-Sforza, L. L. and M. W. Feldman. 1981. *Cultural Transmission and Evolution: A Quantitative Approach*. Princeton: Princeton Univ. Press. [8, 9, 31, 50, 51, 65, 69, 132, 174, 267, 294]

Cavalli-Sforza, L. L. and M. W. Feldman. 1983. Cultural versus genetic adaptation. *Proc. Natl. Acad. Sci. USA* 80: 4993–4996. [117]

Cavalli-Sforza, L. L., M. W. Feldman, K. H. Chen, and S. M. Dornbusch. 1982. Theory and observation in cultural transmission. *Science* 218: 19–27. [50, 297, 298]

Chaffee, S. H. 1972. Television and adolescent aggressiveness (overview). In: *Television and Social Behavior*, Vol. 3, G. A. Comstock and E. A. Rubinstein, eds. Surgeon General's Scientific Advisory Committee on Television and Social Behavior. Washington, D.C.: Govt. Printing Office, pp. 1–34. [54]

Chagnon, N. A. and W. Irons, eds. 1979. *Evolutionary Biology and Human Social Behavior: An Anthropological Perspective*. North Scituate, Mass.: Duxbury. [12, 298]

Chen, K-H., L. L. Cavalli-Sforza, and M. W. Feldman. 1982. A study of cultural transmission in Taiwan. *Hum. Ecol.* 10: 365–382. [50]

Cheverud, J. 1982. Phenotypic, genetic and environmental morphological integration in the cranium. *Evolution* 36: 499–516. [55]

Chomsky, N. 1976. On the nature of language. *Ann. N.Y. Acad. Sci.* 280: 46–57. [45]

Cloninger, C. R., J. Rice, and T. Reich. 1979a. Multifactorial inheritance with cultural transmission and assortative mating. II. A general model of combined polygenic and cultural inheritance. *Am. J. Hum. Genet.* 31: 176–198. [51, 294, 295, 297]

Cloninger, C. R., J. Rice, and T. Reich. 1979b. Multifactorial inheritance with cultural transmission and assortative mating. III. Family structure and the analysis of separation experiments. *Am. J. Hum. Genet.* 31: 366–388. [51, 294, 295, 297]

Cohen, A. 1974. *Two-Dimensional Man: An Essay on the Anthropology of Power and Symbolism in Complex Society.* Berkeley: Univ. California Press. [274]

Coopersmith, S. 1967. *The Antecendents of Self-Esteem.* San Francisco: Freeman. [50]

Crow, J. F. and K. Aoki. 1982. Group selection for a polygenic behavioral trait: A differential proliferation model. *Proc. Natl. Acad. Sci. USA* 79: 2628–2631. [231]

Cyert, R. M. and J. G. March. 1963. *A Behavioral Theory of the Firm.* Englewood Cliffs, N.J.: Prentice-Hall. [93, 94]

Darlington, C. D. 1969. *The Evolution of Man and Society.* New York: Simon & Schuster. [159]

Darwin, C. 1838 (1974). *The Notebooks on Man, Mind, and Materialism.* Transcribed and annotated by P. H. Barrett. In: H. E. Gruber, *Darwin on Man: A Psychological Study of Scientific Creativity.* New York: Dutton, pp. 263–381. [1]

Darwin, C. 1871. *The Descent of Man and Selection in Relation to Sex.* London: Murray. [19]

Darwin, C. 1872. *The Expression of the Emotions in Man and Animals.* London: Murray. [19]

Darwin, C. 1874 (1885). *The Descent of Man and Selection According to Sex.* 2d ed. London: Murray. [19, 82, 172]

Dawkins, R. 1976. *The Selfish Gene.* New York: Oxford Univ. Press. [37]

Day, R. H. 1967. Profits, learning, and convergence of satisficing to marginalism. *Q. J. Econ.* 81: 302–311. [94]

Day, R. H., S. Morely, and K. Smith. 1974. Myopic maximizing and rules of thumb in a micro economic model of industrial growth. *Am. Econ. Rev.* 64: 11–23. [94]

Diamond, J. 1978. The Tasmanians: The longest isolation, the simplest technology. *Nature* 273: 185–186. [9]

Dickemann, M. 1979. Female infanticide, reproductive strategies and social stratification: A preliminary model. In: *Evolutionary Biology and Human Social Behavior: An Anthropological Perspective,* N. Chagnon and W. Irons, eds., pp. 321–367. North Scituate, Mass.: Duxbury. [276]

Dickemann, M. 1981. Paternal confidence and dowry competition: A biocultural analysis of Purdah. In: *Natural Selection and Social Behavior: Recent Research and New Theory,* R. D. Alexander and D. W. Tinkle, eds., pp. 417–438. Oxford: Blackwell. [298]

Duncan, O. D. 1965. The trend of occupational mobility in the United States. *Am. Sociol. Rev.* 30: 491–498. [50]

Durham, W. H. 1976. The adaptive significance of cultural behavior. *Hum. Ecol.* 4: 89–121. [132, 153, 158, 159, 190, 274]

Durham, W. H. 1977. Reply. In: E. E. Ruyle, F. T. Cloak, L. B. Slobodkin, and W. H. Durham, The adaptive significance of cultural behavior: Comments and reply. *Hum. Ecol.* 5: 49–67. [159, 162]

Durham, W. H. 1978. Toward a coevolutionary view of human biology and culture. In: *The Sociobiology Debate,* A. Caplan, ed., pp. 428–448. New York: Harper & Row. [13, 159, 162, 163]

Durham, W. H. 1979. Toward a coevolution theory of human biology and culture. In: *Evolutionary Biology and Human Social Behavior: An Anthropological Perspective,* N. A. Chagnon and W. Irons, eds., pp. 39–59. North Scituate, Mass.: Duxbury. [162]

Durham, W. H. 1982. Interactions of genetic and cultural evolution: Models and examples. *Hum. Ecol.* 10: 289–323. [159, 162]

Durkheim, E. 1895 (1938). *The Rules of the Sociological Method.* Glencoe: Free Press. [23]

Easterlin, R. A. 1976. The conflict between aspirations and resources. *Pop. Dev. Rev.* 2: 417–425. [295]

Eaves, L. J., K. A. Last, P. A. Young, and N. G. Martin. 1978. Model-fitting approaches to the analysis of human behavior. *Heredity* 41: 249–320. [51, 295, 297]

Edgerton, R. B. with W. Goldschmidt. 1971. *The Individual in Cultural Adaptation: A Study of Four East African Peoples*. Berkeley: Univ. California Press. [57–59, 161]

Einhorn, H. J. and R. M. Hogarth. 1981. Behavioral decision theory: Processes of judgment and choice. *Ann. Rev. Psychol.* 32: 53–88. [168, 169]

Eiseley, L. C. 1958. *Darwin's Century*. Garden City, N.Y.: Anchor. [75]

Eiseley, L. C. 1973. *The Man Who Saw through Time*. New York: Scribner. [81]

Elder, G. 1974. *Children of the Great Depression: Social Change and Life Experience*. Chicago: Univ. Chicago Press. [295]

Engelberg, J. and L. L. Boyarsky. 1979. The noncybernetic nature of ecosystems. *Am. Nat.* 114: 317–324. [35]

Epstein, T. S. 1968. *Capitalism, Primitive and Modern: Some Aspects of Tolai Economic Growth*. Manchester: Manchester Univ. Press. [60]

Ervin-Tripp, S. 1976. Speech acts and social learning. In: *Meaning in Anthropology*, K. H. Basso and H. A. Selby, eds., pp. 123–153. Albuquerque: Univ. New Mexico Press. [273]

Eshel, I. 1972. On the neighborhood effect and the evolution of altruistic traits. *Theoret. Pop. Biol.* 3: 258–277. [231]

Falconer, D. S. 1960. *Introduction to Quantitative Genetics*. New York: Ronald. [121]

Feldman, M. W. and R. C. Lewontin. 1975. The heritability hangup. *Science* 190: 1163–1168. [51]

Finney, B. R. 1972. Big-men, half-men, and trader-chiefs: Entrepreneurial styles in New Guinea and Polynesia. In: *Opportunity and Response: Case Studies in Economic Development*, T. S. Epstein and D. H. Penny, eds., pp. 114–261. London: Hurst. [60]

Fisher, R. A. 1918. The correlation between relatives on the supposition of Mendelian inheritance. *Trans. Roy. Soc. Edinburgh* 52: 399–433. [75, 173]

Fisher, R. A. 1958. *The Genetical Theory of Natural Selection*. Rev. ed. New York: Dover. [72, 75, 243, 259]

Fishman, J. A. 1972. *The Sociology of Language: An Interdisciplinary Social Science Approach to Language in Society*. Rowley, Mass.: Newbury House. [246]

Flacks, R. 1967. The liberated generation: An exploration of the roots of student protest. *J. Social Issues* 23: 52–75. [50]

Flinn, M. V. and R. D. Alexander. 1982. Culture theory: The developing synthesis from biology. *Hum. Ecol.* 10: 383–400. [230, 243, 257, 287]

Freedman, R. 1979. Theories of fertility decline: A reappraisal. In: *World Population and Development: Challenges and Prospects*, P. M. Hauser, ed., pp. 63–79. New York: Syracuse Univ. Press. [201–202]

Freilich, M. 1980. Smart-sex and proper-sex: A paradigm found. *Central Issues Anthropol.* 2: 37–51. [37, 276]

Fuller, J. L. and R. W. Thompson. 1960. *Behavior Genetics*. New York: Wiley. [52]

Fuller, J. L. and R. W. Thompson. 1978. *Foundations of Behavior Genetics*. St. Louis: Mosby. [52]

Galef, B. G. J. 1976. Social transmission of acquired behavior: A discussion of tradition and social learning in vertebrates. *Adv. Study of Behavior* 6: 77–100. [34, 82, 130]

Galef, B. G. J. 1980. Diving for food: Analysis of a possible case of social learning by wild rats (*Rattus norwegicus*). *J. Comp. Physiol. Psychol.* 94: 416–425. [39]

Garcia, J., F. R. Ervin, and R. Koelling. 1966. Learning with prolonged delay of reinforcement. *Psychonam. Sci.* 5: 121–122. [84, 86]

Geertz, C. 1972. Deep play: Notes on the Balinese cockfight. *Daedalus* 101: 1–37. [37]

Geertz, C. 1973. *The Interpretation of Cultures*. New York: Basic Books. [36, 281]

Gewirtz, J. L. 1971. Conditional responding as a paradigm for observational, imitative learning and vicarious reinforcement. In: *Advances in Child Development and Behavior*, H. W. Reese, ed., 6: 273–304. New York: Academic Press. [46]

Gewirtz, J. L. and K. G. Stingle. 1968. Learning of generalized imitation as a basis for identification. *Psychol. Rev.* 75: 374–397. [42]

Ghiselin, M. T. 1969. *The Triumph of the Darwinian Method*. Berkeley: Univ. California Press. [172]

Gifford, E. W. 1929. *Tongan Society*. Bernice P. Bishop Museum, Bulletin 61. [270]

Gillespie, J. H. 1981a. The role of migration in the genetic structure of populations in temporally and spatially varying environments. III. Migration modification. *Am. Nat.* 117: 223–233. [112]

Gillespie, J. H. 1981b. Mutation modification in a random environment. *Evolution* 35: 468–476. [112]

Glass, D. V. and J. R. Hall. 1954. Social mobility in Great Britain: A study of inter-generation changes in status. In: *Social Mobility in Great Britain*, D. V. Glass, ed., pp. 177–217. Glencoe: Free Press. [39, 50]

Goode, W. J. 1978. *The Celebration of Heros: Prestige as a Control System*. Berkeley: Univ. California Press. [241, 276]

Goodenough, W. H. 1957. Cultural anthropology and linguistics. In: *Report of the Seventh Annual Round Table Meeting on Linguistics and Language Study*, P. Garim, ed. Washington, D.C.: Georgetown Univ. Monogr. Ser. Lang. and Ling. 9: 167–173. [33, 37]

Goodenough, W. H. 1981. *Culture; Language, and Society*. McCaleb Module in Anthropology. Menlo Park, Calif.: Benjamin/Cummings. [37]

Gould, S. J. 1982. Darwinism and the expansion of evolutionary theory. *Science* 216: 380–387. [290]

Gould, S. J. and R. C. Lewontin. 1979. The Spandrels of San Marco and the Panglossian paradigm: A critique of the adaptationist programme. *Proc. R. Soc. London* B205: 581–598. [3, 13, 282]

Greeley, A. M. and W. C. McCready. 1975. The transmission of cultural heritages: The case of the Irish and Italians. In: *Ethnicity: Theory and Experience*, N. Glazer and D. P. Moynihan, eds., pp. 209–235. Cambridge, Mass.: Harvard Univ. Press. [59]

Greene, P. J. 1978. Promiscuity, paternity, and culture. *Am. Ethnol.* 5: 151–159. [13, 202]

Gruber, H. E. with P. H. Barrett. 1974. *Darwin on Man: A Psychological Study of Scientific Creativity*. New York: Dutton. [1, 19]

Hadley, G. 1967. *Introduction to Probability and Statistical Decision Theory*. San Francisco: Holden-Day. [87]

Hagman, E. R. 1932. A study of fears of children of pre-school age. *J. Exp. Educ.* 1: 110–130. [50]

Hagoromo Society. Kamikaze Divine Thunderbolt Corps Survivors. 1973. *Born to Die: The Cherry Blossom Squadrons*. Los Angeles: Ohara. [204]

Haldane, J. B. S. and S. D. Jayakar. 1963. Polymorphism due to selection of varying direction. *J. Genet.* 58: 237–242. [112]

Hamilton, W. D. 1964. The genetical evolution of social behavior I, II. *J. Theoret. Biol.* 7: 1–52. [202]

Hamilton, W. D. 1967. Extraordinary sex ratios. *Science* 156: 477–488. [286]

Hamilton, W. D. 1972. Altruism and related phenomena, mainly in the social insects. *Ann. Rev. Ecol. Syst.* 3: 193–232. [16]

Hamilton, W. D. 1975. Innate social aptitudes of man: An approach from evolutionary genetics. In: *Biosocial Anthropology*, R. Fox, ed., pp. 133–155. London: Malaby. [231, 275]

Handy, E. S. G. and W. C. Handy. 1924. *Samoan House Building, Canoeing, and Tattooing*. Bernice P. Bishop Museum, Bulletin 15. [270–271]

Handy, W. C. 1922. *Tattooing in the Marquesas*. Bernice P. Bishop Museum, Bulletin 1. [270–271]

Hardin, R. 1982. *Collective Action*. Baltimore: Johns Hopkins Univ. Press. [229, 241]

Harlow, H. F. and M. K. Harlow. 1969. Effects of various mother-infant relationships on rhesus monkey behaviors. In: *Determinants of Infant Behavior*, Vol. 4, B. M. Foss, ed. London: Methuen. [35]

Harris, M. 1968. *The Rise of Anthropological Theory*. New York: Crowell. [281]

Harris, M. 1971. *Culture, Man and Nature*. New York: Crowell. [33, 36]

Harris, M. 1974. *Cows, Pigs, Wars and Witches: The Riddles of Culture*. New York: Random House. [293]

Harris, M. 1977. *Cannibals and Kings: The Origins of Cultures.* New York: Random House. [293]

Harris, M. 1979. *Cultural Materialism: The Struggle for a Science of Culture.* New York: Random House. [132, 158, 281, 293]

Hartung, J. 1976. On natural selection and the inheritance of wealth. *Curr. Anthropol.* 17: 607–622. [202]

Hartup, W. W. 1970. Peer interaction and social organization. In: *Carmichael's Manual of Child Psychology,* P. H. Mussen, ed., 3d ed., 2: 361–456. [54]

Hartup, W. W. and B. Coates. 1967. Imitation of a peer as a function of reinforcement from the peer group and rewardingness of the model. *Child Dev.* 38: 1003–1016. [54]

Henderson, N. D. 1982. Human behavior genetics. *Ann. Rev. Psychol.* 33: 403–440. [39, 51, 52]

Hetherington, E. M. 1972. Effects of father absence on personality development in adolescent daughters. *Dev. Psychol.* 7: 313–326. [47]

Hill, R. C. and F. P. Stafford. 1974. Allocation of time to preschool children and educational opportunity. *J. Hum. Res.* 9: 323–341. [200]

Hiroa, T. R. 1930. *Samoan Material Culture.* Bernice P. Bishop Museum, Bulletin 75. [270–271]

Hiroa, T. R. 1938. *Ethnology of Mangareva.* Bernice P. Bishop Museum, Bulletin 157. [270–271]

Hirshleifer, J. 1977. Economics from a biological viewpoint. *J. Law Econ.* 20: 1–52. [242]

Hirshleifer, J. and J. Riley. 1979. The analytics of uncertainty and information—an expository survey. *J. Econ. Lit.* 17: 1375–1421. [83]

Hirshleifer, J. 1983. From the weakest link to the best shot: The voluntary provision of public goods. *Public Interest* 41: 371–386. [229]

Hoffman, M. L. 1971. Father absence and conscience development. *Dev. Psychol.* 4: 400–406. [47]

Hoffman, M. L. and H. D. Saltzstein. 1967. Parent discipline and the child's moral development. *J. Personal. Soc. Psychol.* 5: 45–57. [47]

Horn, J. M., Y. C. Loehlin, and L. Willerman. 1979. Intellectual resemblance among adoptive and biological relatives: The Texas adoption project. *Behav. Genet.* 9: 177–207. [298]

Houston, A. and J. McNamara. 1981. How to maximize reward rate on two variable interval paradigms. *J. Exp. Anal. Behav.* 35: 367–396. [93]

Hudson, E. A. and D. W. Jorgenson. 1974. U.S. energy policy and economic growth, 1975–2000. *Bell J. Econ. Mgmt. Sci.* 4: 461–514. [24]

Immelman, K. 1975. Ecological significance of imprinting and early learning. *Ann. Rev. Ecol. Syst.* 6: 15–37. [82, 130]

Inkeles, A. and D. H. Smith. 1974. *Becoming Modern: Individual Change in Six Developing Countries.* Cambridge, Mass.: Harvard Univ. Press. [54]

Insko, C. A., R. Gilmore, S. Drenan, A. Lipsitz, D. Moehle, and J. Thibaut. 1983. Trade versus expropriation in open groups: A comparison of two types of social power. *J. Personal. Soc. Psychol.* 44: 977–999. [297]

Insko, C. A., R. Gilmore, D. Moehle, A. Lipsitz, S. Drenan, and J. W. Thibaut. 1982. Seniority in the generational transition of laboratory groups: The effects of social familiarity and task experience. *J. Exp. Soc. Psychol.* 18: 577–580. [297]

Insko, C. A., J. W. Thibaut, D. Moehle, M. Wilson, W. D. Diamond, R. Gilmore, M. R. Soloman, and A. Lipsitz. 1980. Social evolution and the emergence of leadership. *J. Personal. Soc. Psychol.* 39 (3): 431–448. [297]

Irons, W. 1979a. Natural selection, adaptation, and human social behavior. In: *Evolutionary Biology and Human Social Behavior: An Anthropological Perspective,* N. Chagnon and W. Irons, eds., pp. 4–39. North Scituate, Mass.: Duxbury. [13, 153]

Irons, W. 1979b. Cultural and biological success. In: *Evolutionary Biology and Human Social Behavior: An Anthropological Perspective,* N. Chagnon and W. Irons, eds., pp. 257–272. North Scituate, Mass.: Duxbury. [258, 276, 281, 298]

Isaac, G. L. 1976. States of cultural elaboration in the Pleistocene: Possible archeological indicators of the development of language capabilities. *Ann. N.Y. Acad. Sci.* 280: 275–288. [36, 60]

Jacobs, R. C. and D. T. Campbell. 1961. The perpetuation of an arbitrary tradition through several generations of laboratory microculture. *J. Abn. Soc. Psychol.* 62: 649–658. [225–227, 297]

Jain, A. K. 1981. The effect of female education on fertility: A simple explanation. *Demography* 18: 577–594. [201]

Jakobson, R. 1971. Quest for the essence of language. In: *Selected Writings* II. *Word and Language*. R. Jakobson, ed. The Hague: Mouton. [272]

Janssen, S. G. and R. M. Hauser. 1981. Religion, socialization and fertility. *Demography* 18: 511–528. [176]

Jencks, C., M. Smith, H. Acland, M. J. Bane, D. Cohen, H. Gintis, B. Heyns, and S. Michelson. 1972. *Inequality: A Reassessment of the Effect of Family and Schooling in America*. New York: Basic Books. [180]

Jenkin, F. 1864. The origin of species. *N. Br. Rev.* 46: 277–318. [75]

Jensen, G. F. and M. L. Erickson. 1979. The religious factor and deliquency: Another look at the Hellfire hypotheses. In: *The Religious Dimension: New Directions in Quantitative Research*, R. Wuthnow, ed., pp. 157–177. New York: Academic Press. [177]

Jessor, R. and S. L. Jessor. 1977. *Problem Behavior and Psychosocial Development: A Longitudinal Study of Youth*. New York: Academic Press. [50]

Kalat, J. W. and P. Rozin. 1972. You can lead a rat to poison, but you can't make him think. In: *Biological Boundaries of Learning*, M. E. P. Seligman and J. L. Hagar, eds., pp. 115–122. New York: Appleton-Century-Crofts. [87]

Karlin, S. 1979. Models of multifactorial inheritance. I. Multivariate formulations and basic convergence results. *Theoret. Pop. Biol.* 15: 308–355. [1256, 294]

Karlin, S. 1980. Models of multifactorial inheritance. V. Linear assortative mating as against selective (nonlinear) assortative mating. *Theoret. Pop. Biol.* 17: 255–275. [51]

Karlin, S. and J. M. McGregor. 1974. Towards a theory of the evolution of modifier genes. *Theoret. Pop. Biol.* 5: 59–103. [112]

Katz, S. H. and J. Schall. 1979. Fava bean consumption and biocultural evolution. *Med. Anthropol.* 3: 459–476. [177–178]

Katz, S. H., M. L. Hediger, and L. A. Valleroy. 1974. Traditional maize processing techniques in the New World. *Science* 184: 765–773. [153]

Kawai, M. 1965. Newly acquired pre-cultural behavior of the natural troop of Japanese monkeys on Koshima Islet. *Primates* 6: 1–30. [35]

Keesing, R. M. 1974. Theories of culture. *Ann. Rev. Anthropol.* 3: 73–97. [33]

Keisler, C. A. and S. B. Keisler. 1969. *Conformity*. Reading, Mass.: Addison-Wesley. [10, 223–224]

Kimura. M. 1965. A stochastic model concerning the maintenance of genetic variability in quantitative characters. *Proc. Natl. Acad. Sci. USA* 54: 731–736. [75]

King, J. A. 1951. Social behavior, social organization, and population dynamics in a black-tailed prairiedog town in the Black Hills of South Dakota. Ph.D. thesis, Univ. Michigan. [35]

King, J. A. 1959. The social behavior of prairie dogs. *Sci. Am.* 201: 128–140. [35]

Kirkpatrick, C. 1936. A comparison of generations in regard to attitudes toward feminism. *J. Gen. Psychol.* 49: 343–361. [50]

Kirkpatrick, M. 1982. Sexual selection and the evolution of female choice. *Evolution* 36: 1–12. [260]

Klaus, R. A. and S. W. Gray. 1968. The early training project for disadvantaged children: A report after five years. *Monogr. Soc. Res. Child Dev.* 33(4): 1–66. [54]

Kobasigawa, A. 1968. Inhibitory and disinhibitory effects of models on sex-inappropriate behavior in children. *Psychologia* 11: 86–96. [54]

Koestler, A. 1971. *The Case of the Midwife Toad*. New York: Random House. [172]

Kohlberg, L. 1964. Development of moral character and moral ideology. In: *Review of Child Development Research*, Vol. 1, M. L. Hoffman and L. W. Hoffman, eds., pp. 383–431. New York: Russell Sage. [45]

Kohn, M. L. 1981. Personality, occupation, and social stratification: A frame of reference. In: *Research in Social Stratification*, Vol. 3, D. Y. Treiman and R. V. Robinson, eds., pp. 267–297. Greenwich, Conn.: JAI Press. [179]

Krebs, C. 1978. Optimal foraging: Decision rules for predators. In: *Behavioral Ecology*, J. R. Krebs and N. B. Davies, eds., pp. 23–64. London: Blackwell Scientific. [93]

Krebs, J. R. and N. B. Davies. 1981. *An Introduction to Behavioral Ecology*. Sunderland, Mass.: Sinauer. [13]

Kroeber, A. L. and C. Kluckhohn. 1952. Culture, a critical review of the concepts and definitions. *Papers Peabody Mus. Am. Archeol. Ethnol.* 47(1): 1–223 [33–38]

Kurland, J. A. 1979. Paternity, mother's brother, and human sociality. In: *Evolutionary Biology and Human Social Behavior: An Anthropological Perspective*, N. A. Chagnon and W. G. Irons, eds., pp. 145–180. North Scituate, Mass.: Duxbury. [13, 202]

Labov, W. 1972. *Sociolinguistic Patterns*. Philadelphia: Univ. Pennsylvania Press. [54, 246–247, 261, 273]

Labov, W. 1980. The social origins of sound change. In: *Locating Language in Time and Space*, W. Labov, ed., pp. 251–265. New York: Academic Press. [246]

Lande, R. 1976. The maintenance of genetic variability by mutation in a polygenic character with linked loci. *Genet. Res.* 26: 221–235. [75, 121]

Lande, R. 1977. The influence of mating system on the maintenance of genetic variability in polygenic characters. *Genetics* 86: 485–498. [121]

Lande, R. 1979. Quantitative genetic analysis of multi-variable evolution, applied to brain, body size allometry. *Evolution* 53: 402–416. [121, 173, 256]

Lande, R. 1980. The genetic covariance between characters maintained by pleiotropic mutations. *Genetics* 94: 203–215. [121]

Lande, R. 1981. Models of speciation by sexual selection on polygenic traits. *Proc. Natl. Acad. Sci. USA* 78: 3721–3725. [260, 293]

Landy, D. and H. Sigall. 1974. Beauty is talent: Task evaluation as a function of performer's physical attractiveness. *J. Personal. Soc. Psychol.* 29: 299–304. [244]

Larson, L. E. 1974. An examination of the salience hierarchy during adolescence: The influence of the family. *Adolescence* 35: 317–332. [54]

Laughlin, C. D., Jr., and E. G. d'Aquili. 1974. *Biogenetic Structuralism*. New York: Columbia Univ. Press. [45]

Layzer, D. 1974. Heritability analyses of I.Q. scores: Science or numerology? *Science* 183: 1259–1266. [51]

Lesser, G. S. and D. Kandel. 1969. Parent-adolescent relationships and adolescence in the United States and Denmark. *J. Marriage and the Family* 31: 348–358. [47]

Levin, B. R. and W. L. Kilmer. 1974. Interdemic selection and the evolution of altruism: A computer simulation study. *Evolution* 28: 527–545. [231]

LeVine, R. A. 1966. *Dreams and Deeds: Achievement Motivation in Nigeria*. Chicago: Univ. Chicago Press. [59, 201]

LeVine, R. A. 1973. *Culture, Behavior, and Personality*. Chicago: Aldine. [41, 162]

LeVine, R. A. and D. T. Campbell. 1972. *Ethnocentrism: Theories of Conflict, Ethnic Attitudes, and Group Behavior*. New York: Wiley. [238–239]

Levins, R. 1966. The strategy of model building in population biology. *Am. Sci.* 54: 421–31. [25]

Levins, R. 1968. *Evolution in Changing Environments: Some Theoretical Explorations*. Princeton: Princeton Univ. Press. [25]

Lewontin, R. C. 1974. *The Genetic Basis of Evolutionary Change*. New York: Columbia Univ. Press. [3, 5]

Liebenstein, H. 1976. *Beyond Economic Man: A New Foundation for Microeconomics*. Cambridge, Mass.: Harvard Univ. Press. [24]

Lieberman, P. 1975. *On the Origins of Language: An Introduction to the Evolution of Human Speech*. New York: Macmillan. [24, 36]

Linton, R. 1939. Marquesan culture. In: *The Individual and His Society: The Psychodynamics of Primitive Social Organization*, A. Kardiner, ed., pp. 138–196. New York: Columbia Univ. Press. [270]

Lipset, S. M. and R. Bendix. 1964. *Social Mobility in Industrial Society*. Berkeley: Univ. California Press. [50]

Lumsden, C. and E. O. Wilson. 1980a. Translation of epigenetic rules of individual behavior into ethnographic patterns. *Proc. Natl. Acad. Sci. USA* 77: 6248–6250. [206, 294]

Lumsden, C. and E. O. Wilson. 1980b. Gene-culture translation in the avoidance of sibling incest. *Proc. Natl. Acad. Sci. USA* 77: 4382–4386. [294]

Lumsden, C. and E. O. Wilson. 1981. *Genes, Mind, and Culture*. Cambridge, Mass.: Harvard Univ. Press. [10, 37, 46, 69, 131, 132, 153–166, 177, 190, 212, 294]

Lynn, D. B. 1974. *The Father: His Role in Child Development*. Monterey, Calif.: Brooks/Cole. [47]

Lynn, D. B. 1979. *Daughters and Parents: Past, Present and Future*. Monterey, Calif.: Brooks/Cole. [47]

Maccoby, E. E. 1980. *Social Development: Psychological Growth and the Parent-Child Relationship*. New York: Harcourt Brace Jovanovich. [47]

Maccoby, E. E. and C. N. Jacklin. 1974. *The Psychology of Sex Differences*. Stanford, Calif.: Stanford Univ. Press. [47]

Mainardi, D. 1980. Tradition and social transmission of behavior in animals. In: *Sociobiology: Beyond Nature-Nurture?* G. Barlow and J. Silverberg, eds., pp. 227–255. Boulder, Colo.: Westview. [82, 130]

Marshack, A. 1976. Implications of the paleolithic symbolic evidence for the origin of language. *Am. Sci.* 64: 136–145. [36]

Mason, K. O. and V. T. Palan. 1981. Female employment and fertility in peninsular Malaysia: The maternal incompatibility hypothesis reconsidered. *Demography* 18: 549–575. [201]

Masters, R. 1973. Functional approaches to analogical comparison between species. *Soc. Sci. Inform.* 12(4): 7–28. [31]

Matessi, C. and S. D. Jayakar. 1976. Conditions for the evolution of altruism under Darwinian selection. *Theoret. Pop. Biol.* 9: 360–387. [231]

Maynard Smith, J. 1976. Group selection. *Q. Rev. Biol.* 51: 277–283. [231]

Maynard Smith, J. 1978. Optimality theory in evolution. *Ann. Rev. Ecol. Syst.* 9: 31–56. [61]

Maynard Smith, J. and N. Warren. 1982. Models of cultural and genetic change. *Evolution* 36: 620–627. [164]

McCall, R. B. 1977. Childhood I.Q.'s as predictors of adult education and occupational status. *Science* 197: 482–483. [50]

McEvoy, L. and G. Land. 1981. Life-style and death patterns of Missouri RLDS Church members. *Am. J. Public Health* 71: 1350–1357. [176–177]

McNamara, J. and A. Houston. 1980. The application of statistical decision theory to animal behavior. *J. Theoret. Biol.* 85: 673–690. [93]

Michod, R. E. 1982. The theory of kin selection. *Ann. Rev. Ecol. Syst.* 13: 23–56. [231]

Milgram, S. 1965. Some conditions of obedience and disobedience to authority. *Hum. Rel.* 18: 57–76. [38]

Miller, N. E. and J. Dollard. 1941. *Social Learning and Imitation*. New Haven: Yale Univ. Press. [42]

Millot, B. 1970. *Divine Thunder: The Life and Death of the Kamikazes*. New York: McCall. [204]

Mowrer, O.H. 1960. *Learning Theory and the Symbolic Processes*. New York: Wiley. [45]

Mussen, P. H., J. J. Conger, and J. Kagan. 1979. *Child Development and Personality*. 5th ed. New York: Harper & Row. [46, 47]

Nelson, R. R. and S. G. Winter. 1982. *An Evolutionary Theory of Economic Change*. Cambridge, Mass.: Harvard Univ. Press. [295–296]

Newcomb, T. and G. Svehla. 1937. Intra-familial relationships in attitude. *Sociometry* 1: 180–205. [50, 52]

Nisbett, R. and L. Ross. 1980. *Human Inference: Strategies and Shortcomings of Social Judgment*. Englewood Cliffs, N.J.: Prentice-Hall. [38, 93, 168–170]

Nisbett, R. E. and T. D. Wilson. 1977. Telling more than we can know: Verbal reports of mental process. *Psychol. Rev.* 84: 231–259. [38]

Norberini, M. 1966. Ethnocentrism and feuding: A cross-cultural study. M.A. thesis, Univ. Chicago. [238]

Nuttin, J. M., Jr. 1975. *The Illusion of Attitude Change: Towards a Response Contagion Theory of Persuasion.* London: Academic Press. [38]

Oliver, S. C. 1962. Ecology and cultural continuity as contributing factors in the social organization of the Plains Indians. *Univ. California Publ. Archaeol. Ethnol.* 48(1): 1–90. [57]

Olson, M. 1971. *The Logic of Collective Action: Public Goods and the Theory of Groups.* Cambridge, Mass.: Harvard Univ. Press. [228]

Opie, I. and P. Opie. 1959. *The Lore and Language of Children.* Oxford: Clarendon. [54]

Opie, I. and P. Opie. 1969. *Children's Games in Street and Playground.* London: Oxford Univ. Press. [54]

Opie, I. and P. Opie. 1976. Street games: Counting out and chasing. In: *Play—Its Role in Development and Evolution*, J. S. Bruner, A. Jolly, and K. Sylva, eds., pp. 394–412. London: Penguin. [54]

Orlove, B. S. 1980. Ecological anthropology. *Ann. Rev. Anthropol.* 9: 235–273. [57]

Pearson, K. 1901. Mathematical contributions to the theory of evolution. IX. On the principle of homotyposis and its relation to heredity, to the variability of the individual and to that of the race. *Phil. Trans. R. Soc. London,* Ser. A 197: 285–379. [173]

Pearson, K. 1902. Mathematical contributions to the theory of evolution. XI. On the influence of natural selection on the variability and correlation of organs. *Phil. Trans. R. Soc. London,* Ser. A 200: 330–333. [173]

Peoples, J. E. 1982. Individual or group advantage? A reinterpretation of the Maring ritual cycle. *Curr. Anthropol.* 23: 291–310. [237]

Petersen, W. 1975. *Population.* New York: Macmillan. [176]

Piaget, J. 1962. *Play, Dreams and Imitation in Childhood.* New York: Norton. [45]

Pilbeam, D. 1972. *The Ascent of Man: An Introduction to Human Evolution.* New York: Macmillan. [155]

Plotkin, H. C. and F. J. Odling-Smee. 1981. A multiple-level model of evolution and its implications for sociobiology. *Behav. Brain Sci.* 4: 225–268. [158]

Portuges, S. H. and N. D. Feshbach. 1972. The influence of sex and socioethnic factors upon imitation of teachers by elementary school children. *Child Dev.* 43: 981–989. [55]

Posner, R. A. 1980. A theory of primitive society, with special reference to primitive law. *J. Law Econ.* 23: 1–53. [241]

Pospisil, L. 1978. *The Kapauku Papuans of West New Guinea.* 2d ed. New York: Holt, Rinehart & Winston. [60]

Provine, W. B. 1971. *The Origins of Theoretical Population Genetics.* Chicago: Univ. Chicago Press. [179, 290]

Pulliam, H. R. 1982. A social learning model of conflict and cooperation in human societies. *Hum. Ecol.* 10: 353–363. [202]

Pulliam, H. R. 1983. On the theory of gene-culture co-evolution in a variable environment. In: *Animal Cognition and Behavior*, R. L. Mellgren, ed. Amsterdam: North-Holland. [145, 157, 164]

Pulliam, H. R. and C. Dunford. 1980. *Programmed to Learn: An Essay on the Evolution of Culture.* New York: Columbia Univ. Press. [83, 93, 202, 295]

Rancour-Laferriere, D. 1981. Sociobiology and psychoanalysis: Interdisciplinary remarks on the most imitative animal. *Psychoanal. Contemp. Thought* 4: 435–526. [244]

Rapoport, A. 1967. Escape from paradox. *Sci. Am.* 217 (July): 50–56. [282]

Rappaport, R. A. 1968. *Pigs for the Ancestors.* New Haven, Conn.: Yale Univ. Press. [237]

Rappaport, R. A. 1979. *Ecology, Meaning, and Religion.* Richmond, Calif.: North Atlantic Books. [276]

Rice, J., C. R. Cloninger, and T. Reich. 1978. Multi-factorial inheritance with cultural transmission and assortative mating. I. Description and basic properties of the unitary model. *Am. J. Hum. Genet.* 30: 618–643. [51, 294]

Rice, J., C. R. Cloninger, and T. Reich. 1980. Analysis of behavioral traits in the presence of cultural transmission and assortative mating: Application to I.Q. and SES. *Behav. Genet.* 10: 73–92. [50, 51, 52, 294]

Richerson, P. J. and R. Boyd. 1978. A dual inheritance model of the human evolutionary process. I. Basic postulates and a simple model. *J. Social Biol. Struct.* 1: 127–154. [202]

Roff, M. 1950. Intra-family resemblances in personality characteristics. *J. Psychol.* 30: 199–227. [51]

Rogers, E. M. 1983. *Diffusion of Innovations*. 3d ed. New York: Free Press. [167]

Rogers, E. M. with F. F. Shoemaker. 1971. *The Communication of Innovations: A Cross-cultural Approach*. New York: Free Press. [167, 245–246]

Roher, J. H., S. H. Baron, L. E. Hoffman, and D. V. Swander. 1954. The stability of auto-kinetic judgments. *J. Abn. Soc. Psychol.* 49: 595–597. [224]

Rosenberg, A. 1980a. Obstacles to the nomological connection of reasons and actions. *Phil. Soc. Sci.* 10: 79–91. [38]

Rosenberg, A. 1980b. *Sociobiology and the Preemption of the Social Sciences*. Baltimore: Johns Hopkins Univ. Press. [241]

Rosenhan, D., F. Frederick, and A. Burrowes. 1968. Preaching and practice: Effects of channel discrepancy on norm internalization. *Child Dev.* 39: 291–301. [55]

Rosenthal, T. and B. Zimmerman. 1978. *Social Learning and Cognition*. New York: Academic Press. [36, 37, 40, 43, 44, 80, 244]

Roughgarden, J. 1979. *Theory of Population Genetics and Evolutionary Ecology: An Introduction*. New York: Macmillan. [112]

Ruyle, E. E. 1973. Genetic and cultural pools: Some suggestions for a unified theory of biocultural evolution. *Hum. Ecol.* 1: 201–215. [10, 132, 158]

Sahlins, M. 1963. Poor man, rich man, big-man, chief: Political types in Melanesia and Polynesia. *Comp. Stud. Soc. Hist.* 5: 285–303. [57]

Sahlins, M. 1976a. *Culture and Practical Reason*. Chicago: Univ. Chicago Press. [38, 242, 271–272, 277–279, 281, 290, 293]

Sahlins, M. 1976b. *The Use and Abuse of Biology: An Anthropological Critique of Sociobiology*. Ann Arbor: Univ. Michigan Press. [132, 271–272, 279, 281, 293]

Savage, L. J. 1954. *The Foundations of Statistics*. New York: Wiley. [87]

Scarr, S. 1981. Toward a more biological psychology. In: *Science and the Question of Human Equality*, M. S. Collins, I. W. Wainer, and T. A. Bremner, eds., pp. 71–87. AAAS Selected Symp. 58. Boulder, Colo.: Westview. [52, 56]

Scarr, S. and W. B. Barker. 1981. The effects of family background: A study of cognitive differences between black and white twins. In: *Race, Social Class, and Individual Differences in I.Q.*, S. Scarr, ed., pp. 261–315. Hillsdale, N.J.: Erlbaum. [56]

Scarr, S., A. J. Pakstis, S. H. Katz, and W. B. Barker. 1977. Absence of a relationship between degree of white ancestry and intellectual skills within a black population. *Hum. Genet.* 39: 69–86. [56]

Scarr, S. and R. A. Weinberg. 1976. I.Q. performance of black children adopted by white families. *Am. Psychol.* 31: 726–739. [51, 56]

Schelling, T. C. 1978. *Micromotives and Macrobehavior*. New York: Norton. [295]

Schiff, M., M. Duyme, A. Dumaret, J. Stewart, S. Tomkiewicz, and J. Feingold. 1978. Intellectual status of working-class children adopted early into upper-middle-class families. *Science* 200: 1503–1504. [51]

Schneider, D. M. 1968. *American Kinship: A Cultural Account*. Englewood Cliffs, N.J.: Prentice-Hall. [37]

Schneider, D. M. 1976. Notes toward a theory of culture. In: *Meaning in Anthropology*, K. H. Basso and H. A. Selby, eds., pp. 197–220. Albuquerque: Univ. New Mexico Press. [36, 273]

Schneider, H. K. 1974. *Economic Man: The Anthropology of Economics*. New York: Free Press. [241]

Schopf, T. J. M. 1982. A critical assessment of punctuated equilibria. I. Duration of taxa. *Evolution* 36: 1144–1157. [60]

Schultz, T. W. 1979. Investment in population quality throughout the low-income countries. In: *World Population and Development*, P. M. Hauser, ed., pp. 339–360. New York: United Nations Fund for Population Activities. [201]

Schwimmer, E. 1978. *The Yearbook of Symbolic Anthropology I*. London: Hurst, pp. vii–xiii. [272]

Seligman, M. E. and J. L. Hager. 1972. *Biological Boundaries of Learning*. New York: Appleton-Century-Crofts. [86]

Sherif, M. 1935. A study of some social factors in perception. *Arch. Psychol*. 187. Reprinted in: 1967, *Social Interaction*, M. Sherif, pp. 125–135. Chicago: Aldine. [224]

Shils, E. 1981. *Tradition*. Chicago: Univ. Chicago Press. [56]

Shubik, M. 1970. Game theory, behavior, and the paradox of the Prisoner's Dilemma: Three solutions. *J. Conflict Resol*. 14: 181–193. [230]

Silk, J. B. 1980. Adoption and kinship in Oceania. *Am. Anthropol*. 82: 799–820. [272]

Silverstein, M. 1976. Shifters, linguistic categories, and cultural description. In: *Meaning in Anthropology*, K. H. Basso and H. A. Selby, eds., pp. 11–55. Albuquerque: Univ. New Mexico Press. [272]

Simon, H. A. 1957. *Models of Man: Social and Rational*. New York: Wiley. [94, 273]

Simpson, R. L. 1962. Parental influence, anticipatory socialization and social mobility. *Am. Sociol. Rev*. 27: 517–522. [47, 55]

Skinner, B. F. 1953. *Science and Human Behavior*. New York: Macmillan. [46]

Skinner, B. F. 1966. The phylogeny and ontogeny of behavior. *Science* 153: 1205–1213. [86]

Slatkin, M. 1978. On the equilibration of fitnesses by natural selection. *Am. Nat*. 112: 845–859. [61, 112]

Slatkin, M. and R. Lande. 1976. Niche width in a fluctuating environment–density independent model. *Am. Nat*. 110: 31–55. [112]

Slatkin, M. and M. J. Wade. 1978. Group selection on a quantitative character. *Proc. Natl. Acad. Sci. USA* 75: 3531–3534. [231]

Slovic, P., B. Fischhoff, and S. Lichtenstein. 1977. Behavioral decision theory. *Ann. Rev. Psychol*. 28: 1–39. [168–169]

Smith, A. 1790. *The Theory of Moral Sentiments*. London: Bohn. [241]

Smith, E. A. 1983. Anthropological applications of optimal foraging theory: A critical review. *Curr. Anthropol*. 24: 625–651. [298]

Smith, S. M. 1975. *The Battered Child Syndrome*. London: Butterworths. [48, 51]

Spinetta, J. J. and D. Rigler. 1972. The child-abusing parent: A psychological review. *Psychol. Bull*. 77: 296–304. [48]

Staddon, J. E. R. 1983. *Adaptive Behavior and Learning*. Cambridge, Mass.: Cambridge Univ. Press. [4, 83]

Stanley, S. M. 1979. *Macroevolution, Pattern and Process*. San Francisco: Freeman. [60, 282]

Stebbins, G. L. and F. J. Ayala. 1981. Is a new evolutionary synthesis necessary? *Science* 213: 967–971. [290]

Stevens, G. 1981. Social mobility and fertility: Two effects in one. *Am. Sociol. Rev*. 46: 573–85. [201]

Steward, J. 1955. *Theory of Culture Change: The Methodology of Multilinear Evolution*. Urbana: Univ. Illinois Press. [290]

Stigler, G. J. and G. S. Becker. 1977. De gustibus non est disputandum. *Am. Econ. Rev*. 67(2): 76–90. [241]

Symons, D. 1979. *The Evolution of Human Sexuality*. New York: Oxford Univ. Press. [12]

Tarde, G. 1903 (1962). *The Laws of Imitation*. Gloucester, Mass.: Peter Smith. [280–281]

Taylor, M. 1976. *Anarchy and Cooperation*. New York: Wiley. [228, 230]

Terhune, K. W. 1974. A review of the actual and expected consequences of family size. Calspan Report N. DP-5333-G-1, Center for Population Research, National Institute of Child Health and Human Development, U.S. Dept. of Health Education and Welfare. Publ. (NIH) 75–779. [201]

Thelen, M. H., S. J. Dollinger, and K. D. Kirkland. 1979. Imitation and response uncertainty. *J. Genet. Psychol*. 135: 139–152. [224]

Trivers, R. 1971. The evolution of reciprocal altruism. *Q. Rev. Biol*. 46: 35–57. [230]

Tukey, J. W. and F. Mosteller. 1977. *Data Analysis and Regression.* Reading, Mass.: Addison Wesley. [222]

Turelli, M. 1984. Heritable genetic variation via mutation selection balance: Lerch's zeta meets the abdominal bristle. *Theoret. Pop. Biol.* 25: 138–193. [75]

Tversky, A. and D. Kahneman. 1974. Judgment under uncertainty: Heuristics and biases. *Science* 185: 1124–1131. [93, 168]

Twain, M. 1923 (1962). Corn-pone opinions. In: *On the Damned Human Race.* New York: Hill & Wang. [32]

Tylor, E. B. 1871 (1920). *Primitive Culture: Research into the Development of Mythology, Philosophy, Religion, Art and Custom.* London: Murray. [38]

United Nations. 1973. *The Determinants and Consequences of Population Trends: New Summary of Findings on Interaction of Demographic, Economic and Social Factors.* Population Studies 50. New York: U.N. Dept. of Economic and Social Affairs. [176]

Uyenoyama, M. K. 1979. Evolution of altruism under group selection in large and small populations in fluctuating environments. *Theoret. Pop. Biol.* 15: 58–85. [231]

Uyenoyama, M. and M. W. Feldman. 1980. Theories of kin and group selection: A population genetics perspective. *Theoret. Pop. Biol.* 17: 380–414. [231]

Van den Berghe, P. L. 1979. *Human Family Systems.* New York: Elsevier. [12]

Van den Berghe, P. L. 1981. *The Ethnic Phenomenon.* New York: Elsevier. [231]

Van Maanen, J. and E. H. Schein. 1979. Toward a theory of organizational socialization. In: *Research in Organizational Behavior,* B. Staw, ed., pp. 209–263. Greenwich, Conn.: JAI Press. [237]

Vayda, A. P. and R. A. Rappaport. 1968. Ecology, cultural and noncultural. In: *Introduction to Cultural Anthropology,* J. A. Clifton, ed., pp. 477–497. Boston: Houghton Mifflin. [290]

Vogel, S. R., I. K. Broverman, D. M. Broverman, F. E. Clarkson, and P. S. Rosenkrantz. 1970. Maternal employment and perception of sex roles among college students. *Dev. Psychol.* 3: 384–391. [51]

Waddington, C. H. 1957. *The Strategy of the Genes: A Discussion of Aspects of Theoretical Biology.* London: Allen & Unwin. [83]

Wade, M. J. 1978a. Kin selection: A classical approach and a general solution. *Proc. Natl. Acad. Sci. USA* 75: 6154–6158. [231]

Wade, M. J. 1978b. A critical review of the models of group selection. *Q. Rev. Biol.* 53: 101–114. [230, 231]

Wallace, A. R. 1905. *Man's Place in the Universe.* New York: McClure Phillips. [293]

Watson, W., A. Rosenfield, M. Uiravaidya, and K. Chanawongse. 1979. Health, population and nutrition: Interrelation, problems and possible solution. In: *World Population and Development,* P. M. Hauser, ed., pp. 145–173. New York: U.N. Fund for Population Activities. [201]

Watt, K. E. F. 1968. *Ecology and Resource Management.* New York: McGraw-Hill. [24]

Weismann, A. 1893. *The Germ Plasm: A Theory of Heredity,* W. N. Parker and H. R. Ronnefeld, trans. London: Waller-Scott. [118]

Weller, R. H. and L. F. Bouvier. 1981. *Population: Demography and Policy.* New York: St. Martin's. [176]

Weltman, N. and H. H. Remmers. 1946. Pupil's, parent's and teacher's attitudes: Similarities and differences. *Purdue Univ. Stud. Higher Educ.* 56: 1–52. [51, 52]

Werner, E. E. 1979. *Cross-cultural Child Development: A View from the Planet Earth.* Monterey, Calif.: Brooks/Cole. [46, 47, 48, 179–180, 200]

Werner, E. E. and R. S. Smith. 1982. *Vulnerable but Invincible: A Longitudinal Study of Resilient Children and Youth.* New York: McGraw-Hill. [298, 299]

Werren, J. H. and H. R. Pulliam. 1981. An intergenerational model of the cultural evolution of helping behavior. *Hum. Ecol.* 9: 465–483. [202]

Werts, C. E. 1968. Paternal influence on career choice. *J. Couns. Psychol.* 15: 48–52. [51, 52]

Whiting, B. B. and J. M. W. Whiting. 1975. *Children of Six Cultures: A Psycho-cultural Analysis.* Cambridge, Mass.: Harvard Univ. Press. 237 pp. [51]

Wickelgren, W. A. 1981. Human learning and memory. *Ann. Rev. Psychol.* 32: 21–52. [39]

Wilcoxon, H. C., W. B. Dragoin, and P. A. Kral. 1971. Illness-induced aversions in rat and quail: Relative salience of visual and gustatory cues. *Science* 171: 826–828. [87]

Williams, G. C. 1966. *Adaptation and Natural Selection: A Critique of Some Current Evolutionary Thought.* Princeton: Princeton Univ. Press. [231]

Williams, T. R. 1972. *Introduction to Socialization: Human Culture Transmitted.* Saint Louis: Mosby. [41]

Wilson, D. S. 1975. A theory of group selection. *Proc. Natl. Acad. Sci. USA* 72: 143–146. [231]

Wilson, D. S. 1977. Structured demes and the evolution of group advantageous traits. *Am. Nat.* 111: 157–185. [231]

Wilson, D. S. 1980. *The Natural Selection of Populations and Communities.* Menlo Park, Calif.: Benjamin/Cummings. [231]

Wilson, D. S. 1983. The group selection controversy: History and current status. *Ann. Rev. Ecol. Syst.* 14: 159–188. [231]

Wilson, E. O. 1975. *Sociobiology: The New Synthesis.* Cambridge, Mass.: Harvard Univ. Press. [13, 83, 130, 205]

Wilson, E. O. 1978. *On Human Nature.* Cambridge, Mass.: Harvard Univ. Press. [12]

Winter, S. G. 1966. Economic natural selection and the theory of the firm. *Yale Econ. Essays* 4(1): 225–272. [94]

Witkin, H. A. and D. R. Goodenough. 1981. *Cognitive Styles: Essence and Origins.* Psychological Issues Monogr. 51. New York: International Universities. [179]

Witkin, H. A. and J. W. Berry. 1975. Psychological differentiation in cross-cultural perspective. *J. Cross-cultural Psychol.* 6: 4–87. [179–180]

Wright, S. 1921. Systems of mating. I. The biocultural relations between parent and offspring. *Genetics* 6: 111–178. [173]

Yando, R. M, V. Seitz, and E. Zigler. 1978. *Imitation: A Developmental Perspective.* Hillsdale, N.J.: Erlbaum. [40, 45, 244]

Yando, R. M. and J. Kagan. 1968. The effect of teacher tempo on the child. *Child Dev.* 39: 27–34. [55]

Yankelovich, D. 1974. *The New Morality: A Profile of American Youth in the 70's.* New York: McGraw-Hill. [55]

Yarrow, M. R., R. M. Scott, and C. Z. Waxler. 1973. Learning concern for others. *Dev. Psychol.* 8: 240–260. [55]

Young, P. A., L. J. Eaves, and H. J. Eysenck. 1980. Intergenerational stability and change in the causes of variation in personality. *Personal. Indiv. Diff.* 1: 35–55. [52, 55]

Yussen, S. R. and V. M. Levy. 1975. Effects of warm and neutral models on the attention of observational learners. *J. Exp. Child Psychol.* 20: 66–72. [244]

Zajonc, R. B. 1976. Family configuration and intelligence. *Science* 192: 227–236. [201]

Zajonc, R. B. and G. B. Markus. 1975. Birth order and intellectual development. *Psychol. Rev.* 82: 74–88. [201]

Zucker, L. G. 1977. The role of institutionalization in cultural persistence. *Am. Sociol. Rev.* 42: 726–743. [55, 297]

Subject Index and Glossary of Mathematical Terms

Note: See also the section entitled "References and Author Index." In what follows, Greek symbols are alphabetized under the letter corresponding to their English spelling (e.g. θ under "t"). Mathematical symbols, including Greek letters, are indexed before words, regardless of subscripts and other compound elements. A brief definition of each symbol is given here in brackets, followed by a reference to the page on which the formal definition occurs.

a [importance of social relative to individual learning], 96

a(L) [equilibrium importance of cultural transmission in heterogeneous environment], 110

A [weight of parent as model], 183

A_i [transmission weight of parent i], 64–65
In models of: biased transmission, 140; frequency-dependent bias, 209; horizontal transmission, 68–69; multifactor model, 76–77; nonselective formation of sets of parents, quantitative characters, 72

A_{ij} [weight of ith model in the transmission of the jth cultural variant], 249

A_{Ij}, A_{Pj} [the importance of the jth model in the transmission of indicator and preference traits], 252

A_{kj} [weight of parent in role k of set j], 186

$\overline{A}_k$ [average importance of parents in kth social role], 187

$\mathcal{A}$ [importance of genetic or cultural transmission relative to learning], 123

$\mathcal{A}^*$ [optimal value of transmission relative to learning], 126

α_i [basic weight of ith model], 140
use in models of: evolution of biased transmission, 148; frequency-dependent bias, 209

α_{Ij}, α_{Pj} [basic weights of jth model in the transmission of indicator and preference traits], 252

Acquired variation, inheritance of
cultural transmission as, 8, 82, 283–84
Darwin's and Pearson's theories of, 172
See also Guided variation

Adaptation
cultural vs. genetic, 117–31
due to learning, 4, 14, 86, 128
importance in theories of culture, 33, 281

Adaptationist program, critics of, 13–14, 282

Adaptive consequences of cultural transmission, 14–16, 43, 288–89
with direct bias, 146–57
effect of asymmetric life cycle, 15–16, 188–90, 198, 285–86
with frequency-dependent bias, 213–23
with guided variation, 128–31
with indirect bias, 157–59, 266–67

Adaptive theories of culture, anthropologists', 33

Afunctionalism
summary discussion of, 293
and symbols, 277–79

Aggression, and social learning, 41–42

Alexander, R., pure environment hypothesis attributed to, 159–60

Altruism
better models needed, 295
and cooperation, 227–30
and cultural group selection, 232–33, 286
and genetic group selection, 230–32
and group-level functions, 292
problems of explaining, 205
See also Cooperation; Group selection

Analogies, defense of, 30–31

Anchoring heuristic, as evidence for weak bias, 169

Archaeology, and evidence for cultural inertia, 60

Artifacts, not culture, 36

317